Family Ministry

SECOND EDITION

Family
Ministry

Charles M. Sell

ZondervanPublishingHouse
Grand Rapids, Michigan

A Division of HarperCollinsPublishers

Family Ministry: Second Edition
Copyright © 1981, 1995 by Charles M. Sell

Requests for information should be addressed to:
Zondervan Publishing House
Grand Rapids, Michigan 49530

Library of Congress Cataloging-in-Publication Data

Sell, Charles M., 1933–
    Family ministry / by Charles M. Sell.—2nd ed.
      p.   cm.
    Includes bibliographical references and index.
    ISBN 0-310-42910-2 (hard)
    1. Church work with families. 2. Family. 3. Marriage.   I. Title.
BV4438.S44   1995b
259'.1—dc 20

                        94-42822
                        CIP

Edited by Elizabeth Yoder
Interior design by Susan A. Koppenol

Printed in the United States of America

99 00 01 02 / ❖ DH / 12 11 10 9 8 7 6 5

This edition is printed on acid-free paper and meets the American National Standards Institute Z39.48 standard.

♦ ♦ ♦ ♦ ♦ ♦ ♦ ♦ ♦ ♦

I dedicate this book
to my wife Ginger,
our children, and their families:
Chuck, Cheryl, Charlie and Timmy;
Larry, Joni, Daniel and Deanna;
Becky, Wayne, Mandy and Laura;
Howie, Laura, Robbie and Christopher

Contents

Preface

      I first began to study the family to help myself. I became a Christian in my late teens, after being raised in a non-Christian, alcoholic family.[1] Later on, after I was married, I rummaged everywhere I could to find out what a Christian home should look like: listening to sermons, reading books, and eventually taking a course on the subject. That search in due time led me to specialize in family ministry, teaching and writing out of my successes as well as my struggles. I am a typical "wounded healer."

      Perhaps you, too, are looking for information on being a better spouse, parent, son, or daughter. If so, I believe you will find it in this book. Expect to be changed by reading it. Your personal growth is the most important component of family ministry. Helpers of families must first help themselves; then they can model what they teach and explain both the ecstasy and the agony of family.

      You should be well armed to help families after consulting this book. Many churches have built their family-life ministry on the first edition, published fourteen years ago. I have received letters, phone calls, and personal statements as testimony to that fact. This edition is vastly different from the first, partly because of what these people have said. I have included in these pages much of what they have reported to me. There are some new programs and ideas in this edition and much more about the administration of family ministry than before. There are strategies for dealing with dysfunctional family members and single adults. The section on therapy and support groups is also new.

      Besides the up-to-date approaches, you will find fresh, new resources. At the end of many chapters I have listed and evaluated all sorts of accessories for family ministry: books, videos, curriculum, tests, questionnaires, and more.

      Like the earlier edition, theology is at the book's core, and the theological section is now much larger. One of the finest compliments I received about the first edition came from an air force chaplain. Telling me he had arranged for copies to be sent to every air force chaplain, he said, "I am not an evangelical, but what I like about your book is its theology. So much of the training our chaplains get in family life is based on some psychological theory." While neither he nor I shun the social sciences, we agree that Christian family ministry should be grounded in theology. Therefore the overall pattern of this book is theological, though a great deal of material from sociology and psychology has been woven into it. My approach to these sciences is eclectic; my theological stance is evangelical. By that I mean that my method of interpreting Scripture and doing theology is orthodox—using the hermeneutics and theological method that originated in the Protestant Reformation. Even though your viewpoint may be different, you might find the theological discussions helpful to stimulate your own reflection, particularly since there are few comprehensive treatments of the theology of family. Also, you will find many views represented, because I draw on many sources and try as much as possible to compare and contrast my viewpoints with others.

Family Ministry has a sizable section on theory in which I speculate on the shape family ministry should take in the coming decades. In this I especially take into account recent studies of both strong and dysfunctional families. Relatively recent social changes are also considered, particularly the many forms that today's families take. The practical parts of the book flow from this theory, consisting of teaching, therapy, small groups, intergenerational activities, and suggestions for making the whole church family-like. While only a large church could implement all the suggestions in this book, the theory and practice of *Family Ministry* is workable in small congregations. The goal is to equip churches of any size to help families of any type.

I thank the many practitioners of family ministry who have forged the programs delineated here. Also, I express my appreciation to the students and faculty of Trinity Evangelical Divinity School who helped shape my thinking and to the administration for the two quarterly sabbaticals they granted me to write this revision. My thanks to editors Elizabeth Yoder and Jim Ruark for their hard work on this manuscript. And, though I have thanked her often in person, I am glad for this chance to write a public message to my wife: "Ginger, thanks for all the researching, typing, reading, and evaluating you've done for *Family Ministry* as well as encouraging and loving its author."

NOTE

1. Like most alcoholic families, ours was not all bad. My father had a terrible drinking problem which, through a treatment program, he overcame some years after I had left home. Though his condition caused problems in the family and led him to neglect his children, he was always kind to me, never abusive. Along with all the bad times, we had some good ones. My parents always made me feel loved, and I cherish the memory of them.

Introduction: Family Ministry Is Church Ministry

"For my husband on Valentine's Day." Written in pink letters surrounded by hearts, with a picture of two white swans posturing in courtship below, the greeting card is carefully placed beside my word processor. Inside are more treasured words: "I love you for your gentleness and thoughtfulness. I love you for the way you're careful with my feelings. I love your quiet generosity and all the love you share with me. I'm so glad you're a part of my life."

"Interesting, isn't it?" said Ginger, my wife. "We gave each other cards that had the same line: 'I'm glad you're a part of my life.'"

Part? I suppose so: living day by day in the same house, sustained on the same menu; worshipping side by side each week; praying, sometimes agonizingly so, just the two of us; laughing, loving, playing, sleeping together for forty years of life—four children the fruit of that togetherness. And it continues and multiplies. Four children found lovers and brought them to us to love, and now there are eight grandchildren. These they also bring, regularly and often—all eighteen of us together on Valentine's Day to celebrate the birthday of one-year-old Timmy.

Husband, wife, mother, father, grandma, grandpa—happily we play our roles. Grandparenting is best. We are the watchers: "Look at me, Grandma!" "Are you coming to my school musical, Grandpa?" We affirm, hug, encourage, cheer, empathize, teach, and, yes, once in a while, spoil.

Family is important to me. Important? I consult the thesaurus for another word: "Consequential, major, meaningful, momentous, portentous, significant, prominent." Any of these will do.

We have no difficulty recognizing how significant family is to someone like Ginger and me. But what about my friend Frank? He was single, having been divorced years ago. He enrolled at our seminary in his fifties, about to embark on a new career, ministering to singles. Frank spent Christmas with a couple of single friends. His life is unencumbered by children paying a visit or grandchildren coming for him to feed or baby-sit, or a wife to consult with about what TV program to watch. Family isn't important to him, is it?

"Oh yes." I sensed the sadness when he told me he wouldn't be seeing his grown sons at Christmas. He would keep busy to fight the pangs of loneliness. He is still getting over the divorce that tore his life apart and burnt into his soul years ago. He still aches from what happened to him in his childhood family and his struggles with the consequent behavior patterns. Though not every day for Frank includes a family matter, every day family matters, if not in his life, in his mind and heart. Family is important to Frank: sometimes it hurts.

Consider, too, another single: Travis, a thirtysomething single, adult child of an alcoholic. To those in our campus support group he reported a weeklong depression. His father had called, he said, something he often does when he's drunk. As usual his father was griping at length about Travis's mother, blaming her for all the family's problems. Each caustic, slurred word toxic to his soul, the conversation left Travis limp, injured, with a despondency that would not dissolve for many days. Family to him is important: it pains him, and he doesn't know how to cope with it.

Martha, too, is trying to cope. An empty-nester, healthy and energetic, she ought to be enjoying life with her retired husband. And she is, except for one complication: caring for her mother. She did that in her home for a few years, but it was torturous. Every day was an occasion for conflict with the controlling mother with whom she never could relate. For health reasons the mother is now in an institution for the elderly, but Martha knows that the funds will run out soon, and her mother will be back. Out of a mixture of dread and guilt she asked: "Is there a support group for people like me?"

Family doesn't appear to be as crucial to churches as it is to the public.

But surely, family must mean little to carefree Janet, dean of students at a Christian college. Single, occupied with work, cavorting with students on ministry or recreation trips, she appears to have little time or need for family. And, in her late thirties, she doesn't daydream of being married as she often did earlier in life. But in fact, talks and sermons about marriage bother her, she told me, a bit of moisture in her eyes. Although she tries to minimize the role of family in her life, it is still there. Students constantly bring their family issues to her for prayer or counsel. Holiday visits to her Missouri family make her face her own issues. Just how much connection, she wonders, is there between her family of origin conflicts and her present-day struggles—her overweight problem, for instance? Yes, family is important, even for those who don't want it to be.

And family is important even when we are not conscious of it. Lisa, recently off to Great Britain on another of her escapades, has tried everything to evade life: drugs, alcohol, sex, and now travel. For her, family is not something you escape *to*, but *from*. As a teenager she began to turn against the couple who had adopted her as an infant. She snubbed their Christian values, resisted their efforts to stabilize her life—to help her keep a job or stay in college. Why did she rebel? The parents asked themselves that again and again. Like other teens, she seemed to be searching for herself. Perhaps, they surmised, she was unconsciously searching for her biological family. What else could explain the intensity of the rebellion? And why, now, this trip to England, the country in which she had been born and adopted? Although the parents had sought answers they found none: Lisa would not disclose what she was thinking or feeling. Perhaps, however, the answer is this: Family is significant, even when we are not conscious of it.

Men, women, singles, married people, children, teens—family is important to all. Sometimes enjoyable, sometimes hurtful, family plays a major role in our lives, whether we are aware of it or not. It is notable by its presence or its absence, whether we want it to be or not.

Family is, in the words of a social scientist, "the most profound of all influences on who we are and what we do." He explains: "The families to which we are born and those in which we live as adults shape us from birth to death. They are the immediate cause of our best and worst times." No other association links us with one another as family does, and none is more influential.[1]

Americans agree. According to current research, "Family is in." Family takes priority over everything else in life: work, recreation, friendships, or status. "Having a happy marriage," for example, ranks far above "being financially secure" or "having a rewarding job," according to one recent extensive national survey. So does "providing emotional support to your family."[2]

Even high school seniors rank having a good marriage and family above any other goal in life. And apparently there is some basis for their doing so: a good marriage and happiness go together. People who don't assess their marriage as "very happy" report the lowest overall happiness of any category of people.[3]

NEGLECT OF MINISTRY

Yet, family doesn't appear to be as crucial to churches as it is to the public. In the early 1970s, when he surveyed Christian education and youth directors, H. Norman Wright discovered relatively little was being done by the church for families. Two-thirds of those who responded reported that within the past two years their churches had had no family-related programs whatsoever—not even a sermon preached on a family theme.

Today the National Association of Evangelicals has uncovered the same lack of family ministry. In a recent study, few pastors indicated having taken significant steps to help people whose families were in trouble, even though they also said that family disintegration is a relatively common problem in their congregations.[4] Why this shortage of family ministry?

The answer is no doubt complex, but one report speculated that many pastors' families are in so much trouble that the pastors avoid the subject of family. If this is true—if pastors are afraid to tackle family issues lest they call attention to their own ailing home life—it may tell us more about congregations than about pastors. Perhaps pastors are threatened by the widespread attitude that falling short in family life is less tolerable than other failures. We permit our leaders to preach and teach about prayer, evangelism, and other "spiritual" matters without expecting them to have mastered them. Yet we may not allow them to struggle as spouses and parents.

Surely there are other causes for the sparsity of family ministry: frustration because of failed attempts to help, having too much else to do, not knowing what to do. Perhaps some may feel that doing the work of God's kingdom requires sacrificing or ignoring families.

SYMBIOSIS OF CHURCH AND FAMILY

Nevertheless, to ignore enriching, building, and mending families is to ignore what may be the most pressing concern of people in the congregation. It is to overlook the importance of family to the church. There is a solid bond and an enormous interplay between church and home. It is like a symbiotic relationship, common in the world of nature. For example, let us take the relationship between the Claviger beetle and the meadow ant:

The small beetle moves inside the anthill, unconcerned that ants are among its most ferocious enemies. The anthill offers the beetle easy access to life's necessities. It is warm inside, and the ants stock a variety of tasty foods. But the beetle soon stops in its tracks—it spots a fast-approaching ant, one of the hungry predators that call this hill home. The ant, in turn, stops when it reaches the motionless beetle. But instead of striking out, it strokes the beetle. A secretion then appears on the beetle's body; and the ant eagerly consumes it and goes on its way, leaving the visitor unmolested. These two species live in a mutually beneficial way, a pleasant arrangement biologists call "symbiosis."

Church and family, both institutions established by God, ought to live in a similar symbiosis. Fifty years ago, family life advocates put forth this argument: "The family needs the church, the church needs the family."[5] I will try to lay a firm theological base in later chapters, but first I would like to show how family and church are so solidly joined that the success of the church's mission lies in part with the well-being of its families.

Family Ministry Is Spiritual and Moral Ministry

The church needs to help produce strong marriages and families in order to promote Christian morality. What does the term *family* mean? The idea of family fits the category of a *social institution*. Sociologists use this term to refer to the ways and customs of societies as they organize themselves to meet common needs.[6] Economics, transportation, politics, religion, and education are all *universal* social institutions. You can point to a certain high school in your town as an institution, but the school is part of the broad pattern of instruction in your society: the educational institution. The word *family*, too, while designating a specific group of people down the street from you, also refers to this broad-based idea: the way people in a society conduct themselves in certain matters. As such, the family serves various social functions, such as the following:

1. *Reproduction.* Arranging conditions for the reproduction of the race. Children who replace aging and dying members are born and cared for by two committed married people.

2. *Sexual expression.* Providing conditions for satisfaction and control of sexual passions. The idea of family draws boundaries for sexual activity, relegating it to married partners and ruling against incest, adultery, and other types of sexual relationships.

3. *Socialization.* Providing for the nurture of children. The family is relied upon as the primary place where children learn the basic skills needed to survive in society. Obviously, schools and other institutions play a role in this, but the family is most crucial because it shapes the child during the early, formative years.

4. *Status.* Organizing norms related to status given to individuals. A society prescribes roles to family members—giving parents, for example, some authority over their children, or in some societies, husbands authority over their wives.

5. *Economic Cooperation.* Providing rules for economic cooperation between people. For example, parents are to provide for children who are too young to be in the work force.

6. *Emotional Satisfaction.* Creating a context for meeting people's emotional needs.

7. *Social Control.* Exercising social control. Family is a way of keeping people in line. Not only is it given power to demand and restrain behavior, but the family lessens the need for overt control by developing internal controls of self-discipline in its members.[7]

From this perspective it is easy to see why there are clashing views over the idea of family. First, some argue that certain of these functions should not be relegated to family. This was a major issue in the 1992 campaign for President, oddly launched by the Vice-President of the United States in an argument with a fictitious TV character, Murphy Brown. Not so strange was the subject of their debate: the nature of the ideal family.

For decades, people in the Western world have been arguing over the definition of the term *family*. Delegates stalled the work of the 1980 White House Congress on the Family by failing to agree on a simple idea of the family. The creators of *Murphy Brown* challenged the prevailing norms for *social-*

ization, claiming that a child could be reared effectively by a single parent. Not doubting the real existence of one-parent families, the Vice-President contended that two-parent families are a better model.

Other so-called traditional functions of the family have been challenged, such as marriage exerting control of *sexual expression*. Obviously, this is contested by people who want to accept premarital, nonmarital, or extramarital sex.

Even the *reproduction* function is challenged by those who would want it to be acceptable for single women to bear children through artificial insemination and raise them without the help of a father. *Economic cooperation* is also questioned. Are men to be paid higher wages so that their wives can remain at home to care for children? Or should women be freed from child care so they can fulfill themselves in the workplace? The answer to this question is a major issue especially in the Western part of the world. In fact, almost every one of the functions traditionally assigned to the family is debated today.

> **The church that neglects family matters ignores moral matters.**

Upon reflection we realize that the Bible assumes that the family carries at least some of these functions. Three of the ten commandments (those dealing with adultery, obedience to parents, and coveting someone's wife) are tied to the family. Family issues are spiritual and moral issues. Some of today's major issues, such as homosexuality, premarital and extramarital sex, abuse of children, and abortion are family matters. The church that neglects family matters ignores moral matters.

Some may argue that the church faces these issues by preaching against them. But is it enough to tell people what they should not do without teaching and supporting them to do what they should? Couples don't need just to be told not to commit adultery; they need to be helped to commit to a marriage. Biblical writers set the example in this, as Paul did when he taught the Corinthians to overcome sexual temptation by getting married and maintaining a satisfying sex life (1 Cor. 7). Stable, satisfying families preserve morality. Helping married people with their sex lives, emotional adjustment, and communication patterns braces them morally and spiritually.

Even teenage morality is at stake. A high percentage of rebellious and delinquent adolescents come from broken homes. As one expert says, "A vast amount of research has shown that the absence of a parent through divorce, death or a time-consuming job contributes to many forms of emotional disorder, especially to the anger, rebelliousness, low self-esteem and antisocial behavior that characterizes drug use."[8]

Viewed in this way, seminars on marriage and parenting are not nice, optional programs intended to make people selfishly happy. They are necessary to keep people morally and spiritually healthy.

Family Ministry Is Evangelism

There is no question that evangelism is one of the church's highest priorities. This fact, then, makes family ministry essential because it, too, is evangelistic. Family ministry aims to train people how to fulfill parenthood as Christians, which includes nurturing their children in the faith, a task assigned to them in Ephesians 6:4. Parents who evangelize and disciple their own children are doing the work of the church. The home is as much an agency of the church as the Sunday school and children's church. Looking at its families as an arm of the church, church leaders should be concerned about training parents in child development, evangelism, counseling, teaching, personal relationships, and other parenting skills.

Family ministry can extend evangelism beyond the church's own families. Because so many people struggle with family problems, sermons and classes that deal with the family attract the attention of non-Christians. Missionaries and evangelists realize that the greatest opportunity for evangelism today is "the ministry to hurting people." Nowhere in life is there more hurt than in home life. A prominent eighteenth-century preacher, Joseph Parker, put it well: "Preach to the suffering and you'll never lack a congregation."

Evangelism through family ministry can take many forms. Non-churched people often make their way into church-sponsored marriage conferences or parenting classes. A high percentage of nonchurched attend "Adult Children from Dysfunctional Families," "Divorce Recovery," and other such seminars. A New England church rented an auditorium and sponsored evening family-life sessions featuring its pastor as the speaker. More than half of the hundreds who attended came from outside that congregation.

Family Ministry Is Discipling

By "discipling," we usually mean bringing new Christians to a certain degree of maturity and then training them to reach others. Discipling is a central function of the church. A major feature of family ministry is training parents to disciple their children in the Christian faith.

> If a church is to consider itself a discipling church, family ministry cannot be regarded as a mere option.

Family ministry is also critical to discipling in another way. Because many new youth and adult converts come from dysfunctional families, any discipleship training program will no doubt have to include helping them with family matters. Many of the converts are so distressed by personal problems that arise from their family of origin that their spiritual progress is often hindered. Dealing with a dysfunctional family background has become an essential part of the discipling process. For this reason, many pastors and leaders of Christian parachurch organizations claim that it seems to take longer to establish people in the faith today than it did in the past. An experienced leader in the Navigators organization told me that it often takes a year or two longer to train their leaders than it did twenty years ago. If a church is to consider itself a discipling church, family ministry cannot be regarded as a mere option.

Family Ministry Is Biblical Application

Teaching God's truth is obviously the church's business. So is the application of that truth. Whether teaching or applying, a preacher or teacher cannot possibly ignore the family. Peter didn't. After counseling suffering Christians to follow Christ's example, he applies this theme to people in different roles of life, including wives and husbands (1 Peter 3). Paul, too, sought to get truth beyond the front door of people's homes. Having painted in brilliant colors the theme of the new man in Christ, he then portrays what this would look like in families (Eph. 5:22–6:4). Although the church cannot expect its pastors and teachers to be experts on contemporary family life, it can expect them to guide their quest to apply biblical truth to home life. That is family ministry.

Family Ministry Deals with Church Life

From a certain perspective, when the church ministers to families it is actually ministering to itself. Many today take the position that efforts to understand and preserve family life will influence the dynamics of church life, and also serve to stabilize it. "As goes the family—so goes the church."[9]

If the current systems theory of organizations is true, family life and church life may be more closely tied together than we ever realized. Edwin Friedman suggests that ministers are involved in three interlocking family systems: one's own nuclear family, the congregation as a "family," and the nuclear families within the congregation.[10] Imagine that the emotional lives of all these families are like the water in a waterbed, all united and flowing together. Pressure on one spot creates waves of movement throughout the whole.

Cameron Lee uses this image to show how the pastor's own family flows together with all other church families. Suppose a church family suffers from the loss of one of its members while at the same time the minister has a conflict with an adolescent son. Later, the son is arrested for possession of drugs. Lee explains:

> At first glance, these events would seem to be completely unrelated. . . . However, the scenario could be interpreted thus: the family which has lost a member increases its demands for emotional support from the minister; the overloaded minister withdraws from the increased demand and focuses on relationship with the son; this increases the demandingness of the crisis family, whose communications take on a negative and

accusatory tone; the minister transfers this stress to the parent-adolescent relationship; the son acts out.[11]

To many, this insight is not new. In 1960, John Wynn claimed that the minister's interpersonal difficulties would affect his entire parish. "When his professional life and his family life are at odds because he has still to come to terms with both . . . the church membership is certain to feel the effects. Paul's salty word to Timothy is apropos: 'If a man does not know how to manage his own household, how can he care for God's church?'"[12] The implications of this systemic view of the church and its families are too numerous to mention all of them here, but two are critical. First, both leaders and members do well to ponder how their own family life affects what they do in the church and how the church life, as a whole, impacts their families. Second, all will need to fervently support programs that fortify the life of the church's families, realizing that in doing so they will be sustaining the organizational health of the church.

Explaining Church Doctrine

One more inescapable connection between church and family relates to the church's job to teach Bible and theology. So many of the terms and metaphors of Christian theology are taken from family life: God as Jesus' father and ours, to single out the most important. In the worst-case scenario, if people no longer lived in families, our efforts to teach Christian truth would be crippled.

> Efforts to improve our church's families will enhance our ability to teach theological truths conveyed in familial terms.

But families as we know them don't have to become obsolete to make it difficult to convey some biblical concepts. Research confirms that children, even when adults, transfer feelings and thoughts about their parents to God. In Japan, for example, Christians have difficulty sensing the closeness and tenderness of God the Father because traditional Japanese fathers are so emotionally distant from their children. Abused children, in a similar manner, have a hard time feeling the love of God. It follows that efforts to improve our church's families will enhance our ability to teach theological truths conveyed in familial terms.

Family Ministry Is Prevention

So far I have argued that the church should minister to families for the sake of the church. But a strong case can be made for ministering to the family for the sake of families. I have yet to prove theologically that the family institution was created by God. Suppose for a moment, we assume that is true.

God's institution is in trouble. Scores of people from every sector are warning us about its plight. About twenty years ago Nathan Ackerman wrote:

"I am a psychiatrist who has devoted a lifetime to studying the emotional problems of family living. I have pioneered in the field of family therapy. From where I sit the picture of marriage and family in present day society is a gloomy one."[13]

One hour's thumbing through the dozens of texts devoted to the family will convince one that the prophets of family doom are not all within the church. Social experts are often desperate in their appeals to government and society to help the home. Sociologist Betty Yorburg warns, "the nuclear family . . . needs massive help." She writes that the United States is regarded by many analysts as "a bellwether in the trend toward the disappearance of the family as a social form in urban, computerized societies."[14]

> **The church, like no other social institution, is in the best position to prevent family problems.**

And in the words of Edward Shorter: "The nuclear family is crumbling."[15]

Many families are like accident victims in need of emergency treatment; others are accidents waiting to happen. Among the reasons why the church should help the family is simply this: the church is in the best position to do something.

Certainly, the church cannot do everything that needs to be done. It may lack the expertise to counsel many troubled families. Lack of finances and personnel may limit its involvement politically and socially. Yet, there is one arena where it may have the most opportunity, as well as obligation: the area of prevention.

Unfortunately, government and community services are more remedial than preventive. Like physicians, they wait until families are in serious trouble before they offer "intervention." They move in with their resources to try to reverse the destructive process that has been going on for years.[16]

Social and psychiatric professions have reasons for ignoring prevention. Since people are more likely to seek counseling when they are in trouble than when things appear to be going well, there is little demand for prevention services. Thus there is little money to be made in preventing problems. And preventing problems is not as glamorous as solving crises.

Following the old adage that an ounce of prevention is worth a pound of cure, some experts in counseling and social services are crying out for more prevention strategies by professionals. Yet they also are giving more recognition to the so-called "nonprofessionals," like clergy and church lay people.

The church, like no other social institution, is in the best position to prevent family problems. No other institution contains whole families. The church is able to influence people during the crucial transitions of adolescence, early marriage, parenting, etc. In fact, traditionally the church is involved in the lives of its members at crucial family related junctures: baptism, marriage, and death. This gives church leaders an opportunity to identify and deal with problems before they become unmanageable. Marriage and family enrichment, pre- and post-marital seminars, intergenerational programs and many other ministries are easily done in the church, since the church deals with all age groups.

Often, too, the whole family unit is involved in the church, unlike what occurs at school and in other community groups. Because of this, churches are well-suited to work for family wellness. It is the church's business that people live in Christ-like ways in their families at all stages of the life cycle. Some Christian seminaries are turning out family life specialists who are able to counsel, but are not qualified to be licensed therapists, in order to keep them from pursuing remedial counseling at the expense of their devotion to prevention.

Prominent evangelical educator, Ted Ward, has made a forthright plea to the church to help the home: "The family serves a particular and apparently indispensable role within the church."[17] The Christian church and the Christian home, as institutions, are as closely bound together as Siamese twins. If they are cut apart, a major artery may be severed that causes one or both to die.

"Are we willing to do what must be done for the church to help the family face the future?" Larry Richards challenges. "Or will we abandon the nuclear family to face essentially alone these forces it was not designed to overcome without the support of the body?"[18]

The plight of the contemporary family is all too apparent to pastors and other church leaders. Family problems are spilling out into congregational life like sewage from a broken pipe onto the sanctuary carpet. Will the churches do more to help? The next chapter will paint a portrait of the contemporary family. After a closer look, we may be forced to decide that we really have no choice.

NOTES

1. Steven L. Nock, *Sociology of the Family* (Englewood Cliffs, N.J.: Prentice-Hall, 1987), xi.

2. Norval D. Glenn, "What Does Family," *American Demographics* 14:4 (June 1992): 37.

3. Ibid., 34. This is a report of the General Social Surveys conducted by the National Opinion Research Center.

4. Ted Ward, "Unpublished Report of the Task Force on the Family of the National Association of Evangelicals" (1988), 1.

5. Robert Lynn, *Protestant Strategies in Education* (New York: Association Press, 1964), 25.

6. Harold T. Christensen and Kathryn P. Johnsen, "The Family as a Changing Institution," *Marriage and Family in a Changing Society*, 3d ed.; ed. James M. Henslin (New York: Free Press, 1989), 16.

7. Ibid., 15–26.

8. Armand M. Nicholi, "Commitment to Family," *Family Building: Six Qualities of a Strong Family*, ed. George Rekers (Ventura, Calif.: Regal, 1985), 63.

9. Ron Rose, "The Family Unit: Turn the Key—Open the Door," *Christian Bible Teacher* (May 1972): 188–89.

10. Edwin H. Friedman, *Generation to Generation* (New York: Guilford, 1985), 36.

11. Cameron Lee, "Toward a Social Ecology of the Minister's Family," *Pastoral Psychology* 36:4 (1988): 249–59.

12. Ibid.

13. Nathan Ackerman, *Marriage: For and Against* (New York: Hart, 1972), 12.

14. Betty Yorburg, *Changing Families* (New York: Columbia University Press, 1973), 130.

15. Edward Shorter, *The Making of the Modern Family* (New York: Basic Books, 1975), 150.

16. Luciano L'Abate, "Prevention as a Profession," *Prevention in Family Services: Approaches to Family Wellness*, ed. David Mace (Beverly Hills: Sage, 1983), 49.

17. Ted Ward, "The Influence of Secular Institutions on the Family," Plenary Session (St. Louis Continental Congress of the Family, 1974), 4.

18. Larry Richards, "How the Church Can Help the Family Face the Future," Plenary Session (St. Louis Continental Congress on the Family, 1975), 15.

◆ *Part One*

The Family
of Family Ministry

A Diverse and Aging Unit

DISAGREEMENT ABOUT THE CONDITION OF THE FAMILY

The introductory chapter began by claiming that the family is important to us. It ended by reporting that the family is in trouble. Why do Americans have so little success with what they prize so much? Part of the answer lies in what seems to be a large gap between what we *say* we value and what we actually practice.

Consider the findings of a nationwide survey. According to this survey, Americans believe that the greatest threat to the family is the inability of parents to spend enough time with their children. Yet while most people surveyed believe they don't have enough time with their children, they also said they would not pass up a more lucrative or more prestigious job even if it meant more time away from home. In an attempt to explain the contradiction, the report said: "Although Americans say . . . they place a higher priority on family than on money, we should not expect to see them cutting back on their incomes to live in accord with their values. Attitudes and behavior often diverge at critical junctures, and this is one of those instances."[1] Sociologist Norval Glenn agrees, saying, "The truth is that many if not most Americans will sacrifice traditional family ties for activities they claim are less important."[2]

Surveys offer another answer to why family is important but in trouble. When asked, people give conflicting answers about the extent of problems in families. People judge other families worse off than their own. Fifty-nine percent predicated that America's family life will be "only fair" or "poor" in the year 1999. Only 5 percent guessed it would be "excellent." Yet, 71 percent of those who rated family life "only fair," claimed they were "extremely satisfied" or "very satisfied" with their own family life.[3]

Some believe this shows that families are better off than supposed, and that the public in general is swayed by the media's negative portrayal of American family life. Others say that people claim their own families are better off because they want to portray a positive image of themselves.

Whatever the answer, it is clear that the vast majority of Americans think that the quality of family life in the U.S. is declining, and people have a dimmer view of marriage than they did twenty years ago.[4] Yet 63 percent of Americans agree with the statement: "The family is, by far, the greatest source of pleasure for Americans." Only 8 percent said the same about religion, and 6 percent about work and friends.[5]

Reasons for Confusion Among Experts

Experts who look at the same statistics about the family often differ about its condition. Some disagree because they approach the topic of family from different theoretical perspectives. Certain theories cause researchers to be more pessimistic about the family than do others. For example, much of the current concern for family deterioration began with what is called "The Chicago School." Social scientists of this school hold to an "interaction" framework. They focus on the type of interaction they see in families.

When they studied city families in the first part of the twentieth century, those of this school compared these families with the extended family system in Europe. Immigrants to America, they found, were departing from the extended family system they left behind. A new family pattern had emerged. Instead of being held together by law, economics, and authority, family members began to be tied together by "sentiment": ties of close relationships and loyalty. This, they said, amounted to a breakdown of the traditional family.[6]

On the other hand, sociologists who held to "structural-functional" family theory were not so alarmed. They focused on how the family relates to other parts of society. That the family was losing some of its functions was no problem. They believed these functions were sufficiently shouldered by other institutions, like the school, community, or government. What family functions remained were critical for the well-being of individuals. The home still uniquely provided an intimate context for personal emotional development. They believed social change actually made the family a stronger, not weaker, institution. From this vantage point, J. Richard Udry optimistically compared the modern family to that of past centuries: "In many ways the nuclear family has become more important as a social unit."[7]

> The very first characteristic of modern families is diversity.

Some disagreement about family is due to the fact that it is such a political issue. In order to support their idea that the traditional family is still very much American, conservatives claim families are alive and well. Liberals, on the other hand, point to the weaknesses of the traditional family and insist that our idea of family has changed and should continue to do so.

Sifting through expert opinion and social research, we can paint a fairly accurate picture of the modern family. Doing that is the first step in devising a theory of family ministry. While we may have some idea of what we would like families to be, we have to start with what they really are. And the very first characteristic is diversity.

Family Forms Are Diverse

There doesn't seem to be any clear-cut, typical family. Diversity is in. Normal is different. What Americans thirty years ago thought of as the "typical family" is no longer in the majority. Typical meant a family with a husband who was the provider, a wife who was the homemaker, and several children. In 1960, 60 percent of all households were like this[8] ; now, only 7 percent are.[9] Even if we add to these families with one or more children in which both the husband and wife work outside the home, this still adds up to only 26.7 percent of the households in the U.S.[10]

For the first time in the United States, the number of married couples without children living at home, 28.4 percent of households, exceeds the number with children at home. Many of these are "empty nesters," people whose children have moved out. Their numbers are increasing rapidly. The number of married-couple households headed by someone 45–64 years old is projected to grow by 40 percent this decade, to 19 million in 2000.[11]

Yet with all these changes, most people still grow up in a family and live with relatives. Family households (where two or more related people live) far outnumber nonfamily households (persons living alone or with a nonrelative) by 70.2 percent to 29.8 percent. The norm is still for people to marry (over ninety percent of adults do) and to bear children in a family context. So, in a sense, some form of the traditional family is very much present. But the statistics cited above indicate some major changes we should consider in more detail.

Large Numbers of Singles

Because of the high rate of divorce (to be viewed in detail later) and because people are remaining single much longer before marriage, there is a large percentage of single people. Single persons living alone make up 24.4 percent of all households.[12] Add to that the singles who live with a relative or nonrelative, and the percentage of single households is 35.6 percent. Comparing this with percentages of years ago will show how swift and dramatic the change in living patterns has been. In 1970 two-thirds (69 percent) of all households were married couples. Twenty years later that portion had slipped to little more than half (55 percent).[13]

Households with Working Wives and Mothers

More women are working outside the home; many of these are mothers. Fifty-eight percent of married women with children under six years of age are in the labor force. Many are part-time workers or work for pay within their homes. Still, the rate of those in the labor force has increased from 28 to 58 percent since 1970. Similarly the rate of married women working who have children aged 6–17 has increased from 49 percent twenty years ago to 73 percent today.

Single Parent Households

The number of single parent households (the fastest growing type) has now reached 9.3 percent of the total. The Family Research Council has estimated that as many as one-third of today's children will experience their parents' divorce and close to one-half will spend some time in a single parent family before the age of 18.[14] Single parent homes headed by fathers are becoming more common (growing 2.5 times as fast as the number headed by women).

Nonmarried Couples Living Together

Another type of household consists of unmarried people who are sexually involved and living together. The number of cohabiting couples has recently increased dramatically. According to the U.S. Census Bureau there were nearly three million of them in 1990, five times the number reported in 1970.[15] Overall, they make up about three percent of the U.S. households.[16]

> Despite current trends, we must not too quickly assume that the family as we know it will become obsolete.

Couples who cohabit do so for different reasons. Some live together for convenience—to save rent money or to have a temporary place to stay. Others are in a sort of dating relationship, but have no intention of marrying. Some live together as a permanent alternative to marriage, while others plan to marry and are using cohabiting as a sort of trial marriage. Especially prone to this trial marriage arrangement are those who have been divorced. In one study 60 percent of those who remarried set up housekeeping with someone beforehand.[17]

The degree to which cohabiting has become socially acceptable today represents a change of American moral standards. The prominent historian, Edward Shorter, observes that such living together "would have been unthinkable in times past."[18]

Some social scientists predict the practice will increase, moving in the direction of Sweden, where 15 percent of all couples living together are not married.[19] One reason for expecting more cohabiting is the shift of college students' attitude toward marriage. In 1968 only one in four students (24 percent) believed that marriage was an obsolete institution. Four years later the figure had increased to 32 percent.[20]

Yet, the practice of living together as an "unstructured trial marriage," may diminish. Couples are finding that living together with a number of people to find the right one is not working. A recent study found that the later marriage of cohabiting partners was not very stable. Within ten years of their wedding, 38 percent of those who had lived together before marriage had split up, as compared with 27 percent of those who simply married.[21] Whether or not it is increasing, the acceptance of cohabiting is a serious threat to the institution of marriage and a moral issue Christians must face.

DIVERSITY IMPACTS CHURCH MINISTRY

Despite some of these trends, we must not too quickly assume that the family as we know it will become obsolete. Alternatives to the family that have been suggested have not succeeded. Communes and group marriages have not caught on. In places like the Soviet Union, where there has been strong encouragement for communal living, the nuclear family has survived.[22]

Yet the changes in family life that have taken place and might still take place will impact Christian churches. Christians will be forced to examine carefully the legitimacy of certain modifications of family living and respond to changes taking place.

In very practical ways, church leaders are now compelled to recognize the diversity of family forms in their congregations. A simple announcement that the Sunday school picnic is for "families" creates confusion. A sermon that stresses the joys of married life sends some single adults home feeling hurt and lonely, even angry. Urban congregations feel confused and helpless in dealing with the poverty and loneliness of single parents and their children. These same economic and emotional struggles challenge the resources of suburban and rural congregations as well.

AN AGING UNIT

The fact that so many families are made up of older people is unique in history, and will continue to have a dramatic effect on family ministry. In 1900, only 4 percent of the U.S. population was 65 years and older. In 1984, it was 12 percent. When the "baby boomers" are part of that age group in 2030, senior citizens will make up 28 percent of the population.[23]

This increased older sector provides the church with blessings as well as burdens. With more elderly, there will be more three generation families. Grandparents, whom research confirms can have a significant impact on

> The increased older sector provides the church with blessings as well as burdens.

grandchildren, will seek to better understand this role. The increased contact between grown children and their parents will be a tremendous boost to both age groups. For some, however, it will provoke agonizing conflict. A counselor at a senior center told me that they always remain open the Friday after Thanksgiving because they receive more calls that day than any other time from older people who were pained by family strife during the holiday. The increased reports of elderly abuse may indicate that, for some, this strife is quite bitter.

Middle-aged families may well benefit from the long-term presence of their parents. Studies show that older adults give more financial support to their children than they receive from them until parents are about age seventy-four.[24] After this, middle-aged adults may need to help their parents with financial and, most certainly, with emotional support. Despite the general opinion that children forsake their elderly parents, relatively few do. Almost always, it is the daughter who becomes the chief caretaker. This, along with the fact that so many women have jobs other than that of housewife, has already limited the amount of time they have for serving in church agencies. These caretakers, many of them restricted by the daily care for severely ill, such as those with debilitating Alzheimer's, will need some relief that other church members can provide.

Yet the elderly, who are usually quite fit despite the contrary stereotype, can provide a massive source of volunteer personnel for church ministry and missions. We have yet to see the impact on the world of this available "Greypower."

Issues of the elderly family will call for more attention from our pulpits and in our educational programs. Since some of their marital difficulties are unique to them, for example those brought on by retirement, they will require separate marriage enrichment sessions.

Large numbers of single people over age 65 will require special spiritual and emotional support. Forty percent of the women from age 65 to 74 will be widowed, compared to only 9 percent of the men. They will face issues such as masturbation and nonmarital sex that they may not have grappled with since adolescence. One study reported that almost 40 percent of people over 70 years of age were masturbating regularly. And large numbers of unmarried elderly are involved in sexual affairs.

Diversity and aging are two major traits of the modern family that face the church. As we will see in the following chapters, the church will have to reckon with other major changes in family life.

NOTES

1. Patrick Reardon, "Top Threat to Family: No Time for the Kids," *Chicago Tribune* (October 11, 1989), sec. 1, 1.

2. Norval D. Glenn, "What Does Family," *American Demographics* 14:4 (June 1992): 34.

3. Ibid., 37.

4. In Mental Health Surveys, the percentage of people who said that marriage changes a person's life in positive ways went down from 42 percent in 1957 to 30 percent in 1976 and negative responses increased from 23 to 28 percent (ibid., 37).

5. Reardon, "Top Threat," 1.

6. Ernest W. Burgess and Harvey J. Locke, *The Family: From Institution to Companionship* (New York: American Book, 1945).

7. J. Richard Udry, *The Social Context of Marriage*, 3d ed. (New York: Harper, 1974), 16. For an overview of the various theories of the family, see texts on the sociology of the family such as Steven L. Nock, *Sociology of the Family* (Englewood Cliffs, N.J.: Prentice-Hall, 1987).

8. Households can be either family or nonfamily types. A *family* household has at least two people related by blood, marriage, or adoption. *Nonfamily* households include people who live alone, unmarried couples, and housemates.

9. Alvin Toffler, *The Third Wave* (New York: Morrow, 1980), 198.

10. "The Changing American Family," Supplement to American Demographics Desk Reference Series 3 (July 1992): 2.

11. Ibid., 23.

12. Sixty percent of people who live by themselves are under 65, and roughly 60 percent who live alone are women.

13. "The Changing American Household," *American Demographics*, 3.

14. *The American Family Under Siege* (Washington, D.C.: 1989), 2.

15. *Current Population Reports: Population Profile of the United States* (Washington, D.C.: U.S. Government Printing Office, 1991), 23.

16. M. Sheils, D. Weathers, L. Howard, and R. Givens, "A Portrait of America," *Newsweek* (January 17, 1983): 20–32.

17. Felicity Barringer, "'Trial Marriage' Is Often a Ticket to Splitsville," *Chicago Tribune* (June 9, 1989), sec. 1, 14.

18. Edward Shorter, *Making of the Modern Family* (New York: Basic Books, 1975), 119.

19. Jesse Bernard, "The Good-Provider Role: Its Rise and Fall," *American Psychologist* 36 (1981): 1–12. In Judy C. Pearson, ed., *Communication in the Family: Seeking Satisfaction in Changing Times*, 2d ed. (New York: HarperCollins, 1993), 36.

20. Daniel Yankelovich, *The New Morality: A Profile of American Youth in the Seventies* (New York: McGraw-Hill, 1972), 88.

21. Felicity Barringer, "'Trial Marriage,'" 1.

22. "The Changing Soviet Family," in *The Nuclear Family in Crisis: The Search for an Alternative*, ed. Michael Gordon (New York: Harper, 1972), 119–42.

23. Ira L. Reiss and Gary R. Lee, *Family Systems in America*, 4th ed. (New York: Holt, Rinehart and Winston, 1987), 375.

24. Ibid., 390.

3

A Nuclear, Isolated, and Intimate Unit

Most current marriages and families take the form of *nuclear families* that are relatively isolated units. The nuclear family consists of a man and woman living alone with or without children. This form is the functional unit of all modern industrial societies. Not only is this true in the so-called developed nations, but it is becoming increasingly the case in any nation where people live in cities and earn their living in industry rather than farming.[1]

The fact that modern families are primarily nuclear has several implications. First, these families are not *extended families* that were common for thousands of years, for example, in China.

Extended families come in two forms: The three-generation family and the joint family. The first of these households includes the older parents, the sons and their wives and the children of these sons. In the three-generation family, marriage represented a social arrangement between two families. In China, when a young man married a woman and brought her to live with him, his brothers, their wives, and his parents, the role of the wife "was to serve her husband and his mother."[2] A modification of the extended family requires the married couple to live with the woman's family, not the man's.

More than a living arrangement is at stake in the extended family. In some cases, the priority given to relationships is included in the arrangement. While in the nuclear family system the husband-wife relationship is primary, in some extended family systems the adult father-son relationship is the primary one. The extended family places greater value on the *consanguinal*, or blood relationship, while the nuclear family emphasizes the *conjugal*, or marital relationship.

The joint family consists of several brothers, their wives, and their children living together. Such households are sometimes found in societies where inheritance is impartible, that is, where the family estate cannot be divided to be passed along to heirs. Under such a system, several brothers share the estate.

Neither of these forms of extended family have played a major role in American life, though they have existed and continue to exist among certain ethnic groups, particularly in rural America where a married couple lived with their parents. In most instances, however, this occurred during the time between the retirement of the parents and their deaths.

Extended families have seldom resided together in the same house; nor in our history has the married couple been subject to the authority of the husband's or wife's father or mother. In the Western world, marriage is considered a union of two individuals. It is true that households sometimes include a married couple with a relative or two living with them for practical reasons, but this arrangement could not be counted as an extended family and is not typical.

NUCLEAR FAMILY IS ISOLATED

Isolated from Extended Kin

In the nuclear family, married couples are more or less isolated from extended family kin (parents, brothers, sisters, cousins, etc.). Not only do they not live with such relatives, but their contact with them and dependence on them is relatively sparse. Even in past centuries this seemed to be the case. John Demos offers evidence that relationships to cousins, uncles, and aunts are no more intense today than they were in seventeenth-century New England.[3]

Yet not all nuclear families are entirely cut off from relatives. Asian-Americans and Hispanics remain more devoted to extended family kin than do other groups. Among them financial support of parents or siblings is common, and adult brothers and sisters loan money to one another or enter together into financial ventures.

This is not to say that among white Anglo-Saxon families there is no interplay between couples and other relatives. One sociologist, Betty Yorburg, observes, "The completely isolated nuclear family with no relatives within

> Functions that were formerly taken care of within the extended family are now performed by specialized agencies not based on kinship.

easy visiting distance is relatively rare."[4] Studies show that extended family members are called on in emergencies and for financial help, as well as for companionship, and that this happens even among city dwellers.[5]

There is a qualitative and quantitative difference in the relationship of nuclear family members to kin now, compared with preindustrial times. Yorburg agrees with others who conclude that today's patterns no longer include "the daily contact and interdependence based on economic necessity that characterized extended families in traditional societies."[6]

Functions that were formerly taken care of within the extended family (caring for the elderly, securing employment, etc.) are now performed by specialized agencies not based on kinship. For many Americans the extended family has gradually ceased to perform any function other than friendship.[7]

For this reason, I have described the nuclear family as "isolated." And this isolation is even more severe because along with this lack of association with kin, the nuclear family also has limited contact with the community.

Isolated from Community

When sociologists compared modern suburban families in America and working-class immigrant families living at the turn of the nineteenth century, they reached the conclusion that families had lost contact with their communities.[8] This story of community loss has been told and retold in popular presentations, beginning with David Riesman's *The Lonely Crowd*.[9] Ralph Keyes, in *We the Lonely People* reported convincingly, "We feel daily our sense of community loss."[10] Think for a moment about this picture of the secluded family. It is not a home with walls broken down, its occupants forced apart by community demands and relationships as was once true. Rather, Edward Shorter contends, "A New York existence in the twenty-first floor apartments that overlook the East River differs from domestic life about the tanner shop in eighteenth-century Memmingen, partly because the one seals out the outside world, while the other is punctured by it at many points."[11]

The recent practice of "cocooning," creating entertainment in the homes rather than going out for it, underscores this withdrawal from community life.

THE EFFECTS OF ISOLATION

This loss of community and break from kin dramatically impacts people today and will profoundly shape the church's family ministry.

Loneliness

Weakened extended-family contacts may be a major factor in the loneliness within many evangelical homes. Several factors make this highly plausible. First, studies have shown that the extended kin contact is less prevalent among Protestants than in Jewish and Catholic homes.[12] Second, the evangelical constituency includes a major proportion of the upwardly mobile class living in suburban America,[13] and this class is distinctively separated, socially and geographically, from extended kin.[14] Besides the suburban isolation, many evangelicals may be separated from their kin when their non-Christian relatives might misunderstand or oppose their Christian commitment.

This insight may help us see the different ways people in our congregation view the local church. Isolated nuclear families may hunger for more social contact in the church. Those who are more in touch with nearby relatives may be indifferent to small groups and other programs that offer intimate fellowship they don't seem to need. We see this difference every time our church asks people if they want to have a New Year's party. Those with relatives nearby typically decline, while more isolated individuals and families say they need the church to provide a place for them to meet with others on this and other holidays.

Loss of Identity

People may feel a loss of identity because of losing touch with family history and tradition. Edward Shorter asserts that this is true of the majority of modern families. The nuclear family, often without contact with older generations to keep family memories alive, lacks a history, a family tradition. In the past, the family was held fast to the larger social order by ties to generations past and future, as well as to kin presently living. "Awareness of ancestral traditions and ways of doing business would be present in people's minds as they went about their day," Shorter

> The nuclear family, often without contact with older generations to keep family memories alive, lacks a history, a family tradition.

explains. "Now, in its journey into the modern world the family . . . has parted from the lineage, that chain of generations stretching across time."[15]

Personal Emotional Problems

This lack of touch with family and kin may occasion personal emotional problems. Couples become self-absorbed and neglect responsibility for the generations to come. Christopher Lasch argues that American's pervasive feelings of "emptiness and insignificance" arise essentially from "the erosion of any strong concern for posterity." He contends that, "We are fast losing the sense of historical continuity, the sense of belonging to a succession of generations originating in the past and stretching into the future."[16]

Anti-child Bias

This lack of continuity may bring with it a certain anti-child bias. The widespread practice of abortion may be just one of several indicators of this attitude.[17] There is evidence that the United States is not caring for its children. Children, who represent less than 27 percent of the overall population, comprise 40 percent of the poor.[18] Jurg Willi, internationally known Swiss psychiatrist, declares, "There is something wrong with a society that cannot maintain appropriate familial structures, and that cannot see a purpose for human life in the succession of generations and in reproduction."[19]

Ill-equipped Families

Being independent, the nuclear family is less equipped to face its tasks and hardships. The first and most obvious problem for the nuclear family is the absence of immediate counsel and practical help. The psychologist represents the loss of the first of these, and the baby-sitter is a vivid symbol of the loss of the latter. One man, harassed by the hectic pace of life partly caused by the need to chauffeur teenagers too young to drive, sighed, "If my father lived nearby, he would be happy to drive the kids around." This was but one of the many ways the extended family could have been significantly helpful to his nuclear family.

This lack of support from relatives and community has a powerful impact on single parent families. Many of them form informal single parent networks from friends and neighbors. They exchange child care and help each other financially and emotionally in what could rightly be termed survival situations.

Fewer Adult Examples for Children

Children in the nuclear family may lack exposure to adult models other than parents. The superficiality or lack of intergenerational contacts outside the home leaves children with fewer adults, apart from their parents, to be examples to them of how to behave and think.

Greater Opportunity for Abuse

The family's detachment from community may also provide a context for abuse. In premodern times, members of the extended family or the community interfered when abuses took place in the home. Today, with virtual isolation from one another, relatives and neighbors are no longer monitoring these atrocities.[20]

Dissatisfaction of Some Housewives

The loss of community may be part of the cause of the dissatisfaction of some housewives with their role in the home. These women feel cut off from others, especially when empathy and companionship are lacking in a faltering marriage.[21] Not only are the doors of the woman's home not as open to the community as they once were, but also the community does not enter into her life in a meaningful way.

> The loss of community may be part of the cause of the dissatisfaction of some housewives with their role in the home.

The one sure entrance she does have into the community is through vocation. Gainful employment provides a sense of identity and usefulness, as well as a means for social contacts. This is one of the reasons that more women are entering the work force.

Greater Stress for Elderly

The elderly in particular often take the brunt of this nuclear family exclusiveness. Having to take the wife's mother on numerous errands is too much for some husbands. And, even though the majority of elderly prefer to live alone, a husband or wife, in quest of privacy, may not permit a widowed mother-in-law, for example, to move in permanently even when it might be advantageous.

In other words, relatives interrupt rather than complete the picture of the American home. Extended kin living alone sometimes find difficulty in meeting their emotional and relational needs.

Increased Emotional Ties Between Nuclear Family Members

Family historians agree that the family's loss of community ties has increased the need for closer ties within the family. But they disagree as to which came first, the loss of community or the desire for closeness. One argues that when the family lost the daily round of activity with other people, the demands on relationships within the family were intensified.[22] Edward Shorter, however, claims that the demand for affection in the family cut it off from community ties. In traditional European communities life was centered in community. Capitalism and urbanization unleashed the individualism and freedom that allowed husbands and wives to strengthen the ties of affection between themselves. This in turn isolated them from community. In the words of Edward Shorter, "the couple terminated its association with . . . outside groups and strolled off into the dusk."[23] Whether cause or effect, the desire for intimacy within the contemporary family is a fact of life that is both a blessing and a burden. To that feature of the family we now turn.

> The lonely nuclear family, removed from kin and community, has become a more intimate unit than ever before.

NUCLEAR FAMILY IS INTIMATE

We have seen that the lonely nuclear family, removed from kin and community, has become a more intimate unit than ever before, and that this compelling quest for intimacy is relatively recent in Western society. An extensive national survey of families conducted in 1989 showed that Americans don't think of the family in structural terms, as a group of people related by blood, marriage or adoption, but in emotional terms, as a group of people who love and care for each other.[24]

Today's *companionship* form has replaced the economic and social form we call *traditional*. This is not to say that love was entirely absent in the traditional family; it simply was not the critical factor holding it together. In

> Today's *companionship* form has replaced the economic and social form we call *traditional*.

the courtship practices of the traditional family the decision to marry was in most cases made by the parents, and parents gave more consideration to material welfare and social standing than to anything else. Sexual intimacy, so highly valued today, may well have been of less concern, especially to lower-class couples who had little opportunity for privacy in a home where everyone slept in the same room.[25]

Edward Shorter's investigation of medieval peasant families convinced him that there was little affection between husband and wife. "There is ample proof," he claims "that the medieval peasant would call a veterinarian for a sick cow before he would call the doctor for his ailing wife. In the peasant's value system, because of his poverty, the cow was more dear to him than his wife was."[26]

Shorter uses an impressive array of statistics to demonstrate that the Western world underwent a sexual revolution that brought about the present-day emphasis on intimacy. Romantic love unseated economic and other practical concerns during the time he dubs "the revolution of sentiment." This revolution affected not only the relationship between husband and wife, but also the ties between mother and child.[27]

EFFECTS OF EMPHASIS ON INTIMACY

First, it is the basis for claiming that marriage and family is more, not less, important to modern society. Societies tend to hold certain relationships in high priority. In some, the relationship between adult son and father is primary. The contemporary West has chosen to emphasize the significance of the heterosexual peer relationships above all else. Listen to our music for an hour and see the extent of our preoccupation with romantic intimacy. The American family system is built upon the affection between the sexes.

Americans expect the male-female relationship to be their most important source of emotional satisfaction and support.[28] This does not suggest that they achieve intimacy; the point is that they value it. Modern individuals look to the family primarily for relational satisfaction. This phenomenon above all others boldly and forcefully makes the modern family more important than ever, since it provides the longest and most significant relationships in life.[29]

Secondly, this preoccupation with romantic intimacy in modern marriage helps explain the high regard for sexual expression of affection. Pressure on couples to perform well sexually may account for the fact that when there are marital problems, the sexual relationship is also affected.

Third, this high regard for intimacy has placed heavy demands on family members. With less satisfying relationships outside the nuclear family, relationships of family members must now bear a heavier emotional load. Left with the task of being the major source of emotional security for adults and children during most of life, the nuclear family becomes almost explosively emotional. Parents must provide for the basic emotional needs of their offspring with little help from outside. Prior to the emergence of the modern family, emotional attachments were diffused over a wider group than just the immediate family. Today the child's emotional attachments are in most cases confined to the few people in his or her immediate family.

If members of the extended family were present in the home, they could dilute family tensions. But friction in a nuclear home dedicated to togetherness produces an atmosphere in which every quarrel can become a crisis, and each misunderstanding threatens to isolate one person from another. "Under contemporary circumstances," says Udry, "it is easy for families to become boiling cauldrons of emotionality."[30]

This desire for intimacy also forces couples to concentrate on their relationship to such a degree that a tremendous pressure to succeed sometimes makes that success elusive. High expectations for marriage may make couples less satisfied with their marriage. Studies show that lower expectations have played a part in the degree of marital satisfaction working class couples achieve. Housewives who do not have, nor greatly expect to have, a close relationship with their husbands, but do have close friendships with other housewives are, on the whole, more satisfied with their marriages than the wives of white-collar workers.[31] This means that when couples are isolated from kin and community and thus more in need of intimacy in their own marriage, their marriage is at greater risk.

One couple I have known illustrates this. A midnight phone call from Ken was the first I knew that his marriage was in trouble. He told me then that his wife announced she was leaving him. What happened to them happens to other seminary couples like them. Their trouble started when these newlyweds left extended family and friends in a state a thousand miles away in order to attend graduate school. With high expectations of closeness, they moved together into their first apartment. One year into their new relationship, they had found no church to attend regularly. They were using Sundays to build their relationship. During the second year, like butterflies, they flitted from church to church, still establishing no meaningful relationships with others.

In the meantime, Ken was busy with studies; other students satisfied some of his need for social contact. But his wife's need for others was not met, her job offering little chance to develop close ties. Her longing for friends and relatives intensified by her loneliness, she called home frequently, running up huge phone bills that created financial worries. Her relationship with her husband was her prime opportunity for closeness, yet he was busy and not as skillful in intimacy as she wanted or needed. Lonely and desperate, the marriage relationship that had become everything for her now looked like nothing to her.

Demos notes that people expect today's families to "provide the interest, the excitement, the stimulation missing from other sectors of our experience."[32] Yet, as he points out, marriage and family don't always make us feel alive and invigorated as we expect. Our experience does not measure up to our expectations.

When we don't measure up to our expectations, we are then left with what Demos dubs an "anti-image" of the family. Seen from this negative viewpoint, domestic relationships look like "a form of bondage."[33] Monogamous marriage is liable to become boring and stultifying. Disappointment sets in. Divorce often follows because modern expectations make success harder to obtain.

> Ironically, the great desire for family togetherness plays a major part in family disintegration.

It is more difficult for a man to be a friend than a provider, to be an intimate companion than a mechanic. A wife, too, may find being an exciting sexual companion more complex than being a housewife or a man's property. By the same token, it is much easier to lose a friend than to lose one's property, and it is much easier to love a friend than to get away from one's owner.[34]

Ironically, the great desire for family togetherness plays a major part in family disintegration. With affection as the cement to hold marriages together, divorces have become more prevalent. How are Christians to handle this? Should we lower our expectations for family life? Should we put more stress on intimacy and help family members achieve it? Or should we urge couples to have more significant contact outside the home to reduce this demand for closeness inside? Must we enlarge our acceptance of divorce? Our strategy of family ministry will need to address the many perplexities modernity has brought us.

NOTES

1. Steven L. Nock, *Sociology of the Family* (Englewood Cliffs, N.J.: Prentice-Hall, 1987), 30–33.

2. Ibid., 32.

3. John Demos, *A Little Commonwealth* (New York: Oxford University Press, 1970), 124.

4. Betty Yorburg, *Changing Families* (New York: Columbia University Press, 1973), 13.

5. Marvin B. Sussman, "The Isolated Nuclear Family: Fact or Fiction?" *Social Problems* (Spring 1959): 330–40.

6. Yorburg, *Changing Families*, 110.

7. Ibid., 16.

8. Edward Shorter, *The Making of the Modern Family* (New York: Basic Books, 1975), 7. See also Richard Sennett, "The Brutality of Modern Families," *Transaction* (Sept. 7, 1970): 31.

9. David Reisman, *The Lonely Crowd* (New Haven, Conn.: Yale University Press, 1950).

10. Ralph Keyes, *We, the Lonely People* (New York: Harper & Row, 1973), 26. This theme was also supported in the more recent *Habits of the Heart* by Ralph Bellah (New York: Harper & Row, 1986).

11. Shorter, *Making of the Modern Family*, 22.

12. Robert F. Winch, "Some Observations on Extended Families in the United States," *Selected Studies in Marriage and the Family*, 4th ed., ed. Robert F. Winch and Graham B. Spanier (New York: Holt, Rinehart and Winston, 1974), 155–59.

13. Frederick H. Stoller, "The Intimate Network of Families as a New Structure," *The Family in Search of a Future*, ed. Herbert Otto (New York: Appleton Century Crofts, 1970), 147.

14. J. Seeley, R. A. Sim, and E. W. Loosley, "Differentiation of Values in a Modern Community," ed. John R. Seeley et al., *Crestwood Heights* (New York: Basic, 1956), as quoted in J. Richard Udry, *The Social Context of Marriage*, 3d ed. (New York: Harper, 1974), 28.

15. Shorter, *The Making of the Modern Family*, 3–4.

16. Christopher Lasch, *The Culture of Narcissism*, (New York: Basic Books, 1980), 5.

17. Mary Ann Lamanna and Agnes Riedmann, *Marriages and Families: Making Choices and Facing Change* (Belmont, Calif.: Wadsworth, 1986), 387.

18. Ibid.

19. Jurg Willi, *Growing Together, Staying Together: Preserving Marriage and Family in the Face of Personal Change*, trans. Vivien Blandford and Tony Hafliger (Los Angeles: Jeremy P. Tarcher, 1992), 13.

20. David Finkelhor, "Common Features of Family Abuse," *Marriage and Family in a Changing Society*, 3d ed., ed. James Henslin (New York: The Free Press, 1989), 407.

21. John and Letha Scanzoni, *Men, Women, and Change: A Sociology of Marriage and Family* (New York: McGraw-Hill, 1975), 269.

22. Sennett, "The Brutality of Modern Families," 31.

23. Shorter, *The Making of the Modern Family*, 255.

24. Patrick Reardon, "Top Threat to Family: No Time for the Kids," *Chicago Tribune* (October 11, 1989), 1.

25. Shorter, *The Making of the Modern Family*, 22–78, 205–54.

26. Ibid., 59.

27. This view is not without its opponents, who claim there is evidence of affect, especially in wealthy families. In the seventh century, one writer called his children "the most beautiful of our possessions." Of those who died, he wrote: "Our little ones, who were so dear to us and sweet, whom we had cherished in our bosoms and handled in our arms, whom we had fed and nurtured with such loving care."

There is also some proof that ordinary people cherished their children. Mothers resorted to magic to save their children. Epitaphs on sixth-century gravestones tell a different story than that of Shorter. Some, like that of Marucius, whose age is painstakingly recorded as three years, six months, and eight days, give the names of the parents, Elcentianus and Palesta, who "placed him here for love."

Yet Shorter's picture of pre-modern peasant families does provide a helpful backdrop for understanding the phenomenal onrush to intimacy during the last one hundred years.

28. Udry, *The Social Context of Marriage*, 17.

29. Ibid., 16.

30. Ibid., 17.

31. Scanzoni, *Men, Women, and Change*, 269.

32. John Demos, *Past, Present, and Personal: The Family and the Life Course in American History* (New York: Oxford University Press, 1986), 36.

33. Ibid.

34. John Scanzoni, "Can Marriages Last Forever?" *U.S. Catholic* (February 1977): 7.

4

A Troubled Unit

After many years of family ministry in the Methodist Church, Hazen Werner quipped, "The American home is falling apart and wall-to-wall carpeting is not holding it together."[1] The facts support his statement: families are troubled and unstable.

FAMILY INSTABILITY

The Reality of Divorce

Divorce is more common today than it was in the past, most certainly in North America as well as in many other parts of the world.[2] In the U.S. in 1860, the divorce rate was 1 in 1000 married women, ages 15 and higher. In 1982 it was 23 per 1000. In 1860, 96 percent of marital dissolutions resulted from death of a spouse, as compared to only 56 percent in 1970.[3]

Exactly how many American marriages will end in divorce is difficult to determine. It's common to say that one out of two will. This is based on the fact that one divorce is awarded for every two marriages each year. But this doesn't translate into a fifty percent divorce rate since many older, currently married people are not divorcing at such a rate. To say half of all married people are divorced is twice as high as reality: actually, only one fourth of Americans who have been married have also experienced one divorce.[4] And we can't easily predict what will take place in the future since we can only predict based on current rates of various age groups. With some degree of certainty, we can expect that two out of five of today's marriages will end in separation or divorce. On the high side, two demographers predict that two out of every three marriages that occur at the present time will not survive as long as both spouses live.[5]

The Acceptance of Divorce

Divorce numbers are not the only way to portray family instability. The wide acceptance of divorce is as crucial as its practice. It is no longer taken for granted that death is the only accepted way to untie the knot. George Barna's research found that seven out of ten Americans accept divorce and remarriage.[6] This change in the meaning of the marriage commitment is a matter of concern for both the church and Western society as a whole. In church ministry, we will not only have to deal with the effects of the high divorce rate, but the reasons behind it. Are people merely less committed to each other, or are they less prepared to build a successful marriage?

Sexual Relationships Without Marriage

While accepting divorce weakens the force of marriage vows, several modern practices ignore them altogether: non-marital sex and sexually active unmarried couples living together, for example. Premarital intercourse became prevalent in the mid-1950s. The chances that young people who were strongly attracted to each other would include sex in their relationship grew greater in the 1960s as youth began to value the various romantic aspects of a relationship less and got more quickly to the hard sexual core.[7] The proportion of sexually active teenage females continued to rise in the 1980s with the biggest increase among whites and in higher income families. One study showed that the proportion of teenage females who had sexual intercourse rose from 47 percent in 1982 to 53 percent in 1988.[8]

Some challenge studies like these because they include married teenagers and girls who experience only one sexual encounter with no ongoing sexual activity. Instead, the challengers claim, "The real news is that two-thirds of today's unwed teenage girls are not currently sexually active."[9]

The teenage pregnancy rate has fluctuated in the last decade. Nationally, the teenage birth rate reached an all-time low in 1986 of 50.6 per thousand after declining steadily since the late 1960s. It began to rise in 1987 and recorded its largest rise two years ago. The teen birth rate rose 6 percent, from 51.1 per thousand in 1987 to 53.6 per thousand in 1988. This rise was among all races.[10]

BREAKDOWN OF TRADITIONAL ROLES

Confusion over family roles offers another challenge to the church. Denying any distinct roles for husband and wife, egalitarians confront the traditional view of the husband as leader and provider. Many couples have brought the confusion and controversy over this issue into their own marriages. Some identify this confusion of roles as one of the most divisive elements in American life. It is difficult to assess how much turmoil this has caused; however, there are some topics surrounding this issue with which we must deal.

First, it is fair to say that the departure from traditional roles has unleashed a struggle for power between husband and wife. Without the constraints of the traditional submission of the wife, and often without newer guidelines in place, striving for power may dominate the husband and wife relationships. For some women, getting a job may be a ploy to give them leverage in financial decisions by their contribution to the family's income.

> Confusion over family roles offers another challenge to the church.

Second, it may not be thirsting for power that drives most women to work outside the home, but a striving for significance. Data confirms that women in the home tend to hold themselves and their work in lower esteem than they do men and the work they do.[11] For them, a life devoted to the care of children is less rewarding than it was for women in the past.

Third, the movement from the traditional role of husband as sole provider has resulted in more work for most women. While most of them have increased their work outside the home, their husbands have not, for the most part, relieved them of much of the domestic tasks. Many women have two full-time careers, one outside and one inside their home. Many are groping for new approaches to dividing up responsibilities for producing income and performing household tasks.

> Society imposes pressures and priorities on all that allow neither time nor place for meaningful activities and relationships between children and adults.

Fourth, by questioning their own role in the home, women have jostled men to reconsider theirs. Sam Keen claims, "The traditional notions of manhood are under attack. . . . At no time in recent history have there been so many restless, questioning men."[12] The women's crusade has triggered various men's movements, some of which may greatly impact the church.

Fifth, stripped of customary guidelines to order their relationships, couples are searching for new ways to solve conflicts and maintain harmony. Even those who hold to traditional roles (husband-lead, wife-submit) are examining how these play out in a day-to-day practical way.

POWERLESS PARENTS

A Christian man, a prominent Wisconsin surgeon, confided to me that being a father was more difficult than practicing medicine. Other parents vigorously agree.[13] The avalanche of books and articles is vivid indication that parents feel confused and are looking for parenting guidelines.

Prominent family expert Urie Bronfenbrenner lays much of the blame for the struggle of people to be good parents on society. Before a congressional hearing, he stated that society imposes pressures and priorities on all that allow neither time nor place for meaningful activities and relationships between children and adults. These priorities, he claims, also downgrade the role of parenthood and prevent parents from doing things they want to do as guides, friends, and companions to their children.[14]

Fathers as well as mothers seem to be hard-pressed to find time for their children. This is especially true for single parents. Since the typical father sees home and job as two separate domains, combining occupation and family roles successfully is among the most common sources of guilt and anxiety for the middle-class male.[15]

Left to themselves, children and teens are greatly influenced by their peers. Often this results in open hostility between parent and adolescent. If not opposed to parental values, many youth are at least indifferent to them. Such peer orientation and alienation from parents has resulted in rising rates of running away, dropping out of school, drug abuse, suicide, delinquency, vandalism and violence.[16]

Obviously, parental failure is a social problem in a society that depends upon the home to teach children moral values and relationship skills that enable them to participate in society. Though school teachers and day care personnel contribute to this socialization process, the family is still the major player in this process. If the home fails its children, it fails society.

For years, some social scientists have claimed the home has failed and that alternatives to the nuclear family must be found.[17] Just how badly homes are failing in raising their children is difficult to determine. Probably, the majority of parents do an acceptable job. But there is grave public concern about the existence of families that do fail, families labeled as dysfunctional.

DYSFUNCTIONAL FAMILY UNITS

Dave Simmons, a former professional football player, tells men who attend his seminar how his own childhood family negatively influenced him. His father Amos, a military man, was a problem drinker and extremely demanding. He rarely said a kind word to Dave. Always prodding him with harsh criticism to do better, he braced his orders with beatings and verbal assaults. By constantly putting new goals in front of Dave, he never permitted him to feel any satisfaction from any success. Once when Dave was six years old,

If the home fails its children, it fails society.

Amos gave him an unassembled bicycle, commanding him to put it together. Unable to read the directions, Dave struggled to the point of tears. "I knew you couldn't do it," his father shouted, then assembled it for him.

When Dave played football in high school, his father was unrelenting in his criticisms. In the backyard of his home, after every game, his dad would point out Dave's errors in play after play. "Most boys got butterflies in the stomach before the game; I got them afterwards," Dave recalls. "Facing my father was more stressful than facing any opposing team." By the time he entered college he hated his father and his harsh discipline. He chose to attend the University of Georgia simply because it was further away from home than any other school that offered him a scholarship.

After college, hearing he had just become the second round draft pick of the St. Louis Cardinals professional football club, he telephoned his father to share the news. Amos responded, "How does it feel to be second?"

Despite the hateful feelings he had for his father, Dave Simmons began to build a bridge to his dad. Christ had come into his life during his college years, and it was God's love that made him turn back to his father. He learned for the first time what Amos's father had been like. A tough lumberjack, he was known for his quick temper, once destroying a pickup truck with a sledgehammer because it wouldn't start. Amos, too, had been beaten by his dad. "By the time my father died, we had become friends," Dave said.

When he married and had children, Dave believed the negative influence of his father was settled. But he was shocked to find out it wasn't. It was after attending an elementary school basketball game that he became aware of the extent of his father's impact upon him. David had gone with his wife and daughter to see Brandon [Dave's son], play in his first athletic event. Brandon had played rather badly, and on their way home David proceeded to tell him so. He critically scoured the small boy sitting beside him in the car, pointing out all the mistakes he had made during the game. Arriving home, Brandon, now in tears, rushed into the house, followed by David's wife and daughter. Dave found his wife waiting at the front door for him. Angrily, she blustered, "Amos! You are just like your father." No jolt on the football field hit any harder than those words. How could he begin to do to his own son what he had so despised his father doing to him?

> Unless something is done for them, the many problems they have today will be repeated in the families of tomorrow.

Dysfunctional Families Reproduce Themselves

The most disconcerting fact about today's families is that unless something is done for them, the many problems they have today will be repeated in the families of tomorrow. Family life in the Western world is caught in a deteriorating downward spiral, generating guilt among those involved and pessimism among professionals who are trying to help them. A concerned politician, congressman Dan Coats bluntly summarized the research conclusions: Incest begets incest, child abuse begets child abuse, and alcoholism seems to beget alcoholism.[18]

Women who come from divorced homes divorce at a higher than average rate.[19] Men with alcoholic fathers have a four times greater chance of becoming alcoholics than those who grew up in nonalcoholic families.[20] In one study as many as seven out of ten abused children became abusive parents.[21]

It was in the early eighties that we began to understand more fully the dynamics of dysfunctional families and the sway they have over people. Much of what we know has been uncovered by those who work with addicts. Until a decade ago, addiction treatment focused on the alcoholics. Now experts are giving heed to the torment of family members and the kind of adults the children turn into. Some of the first to take note of these families were counselors who began to deal with family members in their treatment programs for alcoholics and addicts. They soon discovered traits common to people in such homes. Janet Woititz's best selling book, *Adult Children of Alcoholics*, brought attention to these traits. The family systems theory also played a major part in discovering how family members were destructively linked together. They reminded us of the solidarity between generations that former therapists, concentrating on individuals, had discounted.

Technically, these families are called "multi-generational codependent family systems." First applied to alcoholic and addictive families, the phrase now covers families where there are workaholics, compulsive gamblers, shoplifters, overeaters, anorexics and/or bulimics, and so-called sexual addicts. Other compulsions, like watching TV, are also added to the list. The common core elements in these family systems are called "addictive family dynamics." "Codependency" is the term most used on the personal level.

The term *dysfunctional* isn't synonymous with nonfunctional. A person can have a dysfunctional heart, such as one with a slight valve problem, and still be alive. Yet, her quality of life might be diminished considerably. A dysfunctional family is one sufficiently troubled to impair its ability to properly socialize children so that they grow up fairly mature, emotionally, physically, spiritually, etc.

Like a greenhouse for raising plants, a family provides an environment for children to grow. Some families hinder the child's development. They may be passively abusive, neglecting the children so that they do not get the proper nutrients (affirmation, intimacy, companionship, diet, discipline, etc.) for normal human development. Some homes may be actively abusive, like a greenhouse with poison in the soil or atmosphere. In such homes, children may not only be deprived of essential growth ingredients, but might actually be stifled by any number of abusive experiences: physical violence, verbal assaults, witnessing of violence, gross parental inconsistencies, sexual violation, etc.

Causes of a Dysfunctional Family

Dysfunctional families are usually created by a problem person: one who is alcoholic, abusive, ill-tempered, or mentally ill. Even so-called workaholics or sex addicts or those with eating disorders can make a home malfunction.

What happens in such families is that the system itself is damaging. Unhealthy, unspoken rules govern it: "Don't trust, don't feel, don't talk." A codependent pattern emerges as the family tries to cope with the severely troubled person. The central issue becomes control, as each family member tries to contain the chaos caused by the alcoholic or otherwise troubled person. Life for every member is negatively affected by the roller coaster ride, enduring the ups and downs of the life of the distressed person whose life is out of control.

The system stifles the personal development of its members, producing immature, troubled persons.

Negative Impact of Dysfunctional Families

These families are having a profoundly negative impact on their children, who often carry their problems into adulthood. In an extensive behav-

> Grandchildren of alcoholics may have the same symptoms as adult children of alcoholics, even though neither of their parents was alcoholic.

ioral study of 215 people, researchers at Columbia and Yale found that the incidence of major depression was far more prevalent among children of chronically depressed parents than among children of normal parents. Children of depressed parents showed significantly higher rates of substance abuse, social and school problems, and psychiatric treatment.[22] Prisoners and youth in detention facilities seem to have one major thing in common: they come from dysfunctional families.[23]

Judith Wallerstein has documented how a parent's marital discord and divorce can have effects on some adults that continue in a child's adult life. "Children are especially affected because divorce occurs during their formative years. . . . The early experiences are not erased by divorce. Children who witnessed violence between their parents often found these earlier images dominating their relationships ten and fifteen years later."[24]

Psychologists now speak of the syndrome called Adult Child of Dysfunctional Family (ACDF). Such people take their personality defects and immaturity into their own marriages and in turn produce dysfunctional families, even though they may not be abusers or alcoholics as were their parents. They often do this by repeating the rules and dynamics of the dysfunctional system that they learned in childhood. For this reason, grandchildren of alcoholics may have the same symptoms as adult children of alcoholics, even though neither of their parents was alcoholic.

Number of Dysfunctional Families

Because the dysfunctional system can continue without the adult child having the same problem as the parent, it is difficult to estimate the number of seriously dysfunctional families. We are fairly certain that there are 22 million adult children of alcoholics in the United Sates, almost one out of eight adults. One estimate, which considered not just alcoholics but problem drinkers as well, is even higher: one out of five.[25]

Since not all abusers are also alcoholics, we add to the number those who came from abusive, nonalcoholic families. Statistics about abuse are not very accurate because much of it goes unreported. Active child abuse, such as severely battering a child, happens to about 10,000 children each year.[26] Sexual abuse occurs to at least 100,000, and possibly as many as 500,000, children per year. Another 100,000 children suffer emotional mistreatment. Children in passively abusive families, where they are grossly neglected, either physically, morally, or educationally, number at least 100,000. Estimates, however, go far beyond these numbers, some as high as 2 million children a year.[27] If we include those who have been neglected or hurt by workaholics and physically or mentally ill or otherwise troubled parents, the percentage of ACDF's in the population gets quite large. Add to these the grandchildren of such parents, and the numbers soar.

Although a significant number of people who grow up in troubled homes do not have serious struggles in their personal or family lives, the ACDF problem still seems severe to those who become aware of it. An Inter-Varsity staff worker at a California university claims over seventy percent of the students come from dysfunctional families. I calculate it to be between thirty and forty percent of adults.

More and more sociologists and psychologists are becoming alert to this problem. Speaking for government agencies, Congressman Daniel Coates declared: "We're trying to look at ways to get to the cause of the problem and try to break that chain."[28]

CONCLUSION

After a seminar or class where I have described the contemporary family, people ask typical "why" questions. Why is the family so troubled? Why is today's divorce rate so different from yesterday's? Why the changes in family? I turn the question back to them. "Society is different," suggests one. "No, people are," another proposes. Someone usually claims we are not as skillful in interpersonal relationships. "No," says another, "we are sinful and in spiritual warfare." What is the cause? Are outside forces on the family mainly to blame? Or have changes in people's thinking and values produced the present family situation? To fully understand the modern family, we must understand what has created it.

NOTES

1. Hazen Werner, *Look at the Family Now* (New York: Abingdon, 1970), 19.

2. Katherine Trent and Scott J. South, "Structured Determinants of the Divorce Rate: A Cross-Societal Analysis," *Journal of Marriage and the Family* 51 (May 1989): 392.

3. David B. Larson, "Marital Status," *Family Building: Six Qualities of a Strong Family*, ed. George Rekers (Ventura, Calif.: Regal Books, 1985), 238.

4. George Barna, *The Future of the American Family* (Chicago: Moody Press, 1993), 68.

5. Studies by Larry L. Bumpass and Teresa Castro Martin. Published in the journal *Demography* and reported in "Study Says Two Marriages of Three Will Fall Apart" *World* (25 March 1989), 4. In Russell Chandler, *Racing Toward 2001: The Forces Shaping America's Religious Future* (Grand Rapids: Zondervan, 1992), 98.

6. George Barna, "Future Issues," cited in Chandler, *Racing Toward 2001*, 333, fn. 34.

7. Edward Shorter, *The Making of the Modern Family* (New York: Basic Books, 1975), 79.

8. "More Female Teenagers Having Sex, Study Says," *Chicago Tribune* (November 8, 1990), sec. 1, 16.

9. "News Watch," *Washington Watch* 2:3 (December 1990): 2.

10. "Teen Pregnancy Rate Grows," *Chicago Tribune* (October 1, 1990), sec. 2, p. 1.

11. Douglas C. Kimmel, *Adulthood and Aging* (New York: Wiley, 1980), 165.

12. Sam Keen, *Fire in the Belly* (New York: Bantam Books, 1991), 5–6.

13. E. E. Le Masters and John DeFrain, *Parents in Contemporary America* (Belmont, Calif.: 1989), 1–2.

14. Urie Bronfenbrenner, testimony before the Senate Subcommittee on Children and Youth, "Hearing on American Families," *Congressional Record* (26 September 1973).

15. Ray Fairchild and John Charles Wynn, *Families in the Church: A Protestant Survey* (New York: Associated Church Press, 1961), 37.

16. Bronfenbrenner, "Hearing on American Families."

17. For example, David Cooper, *The Death of the Family* (New York: Random House, 1971).

18. Daniel Coates, "Commitment to Family by National Leaders," *Family Building: Six Qualities of a Strong Family*, ed. George Rekers (Ventura, Calif.: Regal Books, 1985), 169.

19. J. Richard Udry, *The Social Context of Marriage*, 3d ed. (New York: Harper, 1974), 399.

20. "Familial Alcoholism and Problem Drinking in National Drinking Practices Survey," *Addictive Behaviors* 8 (1983): 133–41. Though some studies show that alcoholism may be passed down in the genes, not all of this influence on these sons can be attributed to that. See Peter Steinglass, *The Alcoholic Family* (New York: Basic Books, 1986), 296–98.

21. Bryon Egeland, Deborah Jacobvitz, and Kathleen Papatola, "Intergenerational Continuity of Abuse," *Child Abuse and Neglect: Biosocial Dimensions*, ed. Richard J. Gelles and Jane B. Lancaster (New York: Aldine de Gruyter, 1987), 270.

22. "Depression Tied to Family Problems," *Family Research Today* 3:6 (December 1987/January 1988): 5.

23. When Congressman Daniel Coates asked a counselor from a modern juvenile detention facility why kids ended up there, he was told, "The one common denominator is that every one of the kids in this facility is from what I would call a disoriented family. There is something present in the family that is out of sync, it is not what we would call normal—if there is something such as a normal family. The kids here who are violent have been subject to violence in their families. The kids who are on drugs or drinking have seen drug abuse in their family. We see this cycle being repeated and repeated" (Coates, "Commitment to Family," 170).

24. Judith S. Wallerstein and Sandra Blakeslee, *Second Chances: Men, Women and Children a Decade after Divorce* (New York: Ticknor and Fields, 1989), 297–98.

25. About 76 million Americans (43 percent of U.S. adults) have been exposed to alcoholism in their family, according to the National Center for Health Statistics. These people grew up with or married an alcoholic or a problem drinker, or had a blood relative who was an alcoholic or a problem drinker. They are 46 percent of women and 39 percent of men. Almost one in five American adults (18 percent) lived with an alcoholic when they were children. Whites are more likely than average to have grown up with a problem drinker (19 percent). Hispanics

and blacks are less likely. An estimated 10.5 million Americans are alcoholics, and that is only a fraction of the number of people affected by the disease. Having an alcoholic in the family increases one's chance for adverse social, psychological, and economic outcomes and for biological predisposition to the disease itself, says the report. Children who live with an alcoholic parent are at greater risk of becoming alcoholic. For more information, see "Exposure to Alcoholism in the Family: United States, 1988," Advance Data from Vital and Health Statistics, no. 2054. National Center for Health Statistics, 6525 Belcrest Road, Hyattsville, MD 20782. See also Joe Schwartz, "Everybody Loves a Drunk," *American Demographics* 14:3 (March 1992): 13.

26. Experts argue over whether abuse has gotten worse in the last several decades. Those who think it has not argue that people just didn't report it as they do now, under compulsory child-abuse reporting laws. Moreover, they claim the definition of abuse has changed through the years, now including acts that were not previously thought of as child abuse.

27. Mary Ann Lamanna and Agnes Riedmann, *Marriages and Families; Making Choices and Facing Change* (Belmont, Calif.: Wadsworth, 1986), 435.

28. Coates, "Commitment to Family," 170.

5

A Changing Unit

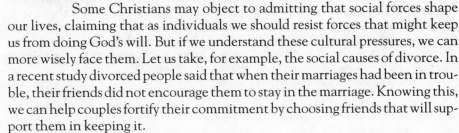

This chapter will examine and evaluate the factors that have shaped the families of today, particularly economic, technological and other social developments. There are many benefits of understanding these forces.

Some Christians may object to admitting that social forces shape our lives, claiming that as individuals we should resist forces that might keep us from doing God's will. But if we understand these cultural pressures, we can more wisely face them. Let us take, for example, the social causes of divorce. In a recent study divorced people said that when their marriages had been in trouble, their friends did not encourage them to stay in the marriage. Knowing this, we can help couples fortify their commitment by choosing friends that will support them in keeping it.

Understanding social conditions that induce family changes will also help us understand what is happening in other parts of the world. Families in many third world countries are experiencing social conditions similar to those that people in the Western world confronted more than a century ago. In parts of Africa, for example, economic conditions force men to leave families in order to pursue work in far-off places, creating havoc in families that used to be quite stable. This follows the same kind of industrialization that took place in our past. And the results are similar: the evidence from around the world, with few exceptions, shows that wherever industrialization and urbanization increase, so does divorce.[1] Two explanations are given for this. When individuals become less economically dependent on their marriages, they develop higher expectations for marriage. The increased economic freedom and greater dissatisfaction lead to more separations and divorces.

> Understanding social conditions that induce family changes will also help us understand what is happening in other parts of the world.

In addition, we can better understand that the church's ministry to families will include attempts to influence church, community and national thinking and policy. One of my African students, for example, believes he must use his official position in his denomination to help change the African Christian's attitude toward the pastor. Many church members believe the pastors should do all the work of the local churches themselves, making it almost impossible for them to invest time in their marriages and families. As a result, the average pastor's family is a troubled one. Until there is a change in the Christian society there, individual pastor's attempts to change the situation will, for the most part, be futile.

THE BEGINNING OF CHANGES IN THE FAMILY

To adequately assess the social factors in changing family life, it will be necessary to note exactly when those changes began.

So much talk about changes in family life in recent decades seems to suggest that the plight of the family is relatively new. There are frequent unfavorable comparisons of today's families with earlier ones. Family expert John Demos notes that Americans have developed the idea of "the family's golden past," that there is some ideal state of domestic life that we have tragically lost.[2] Yet observers of American life have been calling our attention to the decline of family life for a long time. More than five decades ago, Regina Wieman wrote: "The family is going through a long and perilous crisis. Nobody noticed just when it started; nobody can say just how long it will last; nobody knows what the outcome will be."[3]

> By mid-nineteenth century, there was an outpouring in popular literature of the same complaints we hear today.

She was not the first to warn of the predicament of the family. Prominent educator, Herman Horne, in 1909 lamented the "dangers threatening the home." He pointed to the "growing evil of divorce," citing "the present ease with which divorce may be secured. . . ." Home was being forsaken by the women. And for men, home was little more than the place where they slept. Even worse, he lamented, "Family worship is almost an extinct custom. Children are growing up without knowledge of the Bible."[4]

According to this educator, family "decadence" had set in more than eighty years ago, making us wonder exactly when the so-called golden age of the family existed. When, exactly, did the current batch of problems in the American home actually begin?

Yale University professor of history, John Demos, says it was about 1830 when observers first began to notice the plight of the family: "The family, they believed, was set on a course of decline and decay. From a stable and virtuous condition in former times, it had gradually passed into a 'crisis' phase."[5]

By mid-nineteenth century, according to Demos, there was an outpouring in popular literature of the same complaints we hear today: "Divorce and desertion were increasing; child-rearing had become too casual and permissive; authority was generally disrupted; the family no longer did things together; women were more and more restless in their role as homemakers."[6] It was during this period that people began to think back to the family's better days that occurred more than 150 years ago.

About these so-called better days, we can at least point to certain facts. In the last chapter we noted that divorce was comparatively infrequent one hundred years ago compared with today.[7] And as far as we can tell, two hundred years ago, there were almost no battered children in American homes.[8] In 1800 fathers were not only present in the home, they were central figures. Unlike today's child custody disputes, the courts almost always awarded the children to the fathers. And when adult children wrote home, they always addressed their letters to Dad, somewhere inserting a casual, "Say Hello to Mother."[9] Despite these differences between today and two hundred years ago, it is still difficult to say with certainty that families in general were more functional and happy than they are today. We know, for example, that alcoholism, as well as physical and sexual abuse, goes back three or four generations, clearly indicating that such things were present in the mid-nineteenth century.[10] Psychological and spiritual conditions are difficult to assess. Were marriages happier? Were homes more "spiritual"?

THE ROLE OF SOCIAL AND ECONOMIC CHANGES

The family is especially susceptible to economic changes. In fact, economics is behind the major differences between today's and yesterday's family. Going all the way back to the first century, families were the major economic unit. Individuals were primarily dependent on their families for their financial well-being, though the precise form of this dependence changed from time to time over the course of the last two thousand years.[11] Even during the Middle Ages, when peasants worked for the lord of the manor, they usually did so as families. Their right to work the "rented" land was passed down through the family. Wives worked the fields with their husbands and children.

When cities developed, the same pattern continued. Craftsman, shopkeepers, petty merchants, and laborers worked together as families. The shoemaker's family, for example, lived beneath his small roof. His wife was his business partner, working by his side; the children also helped or were put out as apprentices in the same or another trade. Unmarried men and women stayed in their own families, with no place to go except to a convent or to other families to work as servants. Even the later development of "cottage industries," where families clustered together to manufacture goods, did not greatly disturb the family. While men and women worked away from their homes, mothers could still take their children with them and care for them while they worked.

> In the latter part of the eighteenth century middle and upper class white women became primarily homemakers who were consumers instead of producers.

Later with the industrial revolution came the shift from cottage industries to factory. Much has been written about the impact of the industrial revolution on the family. With the development of modern factories, men left home for the workplace, leaving their wives and children alone for a large part of the day. Women could no longer combine employment with care of the home. The increase in income also made it feasible for most wives to devote time solely to housekeeping. It was in the latter part of the eighteenth century that middle and upper class white women became primarily homemakers who were consumers instead of producers.

In this period, lasting until the 1940s, the image of the wife and mother working inside, not outside, the home developed. "Housewife," then, is a relatively modern role.[12] As a result, in 1940 only 14 percent of married women were in the labor force.

Marriages Less Stable

It is easy to see why families might have been more stable prior to the industrial revolution. That there were fewer divorces and rebellious children is not necessarily due to greater religious faith or better marital relationships. To divorce a spouse or rebel against parents would be very costly in economic terms. Bonds of affection were perhaps less important than economic ties. In fact, they were often confused. Seventh-century King Chilperic was said to love his wife, Galswinth, "very dearly, for she had brought a large dowry [a payment to him made by her parents] with her."[13]

Women Employed Outside the Home

Since the nineteenth century, economic forces have continued to change the shape of the family. This, however, does not mean this many women are absent from their families all day. Many of these women are part-time employees outside the home and many others have jobs that keep them at home.[14]

Since World War II many women have left the home for the workplace for economic reasons. By 1986, 55 percent of married women were employed, including over half of mothers with children under age three.[15] Two-income families are becoming the norm for various reasons. Many women work because they are single. For many of them, it was the family breakdown that caused their employment, not their employment that caused the family breakdown. Others work because of the necessity of a two-income family, despite the claim of Larry Burkett that a wife should rarely feel she "has to work." "When that happens, you are living above your means," he advises. "More money won't help."[16] Perhaps his advice applies to some middle- and upper-class couples, but hardly to the millions of poor. According to a report from the Children's Defense Fund, nearly 36 out of every 100 children living in families with parents under thirty years old are classified as poor. Many of these families live without health insurance and in substandard housing.[17]

Such economic issues place a strain on marriage. A recent U.S. Census Bureau report was the first national study on how family stability is affected by poverty and the employment status of parents. They found that couples heading two-parent families are nearly twice as likely to separate or divorce if they

The family became a buffer against stressful jobs and hectic city life.

are living in poverty. Poor African-American families are nearly twice as likely to break up as poor white or Hispanic families, perhaps because their poverty is deeper. The study concluded that the families with the best chance of staying together are those in which the husband works full time and the wife works part time. These families are less likely to break up than families in which both parents work.[18] "Strong family values have to include a strong economic foundation," says Clifford Johnson, support director for the Children's Defense Fund.

The industrial revolution provoked other domestic changes. Workplace and family separated, the family became a haven for people against the rapid social changes that were taking place, a buffer against stressful jobs and hectic city life. It was in nineteenth-century America that people began talking about the "jungle" out there. The home was seen as a place of quiet and repose.

This, according to historian John Demos, contributed to the high value placed on family evident today. Expectations for marriage and family soared. This in turn, as we observed earlier, has led to a great deal of dissatisfaction because families did not live up to their promise.

Globalization

Families worldwide are being touched by the most revolutionary feature of modernity: globalization, a term referring to the close connection between the parts of the world.

In the U.S., the enormous flow of immigrants has produced a plurality of family forms and customs. Peter Berger maintains that the high percentage of Latin-born immigrants in the United States, with their high regard for the family, will help Americans continue to value family life.

Through the media, people in developing countries continue to be affected by Western values, marrying for romantic love and placing more emphasis on marital intimacy. Modern transportation makes it possible for people to find jobs in other countries. Husbands or wives often leave their families behind, hoping within a few years to arrange for spouse and children to join them. In the meantime, they spend only a week or two with their families each year. Separated, spouses are subject to sexual and romantic involvement with other partners, leading to divorce.

Technological Changes

Innovations in architecture, medicine, transportation, and other areas of technology can produce ripples of change in a nation's households. Sociologists enjoy pointing out that when elevators were installed in apartments, the U.S. birth rate rose. Imagine carrying a toddler and a wagon load of toys up three flights of stairs and you'll know why. Central heating in homes separated family members who no longer had to spend their evenings together in the family room to stay warm.[19]

On the other hand, it is obvious that the "pill" and other modern contraceptive devices contributed to the lowering of the birth rate as well as to the change in women's sexual practices. Freed from the fear of pregnancy, females have come closer to males in their casual attitude toward nonmarital sex.

Innovations in medical technology equip people to do things that challenge traditional family norms. For example, artificial insemination and embryo transplants raise new questions: Is it adulterous for a surrogate mother to be implanted artificially with the sperm of another woman's husband so that she bear a child for her? What if a couple hires the surrogate to bear a child by having their own fertilized egg transplanted into her womb?

Politics

That a government can alter family life is obvious from what is happening in China. By law a couple is encouraged to have only one child. Parents who have a second child are penalized by large fines or the withholding of bonuses from their employment.[20] In the United States, the battle over abortion shows how family matters are issues in all the sectors of government: executive, legislative, and judicial; federal, state, and local.

Sometimes political policy affects the family more subtly. Until recently in the U.S. a romantically involved elderly couple would receive more Social Security money if they remained single than if they married. For this reason, senior citizens made up a large portion of the couples who lived together without marrying. Fewer of them are among the "live-ins" now that the Social Security regulations have been changed.

The way the government offers child care support affects the family. For many years, a tax break was given only to parents who placed their children in day care centers. There was no financial incentive for couples to care for their own children. Recently, this has been changed. In the government's 1990 budget, a Young Child Tax Credit was added to the package. Up to $355 in direct tax assistance is available to families with incomes below $21,000 if they have a child under age one.[21]

Shifts in Values

Sociologist Norval Glenn claims that surveys indicate that shifting ideas about the family are also "driving the changes" occurring in families.[22] Economic and social forces, powerful as they are, do not make changes in family life inevitable. Change in personal values alter the way people relate in families.

For example, not all married women who work outside the home do so for financial reward. They may be motivated by a quest for self-esteem since homemaking is no longer as highly valued as other types of work. Homemakers are not direct producers; they serve others (husbands) who participate directly in the economic and political world by meeting their needs for everyday maintenance and emotional support. Observes one expert: "Work that is directly more productive is more highly valued and rewarded in most modern, industrialized societies."[23]

Another example of a shift in values relates to divorce. In the 1950s most Americans believed that parents should stay in an unhappy marriage for the sake of the children. By the mid-1970s a majority of Americans rejected that view. Barbara Whitehead explained what happened: "What had once been regarded as hostile to children's best interests was now considered essential to adults' happiness."[24]

FORECAST: RADICAL CHANGES

Current trends in emerging technology and economic, social, and political values compute badly for those dedicated to family values. Not bothering to argue for the survival of the family, some futurists already speak of a "post-marital society."[25]

Suppose, for example, that in the year 2020 most of the practical reasons for not having sexual relationships outside of marriage are gone. AIDS and other sexually transmitted diseases are wiped out. Unwanted pregnancies can be prevented by sterilization, after everyone who wants to deposits sperm and ovum in a "bank," kept to be fertilized in the future whenever two people decide to have a child. Perhaps an "artificial womb" will be available for developing the fetus. Technology will thus make sexual intercourse irrelevant to having babies. That perspective of sex would be radically opposite that of Christians living five hundred years ago. We will have gone from the view that sex was for having babies to the view that sex is for anything but having babies.

Marriage, too, will be unnecessary, some futurists tell us. The government will stop trying to regulate marriage, predicts Bernard Murstein, "couples being allowed to enjoy the pleasures of sex within whatever arrangement they find satisfactory."[26] Intimacy needs will be met "in a variety of relationships with varying intensities and durations." Robert Francoeur predicts: "In a world where sexual-sensual intimacy has expanded into the domain of communication and friendship, we [will] no longer talk about 'homosexual,' 'heterosexual,' or 'bisexual' persons as our ancestors did so emotionally in the 1980s."[27] By separating erotic intimacy from human reproduction, he claims, we will "have finally allowed both experiences to become more fully human and personal."[28] Since marriage will not be necessary for sexual relationships, people can more easily find a satisfying union, after frequent attempts with a number of partners.

By the time a couple is ready to have children, they will have a good basis for a functional, healthy family. At this point, a couple will be tested to determine if they qualify to be parents. Embryo transplants will become the norm so that a couple will be required to have their sperm and ovum genetically tested before they are permitted to have a technician fertilize the egg in a lab. Robert Francoeur predicts that lesbian couples will purchase frozen semen from sperm banks and have their children by artificial insemination. Gay male couples will hire surrogate mothers who will be inseminated with their mixed semen. Single women will have children by calling on sperm banks. Any couple choosing to have children will be required to enter into a contract to stay together until the child is old enough to be independent. Then they are free to separate and join with other partners if they desire.[29] The average person will have at least three long-term sexual relationships in a lifetime.[30]

> Current trends in emerging technology and economic, social, and political values compute badly for those dedicated to family values.

Some foresee the acceptance and practice of polygamy thirty years from now, especially as a way to meet the needs of elderly women who outnumber the eligible men their age.[31]

Surely, all this sexual coupling with different people will wreak havoc on human emotions, won't it? No, we are told that jealousy, which tied people to others when more permanent relationships were useful, will then be viewed as an unnecessary feeling. People will frequent "jealousy workshops" to be free of it.[32]

At first glance, it looks like someone's futurizing has turned to fantasizing—until we stop to consider that some of this is already a reality. Much of the contributing technology is already available and changes are occurring in public thinking and policy. In January of 1993, Mayor David Dinkins signed an executive order to allow unmarried couples, including homosexuals, to register as domestic partners with the city clerk. He called his action a "major step toward ensuring that the thousands of individuals involved in long-term committed and caring relationships are extended the same rights as individuals bonded through the traditional concept of the family unit."[33]

Those who judge human behavior by evolutionary theory will claim these cultural conditions signal a new age of human development. Human sexual pleasure evolved, they claim, in order to keep a couple together during the years when the children needed them. However, when sex will not be related to producing children, this need will no longer be present. Francoeur judges we will be "liberated" from past values and traditions by the year 2020. By then, only three or four percent of Americans will believe in the traditional family.[34]

Certain or not, this forecast thinking provides some evidence that the society of the future may severely jolt our thinking about the family.[35] The rushing winds of social change create turmoil and confusion for Christians as well as for others. Just as in a storm, we must be somewhat flexible, swaying with the gusts to keep from getting blown over. Yet we need to hang on to something sturdy and fixed to keep from being swept away.

SEARCH FOR NORMS FOR FAMILY

As a goal for family ministry, some ideal model of family must be created, but by what process and criteria?

Attempting to find a workable plan, anthropologists observe cultures to see if there is any worldwide idea of family, supposing what is practiced by all could be accepted by all. But social scientists don't agree on what family practices are common to all cultures.[36] And often what they do find is quite limited. After surveying the world's approach to the functions of family, two sociologists could find only one factor common to all of them. Everywhere, the early nurture of children is done by some family members. "We know of no society in which the function of nurturant socialization of the newborn is not performed by a small kinship-structured group," they reported. In this aspect, and in this alone, they contend, "family" is universal.[37] Though meager, this finding is meaningful; it confirms the crucial role of kin in early childhood and serves as a warning, from scientific quarters, to those who would dismiss worries about institutional day care and other nonfamily forms of child care.

> Social scientists don't agree on what family practices are common to all cultures.

Using Research to Discover What Works

Still, there is another way to determine what family ought to be: scientific research that confirms the best practical approaches to family functions. We would look for research that shows whether keeping sex inside marriage is best for humans; whether a patriarchal style of the husband's role as leader is best for marriage and for society; whether mothers employed outside the home are less effective in childrearing, etc. Establishing norms and standards through science is a common approach to issues today.

For example, Ira Reiss and Gary Lee argue logically and scientifically for the infant's need of warm, emotional and physical contact supplied by "family." They cite the case of the Ik culture, in which newborns are neglected in many ways, often left to die. This is obviously dysfunctional, since this practice, along with severe econimic strains, is causing the Iks to go out of existence.[38] Thus, this "family" nurture of children is essential.

Studies of nonhuman primates also prove the need for such care, according to Reiss and Lee. They point to Harry Harlow's classic work on rhesus monkeys, as well as other research, to show the impor-

It is questionable whether the family of yesterday can be the model for the family of a vastly different today. Retreat is virtually impossible.

tance of physical contact in an infant's emotional development. Monkeys raised by receiving "comfort" from close contact with a mother were emotionally stable. Those raised by surrogate mothers made of cloth or wire became emotionally disturbed and were unable either to relate to other monkeys or to perform sexually.

Another type of evidence is drawn from studies of human infants raised in institutional settings, separate from their mothers. In short, this data indicates that maternal separation has damaging effects on children.[39]

This practical, scientific approach to defining family is certainly useful. In this book, I draw upon such evidence from time to time to support conclusions. But there are limits to this approach. Studies are lacking in some areas, and issues that are well researched are not settled because the findings are so contradictory. Often the matters are so politically and socially controversial that all sides of the problem cite research that proves their viewpoint.

Looking to the Past

Another way to find the ideal family is to look to the past. This is the approach of many religious and political conservatives who constantly refer to superior forms of family during America's conformity to its Judeo-Christian heritage. This may be accepted as a political strategy, since advocates can argue that their views should be America's because they once were American. But, as an approach to discover the ideal family, this approach is inadequate for Christians. In the first place, we can't be certain that the so-called traditional family was the best form of the family. Developed in the latter part of the nineteenth century, during America's "Victorian era," this model had its shortcomings, as historians are quick to point out. And they tell us that what people want to get back to, "the classical family of Western nostalgia," may never have existed in the first place.[40] Moreover, it is questionable whether the family of yesterday can be the model for the family of a vastly different today. Retreat is virtually impossible.

In fact, many Christian advocates of strong families contend that we must look not back, but ahead. George Barna, among others, claims that churches too often hold onto a traditional model of the family. And although many people claim to believe in this traditional approach, they do not act on these beliefs. "Because of this, they are uncomfortable with what the church is preaching."[41]

This tension between what exists in people's minds and in their lives must be confronted. One expert counsels the church to dispel current

> A strategy of family ministry must spring from an in-depth analysis of the contemporary family and a careful, continuous scrutiny of our theology.

family myths: "The good family has no problems." "There are no bad children, only bad parents." "All two-parent families are healthier than single-parent families." "The good family has its children involved in many activities." "A father's primary responsibility is to his work." "A good mother doesn't work outside the home." "Good families stay rooted in one community." Delores Curren admits there is some truth in all of these, but she warns: "Automatically assuming that they are all true takes a toll on families in loss of confidence and despair."[42]

These swift cultural changes in family living put Christians in a risky situation, since the drift seems to be away from biblical norms. The temptation is to cling to the present or wish for a return to the past, believing the only Christian form of the family is preserved there. "Too much church literature," wrote R. W. Fairchild, "betrays a wish for today's families to remain just as they were in the 1890s." This strategy runs the risk of leaving the church behind the times, ineffectively out of touch. On the other hand, those too quick to sail the currents of a changing culture may be swept from their Christian convictions.

Using an Integration Approach

Our challenge lies in integrating our Christianity with modernity. A strategy of family ministry must spring from an in-depth analysis of the contemporary family and a careful, continuous scrutiny of our theology. In this process, our theology must remain supreme, providing the standards for the family. We will be forced to look at new issues in the light of Christian truth. What will we say about nonmarital sex if fear of pregnancy and disease are erased? Will it be enough to shout that God is against it? Or can we propose other reasons for nonmarital sexual abstinence? If so, we will have to probe deeply the theological, psychological and spiritual aspects of marriage and sexuality. The family model that emerges will not be a biblical family, if by that we mean it will resemble families of biblical times. Rather, it will be a modern model—based on biblical principles.

We cannot begin to talk about a family ministry strategy until we have first constructed a theology of the family, the subject of the next section. Not all the many issues will be decided for you. Rather they will be introduced and explored, garnished with arguments pro and con, equipping you to settle them for yourself.

> The family model that emerges will not be a biblical family, if by that we mean it will resemble families of biblical times. Rather, it will be a modern model—based on biblical principles.

EXCURSUS ON THE THEOLOGICAL TASK

Theology, simply put, is thinking Christianly about anything and everything. It's not quite the same as thinking biblically. Though the Scriptures are the basis for theology, theology does more than interpret every passage of Scripture dealing with marriage and family. The following are the distinguishing features of the theological task that I have followed in developing a theology of the family.

Selecting Relevant Scripture

Since God's revelation was given in different periods of history and under varying circumstances, we cannot simply assume that every statement of Scripture applies directly to us today. Jesus showed he understood this when, debating divorce with the Pharisees, he dismissed their appeal to Moses (Deut. 24:1–4) as irrelevant. Saying this does not deny that all Scripture is relevant, since any passage contains some principle that we could apply to ourselves. Rather, not all Scripture as stated was meant for all people in all eras. If we were merely to list and arbitrarily apply the statements of Scripture about marriage and family we would insist that: adulterers should be stoned and illegitimate children ostracized; a man would be obligated to marry his sister-in-law; rebellious teenagers would be put to death; sex would be prohibited during a wife's menstrual period, etc.

Theology looks at all of Scripture, examining each book and its message in order to make sense of the whole biblical message, which is the basis for selecting what is relevant for Christians. Dispensationalists, for example, sometimes qualify Jesus' strong prohibition against divorce by claiming this ideal was to be applied only in the millennium, when it is possible to do God's will. In the present age of grace, under certain circumstances, forgiveness for those who fail in marriage makes divorce and remarriage a workable solution in some cases. Whether their interpretation is correct or not, they are right in their effort to interpret individual Scripture in the light of the whole biblical message.

Dealing with Moral and Practical Questions

In its effort to make biblical principles relevant to today, theology goes beyond the exegesis of Scripture. It moves in two directions: sometimes theology starts from Scripture and advances to application to life; other times, it starts with some contemporary issue and then consults Scripture for an answer. Revealed in the context of ancient cultures, biblical truth obviously does not always deal directly with modern practices like artificial insemination, sterilization, embryo transplants, and the like. It offers no specific guidelines for dealing with child or spouse abuse. Besides bringing such specific issues to Scripture, we will also need to bring modern psychological, sociological, and ethical perspectives that are foreign to Scripture, but may or may not be compatible with its overall principles. For this reason, theology will embrace other disciplines, while Scripture remains its final authority.

Searching for Reasons

To speak to ethical and practical issues, theology attempts to get to the foundation of matters. While it may affirm that adultery is wrong, it also asks why. It tries to get at the heart and essence of things. It establishes basic explanations and meaning of things as they are in Scripture and then draws implications from them. Jesus practiced this. He drew his conclusion about divorce from his view of marriage. "They are no longer two, but one," he said, referring to the "one flesh" statement of Genesis 2:24. Reasoning from this, Jesus then said: "What God has joined together, let no man separate."

In this reasoning, the theologican will attempt to get back to basics. What, for example, is marriage? Is it a contract between two people, or is it a love relationship? Knowing the answer to questions such as these, we can then explain specific passages of Scripture more in depth. We may more fully understand why God says, "I hate divorce," or on what grounds God forbids nonmarital sex. We are then in a better position to answer contemporary issues that are not addressed by a specific passage of Scripture. Take, for instance, the matter of embryo implants. Is it wrong for a woman to be implanted with another woman's egg that was fertilized by her husband's sperm? Answering this requires delving into the meaning and reasons for adultery. Is adultery primarily forbidding illegitimate sexual contact or illegitimate conception? Other biblical themes will also need to be consulted to answer such questions.

In appealing to broad-based Christian principles we will have to be careful not to use these to justify ignoring answers derived from specific passages of Scripture.

Catholic moralist Andre Guindon is one of many who do this, elevating theological thinking above biblical assertions. He first argues that marriage is based on love, not upon an institutional contract. Then he moralizes that when love is gone from a marriage, persons should be free to divorce. Homosexuality is also then judged by this general rule, not by specific scriptural passages: "When gay sex is loving, it is difficult to discover . . . what Christian law is broken." Employing this method of thinking, Guindon sees no need to carefully exegete Scripture that deals with divorce or homosexuality.

Evangelicals, who rely on the authority of all Scripture, insist we not use broad theological themes to unfairly disregard clear statements of Scripture when they are present.

Basing Guidelines in the Person of God

Ultimately, any theological conclusion about marriage and family must be grounded in the person of God; the term *theology* literally means discourse about God. While attempting to describe what God created, theology will also try to see how the creation is connected to the person of the creator. Any link that is found will give profound meaning to our model of the family since a prescribed feature of family would spring from the very nature of God. For this reason, complying with God's norms for sex, marriage, and family will not just be conformity to what God says, but who God is.

Furthermore, the theology of family will need to be linked to God as redeemer. The theology of creation will tell us what was and is. Redemption will tell us what will be. Family must ultimately derive its value and nature from the Sovereign King's future plan. Family, like everything else, will finally be engulfed by God's kingdom. For this reason, our quest for a theology of the family will begin with God's work of redemption.

NOTES

1. Katherine Trent and Scott J. South, "Structural Determinants of the Divorce Rate: A Cross-societal Analysis," *Journal of Marriage and the Family* 51 (May 1989): 392.

2. John Demos, *Past, Present, and Personal: The Family and the Life Course in American History* (New York: Oxford University Press, 1986), 30.

3. Regina Wieman, *Family and the Church* (New York: Harper, 1937), 18.

4. Herman Horne, *Psychological Principles of Education* (New York: Macmillan, 1909), 367–73.

5. Demos, *Past, Present and Personal*, 30.

6. Ibid.

7. David B. Larson, "Marital Status," *Family Building: Six Qualities of a Strong Family*, ed. George Rekers (Ventura, Calif.: Regal Books, 1985), 238.

8. Demos, *Past, Present, and Personal*, 70–88, argues that child abuse was not prevalent in the past and that it is a new phenomenon. See also Dorcas Hardy, "How Government Can Serve Children and Families," in *Family Building*, ed. George Reker (Ventura, Calif.: Regal, 1985), 213.

9. Demos, *Past, Present, and Personal*, 41–67.

10. Comparing past homes with today's is a complex operation because digging up the specific details of past family life is painstakingly difficult. We have no survey results to compare with. For example, in certain communities of eighteenth-century America, 30 to 40 percent of all brides were pregnant. That is demonstrated by comparing their wedding dates with the birthdays of their eldest children. From this some scholars assume that older generations had lost control of their children. But, as Demos argues, "The factors involved here are too numerous, and the relationships between them are too complex, to permit such . . . inference" (ibid., 7).

11. For a detailed survey of how changing social and economic factors impacted family lifestyles from A.D. 500 to A.D. 1500, see Frances Gies and Joseph Gies, *Marriage and the Family in the Middle Ages* (New York: Harper & Row, 1987).

12. Mary Ann Lamanna and Agnes Riedmann, *Marriages and Families; Making Choices and Facing Change* (Belmont, Calif.: Wadsworth, 1986), 352–53.

13. Gregory of Tours, *The History of the Franks*, trans. Lewis Thorpe (n.p.: Harmondsworth, 1974), 222, quoted in Gies and Gies, *Marriage and the Family in the Middle Ages*, 60.

14. "Is the 'Traditional' Family Dead?" *Family Policy*, published by the Family Research Council of America (September/October 1988): 1–5.

15. Lamanna and Riedmann, *Marriages and Families*, 353.

16. Larry Burkett, *The Complete Financial Guide for Young Couples* (Wheaton, Ill.: Victor Books, 1989), 198.

17. Eileen Ogintz, "Young Parents Sink in Poverty, Study Says," *Chicago Tribune* (August 31, 1989), sec. 1, p. 12.

18. Patrick T. Reardon, "How Poverty's Weight Cracks Families," *Chicago Tribune* (January 15, 1993), sec. 1, p. 1.

19. George Barna lists five major technological breakthroughs and their effects on the family: the automobile, telephone, movies, central heating, and electricity (*The Future of the American Family* [Chicago: Moody Press, 1993], 32).

20. Ziangiming Chen, "The One-Child Population Policy, Modernization, and the Extended Chinese Family," *Journal of Marriage and the Family* 47 (February, 1985): 193.

21. "Child Care Victory," *Washington Watch*, published by the Family Research Council, vol. 2:2 (November 1990): 1.

22. Norval D. Glenn, "What Does Family," *American Demographics* 14:4 (June 1992): 34.

23. Joan Huber and Glenna Spitze, *Sex Stratification* (New York: Academic, 1983); Lamanna and Riedmann, *Marriages and Families*, 353.

24. Barbara Whitehead, "Dan Quayle Was Right," *Atlantic Monthly* 271: 4 (April 1993): 50.

25. Lester A. Kirkendall and Arthur E. Gravatt, eds., *Marriage and the Family in the Year 2020* (New York: Prometheus Books, 1984).

26. Bernard Murstein, "'Mate' Selection in the Year 2020," *Marriage and the Family in the Year 2020*, ed. Kirkendall and Gravatt, 74.

27. Robert Francoeur, "Transformations in Human Reproduction," *Marriage and the Family in the Year 2020*, ed. Kirkendall and Gravatt, 101–2.

28. Ibid., 89–105.

29. Ibid.

30. Murstein, "'Mate' Selection in the Year 2020," 74.

31. Lester Kirkendall and Arthur E. Gravatt, "Marriage and Family: Styles and Forms," *Marriage and the Family in the Year 2020*, ed. Kirkendall and Gravatt, 67.

32. Murstein, "'Mate' Selection in the Year 2020," 81–82.

33. "Unmarried Partners Status OKd in N. Y.," *Chicago Tribune* (January 8, 1993), sec. 1, p. 1.

34. Robert Francoeur, "Moral Concepts in the Year 2020: The Individual, the Family and Society," *Marriage and the Family in the Year 2020*, ed. Kirkendall and Gravatt, 198–99.

35. Futurists are not always to be taken seriously. For one thing, they are almost always optimistic about technological development. That all sexually transmitted diseases and other pragmatic problems related to promiscuous sex will be eliminated within the next thirty years is rather idealistic. Also, futurists tend to project their own value system into their portrait of things to come. We do well to remember, as we said in chapter 2, that despite some current trends, we must not too quickly assume that the family as we know it will become obsolete.

36. For example, there is considerable debate over whether or not the nuclear family form of the family exists everywhere. See Steven L. Nock, *Sociology of the Family* (Englewood Cliffs, N.J.: Prentice-Hall, 1987), 31.

37. Ira L. Reiss and Gary R. Lee, *Family Systems in America,* 4th ed. (New York: Holt, Rinehart and Winston, 1988), 25–30. They particularly point to the need of the infant to have adults respond to him or her and provide emotional support. Essentially, it is the mother who provides this. However, in some cases care may come from some socially recognized kin.

38. Ibid., 25.

39. Ibid., 25–27.

40. A thorough description of the nineteenth-century family, with comparison to today's family, can be found in William J. Goode, *World Revolution and Family Patterns* (New York: Free Press, 1963), 6–7.

41. George Barna, "The American Family and Church Ministry," news release from the Barna Research Group (30 July, 1990), 3, cited in Russell Chandler, *Racing Toward 2001: The Forces Shaping America's Religious Future* (Grand Rapids: Zondervan, 1992), 90.

42. Delores Curran, "Community Leaders Can Develop Programs," in *Family Building: Six Qualities of a Strong Family*, ed. Rekers, 276.

◆ *Part Two*

The Theology of Family Ministry

Importance and Form of Family

THEOLOGICAL SIGNIFICANCE OF FAMILY

Some church leaders suggest that our churches can become *too* family-centered. Christians can become so wrapped up in their family life that it becomes a form of idolatry.[1] Evangelical Rodney Clapp calls this *hyperfamilism*, which is the tendency to spend so much time enriching family life that one has little regard for other important responsibilities, especially those related to the work of the church.[2] When church members become so involved in their families that they neglect building close relationships in the church, single people may suffer because they need intense participation in church life and activities. Clapp argues: "For years it has been popular among evangelicals to list three lifetime priorities in this order: God, family, and church . . . in these popular rankings, family usurps the place the New Testament assigns to the church."[3]

SCRIPTURE THAT SEEMS TO DIMINISH THE ROLE OF MARRIAGE AND FAMILY

To try to settle this family versus church debate, let's consider the biblical arguments that seem to place a higher priority on the church. Quite a few New Testament passages seem to demean, if not diminish, marriage and family. Did Jesus, for example, subordinate marriage and family to the church when he told his followers to seek first God's kingdom (Matt. 6:33)? What are the implications of his assertion that at the resurrection people will neither marry nor be given in marriage, but be like the angels in heaven (Matt. 22:30)? Marriage is apparently temporal, not eternal.

Other statements and actions of Jesus seem to lessen the importance of marriage and family. Never married, Jesus pressed for supreme allegiance to himself, sometimes by gross exaggeration: "If anyone comes to me and does not hate his father and mother, his wife and children, his brothers and sisters—yes, even his own life—he cannot be my disciple" (Luke 14:26). That some of his followers did sacrifice their family life for Christ's mission is evident by Peter's remark: "We have left all we had to follow you!" Replies Jesus, "I tell you the truth . . . no one who has left home or wife or brothers or parents or children for the sake of the kingdom of God will fail to receive many times as much in this age and, in the age to come, eternal life" (Luke 18:28–30).

Jesus himself, on one occasion, stressed the priority of "spiritual family" relationships over blood relationships by seeming to snub his own family. Having received a message that his family had come to see him, he refused to welcome them. Instead he responded, "Who are my mother and my brothers?" And looking at those who sat around him, he said, "Here are my mother and brothers! Whoever does God's will is my brother and sister and mother" (Mark 3:33–35).

The apostle Paul also shows this concern for the superiority of the kingdom. Wanting Christians to be free from the concerns of this world, which "in its present form is passing away," he suggests that unmarried people would be better off remaining single (1 Cor. 7:26–31). In this he follows Jesus who spoke of those who "have renounced marriage because of the kingdom of heaven" (Matt. 19:12). "An unmarried man is concerned about the Lord's affairs," he affirms, "But a married man is concerned about the affairs of this world . . . and his interests are divided" (1 Cor. 7:32–33). The same holds true for a woman. Paul seems to show total lack of regard for any Christian responsibility to continue to populate the earth as commanded in Genesis 1:27. "Clearly, Jesus (and Paul) departed from the view of the Hebrews of universal marriage," says David Mace.[4]

However, this view is not all the New Testament has to say about family.

REASONS FOR THE IMPORTANCE OF THE FAMILY

When we look more closely at the Gospels, we see that Jesus never really opposed or attacked marriage.[5] To the contrary, he honored it by attending the marriage in Cana (John 2:12ff.). Though he asked Peter and others to leave everything and follow him, he didn't seem to require their abandoning their families. At one time, he healed Peter's wife's mother while in Peter's home (Mark 1:30ff.). Later, Peter and the other apostles apparently took their wives with them on the missionary journeys (1 Cor. 9:5). Most important, Jesus used marriage and family repeatedly as the basis for parables and analogies. For example, the parable of the ten virgins uses the metaphor of the wedding (Matt. 25:1ff.). Jesus spoke of feasting with his disciples in the future that later Scripture calls the marriage feast of the lamb (Luke 22:30; Rev. 19:9).

Paul too dignifies marriage and family in his writings. To the Ephesians he wrote a profound treatment of marriage in which Christ's love for the church is compared to a groom's love for his bride.

The New Testament, then, seems to portray two contradictory views of marriage and family. In part, the reason for this is that the statements are couched in three different contexts: creation, redemption, and eternity.

Three Contexts for Family: Creation, Redemption, Eternity

Some Scriptures refer to God's original purposes; others are given in the present context of a fallen world; and still others are made in the framework of God's redemption, his Kingdom, and "New Creation." Statements about marital sex, for example, will reflect all three of these contexts. In God's creative order, sex is needed to populate the earth (Gen. 1:28). In the present sinful era, its regular practice in marriage keeps men and women from burning with passion and thus guards them from immorality (1 Cor. 7:1–9). But for the sake for the kingdom of heaven, some will renounce marital sex (Matt. 19:12).

Acknowledging the existence of these three spheres will help us gain a better perspective of the importance of family. It is true that marriage and family are part of God's present creation and are temporary. In a certain sense, they are not part of the "new creation," which is eternal and ranks above the original creation. However, in the present age, marriage and family are related to the kingdom in a crucial way: they become the place where kingdom values, ethics and virtues are to be practiced and displayed. In this respect, they are temporary institutions that embody eternal ideals.[6]

> The family's place in the kingdom is often overlooked by those who tell us that family competes with church.

The family's place in the kingdom is often overlooked by those who tell us that family competes with church. Rodney Clapp, for instance, urges Christians not to put their families ahead of the church. Clapp arrives at this ranking because he equates the church with the kingdom.[7] However, both family and church participate in the redemptive work of Christ and are under his kingdom rule. Clapp's ranking is unnecessary and misleading since Christians have so-called kingdom privileges and responsibilities in both church and home as well as in society.

Sometimes the Scriptures warn us that the family should not interfere with our commitment to the kingdom. Yet Scripture also cautions us not to neglect marital responsibilities for spiritual pursuits, as when Paul tells Christians not to allow fasting and praying to interfere with meeting their mate's sexual needs. Putting the church first does not justify ignoring marriage and family obligations. The church is not always first any more than the family is always first. For example, if the church family were to be put first, we would expect it would be first in taking care of widows. However, 1 Timothy 5:3–5 indicates that families should take care of their own widows; only after they cannot do this should the church do it.

What is true of responsibilities is also true of privileges. God has given us all things to enjoy, including marriage. Certainly we should not allow our enjoyment of marriage to interfere with our commitment to the church, for

> ## While temporary sacrifice is proper, abandonment is not.

example having frequent romantic weekends that exclude Sunday church involvement. But we should not permit enjoyment of church to neglect our family life, as when church members immerse themselves in "church work" at the expense of their spouses and children. There may be times when we temporarily sacrifice family for church (during crises, or special missions, etc.) or church for family (as when a mate's serious illness demands a person's time). But while temporary sacrifice is proper, abandonment is not. Seeing both the temporary and eternal qualities of marriage and family will keep us from unduly idolizing them while at the same time not underrating their importance.

Conclusion: Family Life Restored

In summary, we have established that marriage is part of God's created order, still in effect today, and that the "new creation" Christ has begun in his believers is intended to restore marriage and family to what God intended. Now, we must determine exactly what marriage and family ought to be.

THE BIBLICAL FORM OF THE FAMILY

It is rather surprising to discover that there is no clear definition of the word "family" in the Bible, either in the Old Testament or in the New Testament. The Hebrews had no actual word for family. And in the New Testament, *okkia* ("household"), the word most often translated "family" isn't an exact equivalent of our word family, since it refers to everyone living in a house, including servants and various relatives.

There is, nevertheless, plenty of scriptural material for constructing a model of what the family should be.

Marriage Instituted by God

Although today it is generally accepted by Christians that marriage, as we know it, was created by God, some of the early Hebrews accommodated themselves to the marriage practices of neighboring cultures. For example, Abraham married his half-sister (Gen. 20:12); Sarah gave her maid to Abraham as a wife (16:1–3); and Jacob had two wives (29:26–28). These examples might suggest that marriage and its customs were merely human inventions, subject to the definition and control of society.

But both testaments view marriage as being of divine origin and under God's regulation. Genesis 2 provides the basic ideal: "For this reason a man will leave his father and mother and be united to his wife, and they will become one flesh" (2:24). Jesus refers to this foundational statement about marriage, seeing marriage not as an institution of Mosaic law or the patriarchal social system of Moses's day, but as a part of God's order of creation. Marital ideals are to be traced "from the beginning" (Matt. 19:8).

The apostle Paul too seems to base his attitude toward marriage on its being created by God. In his appeal to Timothy to combat those "liars" who would forbid marriage (1 Tim. 4:1–5), Paul seems to be including marriage in his statement that "everything God created is good" (v. 4). Perhaps he had in mind God's pronouncement after creating man and woman: "And it was very good" (Gen. 1:27–28, 31).

Biblical scholars tend to agree that the basic form of family created by God is the nuclear family, which gives the highest priority to the husband-wife relationship. Elements of Genesis 2:24 make it clear that a husband and wife's first loyalty are to each other and not to any extended family relationship. That the man is said to leave his father and mother to be united to his wife suggests he replaces one commitment with another. The fact that husband and wife become one flesh supports the priority of the nuclear pair. That Adam says of his wife, "This is now bone of my bones and flesh of my flesh" is especially significant. The Hebrew words for bone and flesh are frequently used to describe extended family relationships (Gen. 29:14; Judg. 9:2; 2 Sam. 5:1; 2 Sam. 19:12–13; 1 Chron. 11:1). That the same terms are used to describe both the marriage (conjugal) relationship and blood (consanguinal) relationships shows that blood ties are not superior to the marital union. It is true that in Old Testament times, for political and economic reasons whole groups of families joined

> The basic form of family created by God is the nuclear family, which gives the highest priority to the husband-wife relationship.

together to make a unit. A major political unit, tribes, were made up of extended kin. Yet, the nuclear family identity was pronounced within these groupings and there is nothing to suggest that any extended family arrangement was part of God's creative order. This is especially significant for Christians in societies where non-Christian traditions dictate that the parent-adult child relationship should have priority over the husband-wife union. It also has crucial practical application to Christians whenever parents interfere or compete with their son's or daughter's marriage.

The concepts of *husband*, *wife*, and *marriage* are in both testaments. Having become "one flesh," the pair is recognized by society as a social unit with privileges, responsibilities, and restrictions that we will describe in detail later on. This means that persons of the same sex cannot marry, since it requires a man and woman to create a "one flesh" relationship.[8] In addition, there must be only one man and one woman, making monogamy the norm.

Marriage Is Monogamous

Not all scholars of the Bible hold to the view that Scripture promotes monogamy. Gerhard von Rad, an Old Testament scholar, claims monogamy is not implied in Genesis 2. In fact, he contended that polygamy was the norm in the nation of Israel until the time of the Exile.[9]

By contrast, Scripture seems to point to monogamy as the norm. In an excellent article on the nature of the family in the Old Testament, Professor Walter Wegner provides convincing evidence for his contention that throughout history Israel's ideal for marriage was monogamy. He points first to the prototype of Adam and Eve, which was clearly monogamous. And he explains that the Old Testament proposes a one-husband and one-wife pattern, even though Israel's actions did not always match God's plan.[10]

In particular, the prophets, who cover half a millennium of Israel's life, affirm monogamy in their messages. Using the marriage relationship as a

> We must accept the fact that family situations that are less than ideal are still acceptable.

metaphor of God's relationship to Israel, Hosea is a shining example of love and faithfulness to one's partner in marriage. David Schuller asserts, "The portrait of Hosea's marriage suggests that monogamy union is under discussion and that such a marriage would be regarded as normative by the prophet's audience."[11] The book of Hosea makes it clear that God will have no other wife but Israel, just as Israel is to have no other husband but Jehovah. This same emphasis is found in Isaiah and Ezekiel (Isa. 54; 62:1–5; Ezek. 16).

L. Koehler explains the exceptions to monogamy in Israel as being primarily the practice of the kings. This, he says, does not cancel the standard of Genesis 2:24. Departure from the ethical and religious will of God was frequent among Israel's leaders. It is erroneous, however, to conclude from this that polygamy was the norm for the ordinary people.[12]

For the Christian, Jesus' interpretation of Genesis 2:24 is definitive (Matt. 19:1–2). In maintaining that remarrying after one is divorced constitutes adultery for both the man and the woman (v. 9), Jesus by implication upholds the ideal of monogamy. Here Jesus quotes the Septuagint, the most important Greek translation of the Old Testament. In Genesis 2 the Septuagint uses the word *two*, meaning two people will become one in marriage. This indicates that only a pair is to be involved in marriage, not more. Paul, too, supports monogamy when listing qualifications for church leaders and criteria for church support of widows (1 Tim. 3:2, 5:9; 12; Titus 1:6).

Family Instituted by God

That God's design was for children to be raised by a man and woman is also well established in Scripture. A command to "be fruitful and increase in number and to fill the earth" was given to Adam and Eve. That children were only to be born to married couples is clear from the fact that sex was to be practiced within a monogamous marriage, as we have already seen. That ideally children are to be raised by their parents and not by the extended family, tribe, or community seems clear by the fact that one of the ten commandments was for children to honor their parents (Ex. 20:12). Parents were commanded to teach their children about God (Deut. 6:7). Though the word "parents" is not actually used, it seems clear that the teaching is to be done at home: "Talk about them when you sit at home and when you walk along the road, when you lie down and when you get up" (Deut. 6:7).

The apostle Paul also places the responsibility for spiritual nurture in the home: "Fathers, . . . bring [your children] up in the training and instruction of the Lord" (Eph. 6:4). Obviously this doesn't mean that children learn only from their parents; in the book of Proverbs wise men are also the teachers of children. But even in this case the wise men point children to their parents, urging them to "listen . . . to your father's instruction and do not forsake your mother's teaching" (Prov. 1:8).

So far, we have been picturing the ideal family: a husband and wife with children. However, we must accept the fact that family situations that are less than ideal are still acceptable. In the case of the death or desertion of a spouse, a parent may be forced to raise a child alone. Other conditions sometimes make it necessary for children to be raised by other relatives or even non-relatives. It may even be proper for a single person to adopt a child. But such cases should be seen as exceptions to God's ideal pattern. And in these situations, care should be taken to see that children have close contact with both males and females to provide appropriate role models and satisfying relationships with both sexes, as would be the case if they were raised by both a father and mother.

At this point, another question arises: is it proper for a husband and wife to remain childless? Certainly some couples cannot have children. But should they choose not to have them? The answer to this question is bound up in another: what is the purpose of marriage? Did God create marriage primarily for its childbearing function? Or is it designed for some other purpose? If marriage is primarily for having children, then its most important function is to reproduce and care for them. Other features of marriage—companionship, romance, intimacy and sexual pleasure—would then be considered less significant and even optional. Everything in the marriage would revolve around the child-rearing function. Later, when we consider the theological feasibility of love, sex, and other companionship aspects of marriage, we will deal with this question. Right now, it is enough to point out that Scripture affirms husband and wife as a distinct social unity, a family. And that unit is the ideal place for bearing and raising children.

Extended Kin Relationships Regulated by God

Theologically defining extended kin relationships is a crucial issue for modern times. Many people are angry with their parents and aggravated by other relatives. They deal with extended family by ignoring them. Relatives pose annoying questions and troubled emotions. Feeling guilty over her anger with her parents, one woman asked me: "What does it mean to honor my parents when my father repeatedly sexually abused me and my mother stood by without helping me?" Others ask: "Must I try to help my thirty-year-old brother with his financial problems?" "Just how much effort should I put into keeping in touch with my sister, or my aunt?"

As a separate unit, husbands and wives answer to one another and are no longer under the authority of their parents or other relatives (Gen. 2:24).

> Theologically defining extended kin relationships is a crucial issue for modern times.

Biblically, it is clear that these extended kin relationships have some significance. We have already seen that the phrases Adam used to describe his relationship to Eve, "bone of my bones and flesh of my flesh" (Gen. 2:23), are later used to refer to other relatives (Gen. 29:14; Judg. 9:2; 2 Sam. 5:1; 19:13; Neh. 5:5). While this validates the strength of the conjugal union, it also attaches some importance to blood relationships. Some obligations are spelled out. Incest is forbidden between "close relatives," such as brother, sister, aunt, uncle, etc. (Lev. 18:6–18).

Other Extended Kin Relationships

Nothing is said in Scripture of any special obligation between brothers and sisters, except those embodied in the kinsman-redeemer edict. "If one of your countrymen becomes poor and sells some of his property, his nearest relative is to come and redeem what his countryman has sold" (Lev. 25:25). Because of the enormous need to own land, this provision helped guarantee the passing of land from one generation to another. Also, to continue a family line the Old Testament law pressured a man to consider marrying his dead brother's childless wife in order to father a son who could continue his brother's name and inheritance (Deut. 25:5–10). Despite the lack of specific obligations of siblings for one another, there are other passages of Scripture that suggests a distinct relationship between them. The Bible speaks of "brotherly love" as something unique, and elevates that relationship by saying, "there is a friend that sticks closer than a brother" (Prov. 18:24). The sentiment of Scripture seems to be that the nuclear family is the prime relationship; however, extended kin relationships should not be taken lightly.

NOTES

1. Roy Fairchild and John Charles Wynn, *Families in the Church: A Protestant Survey* (New York: Association Press, 1961), 16.

2. John Charles Wynn, "The Home and Christian Education," *Introduction to Christian Education*, ed. Marvin Taylor (Nashville: Abingdon, 1966), 292.

3. Rodney Clapp, "Is the 'Traditional' Family Biblical?" *Christianity Today* 32 (September 16, 1988): 25.

4. David and Vera Mace, *The Sacred Fire: Christian Marriage Through the Ages* (Nashville: Abingdon Press, 1986), 57.

5. Geoffrey W. Bromiley, *God and Marriage* (Grand Rapids: Eerdmans, 1980), 37.

6. Ray Anderson, *On Being Human* (Grand Rapids: Eerdmans, 1982), 52.

7. Clapp, "Is the 'Traditional' Family Biblical?"

8. Prior to the Reformation, marriage was not respected for its being created by God perhaps because of a negative attitude toward sex. In the sixteenth century, the one factor that kept theologians from a total disregard for marriage was its sacramental nature. It was thought to be one of a number of avenues by which God dispenses grace in a special way along with baptism, the Lord's Supper, and others. This view of marriage was based chiefly on the fact that Paul asserted that it was a symbol of the union of Christ and the church.

Combining a sacramental view of marriage with such a negative attitude toward sex created a major problem. How could a sacrament encourage acts that could easily be sinful? The way they defined marriage answered the question. Normally, we think of marriage consisting of two elements: the public consent of the partners and their private consummation in sexual intercourse. After centuries of debate, the church leaders decided that consent alone was necessary for the sacrament of marriage to take place, thus avoiding making sex a part of the sacrament.

Some church reformers began to see the confusion in this position. In the seventeenth century, John Calvin attacked the church for its "low view of marriage" when he wrote: "But, having graced marriage with that title of sacrament, to call it afterward uncleanness and pollution and carnal filth—what giddy levity is this?"

9. Gerhard von Rad, *Genesis: A Commentary*, rev. ed. (Philadelphia: Westminster, 1973), 85.

10. Walter Wegner, "God's Pattern for the Family in the Old Testament," *Family Relationships and the Church*, ed. Oscar Feucht (St. Louis: Concordia, 1970): 29. See also *New Bible Dictionary*, s.v. "Marriage."

11. Quoted in Wegner, "God's Pattern for the Family," 29.

12. L. Koehler, *Hebrew Man* (New York: Abingdon, 1956), 78.

7

Commitment: The Family's Foundation

Having described the family in its nuclear form, we must now confront the many questions about its nature. What is unique about marriage? What is the purpose of sex? How intimate should husband and wife be? Should marriage be romantic? Should husbands lead? May a wife choose a career outside the home? Disagreement and confusion over these questions create havoc in some marriages. Like two carpenters building a house together, each with a different set of blueprints, a couple with differences over the nature of the family inevitably clash. The resulting conflict leads to disappointment and despair. Their dedication to each other is not always enough to successfully confront their confusion. They separate or else stay together, settling down in a mediocre union, turning outside the home for something meaningful to fill the void of an empty marriage.

Parents and children, too, are not sure what to expect in their relationship. We should try to clear up some of this ambiguity by describing as clearly as we can what God defines as the nature of marriage and family. We can then point people to the kind of structure they are to build.

COMMITMENT'S COMPONENTS

The basis of marriage and family is commitment. Scripture makes it strikingly clear that this is the basic glue that holds a marriage together. Marriage as a legal contract may be implied in Genesis 2:24, since other passages call it a covenant.[1] The term *davak*, "be united," used in Genesis 2:24 may suggest a contractual arrangement since the Hebrew word means "to adhere to" or "hold fast to," as in a covenant (Deut. 4:4; Josh. 22:5).

> Scripture makes it strikingly clear that commitment is the basic glue that holds a marriage together.

Social Commitment

Marriage is a socially sanctioned commitment. The practice of living together without making a public declaration of marriage is neither biblical nor socially acceptable. The public nature of marriage is clearly seen in that the man is portrayed as leaving father and mother to marry (Gen. 2:24). From earliest Hebrew times, at least both families arranged, approved of, and witnessed the couples' intent to live as husband and wife. Later Hebrew marriage customs such as the public procession from the bride's home to the groom's affirmed the public nature of the marriage pledge. And the legal sanctions in the Old Testament make it clear that marriage is regulated by society for the couple's and society's sake. It costs extended kin and society whenever marriages break down, since abandoned women and children sometimes become their responsibility. Society has a stake in marriage and should have some say in it as well.

A Divinely Sanctioned Commitment

Another aspect of the marriage contract relates to God. Jesus said that God joins couples together (Matt. 19:6). In fact, this is his chief argument against divorce. Exactly how Jesus tied the indissoluble nature of marriage to his statement, "they are no longer two but one," is not exactly clear. It could be a mere reference to the fact that God is witness to the union, since Proverbs 2:17 calls marriage a covenant "made before God." Taken thus, it would refer to marriage as an institution created by God, since those who enter it are joined together by God. On the other hand, it might point to a more personal, mysterious fusion of individuals who are so intimately tied together in marriage.

How we interpret Jesus' statement influences what we will think about divorce, since marriage as a mere institution may more easily be nullified than some highly personal metaphysical union. Whatever we decide, it is quite clear that when two people marry, they do so before God; Jesus based his view of divorce on that reality.

Personal Commitment

Scripture views marriage as a profoundly personal commitment, a pledge of personal loyalty to another human being. Some people have argued that making the marriage contract legal makes it less personal. Deciding to live together without ceremony or license, some couples have said they want their marriages to be held together by love, not a piece of paper. Yet requiring it be socially sanctioned need not make the marriage commitment less personal. It is not the church or society or even God that unite a couple in marriage; each is joined to the other by a personal decision.[2]

Speaking about the betrayal of the adulterous woman, Proverbs 2:17 stresses both the divine and the personal components of the marriage vow. Not only has she ignored the covenant made before God, but she has forsaken the partner of her youth. This is not, by the way, the youthful partner, but the one *taken in youth*, indicating personal betrayal of one with whom she may have lived for some time.

All of these components of commitment—social, divine, personal—combine to support couples staying together through the rough spots of their relationship. About four years into our own marriage, my wife confided to me that she had wanted to leave me during the first two years. Her words so shocked me that I can recall precisely what came next: "I didn't leave you because I don't believe in divorce, God doesn't believe in divorce, and my Aunt Vea didn't believe in divorce." Prior to our wedding, her aunt, whom she respected, took her aside and said: "You stick with that man." She did, and we have built a terrific relationship, not because we were instantly compatible, but because we were intensely committed.

A Commitment Patterned After God's Covenant

For the Christian, we must add the fact that the marriage covenant is patterned after the covenant that God makes with us, a covenant of love. The apostle Paul profoundly blends together the marriage themes of oneness and love in Ephesians 5 where he compares the union of Christ and the church to the relationship of husband and wife. In verse 25 he commands husbands to love their wives just as Christ loved the church. Paul appeals to the redemptive, not the created order of things. There is even a futuristic, prophetic tone to the passage, since Paul's definition of Christ's love for the church is that of the bridegroom for his bride, who has made her "holy, cleansing her . . . to present her to himself . . . without stain or wrinkle or any other blemish" (Eph. 5:26).

Love is to be present, claims Paul, because the husband and wife are "one flesh," just as Christ and the church are one. In verses 31 and 32 of Ephesians he quotes Genesis 1:27 to establish this fact: "We are members of his body. 'For this reason a man will leave his father and mother and be united to his wife, and the two will become one flesh.' This is a profound mystery—but I am talking about Christ and the church." Christ is one with the church because he loves it; but he also loves it because he is one with it. The same is true for the husband. "In the same way, husbands ought to love their wives as their own bodies" (Eph. 5:28). Paul is not saying by this that a man's self-love should be a pattern for loving his wife. Rather, since he has already made Christ's love the model of that love, he no doubt means that a man's wife is also a man's "body," since he is one with her in marriage. Thus he reasons: "He who loves his wife loves himself" (v. 28).

> We have built a terrific relationship, not because we were instantly compatible, but because we were intensely committed.

What Paul gives us, then, is this: marriage somehow provides a unique arena for the display and experience of redemptive love and has, thereby, a special place in God's creative and redemptive plan.

Karl Barth and other theologians have placed much emphasis on the fact that God's covenant of love with his people is behind the husband-wife love covenant. Writes Barth: "God Himself, Lord and King of all, did not will to be alone but chose to have a partner in the people of Israel. So man was not to be alone, but to have his helpmeet in woman."[3] At times, married love is used for an analogy of God's love. At other times, as in Ephesians 5, God's love becomes the analogy for marital love.

Geoffrey Bromiley explains that this comparing of these two loves is made possible because there is, in reality, a close connection between the two. He claims that God created earthly marriage in the image of his own eternal marriage with his people. This means that we are not really to understand God's relationship to us in terms of what we understand of marriage. Rather, it is the other way around; we understand marriage by what we know of God's union with his people.[4] This thought gives marriage great significance: marriage and family are based not merely on the creation of God, but on the very person of God. And one of the most distinctive features of God, the lover, is faithfulness. The "husband" of Israel swears to his people: "Though the mountains be shaken and the hills be removed, yet my unfailing love for you will not be shaken" (Isa. 54:10). It is this feature of marital love that led the church to bring marriage under the control of the church and shaped its view of divorce. Before the twelfth century the church had differing views on divorce, but when theologians made this comparison of God's love and marital love, their view became more strict. Today, if and when divorce might be acceptable is still a hotly debated issue.

> Marriage and family are based not merely on the creation of God, but on the very person of God.

The Divorce Issue

Foremost in this debate is the matter of theological change itself. Some maintain that theology concerning marriage must change due to contemporary marital problems, but only after a careful scrutiny of the Bible. The historical Protestant position has been to permit divorce in cases of adultery or desertion, but to deny remarriage. Bernard Ramm accuses those who hold to this view of divorce and remarriage of being "naive or unrealistic in facing the thousands of facts we now know about marriage and divorce from medicine, psychology, and sociology."[5] And Dwight Small's departure from the traditional view is based in part on his belief that new insights have been forged by the pressure of changing times.[6]

On the issue of a biblical ethic of divorce and remarriage, there are scores of opinions, yet basically they may be subsumed under two major viewpoints. Ramm calls one of these approaches "the strict Protestant view." In general, those who hold this view believe that Matthew 19:9 and 1 Corinthians 7:15 allow divorce in cases of unfaithfulness or desertion,[7] but they deny divorced persons the right to remarry. Many evangelicals today, as well as earlier Protestant ethicists, however, allow the innocent party the privilege of remarrying, because the marriage was broken by the unfaithful or deserting partner. There is, they say, no sin in the innocent partner's remarrying.

The hallmark of this viewpoint is the strict interpretation of Jesus' words on the subject of divorce: "What God has joined together, let man not separate" (Matt. 19:6). Proponents of this view hold that there is additional biblical evidence that Jesus taught a strict view of divorce: "I tell you that anyone who divorces his wife, except for marital unfaithfulness, causes her to become an adulteress, and anyone who marries the divorced woman commits adultery" (Matt. 5:32).

Those holding this view are divided primarily over what exceptions there are to the general rule. Some dispute the textual validity of the exception clause in Matthew 19:9, denying that there is any exemption whatsoever that allows divorce. Others would permit divorce and remarriage in the case of unchastity, explaining that the exception clause applies to unchastity but not to desertion. They would disagree with the interpretation of 1 Corinthians 7:15 that puts forth what has come to be known as the "Pauline privilege." This verse is instead taken to mean that the Christian should remain unmarried.[8]

The Broad Protestant Principle

Ramm calls the opposite viewpoint on this matter of divorce and remarriage the "broad Protestant principle."[9] Those who hold this view maintain that the New Testament gives the church the fundamentals of Christian marriage but not an exhaustive treatment on the subject of divorce.[10] On the contrary, they say, only a minimum treatment is given. Thus the traditional camp is accused of using a simple proof-text approach to a complicated ethical problem.

Ramm argues that the pastor who thinks the New Testament contains an exhaustive body of ethics concerning marriage and divorce is at a loss to handle the kind of problems faced in modern society. As an example, he points to the person with neurotic or psychotic symptoms that were masked during courtship. Also, there are the persons dependent on alcohol who marry. Again, what should be done with homosexual spouses, especially those who marry to conceal their sexual orientation? And certain states allow automatic divorce if either partner is sentenced to prison for ten years or more. None of these matters are specifically discussed in Scripture, yet the Christian church must deal with these problems, argues Ramm.[11]

Modern society contributes in another way to the wide range of problems confronting marriage partners, according to those who hold this view. They explain that it has become more difficult to succeed in marriage in the last five decades. In our complex society, divorce is seen as a necessary safety valve for the preservation of the institution of marriage. Historian William O'Neill argues that divorce prevents explosions in the family that might undermine the very foundation of marriage. If there were no divorce, dissatisfaction would build up suddenly, and could result in violence. People might repudiate the institution of marriage, much as governments are overthrown.[12]

Advocates of the broad view of divorce and remarriage do not seek to break from a conservative view of Scripture. They attempt, rather, to get a different perspective on the statements of Jesus on this subject. Dwight Small takes a dispensational approach to Christ's statements on this matter, explaining that they pertain to the kingdom age of the future. Small does not deny that Christians of today should take their standard for marriage from Christ's words, but he maintains that there is a different application of these words during the present age of grace than there will be during the kingdom age. Thus, the indissolubility of marriage is the ideal, as stated in the beginning of Genesis and as it will be again in the kingdom age; but because of our continued sinfulness and hardness of heart, there is forgiveness for those who fail today.

Small maintains, moreover, that divorce is possible only because of grace.[13] Marriage is supposed to be permanent. Divorce is always wrong. It is allowable only under special circumstances and then only under the permissive will of God, not his ideal will. Small builds his case on the concept of "realized forgiveness," a term put forth by Presbyterian James G. Emerson, Jr., in

> **The indissolubility of marriage is the ideal; there is forgiveness for those who fail.**

1961.[14] Realized forgiveness is the Christian's awareness that one always lives in the presence of God's forgiveness. Christians are to realize this truth to such a degree that they are free from excessive guilt. Therefore, according to Small, pastoral ministry in cases of divorce and remarriage should be based on God's forgiving grace, not only on his ideal law.

According to those who hold the broad view, even if Jesus' words were meant to be directly applied to present-day Christians in situations of divorce and remarriage, they were not meant to be used in a legalistic way. They develop this argument as follows: Christ refused to deal with divorce within the confines of Mosaic law. He held up God's ideal standard for marriage, which prevailed before the fall into sin—in the beginning. Jesus' statement about divorce is not unlike other declarations, such as, "Be perfect, therefore, as your heavenly Father is perfect" (Matt. 5:48). The indissolubility of the marriage bond is a standard of perfection, just as holiness is. Permanence of marriage was God's intention.

> Marriage is part of the created order; divorce is part of the redemptive order.

Proponents of the broad view explain that the question of whether this perfect standard can be applied to every couple considering divorce is the major issue. Their explanation is as follows. Even in Old Testament times divorce laws were not always enforced so as to uphold God's perfect standard. To interpret Jesus' words as law does not allow for contingencies such as partners who deny or forfeit their commitment through adultery, perversion, desertion, impotence, frigidity, or severe neurosis or psychosis. Under the Mosaic law there was no difficulty in dealing with, for example, adultery—the guilty person would have been stoned. But situations that were not problems under the law have become problems for Christians under grace.

Those who hold the above view of the words of Jesus concerning divorce call attention to the context of his words. They say that he was affirming God's ideal for marriage against Jewish leaders who made the termination of marriage an arbitrary decision of the husband. As at other times, the Lord intended to show these leaders their own sinfulness. He appealed to the creative order, which constitutes the spirit of the law.[15] These leaders were denying their own selfishness and sinfulness by stretching the letter of the law.

According to those who hold the broad view, it is possible to take Jesus' words and codify them into law, thereby doing exactly what he was trying to avoid. So it is, according to this view, that evangelical pastors and theologians juggle verses and argue about exceptions and motives, much like canon lawyers. And lay people go from one clergyperson to another to find sanction for their actions, attempting to resolve their guilt and restore order in their lives by a legalistic appeal to a verse in the Bible. Rather, Small and others are saying, we should appeal to God's forgiveness. The answer is not to be found in analyzing an exception clause; it is to be realized in God's indisputable words about grace. Marriage is part of the created order; divorce is part of the redemptive order.

To hold that forgiveness extends to the divorced person who has remarried has been most difficult because of Jesus' explicit statements that one commits adultery by remarrying (Matt. 19:9). However, the editors of *Christianity Today* recognize this problem and come to the following conclusion:

> Murder and theft the evangelical freely forgives, but not divorce. In part, this different attitude is based on the conviction that others sins are completed and have been repented of, but divorce and remarriage involve a

continuous living in adultery. The conclusion is not warranted on biblical grounds. The guilty partner in a divorce on the grounds of adultery has already broken the original marriage. . . . The fact that the original marriage is dissolved means also that the guilty party who remarries is not living in adultery, for his original marriage was dissolved. His sin was in the adultery that brought on the divorce. Since he is no longer married, he new alliance is not adulterous. Similarly in the case of divorces secured on trivial grounds, a move to marriage by either partner serves (as does adultery) to break the original marriage; and on biblical grounds the church is not justified in treating the remarried as though they were continuing to live in adultery.[16]

Remarriage would not be acceptable if Jesus' phrase "God has joined together" was taken as a personal, not an institutional, joining.[17] However, it seems clear that since marriage is foremost a covenant, only the institution is grounded in creation.[18]

The distinctive mark of this new stance on divorce, then, is that divorce now becomes primarily an ethical issue. While they do not deny that God's standard for marriage is permanence, those of this persuasion place the question of breaking God's standard in the broader context of the whole New Testament ethic. According to this view, divorce and remarriage are moral choices that are sometimes acceptable, though never the Creator's ideal. Dwight Small sees them as being acceptable when it is a matter of choosing between the lesser of two evils. At times remaining together may be intolerable for a couple and possibly also for their children. James Montgomery Boice concurs with Small's conclusion: "We live in an imperfect world. And this means that there will always be circumstances in which the Christian will have to choose the lesser of two evils."[19] Boice cites an imaginary case in which a woman is married to a brute of a husband, a man who spends her money on drink and deserts her with the result that she must raise the children alone. Should the husband return, he might seize the money she has saved for her children's college expenses. A woman in such circumstances is justified, says Boice, in initiating a divorce.[20]

Small explains that since divorce and remarriage are always wrong, the persons involved must claim the forgiveness of God.[21] Certainly, a Christian husband or wife may have contributed to the failure of a marriage, and they should confess that sin. But divorce in a marriage in which the relationship is becoming more and more destructive is not sin. Remarriage may be best for divorced persons who burn with passion and are continually subject to sensual temptation.

Whether holding to the strict Protestant view or the broad Protestant principle, no evangelical writer today endorses easy divorce. Marriage is to be honored as a serious personal and socially sanctioned commitment made in the presence of God.

The next question we will consider logically follows: What are the obligations that arise out of this commitment? But before we consider that, we will explore two other areas of commitment in the nuclear family: parents' commitment to children, and children to their parents.

Parents' Commitment to Children

Surprisingly, the Scriptures say little about what commitments parents are to have to their children. The idea that parents are to provide for their children seems to be taken for granted. Whenever parental obligations are spelled out, they mostly deal with disciplining and teaching the children, matters we will deal with elsewhere.

Yet, there is some basis for maintaining that parental commitment involves love. Only one Scripture actually tells parents to love their children; even there, it is only the wife who is addressed (Titus 2:4). Jewish scholars wondered why there was no such command in the Old Testament; they solved the problem by maintaining, no doubt rightly so, that such love was included in the command to love our neighbor as ourselves (Lev. 19:18).

A number of passages, however, mention parental love or assume it to be a virtue. A parent who loves a child will discipline him (Prov. 13:24). A special love parents have for their children seems to be implied in the psalmist's cry: "Though my father and mother forsake me" (27:10). Suggesting parents would be the last people on earth to abandon him, he seems to hold a very high view of parental love. This same lofty view shines through the references to God as a parent. In the Psalms, God is a father who pities his children, showing that compassion was included in the Hebrew concept of father.

But the most clear-cut description of parental love comes from the New Testament, from the lips of Jesus. His parable of the lost son who is welcomed back to the family after he had wasted his inheritance is a picture of intense love, both divine and parental. In addition, Jesus discloses how important he considers parental love when he points to God as a loving Father: "Love your enemies . . . that you may be sons of your Father in heaven. He causes his sun to rise on the evil and the good, and sends rain on the righteous and the unrighteous" (Matt. 5:44–45). Jesus appeals to the same analogy in Luke 6:36, this time speaking of mercy: "Be merciful, just as your Father is merciful."

> A parent's love, like God's, is to be characterized by mercy, acceptance, and forgiveness.

These statements suggest that a parent's love, like God's, is to be characterized by mercy, acceptance, and forgiveness. Parental love should be loyal and steadfast, like God's love, who loves even his evil children. The parents' commitment to their children is grounded in God the Father just as the commitment of husband and wife is based on God the lover.

Children's Commitment to Parents

Nowhere in Scripture are children ordered to love their parents. Rather, the children's commitment is defined in terms of respect. So serious is this that it is one of the Ten Commandments: "Honor your father and your mother" (Exod. 20:12). Other scriptures spell out only three specific guidelines for doing this. First, children are to obey their parents and listen to their teaching (Eph. 6:1; Col. 3:20). Second, no one should curse his father or mother (Exod. 21:17). Third, adult children are to care for aged or infirm parents. Jesus strongly criticized religious leaders who schemed to make it possible for people to shirk this duty (Mark 7:9–13). The apostle Paul referred to the financial care of parents and grandparents when he wrote: "If anyone does not provide for his relatives, and especially for his immediate family, he

> The children's commitment is defined in terms of respect.

has denied the faith and is worse than an unbeliever" (1 Tim. 5:8). Not only did Paul extend the obligation to the care of grandparents, but he said that such care was a way to repay them, which is "pleasing to God" (1 Tim. 5:4).

So far we have determined that what holds a nuclear family together is commitment. We have determined *whom* each person is committed to, but in a few instances we have not described *what* each is committed to. We now turn to depicting exactly what those responsibilities are.

NOTES

1. Proverbs 2:17 and Malachi 2:14.
2. This is true even of the Roman Catholic view of marriage as a sacrament, a rite receiving a special blessing from God. Roman Catholics stress the personal aspect by alleging: "The parties, not the priests, are the ministers of the sacrament."
3. Barth observes this paradigm of love throughout the Old and New Testaments, seeing God's love behind the man-woman relationship in the Song of Songs and Genesis 2:17:

> The immutable covenant relationship between Yahweh and Israel, and therefore the center of the Old Testament witness, stands dominatingly behind Genesis 2 and the Song of Songs. It was an unattainable model of humanity because love such as that of Yahweh for Israel is beyond the reach of a human husband in relation to his wife. Even God Himself, the Lord and King of the heavenly and earthly space created by Him, did not will to be alone, but to have His concrete counterpart in the people Israel, man was not to be alone, but to have his helpmeet or counterpart in woman (Karl Barth, *Dogmatics*, 2:297).

4. Geoffrey W. Bromiley, *God and Marriage* (Grand Rapids: Eerdmans, 1980), 43.
5. Bernard Ramm, "To Love and Cherish Till," *Eternity* (June 1976): 51.
6. Dwight Small, *Right to Remarry* (Old Tappan, N.J.: Revell, 1975), 12.

7. Guy Duty, *Divorce and Remarriage* (Minneapolis: Bethany Fellowship, 1967), 45–51.

8. James Montgomery Boice, "The Biblical View of Divorce," *Eternity* (December 1970): 21.

9. Ramm, "To Love and Cherish," 51.

10. Ibid.

11. Ibid.

12. John Scanzoni, "Can Marriages Last Forever?" *U.S. Catholic* 42:2 (February 1977): 7.

13. Small, *Right to Remarry*, 183–87.

14. James G. Emerson, Jr., *Divorce, The Church and Remarriage* (Philadelphia: Westminster Press, 1961), 34–83.

15. Ibid.

16. "Divorce and Remarriage," *Christianity Today* 23:16 (May 25, 1979): 8.

17. This is the argument of D. A. Carson, "Matthew," *The Expositor's Bible Commentary,* vol. 8, ed. Frank E. Gabelein (Grand Rapids: Zondervan, 1984), 412.

18. For a thorough discussion of this point and an exhaustive exegesis of Jesus' words in Matthew 19:3–12 see Craig L. Blomberg, "Marriage, Divorce, Remarriage, and Celibacy: An Exegesis of Matthew 19:3–12," *Trinity Journal* 11 (n.s., 1990): 161–96.

19. Boice, "The Biblical View," 19.

20. Ibid.

21. Small, *Right to Remarry*, 184.

External Duties of Family

Commitment is the foundation of marriage and family—but it is only a foundation. It is not enough for a couple to stay together; they must build together. An individual can be unfaithful to the marriage contract even if he or she has never had an affair with another person. Faithfulness is not measured in terms of what a married partner does not do, but what he or she does do.

This, too, is true in the parent-child relationship. It is not enough that family members live under the same roof. They must participate in a quality of life God has prescribed, which I will now try to describe.

ISSUE OF INSTRUMENTAL AND EXPRESSIVE DUTIES

To depict the essence of family life, I will follow the lead of some sociologists who distinguish two major categories of relating: instrumental and expressive. The first set involves task-oriented matters; for example, parents providing food, shelter, clothing, and other necessities for children. Expressive obligations consist of relational matters: listening, affirming, being emotionally close, and the like. Both are expressions of love, but markedly different. Marriage, too, includes both. Sex, for instance, has an instrumental function (to conceive a child), but it also might have an expressive element (to create intimacy).

In the Broadway musical *Fiddler on the Roof*, the middle-aged wife of the Russian Jew, Tevye, said he was a fool because he asked: "Do you love me?" Refusing to answer, she cited twenty-five years worth of things she had done for him: washed his clothes, cooked his meals, given him children, milked the cow, fought and starved with him, and shared his bed. Then she asked, "If that isn't love, what is?" At that moment, Tevye wanted more than the instrumental side of love, signified in tasks his wife performed. He was yearning for the emotional and expressive things of marriage.[1]

> Commitment is the foundation of marriage and family—but it is only a foundation. It is not enough for a couple to stay together; they must build together.

We will need to explore biblical terrain to see if these expectations are legitimate. First, however, we must explain what Scripture has to say about the instrumental side of family.

INSTRUMENTAL DUTIES OF MARRIAGE AND FAMILY

Financial Duties

Foremost among the so-called external duties is the financial. Spouses and parents are to provide for one another and for their children. Paul the apostle underscores the seriousness of this burden: "If anyone does not provide for his relatives, and especially for his immediate family, he has denied the faith and is worse than an unbeliever" (1 Tim. 5:8).

Husband Not Only Provider

At this point, we must ask whether or not Scripture supports the traditional idea that the husband is to be the primary, if not sole, provider for the family. Most of the debate about this centers on whether the man should be the primary provider, as hardly anyone argues he should be the only provider. That women in past agriculturally based societies were very much involved in contributing to family finances is obvious; such was true in biblical times and is confirmed by biblical principles. The woman portrayed in Proverbs 31 was very much involved in business affairs.[2]

Debate Over Wife as Provider

Those who contend that the husband should be the primary provider base their views on chapter 3 of Genesis, where in laying down the curse on mankind, God designated two different spheres for the lives of men and women. The wife's role is to bear children; the husband's is to work. "Evidently, God has in mind from the beginning that the man should take special responsibility for sustaining the family through bread-winning labor," argues John Piper.[3] In addition, woman was created to be man's "helper," (Gen. 2:18), indicating that she was to assist man in his God-given mission.

> Most of the debate centers on whether the man should be the primary provider, as hardly anyone argues he should be the only provider.

Those opposed to making man the primary provider (and leader) of the home call attention to the fact that the Hebrew word *ezer*, translated "helper," refers to God in most Old Testament references. Therefore, the word conveys no sense of subordination; the man is also to be the helper to the woman in the sense that both need companionship. Another argument for equal share in providing and leadership is that both the man and woman, created in God's image, were to have dominion over the earth. Since the Bible teaches the full equality of men and women in creation and redemption, it is said we should not prescribe special roles to males and females in family, church, or society.

It would seem that the most prominent New Testament statement about providing for the family would settle this argument. Doesn't Paul maintain that if anyone does not provide for his relatives, and especially for his immediate family, he has denied the faith? (1 Timothy 5:8). He does, but still leaves the issue undecided since the statement could apply to both males and females.

In fact, Paul does, in that context, apply it to women: "If any woman who is a believer has widows in her family, she should help them" (1 Tim. 5:16).

> The socialization of children includes teaching them basic practical and relational skills necessary to function in society.

The chapter thus interwoven with the issue of husband and wife roles, I am going to postpone until later any final comment on this matter. Whatever our conclusion, Scripture makes it clear that family members are responsible to care for one another's physical needs. Able men and women should be cautioned not to shirk this duty and expect others to shoulder it for them.

Socialization of Children

Ideally, children should be raised by their parents. Previously, when defining the family, I cited Scripture from both testaments to prove this point. The socialization of children includes teaching them basic practical and relational skills necessary to function in society. Scripture stresses two major components of this process: training (disciplining) and teaching (Eph. 6:4). The Hebrew work *musar*, often translated "to discipline," embodies both of these ideas. Spiritual truth should be integrated into this training and teaching.

This spiritual nurture of children has been a major theme of theological systems, the Lutheran and Reformed being the most explicit.

Lutheran View

Many theologians, like Luther, place the child-rearing role of the family only in the creative realm, not the redemptive. In other words, being a Christian will enable a person to function better in a family, but there are no "Christian families," only Christians living in families. While parents are to participate in the spiritual training of their children, Lutherans tend to place a strong emphasis on the church's role. This is due in large measure to their view of baptism, whereby the child is regenerated. Sacerdotal churches, where grace is dispensed to people through the church's ordinances (or sacraments) tend to stress the church's role in promoting the spiritual development of its youth. Theologically, such churches contend God uses the church, not the family, to nurture the children in Christ.

Covenant View

The theological system that most underscores the parent's role in Christian nurture is the covenant position of Reformed and Presbyterian churches. They place family life squarely in the mainstream of redemption.

Believing the church began with Abraham, they have maintained that children of Christians, like Abraham's offspring, participate somehow in the covenant of salvation. This covenant of redemption was in the mind of God prior to the creation of the world and is the basis for all history. God's primary purpose in creation and history is to redeem the elect that he has chosen in eternity past.[4] As the Abrahamic covenant was "sealed" with Jewish children by circumcision, it is "sealed" in the present age by infant baptism, which places the child in the covenant. Because this does not truly regenerate the child, theologians have discussed for decades exactly what it means for the child to be in a covenant relationship with God. Some say it makes certain that the child will eventually place faith in Christ. Others see no such guarantee. What they do see is a "spiritual solidarity of the family, with parents having a heavy responsibility to teach their children."[5] The fulfillment of the promise of salvation depends on their doing their job.

Covenant theology is faulted by others, namely Baptists and dispensationalists. They charge that the Reformed and Presbyterian idea of covenants are never mentioned in the Bible. Also, they contend that the vagueness of covenant theologians on what it means for children to participate in the covenant makes that participation worthless. This is particularly true when some baptized children, supposedly within the covenant, never do become Christians, living and dying as unbelievers. Further, dispensationalists argue that while there may be some spiritual relationship with believers in the Old Testament, the church actually began at Pentecost, not with Abraham, ruling out the idea that baptism takes the place of circumcision.

> Unselfish devotion to the quality of life, spiritually and otherwise, of generations to come is something that must run through the whole fabric of a society, including its political, educational, and ecclesiastical institutions.

No matter what our judgment about the truthfulness of covenant theology, it does remind us of two important biblical assertions about the family. First, somehow children of believers are unique. Writing to spouses of non-Christians, Paul says: "The unbelieving husband has been sanctified through his wife, and the unbelieving wife has been sanctified through her believing husband. Otherwise your children would be unclean, but as it is, they are holy" (1 Cor. 7:14). Because we have no further word than this, we cannot be exactly sure what Paul means by this, but it does make believers' children special in some way.

In addition, covenant theologians rightly assign to parents the primary responsibility for nurturing their children in the faith. Some of the denominations built on this theology have been unusually faithful in making families central in their members' lives.

Reproduction Function

Having earlier established that children are to be born in the context of marriage, we return to the question of whether or not a married couple is obligated to bear children if they are able. The answer to this is wrapped up in the controversy about instrumental and expressive aspects of marriage and family.

If marriage and sex is primarily (or only) for having children, then sex is more of an instrumental than expressive element and, therefore, if a couple does not intentionally conceive children they are betraying the primary purpose of marriage. Recently, author Mary Pride has argued forcefully for the view that marriage is for childbearing. "Without Eve, Adam could not possibly be fruitful and multiply

> Until recently, church leaders seldom spoke of marriage and family in expressive terms. Sex was for producing children, not for intimacy.

. . . Eve was needed for the couple to bear fruit. The biblical reason for marriage is to produce fruit for God. Marriage is to produce children, and to make the earth fruitful for God."[6]

We have no reason to believe God's commission to bear fruit and fill the earth is no longer in force. Unselfish devotion to the quality of life, spiritually and otherwise, of generations to come is something that must run through the whole fabric of a society, including its political, educational, and ecclesiastical institutions. In chapter two, I pointed to a possible serious weakening of motivation to make the sacrifices necessary to accomplish this.

Yet the crucial question remains: Does God intend that marriage exists for more reasons than the conception and care of children so that a couple may choose to be married for these reasons and choose to not have children?

This question is central to the controversy over the so-called expressive features of marriage and family.

CONTROVERSY OVER EXPRESSIVE SIDE OF MARRIAGE AND FAMILY

Until recently, church leaders seldom spoke of marriage and family in expressive terms. Emphasis was placed on instrumental matters. Sex was for producing children, not for intimacy. Marriage was not a companionship, but a partnership to carry out the external duties for each other, the children, society, the church, and God.

Relationships between parents and children were treated in much the same way. Christian parents were not often counseled to be emotionally close to their children or to verbalize their love for them.

In the early centuries of the Christian church, the issue of sex dominated discussions about marriage. Judging that sexual pleasure was not part of

God's original creation, but was a consequence of man's fall into sin, sexual intercourse was only legitimate insofar as it was directed toward conceiving a child.[7]

AUGUSTINE'S THREE REASONS FOR MARRIAGE

The fourth-century Augustine, who influenced thought for more than a thousand years afterward, never mentioned any expressive features in his reasons for marriage. The first of these, "offspring," was the primary, almost exclusive, justification for sex.[8] Augustine said even sex for procreation could be sinful, if it was done with too much lusting, because he believed sexual activity in marriage was the greatest threat to the spiritual life.[9]

The second reason Augustine gave for marriage, "fidelity," referred to paying the marriage debt. Following Paul's advice in 1 Corinthians 7, Augustine believed that married partners could avoid illicit intercourse if by marital intercourse they sustained "each other's weakness."

The term "sacrament" he used for the third reason for marriage, meaning Christian marriage must be indissoluble—a sacrament is a symbol of stability. In all his discussion, Augustine never mentioned love, companionship, or intimacy as elements for marriage. His commentary on Genesis shows how he completely ignored them. Asking why Eve was made as a helper for Adam, he denied she should serve as a companion. Adam had no need of that. Besides, Augustine asked: "How much more agreeably could two male friends, rather than a man and woman, enjoy companionship and conversation in a life shared together?"[10] He then concluded: "I do not see in what sense the woman was made a helper for the man if not for the sake of bearing children."[11]

Among contemporary Christian writers, Pride represents this same viewpoint. The statement of Genesis 2:18, "It is not good for the man to be alone," in no way implies Adam needed a companion, according to Pride. "God could have given a dog if all Adam needed was a companion . . . God gave Eve to Adam to be his helper. Why? Because Adam had been assigned a project. God told them to 'be fruitful and increase in number. . . .' Marriage is to produce children."[12]

Pride wants to help people avoid the frustration that sometimes comes by expecting too much of marriage. Marriage was created to bear children and to serve God, she argues. Romantic love, intimacy, and sexual pleasure are okay, but they are not what God requires. What is required is that Christian husbands and wives are faithful to family duties and that they love each other as brothers and sisters in Christ. She tells of a satisfied married pair who jogged along happily in their marriage until someone talked them into a "romantic weekend." Until then, she claims, they were doing fine: they shared interest in the kids, the house, the husband's job, and so on. But when they packed their bags and headed off to be "intimate," their troubles began. Pride explains what happened: "On the way to their resort, they began to talk about 'us' rather than their common interests, as they had always done before. After only one day they returned, shocked to discover that when it came to talking about 'us' they had nothing to say."[13]

Their problem, according to Pride, was not that they couldn't be intimate; their mistake was that they even tried. According to her, they had a perfectly good marriage until someone happened along to raise their expectations. "Intimate marriage isn't biblical," she asserts. "Intimate marriage demands that marriage be self-centered. It insists that kicks and thrills are the reasons for marriage. It tries to squash everyone into one mold—that of hedonistic teenagers—and destroys all who can't fit."[14]

The majority of writers from the early church through the medieval ages expressed this same attitude toward marriage.[15] There were a few exceptions. John Chrysostom spoke of the divine origins of marriage and the benefit of shared love in the lives of children. Clement of Alexander wrote about mutual love, support, and assistance that married partners extended to each other.

TOWARD A MORE POSITIVE VIEW OF THE EXPRESSIVE ELEMENTS OF MARRIAGE

In Catholic circles, new ideas about marriage surfaced when Thomas Aquinas, celebrated theologian of the thirteenth century, wrote of marriage as "the greatest friendship."[16] Then, in 1566, the phrases "mutual help" and aiding one another to "more easily bear the discomforts of life and sustain weakness of old age," were first added to the purposes of marriage in the Catholic Counter-Reformation catechism.[17]

> New ideas about marriage surfaced when Thomas Aquinas wrote of marriage as "the greatest friendship."

Protestant Views

Views of marriage and family continued to change during the time of the Reformers of the sixteenth century. Luther lamented the lack of emphasis on the family in his day. He explained that it was in part the result of the priority given to both monastic life and the institutional church. He accused the church leaders of his day of misunderstanding the glory of family living because of the "counter-glory" given to monastic life.[18]

Calvin and others contributed to a swing in the direction of marriage as a companionship. Calvin differed radically from Augustine. Why had God said Adam was alone? He answered: "Man has been created that he may not lead a solitary life, but may enjoy a helper joined to himself." Marriage, to Calvin, was a "fellowship."[19]

The Christian humanist, Erasmus, had no problem identifying companionship with marriage, asserting, "For at the begynnying when he had made man of the slyme of the earthe he thought that his lyfe should be utterly myserable and unpleasaunt, if he joyned not Eve a compangion unto him."[20]

The Puritan Contribution

The Puritan movement within the Church of England produced the most biblical and positive view of marriage up to their time in history. One historian summarizes: "From the 1620s to the 1660s, in the great age of their writings on marriage, almost all the Puritan preachers and theologians urged spouses to maintain a steady and reliable delight in the mates, a pleasure both sensuous and spiritual."[21] They wrote eloquently of marriage for companionship, including its sensual side.[22] Their appeal to Scripture caused them to break with the past.

The Puritan's high views of marriage were not representative of their age, nor did they carry over into later centuries. Neither the Renaissance nor Reformation succeeded in building a bridge between the spiritual and the sensual. Even Shakespeare, "whose instinct for the natural is his principal title to undying fame," notes one historian, "speaks of the act of love as 'the expense of spirit in a waste of shame.'"[23]

In contrast to the past, today's Christian writers, Catholic or Protestant, liberal or conservative, have been giving considerable attention to the expressive side of marriage and family. Intimacy, sensual love, and emotional love are given biblical and profound theological support.

> The Puritan movement within the Church of England produced the most biblical and positive view of marriage up to their time in history.

Before we examine that support in the next chapter, we need to answer some nagging questions: How can we justify these novel ideas about marriage that challenge so many centuries of Christian thinking? Are we being influenced more by our modern times than Christian truth?

A number of historians have dealt with these matters. They claim that past writers simply overlooked the biblical evidence for the expressive side of marriage and family. They cite a number of reasons why they did.

REASONS FOR THE EARLY CHURCH'S NEGATIVE VIEW OF MARRIAGE

Concentration on Certain New Testament Texts

John Noonan, church historian, claims the leaders of the first several centuries of Christianity were greatly influenced by certain New Testament texts. When these Christian leaders grappled with the issues of their day, they allowed Scriptures that exalt virginity, that seem to show disinterest in marriage and exclude it from the resurrected state to blot out other texts.[24]

High Regard for Celibacy

That more and more of the clergy voluntarily chose celibacy no doubt had something to do with the prominence given to Scripture that ratified their lifestyle. Being under persecution, the church's heroes tended to be those who had denounced earthly ties.[25] The result, notes Noonan, was that: "the treatises of the Fathers on the virginal life seem to express a disregard for marriage."[26] With the emergence of a high view of celibacy, by the time of the Middle Ages (A.D. 500—1500), marriage was, more or less, a necessary evil. Levin Schucking reports of numerous utterances where unmarried and married men are compared in numerical terms: "marriage counts as 30, widowhood 60, and virginity 100."[27]

Add to all of these reasons the fact that almost all that was written and taught about marriage was done by unmarried monks and clergy. Those who put together the standards about marriage regarded married life as an inferior level of Christianity. "This set marriage back for 1000 years," claims David Mace.[28] So high was the regard for celibacy that even married couples were praised for not practicing sex in their marriage.

Immoral Society

Another reason that certain New Testament texts captured attention was their use in combating the low moral standards of the Greco-Roman world. Prostitution was common, even practiced in religious temples. Fighting these evils, preachers and teachers spoke often of the corrupt aspects of sex.

Dualistic View of Life

Most of all, sex became dubious to early church and medieval theologians because of the way they thought about body and spirit. Adopting the dualistic views of Greek philosophy and oriental religion, they regarded anything physical to be the enemy of the soul. The aim of every true Christian was to attain perfection through renunciation of the world and subjugation of the body. To this end, every means was employed—fasting, solitude, prayer, mortification; but always, as one historian notes: "The decisive test, the critical discipline, was that of sexual continence."[29]

Idea of Salvation: Easy Forgiveness

Some historians believe the Roman Catholic idea of salvation played a part in ambivalent attitudes toward sex and marriage. They claim that most professing Christians really didn't follow the strict guidelines handed down to them. Sexual sins were so common they weren't taken seriously. "Confess them to the priest, and for a few routine prayers and a small cash contribution, he could release them from your spiritual record."[30]

This resulted in a lot of extra-marital sex. In some historical periods, clerics and Popes had mistresses. Evidence is plentiful to suggest that it was grossly more sinful for a priest to marry than it was for him to have a mistress. In all the popular literature of the thirteenth century, clerical celibacy was a joke.[31] In Spain in the twelfth century it was quite acceptable for a young bachelor to keep a *barrangana* (mistress) until he was ready for marriage. Celibate priests in Spain and elsewhere did the same. "Everyone who entered the clergy made a vow of chastity," claims Esmein, "but almost none observed it."[32]

> Having abandoned the Greek dualistic view of humanity, with its disdain for anything physical, Christians now notice the beauty and importance of certain family relationships overlooked in the past.

In the next chapter we will move toward a theology of marriage and family that embraces wholeheartedly the expressive side of marriage and family. In the past fifty years, theologians have looked more carefully at what all Scripture has to say about marriage and family. Having abandoned the Greek dualistic view of humanity, with its disdain for anything physical, Christians now notice the beauty and importance of certain family relationships overlooked in the past.

NOTES

1. Sheldon Harnick, "Fiddler on the Roof," *The Ultimate Broadway Fake Book* (Winona, Minn.: Hal Leonard Publishing, 1988), 106.

2. Even one of the most conservative views of the roles of husband and wife does not argue that the women should not be gainfully employed. See John Piper and Wayne Grudem, *Recovering Biblical Manhood and Womanhood: A Response to Evangelical Feminism* (Wheaton, Ill.: Crossway, 1991), 42.

3. Ibid., 42–43.

4. L. Berkhof, *Systematic Theology* (Grand Rapids: Eerdmans, 1941), 265.

5. Pierre Marcel, *The Biblical Doctrine of Infant Baptism*, trans. Philip Edgcumbe Hughes (London: James Clarke, 1953), 113.

6. Mary Pride, *The Way Home: Beyond Feminism, Back to Reality* (Westchester, Ill.: Crossway, 1985), 16, 17, 18, 22, 25, 26.

7. Anthony Kosnik, ed., *Human Sexuality: New Directions in American Catholic Thought* (New York: Paulist Press, 1977), 37.

8. For a lengthy discussion of Augustine's views, see John T. Noonan, *Contraception: A History of Its Treatment by Catholic Theologians and Canonists* (Cambridge, Mass.: Harvard University Press, 1966), 113–38.

9. Ibid., 126.

10. St. Augustine, *The Literal Meaning of Genesis*, trans. John Hammond Taylor, *Ancient Christian Writers*, vol. 2, ed. Johannes Quasten et al. (New York: Newman Press, 1982), 75.

11. Ibid.

12. Ibid., 16, 22.

13. Pride, *The Way Home*, 18.

14. Ibid.

15. During the Middle Ages all moral guidelines concerning marriage from A.D. 400 onward came out of this idea that sexual intercourse is sinful and that it is only right when its purpose is procreation. The prohibition of sexual fantasies, masturbation, homosexual acts, premarital, extra-marital or post-marital sex, conception, and all other forms of sexual activity cluster around the concept of fertility.

Even the justification of sex when conception is not possible, as in the case of infertile couples or older people, is dealt with in this way. Since, in these cases, conception was not possible, it was argued that sex at these times was acceptable, because the couple was not giving up their intention to conceive, which was the real issue.

Judgments about anal intercourse or position of intercourse were made on this basis of intention to conceive. The woman being on top was considered "against nature," because she was more likely to aid conception by retaining the seed if she were underneath.

Some church fathers "taught that sexual intercourse was forbidden when a man's wife was already pregnant. It was regarded as unreasonable to sow seed in a field that had already been planted." In the thirteenth century, Albert the Great warned about the seriousness of the sin of intercourse during a wife's pregnancy.

To have sex for pleasure alone was to consent to the depravity of the fallen nature. Even those who were more moderate in their regulations still conceded that sex, even in marriage, always included "an element of evil."

16. Thomas Aquinas, *Summa Contra Gentiles*, 3, 124, quoted by Edmund Leites, *The Puritan Conscience and Modern Sexuality* (New Haven, Conn.: Yale University Press, 1986), 79.

17. Leites, *The Puritan Conscience and Modern Sexuality*, 77.

18. Edward H. Schroeder, "Family Ethos in the Light of the Reformation," *Family Relationships and the Church* (St. Louis: Concordia, 1970), 111.

19. John Calvin, *Institutes*, Book 1, chaps. 8, 41, ed. John T. McNeill (Philadelphia: Westminster Press, 1960), 2:405.

20. *Ecomium Matrimonii*, quoted by Leites, *The Puritan Conscience and Modern Sexuality*, 80.

21. Leites, *The Puritan Conscience and Modern Sexuality*, 3.

22. Ibid.

23. Sonnet 129, cited by Levin L. Schucking, *The Puritan Family: A Social Study From the Literary Sauces*, trans. from the German by Brian Battershaw (New York: Schocken, 1970), 37.

24. Noonan, *Contraception*, 39–40.

25. David Mace and Vera Mace, *The Sacred Fire: Christian Marriage Through the Ages* (Nashville: Abingdon, 1986), 82.

26. Ibid., 89–90.

27. Schucking cites Dan Michel's Middle English Ayenbite of Inwyt (p. 234), adding that there are "plenty of similar utterance" (Schucking, *The Puritan Family*, 21).

28. Mace and Mace, *The Sacred Fire*, 82.

29. Derrick Sherwin Bailey, *Sexual Relation in Christian Thought* (New York: Harper Bros., 1959).

30. Ibid., 129.

31. Barbara Tuchman, *A Distant Mirror: The Calamitous 14th Century* (New York: Ballantine Books, 1978).

32. Esmein Adhemar, *Le Marriage en Droit Canonique*, vol. 1, ed. R. Genestal (Paris: n.p., 1929–35), *Marriage and the Family in the Middle Ages*, ed. Frances Gies and Joseph Gies (New York: Harper, 1987), 155.

Expressive Features of Marriage and Family

9

Popular songs, movies, radio and TV commercials, books, and magazines bombard modern people daily with notions of romance, sensual love, and intimacy. Phone companies invite us to use their services to call Mom or a grandchild to say, "I love you." The value people place on these expressions of affection is woven tightly into the fabric of modern life in the Western world.

Yet, we have seen that during most of church history, church leaders have seldom depicted the expressive features of marriage and family. We will now explore the biblical foundation for the three elements they ignored: intimacy, sensual love, and emotional love.

INTIMACY IN MARRIAGE AND FAMILY

Intimacy occurs whenever two people, moving beyond a superficial knowledge of one another, share some inner thoughts and feelings. In common terms, it's "being close." A theological basis for marriage and family intimacy is first of all found in the Old Testament, particularly in those passages that define the marriage relationship.

Old Testament Support for Intimacy in Marriage

The most appropriate place to look for some thread of intimacy in the biblical notion of marriage would be in the passage in Genesis where marriage is first described. "For this reason a man will leave his father and mother and be united to his wife, and they will become one flesh" (Genesis 2:24). Yet, this verse does not immediately yield clear-cut support for an intimate relationship. The term "one flesh," is not defined; it could simply refer to the fact that they are now to be considered a family-like people who are related by blood.

> Intimacy occurs whenever two people, moving beyond a superficial knowledge of one another, share some inner thoughts and feelings. In common terms, it's "being close."

Some have found a reference to intimacy in the following verse: "The man and his wife were both naked, and they felt no shame" (Gen. 2:25).

Jack and Judith Balswick claim intimacy was an essential feature of the pre-Fall family and that it was only after their sin that the family began to play deceptive games with one another.[1] Prior to this they had the ability to be themselves without any pretense because they were said to be naked and without shame. It was only after disobedience that the family began to play deceptive games with one another. That the idea of physically shameless nakedness refers to personal closeness is quite possible, but not certain. The words are so symbolic they are subject to a variety of interpretations. Being without shame may refer to their moral purity before God, not their attitude toward one another. Yet, other Old Testament references tend to lend weight to the idea that God's ideal for the family at creation was that it be intimate.

For one thing, we know that marriage, from the beginning, was to be a sexual relationship, at least suggesting a physical intimacy. Many scholars note the sensual overtones in the phrases in Genesis 2:24. The term *united* literally means to be "joined to," suggesting the sexual union. Even the idea of being "one flesh," might convey a hint of sensuality. However, proving that marriage is to be a sexual union does not prove it to be an intimate one. The kind of intimacy for which we are seeking evidence is more than physical, being personal and emotional.

Support for this broader intimacy does build with the addition of certain other matters. (1) The Hebrew term for *flesh* is sometimes used for the whole person. Thus, being "one flesh," may suggest that marriage is to be a union of persons, not just bodies. (2) The Old Testament uses the word *yada*, "to know," to refer to sexual intercourse. Scholars believe this contributes to the idea that sex is supposed to be a very intimate union, not just a physical one. They did this because they viewed sex as a very personal union. (3) Comparing the phrase "leave father and mother" with "be united to his wife" offers some insight into the idea of marriage in Genesis 2:24. Leaving a personal relationship with parents to enter into one with his wife, suggests the man's union with his wife is broader than sexual.

All these bits and pieces of evidence for intimacy as a biblical ideal in marriage are not quite conclusive in themselves. But they really become persuasive when they are viewed within the whole second chapter of Genesis.

Context of Statement about Marriage

The description of marriage in Genesis 2:24 is greatly impacted by the statement that comes earlier in the passage: "It is not good for the man to be alone." Eve, marriage, and family were all created because of Adam's aloneness (Gen. 2:18). This indicates humans are in need of intimacy that is to be found in marriage and family. Marcus Barth concludes that the phrase *be united*

(Hebrew *dabaq*) and its Greek equivalents mean a voluntary, passionate, close relationship that involves a man's soul and body.[2]

Old Testament scholars saw this even before Christians began to stress marital intimacy. In 1888, Franz Delitzsch declared, "Marriage is a relation . . . of the most intimate, personal, spiritual and corporeal association."[3] S. R. Driver stresses intellectual intimacy: Eve is to be "a help, who may in various ways assist him, and who may at the same time provide a companion, able to interchange thought with him, and be in other aspects his intellectual equal."[4] He concludes that the attachment between the man and wife become "greater, and the union closer, even of that between parent and child."[5]

Marriage in Proverbs and Song of Songs

Further proof for this companionship concept of marriage is found in later books of the Old Testament. God speaks of the wife as "your companion and your wife by covenant" (Mal. 2:14 NRSV). Proverbs 2:17 tells us the wayward wife has left her "partner." Using the term "partner" to translate the Hebrew word *aloof* is misleading. *Aloof* denotes the closest possible relationship a person can have, translated in other places "close friend" (Prov. 16:28; 17:9).

Song of Songs gives more evidence for injecting intimacy into the idea of marriage. No matter how it is interpreted, this Song celebrates marital love, and is used by Jews even today in their wedding ceremonies. "This my lover, this my friend," she says of him (5:16). Marveling in the revelation of each to the other, he invites her to be like a dove in the cleft of the rock to "show me your face, let me hear your voice" (2:14).

So far, our proof for intimacy in marriage is embedded in God's creative purpose. If we are to follow our assertion that God's redemptive purpose is of greater priority, we must now ask if the intimate feature of marriage is incorporated into God's new creation. The following arguments will not only demonstrate that it is, but that the Godly, spiritual, eternal basis for the husband-wife relationship will justify any elegance we currently bestow on marriage.

THE REDEMPTIVE BASIS OF INTIMACY IN MARRIAGE

Husband and Wife Reflecting the New Image

We have seen that Christians sometimes ignore marriage and family life in order to give the kingdom of God first place in their lives, which may be called for at times (Matt. 19:12). Yet we should be cautious not to separate so drastically God's new creation (signified by kingdom) and his old creation.

Though the new creation is greater and distinct from the old creation, it is also a continuation of the old. This is true for three reasons: (1) The new creation is described as a renewal of mankind in the image of God after which he was originally created. Paul described the Christian life in these terms: "Do not lie to each other, since you have taken off your old self with its practices and have put on the new self, which is being renewed in knowledge in the image of its Creator" (Col. 3:9). (2) The image of God to which we are being renewed is God's Son, Jesus Christ (Rom. 8:29).[6] (3) Thus the Christlikeness to which we are called and destined is, in part, a renewal of what God originally intended for man. In his book, *The True Image*, Philip Hughes summarizes this truth:

> Conformity with the image of God's Son is . . . conformity with the image of God in which man was originally created and into which, now through redeeming grace, it is his destiny to be recreated. The destiny that was planned from the very beginning is fulfilled redemptively and re-creatively in the Son by God who proclaims: 'Behold I make all things new!' (Rev. 21:5).[7]

In redemption, all aspects of created humanity, including our roles as male and female, are enhanced and elevated.[8] Thus marriage and family play a role in the new creation. Jesus affirmed this by grounding his standards for marriage "in the beginning." Geoffrey Bromiley explains that it is only those who give priority to the Kingdom ethics and values who can have a truly ordered marriage.[9] Married partners, discarding deceit and manipulation, should relate to one another honestly and intimately as God intended in creation and now makes possible in salvation. Richer and deeper support for intimate marriage comes from seeing how marital intimacy reflects something of the very person of God.

> In redemption, all aspects of created humanity, are enhanced and elevated. Thus marriage and family play a role in the new creation.

Husband and Wife Reflecting God

No one has given more profound meaning to the male-female relationship than Karl Barth, who uniquely claimed our sexuality is rooted in our being created in the image of God (*imago dei*). Simply put, we are in God's likeness because we are male and female: "In the image of God he created him; male and female he created them" (Gen. 1:27). Just as God is a being with capacity for relationships, so, too, are we.[10]

EXCURSUS ON THE *IMAGO DEI*

Karl Barth comments on Genesis 1:27, which reads, "In the image of God he created him; male and female he created them." "Could anything be more obvious than to conclude from this clear indication that the image and likeness of the being created by God signifies existence in conformation . . . in the juxtaposition and conjunction of man and woman which is that of male and female?" (*Church Dogmatics*, vol. 3, pt. 1, trans. G. W. Bromiley [Edinburgh, 1958], 195). By claiming that the male-female distinction is the essence of the *imago dei*, Barth affirms two truths that are basic to his theological system. First, the original creation of man was an expression of the person of Jesus Christ. Sourcing all his theological thinking in the person of Christ, he maintains that the essential aspect of being human is the capacity for encounter with God and with one another. He begins with Christ because he is the revelation of God, which he calls the revelation of the Word. Also, he draws his concepts from redemption in Christ, not creation, because he maintained that God's redemptive plan was in place prior to the creation.

The foundation of his thinking about man is that God created man to be in covenant with himself. This covenant is a redemptive one of grace that is found in Christ's death for the world. God created the world and man so that man would become God's partner in history. This is the goal of creation and it "is not something which is added later to the reality of the creatures" but it "already characterizes creation itself" (ibid., 231). The covenant between Jesus Christ and his community was, in the beginning, the first and proper object of the divine will and plan and election, and the internal basis of creation (ibid., 299). That mankind includes both male and female expresses the fundamental idea that one person alone cannot fully express who God is. Rather, the two sexes embody the relational dimension of humanity.

Barth goes even further. Ultimately, the likeness of man's being as male and female is not due merely to the covenant relation of God and man but to the very being of God. God has created us male and female (a duality) to express his own essential nature of being Father, Son, and Spirit (a trinity). (See Bromiley, *God and Marriage*, 133.) "Man is no more solitary than God. But as God is One, and he alone is God, so man as man is one and alone, and two only in the duality . . . of man and woman. In this way he is a copy and imitation of God" (Barth, *Church Dogmatics*, vol. 3, pt. 41, 186). Just how central this is to his theology is seen in his blanket statement, "The fact that he created man and woman will be the great paradigm of everything that is to take place between him and God, and also of everything that is to take place between him and his fellows" (Ibid., 186.)

This covenant is not only the basis of our relationship to God, but also to one another. We exist in co-humanity. A person cannot exist alone because God created us to be in encounter with others. Encounter is distinct from mere human relationships; rather in an "I-Thou" encounter we discover something about ourselves, as well as about others. In this encounter we are fully human. This feature of created man he calls our "co-humanity."

All relationships can be the context of this "I-Thou" encounter. But it has special meaning in the "one flesh" experience in marriage.

In Genesis 2, where it is decided that it is not good for man to be alone, where he is to recognize himself in another and another in himself, where humanity relentlessly means fellow-humanity, where the body or existence of woman is the same to man as his own body or existence, where the I is not just unreal but on the far side of al-egoism or altruism—must be the willing and longing of the Thou.

Barth explains how even the sexual aspect of marriage participates in this affirmation of our co-humanity:

> For sexual intercourse means that at the climax and in the completion of their encounter they become one body, belonging wholly to one another in their corporeality, and mutually attesting and guaranteeing their humanity. In this completion the man no longer belongs to himself, but to the woman; and the woman no longer belongs to herself, but to the man. In this completion there takes place between them something final and irrevocable. They are both what they became in this completion—a being belonging to this other (Barth, *Dogmatics*, vol. 3, pt. 45, 306–7).

A few evangelical theologians agree with Barth, but most do not. However, it is not necessary to accept Barth's idea of the *imago dei* in order to see that the human capacity for relationships is a reflection of God's being. Using the phrase "I-Thou" to typify a close, open, quality union, Philip Hughes connects our human capacity for intimacy as a reflection of God's character.

Yet Hughes does indicate that the recovery of personhood in our relationship with God is the new man. And "because that image is in fact a Person, the Son who is the Image of God, it is in him that the vertical I-Thou, person-to-Person, relationship with God is restored, and also, as a necessary consequence, the horizontal I-Thou, person-to-person relationship with our fellow human beings."[11]

> **Much of the meaning of sex in marriage is found in the profound sense of intimacy it affords to humans who, like God, have a capability of relating deeply to others.**

Theologically, we can say that much of the meaning of sex in marriage is found in the profound sense of intimacy it affords to humans who, like God, have a capability of relating deeply to others. The sexual relationship satisfies a deep longing for personal communion.[12]

Comparing it with animal sex, Ray Anderson explains the deep meaning of human sex: "Animals do not experience the other as total 'other' in the sense of the mystery of encounter with being . . . . The mating of dogs does not produce relationships which transcend that natural and instinctive drive. . . . Human persons, however, not only mate but they 'meet.'" That personal "meeting" with another intensifies certain self-knowledge (the I-Self encounter) and enhances the knowledge of the other (I-Thou encounter).[13]

> **Redemption should provide us with the capacity for the richest marital experiences.**

These theological explanations about sex and marriage may help to explain why we humans possess such a powerful yearning for intimacy. It may also help us understand why the sexual arena is such a problem for fallen, sinful mankind, its proper expression being so closely tied to our essential being.

On the other hand, this perspective of the marriage relationship should offer hope to Christians. Redemption should provide us with the capacity for the richest marital experiences.[14]

INTIMACY BETWEEN OTHER FAMILY MEMBERS

The biblical recognition of intimacy between other family members is not as clear as it is for husband and wife. But there are instances where Scripture suggests there ought to be a special closeness among family members, an open expression of emotions. An excellent example of two of the most dramatic aspects of family life, repenting and forgiving, is found in the parable of the prodigal son: "His father saw him and was filled with compassion for him; he ran to his son, threw his arms around him and kissed him" (Luke 15:20). And in a description of true friendship in Proverbs 18:24, our relationship with a friend is compared to our closeness to a brother, indicating expected intimacy between siblings.

> **Singles can experience sensual intimacy without its being sexual.**

By investing families with a high quality of intimacy, I am not suggesting it cannot be had elsewhere. Interpreters generally agree that Eve's being created to overcome Adam's aloneness does not suggest that marriage is the only source of close companionship. Rather, the passage is taken to mean that humans are created as social creatures. Redeemed Christians are to foster intimacy by being honest persons who speak the truth in love and put off falsehood (Eph. 4:15, 25). Single people, too, need a sense of closeness with others, including family. Intimacy with others is achieved by sharing emotions, thoughts, and activities; it includes playing, praying, and serving together. Singles, too, can experience sensual intimacy, without it being sexual: an encouraging hand on the shoulder, a warm hug, etc.

SENSUAL AND EMOTIONAL LOVE IN MARRIAGE

Along with intimacy, love is a major component of the expressive dimension of marriage and family. Just as our craving and capacity for authentic, intimate encounters with others is embedded in our being created and recreated in God's image, so also is our capacity to love.

Love as an Issue

Love Is Sacrificial and Willful

There is little debate about some of love's traits. Scripture throughout affirms that love is to be sacrificial and unselfish. Paul tells husbands to love their wives as "Christ loved the church and gave himself up for her" (Eph. 5:25).

Love that is willful, sacrificial, and action-oriented has usually been referred to as agape. It has not always been thought that agape is also emotional, romantic, and sensual.

That it is willful, under our control, is also clear. Scripture doesn't tell us to fall in love, but it commands us to love. That love involves action, not just feeling, is obvious in Paul's unmatched description of love in 1 Corinthians 13. Love is patient, kind, trustful, and hopeful. It doesn't act rudely, is not easily angered, always protects and perseveres, etc. To paraphrase what James says about faith: "Love by itself, if it is not accompanied by action, is dead. . . . Show me your love without deeds, and I will show you my love by what I do" (James 2:17–18).

Love that is willful, sacrificial, and action-oriented has usually been referred to as *agape*, a Greek word for love. It has not always been thought that *agape* is also emotional, romantic, and sensual.

Agape is normally distinguished from *philia* (friendship love) and *eros* (sexual love). In his pivotal work, *Agape and Eros*, Anders Nygren contrasted *agape*, Christian love, with the love of the ancient Hellenistic world, which he termed *eros*.[15] Among other differences between the two types of love, he claimed *eros* involved getting while *agape* was identified with giving. C. S. Lewis popularized this segregation of love into diverse kinds in his book, *The Four Loves*.[16]

Lewis especially contrasted God's love with man's natural love. Human love, he claimed, is always directed to objects that the lover finds in some way intrinsically lovable. But divine love in us enables us to love what is not naturally lovable—lepers, criminals, enemies, morons, and so on.[17]

Designated as a fruit of the Holy Spirit, this type of spiritual love is necessary in marriage and family. By means of this love, family members forgive and endure the disappointment and heartbreak that they, because of their imperfection, inflict upon one another. God's love in them enables them to be kind to one another when they least of all deserve it.

It is this love that elevates all other aspects of marital love. When a husband and wife first love God and then love each other by the power of God's love within them, they will be prevented from making an idol of their love to one another. They will realize that their partner cannot meet needs that God alone can meet. Nor will they idolize love itself, believing that erotic love will satisfy their emptiness. With unselfish, Christlike devotion to one another, they will not use sex to dominate or manipulate one another, or use it as a medium of hurt or degradation.

Issue of Romantic, Emotional Love

Limiting the definition of *agape* to acts that are willful and sacrificial raises the question of the role of emotions in the notion of love. That romantic love exists is obvious. It has been celebrated in novels and has been the subject of scientific research. It's also clear that strong feelings can occur between parents and children. The question we are asking is whether these things should occur. Should a wife expect her Christian husband to be romantically involved with her? Must a parent feel love for a child or a child for a parent? Are these part of God's ideal for marriage and family?

To answer this, we need to first of all establish what we mean by romantic and emotional love; then we can determine whether there is any biblical or theological support for insisting this type of love be the norm for Christian marriage and family. Psychologists have sorted out some of romantic love's common traits. Spontaneous attraction: chemically, a couple will sort of fuse together despite little or no previous experience with one another. Intense preoccupation: they will then become engrossed with each other, giving each other the undivided attention of a hound chasing a rabbit. Enjoyable experience: time together is pleasing; there is no complaining about being together. Pain in absence: separation from one another is miserable. Physical reactions: rise in heart rate, sweaty palms, weak knees, and even dizziness. Robust relationship: the relationship will be rather strong, even through it arises quickly. Unselfish concern for the other's welfare: there will be an awesome concern for the well-being of the person loved. Pampering: they will listen to each other for long hours and indulge one another, sometimes buying costly gifts. The lovers will enjoy and be thrilled by unselfish acts lavishly poured out for the benefit of the one loved.[18] Idealism: there will be a strong tendency to lose touch with reality.

> Christlike love in marriage should include romance and passion.

They will be blind to each other's problems and faults. This idealism may extend to all of life. They live in a sort of fantasy land, full of optimism and happiness.[19]

Does the Bible attest to the reality of this type of love? And should we expect some of its features to continue after marriage?[20] Some recent theologians insist that Christlike love in marriage should include romance and passion. Love is so complex that we lose something when we try to fix too explicitly the boundaries between sexual feelings, romantic emotions, passion, affection, compassion, and sacrificial love.[21] Two lines of argument support this view: first, the Old Testament portrays a passionate, romantic side of marital love; second, the New Testament does the same.

Marital Love as Sensual, Emotional, and Romantic

Old Testament View of Marital Love

Traits of romantic love appear frequently in the Old Testament. Take, for example, the idealism associated with romance. Jacob was portrayed as out of touch with reality when he served seven years to get Rachel as his wife (her father's price) but "they seemed like only a few days to him because of his love for her" (Gen. 29:20). Other Scriptures picture the intense, passionate, compulsive nature of love between a man and woman. Elkanah treated Hannah differently from his other wife Peninnah "because he loved her" (1 Sam. 1:5). In Hebrew, there is a special word for the love between a man and woman (*ahaba*). Song of Songs lauded *ahaba*: "Love is as strong as death, its jealousy unyielding as the grave. It burns like blazing fire, like a might flame. Many waters cannot quench love; rivers cannot wash it away" (Song of Songs 8:6–7).

Some passages even command this robust, excited, passionate love. Proverbs 5:18–19 tells a husband to "rejoice in the wife of your youth . . . may her breasts satisfy you always, may you ever be captivated by her love." The prominent Old Testament scholar of the last century, Franz Delitzsch, tells us that to "be captivated" by her is translated from the Hebrew word that is used for being intoxicated by wine.[22] This indicates, he writes, that there should be "an intensity of love connected with the feeling of superabundant happiness."[23] Such a state is to be maintained throughout marriage, since the reference to "wife of your youth" is not about a youthful wife but a wife (perhaps now old) that a man took in his youth. He is to keep the ecstasy in the marriage "ever" and "always."

According to the Song of Songs the intensity of this love may sometimes make a person feel ill: "I am faint with love" (Song 2:5). It eventuates in a feeling of ownership: "I am my beloved and my beloved is mine." It is "as strong as death."

Nygren suggests that such elements of love are never a part of Godly love. Yet in the Old Testament, the love between a man and woman is sometimes used as a model for God's love for his people. The same word for the love between the sexes (which includes sexual love) is used of God's love for his people in a number of places (Deut. 7:8; 1 Chron. 2:11). "I have loved you with an everlasting love," said God through the prophet Jeremiah (Jer. 31:3). "I led them . . . with ties of love," said God (Hos. 11:4). God's love is not only expressed in the medium of marital passion; it is passionate. With this in mind, we now turn to the New Testament view of marital love.

New Testament View of Marital Love

Two major passages in the New Testament touch the subject of love in marriage. In Ephesians 5:25 husbands are told to love their wives "just as Christ loved the church." Titus 2:4 states young wives should be taught to love their husbands. To determine the nature of the love commanded, we must ask whether or not these passages embrace the concept of passionate love the Old Testament asserts.

In his commentary on Ephesians, Marcus Barth denies the idea that the love described here is only sacrificial and willful, even though the word for love is *agapao* (the verb form of *agape*). He boldly asserts that not only should husbands be passionate in their love for their wives, but that Christ himself also loved the church in that way.

He dubs this section of Ephesians "The Romance of Christ and the Church," claiming the

> **We should not exclude something of the idea of *eros* in *agape*.**

tone of the passage is amorous because it uses the analogy of the bridegroom and his bride.[24] Acts done for the bride—giving himself, washing her with water, and preparing her for the wedding—are done because he adores her and looks forward to the future marriage. In this sense, Barth sees the analogy as of the most powerful form of romantic love, the expectant love of the engaged.[25]

The use of the term *agape* in this passage, claims Marcus Barth, includes "passionate desire and sexual fulfillment that have been attributed primarily to *philia* and *eros*."[26]

Barth is only one of many scholars who have recognized the error of so sharply separating *agape* from other types of love. Because the New Testament employs three different Greek words for love, it does not necessarily suggest there are three types of love and that each is always used exclusively for one of those types. The words *agape*, *eros*, and *philia* are sometimes used in place of one another, meaning they are not entirely separate. For example, in the Septuagint translation of the Old Testament, the Hebrew word for sexual love is often translated by the word *agape*.

We should not exclude something of the idea of *eros* in *agape*. "A chief characteristic of agape is irrationality," writes Casmir McCambley. "It creates its own logic, its own way of being, resulting from a kind of affectionate clinging. We must be careful not to separate *agape* and *eros*."[27]

At this point, we should stop to consider whether uniting *eros* and *agape* in this way has subtracted the notion of unselfishness from our idea of Christian love. Nygren claimed that this trait of unselfishness, above all else, separated the two types of love. *Eros* is based on a "selfish self-assertion." He described it as a possessive kind of loving, determined by the quality of the object loved. Yet *agape* overflows spontaneously for a person, whether good or evil.

A closer look at the term *agape*, however, reveals that it does include something of loving for personal gain. Barth notes: "Paul has stated that the 'loving' Father acquires a people for himself that become his 'property' (Eph. 1:11, 14), and that the risen Messiah presents 'to himself' a glorious Bride (5:27), his body, the Church" (5:28–29). With equal freedom Paul speaks of that which a husband gains through his love: a body whom he can love as his own true self (5:28–29). In other words, love can sometimes be a response to the quality of

> **Christlike love can be expressed in many ways and in many types of relationships: sensual, emotional, intimate, and romantic expressions of love, unique to marriage, are also expressions of Christian love.**

the object loved. Christian love may also be generated and directed toward something desirable in the one loved. Would husbands and wives want it any other way? Do they want to be loved by a love that is condescending, costly, and self-sacrificing? Don't they each want to be desired and loved for who they are? While it is true that Christ loved us while we were yet sinners, wholly undeserving, is it not true that even he loved us because he valued us? And, when emulating Christ's love, do not Christians love the so-called undesirable people (enemies, outcasts, the unlovable) because they sense their intrinsic value as humans? Therefore, when Paul commands husbands to love their wives as Christ loved the church, he is not telling them to merely act in love. He is urging them to cultivate a feeling of love, just as God asks of us when he commands us to love him with heart, soul, and strength.

Now we must ask if wives are also to love in such a way, looking closely at the Titus passage. Speaking of the older woman, Paul writes: "Then they can train the younger women to love their husbands and children." (Titus 2:4). Mary Pride represents some who claim that the love wives are to have is different from that of husbands because the term for love used in this passage is the verbal form of *phile*, not *agape*. "The 'love' he asks from us is philea love; brotherly love. It is based on our relationship, not our emotions."[28] There are several reasons why this is not true.

First, as we have already noted, the terms for love cannot be distinguished in this way. Second, in the Bible the verbal form of the word *agape* is applied to wives as well as husbands. In the context of Paul's instructions to wives and husbands, he tells all Christians to be imitators of God and "live a life of love [*agape*], just as Christ loved us." Third, when applying the Old Testament concept of love in marriage to Christians, as we have already done, it is clear that its emotional, passionate expression is true of both men and women.

Christlike love can be expressed in many ways and in many types of relationships: that is what we have been claiming. Therefore, sensual, emotional, intimate, and romantic expressions of love, unique to marriage, are also expressions of Christian love.[29]

C. S. Lewis, connoisseur of love, saw this. Natural loves are like God's love, he claimed:

> Let us here make no mistake. Our Gift-loves are really God-like; and among our Gift-loves those are most God-like which are most boundless and unwearied in giving. All the things the poets say about them are true. Their joy, their energy, their patience, their readiness to forgive, their desire for the good of the beloved—all this is a real and all but adorable image of the Divine life.[30]

This is not to say that marital love must always be expressed in these ways. Passion is broader than sex; love is more than passion. Each couple will, like two artists, create their own marriage masterpiece. Romance for some will be less important than it is for others. When the sexual relationship is restricted or absent because of sickness or age, love continues to find countless channels of expression.

The point of this chapter is this: partners who lavish their affection on one another, delighting in all aspects of their union and communion, need not be made to feel that this love is inferior or even unrelated to a genuine expression of Christian love. This error has no doubt led many Christians to neglect the relationship with their spouses in order to devote themselves unselfishly to helping others outside their families, as if loving those outside were a more important manifestation of the love of God.

> The love of husband and wife will often be costly; loving acts will be required even when feelings are absent.

This does not mean that the love of husband and wife will always be easy, flowing from a vast reservoir of romantic feeling. Actually, it will often be costly; loving acts will be required even when feelings are absent. And feeling will have to be generated when it is not spontaneously there or has been allowed to grow cold. Husbands and wives with low sexual desire may be called upon to develop their sexual appetites through therapy and agonizing effort, in order to express true *agape* to their spouses. Sacrificial Christlike love, a fruit of the Spirit, will be needed if couples are to maintain a satisfying level of romantic, sexual, and emotional attachment to one another.

NOTES

1. Jack O. Balswick and Judith K. Balswick, *The Family: A Christian Perspective on the Contemporary Home* (Grand Rapids: Baker, 1989), 31.
2. Marcus Barth, *Ephesians: Translation and Commentary on Chapters 4–6* (New York: Doubleday, 1974), 640.

3. Franz Delitzsch, *A New Commentary on Genesis* (Edinburgh: T. & T. Clark, 1899), 145.

4. S. R. Driver, *The Book of Genesis* (London: Methven, 1906), 40–44.

5. Ibid. 40–44.

6. Many other passages of Scripture support this fact: "Those whom God foreknew, he also predestined to be conformed to the image of his Son" (Rom. 8:29. See also 1 Cor. 15:4; 2 Cor. 4:4; Col. 1:15).

7. Philip Edgcumbe Hughes, *The True Image* (Grand Rapids: Eerdmans, 1989), 36.

8. Ibid., 19.

9. Geoffrey W. Bromiley, *God and Marriage* (Grand Rapids: Eerdmans, 1980), 67.

10. For those who accept it, see Ray Anderson of Fuller Theological Seminary in *On Being Human* (Grand Rapids: Eerdmans, 1982). Also from Fuller, Jack and Judith Balswick in *The Family: A Christian Perspective on the Contemporary Home*. D. H. Field, "Sexuality," in *New Dictionary of Theology*, ed. Ferguson Sinclair, David F. Wright, and J. I. Packer (Downers Grove, Ill.: InterVarsity Press, 1988), 637–39. Many disagree with Barth. Bromiley questions Barth's basic thesis. "We have the christological and covenantal understanding which controls his whole exegesis. Is this a valid interpretation in the total context of scripture, or is Barth with his rich and fertile mind seeing things that are not actually there?"

Bromiley and others question Barth's interpretation of Genesis 1:17. Barth thinks his exposition is obvious because the concepts image of God and male and female are in the same sentence. "In the image of God, he created him, male and female created he them." Hughes says that to refute this exegesis we need to simply affirm "that the phrase *created man as male and female* is in fact additional and not explanatory which is the more natural way of taking it."

G. C. Berkouwer sees another difficulty with Barth's thinking. Barth's interpretation is confusing because "he sometimes refers to man-woman relationship as image and then later broadens this to fellow-man relationship."

Another problem with this interpretation is that the animals are also created male and female. Though Barth attempts to show how human sexuality is distinct from the animals, it appears a problem to bring that into the first chapter of Genesis and conclude that man's sexuality is the meaning of the likeness of God which distinguishes him from the animal world.

11. Anderson, *On Being Human*, 54.

12. Derrick Sherwin Bailey, *Sexual Relation in Christian Thought* (New York: Harper, 1959), 269–70.

13. Anderson, *On Being Human*, 106.

14. Though our Christlikeness will appear in other forms and in other relationships, it has a unique opportunity for expression within marriage. So has Christlike love, which is also to be one of the major features of marriage.

15. Anders Nygren, *Agape and Eros* (Philadelphia: Westminster, 1953), viii.

16. C. S. Lewis, *The Four Loves* (New York: Harcourt, Brace, 1960).

17. Ibid., 176.

18. Harry Stack Sullivan, *Conceptions of Modern Psychiatry*, 2d ed. (New York: W. W. Norton, 1966), 42–43.

19. Ibid.

20. Mary Pride, *The Way Home* (Westchester, Ill.: Crossway, 1985), 20.

21. Helmut Thielicke, *The Ethis of Sex*, trans. John W. Doberstein (New York: Harper, 1964), 6.

22. Franz Delitzsch, *Biblical Commentary on the Proverbs of Solomon* (Grand Rapids: Eerdmans, 1978), 1:132.

23. Ibid., 131.

24. Barth, *Ephesians*, 623.

25. It may be asked, why did Paul command husbands to love their wives and not wives to love their husbands? It must be remembered that Paul did command wives to love husbands in Titus 2:5, where he uses the word *philandros*, "husband-loving." If we do not distinguish the terms *phile* from *agape*, then it is clear Paul did not single out husbands in his command to love. Remember, too, that Jesus commanded his followers to love one another, a love that can be extended to all relationships. In the Old Testament, love is not specifically commanded of husbands and wives. Yet, it was a practice of rabbis to apply the command to love one's neighbor as one's self to family relationships. Marcus Barth guesses that Paul command husbands to love, and not wives, in Ephesians because he may have been convinced that husbands more than wives are exposed to the temptation to offer cheap or costly gestures as a substitute. See Barth, *Ephesians*, 701.

26. Barth, *Ephesians*, 716.

27. McCambley notes that Gregory joins *eros* and *agape* together at the beginning of his *Commentary on the Song* by quoting from Proverbs 4:6: "ardently long after wisdom" (p. 25). "This text quoted above gives us the proper nuance of eros; it is a passion which moves the soul. Because *eros* is a passion, it is therefore outside the realm of the *nous* [mind], man's most noble faculty. *Eros* is best viewed as an intensification of *agape*; 'the bride is wounded by a spiritual fiery shaft of desire' (*eros*). For *agape* which is aroused is called *eros*" (p. 383). Gregory describes *eros* here as an excess of *agape*, a more intense and fervent manifestation. The bridegroom, the "noble lover of our souls," initiates his *agape*, which the bride passively receives and reflects like a mirror.

Therefore, the noble lover of our souls shows his love by which Christ dies for us sinners. The bride, in turn, is inflamed with love and shows the shaft of love deeply placed in her heart, for this is fellowship with God (Introduction to Gregory of Nyssa, *Song of Songs*, trans. by Casimir McCambley [Brookline, Mass.: Hellenic College Press, 1987], 26–27).

28. Pride, *The Way Home*, 20.

29. Barth, *Ephesians*, 718.

30. C. S. Lewis, *The Four Loves*, 19–20.

10 Marriage and Family as Complementing

ROLES OF HUSBAND AND WIFE

Having dwelt so long on the unity and emotional closeness of family, we must also see the theological basis for difference and distance between family members. Things that go together are often very different: peaches and cream, a horse and carriage. Other metaphors that have been used to picture marriage are a lock and a key, and a violin and a bow.

Scripture makes it clear that oneness in marriage results from the union of two *different* people. When God created the woman for Adam, she had to be like him, "bone of my bones and flesh of my flesh." But she also qualified because she was different; she was female. Partners unite sexually because they are the complement of one another; apparently, they also complement each other in other ways as well. This leads us to the question of what the differences between maleness and femaleness mean in marriage.

Karl Barth, whose idea of gender grows out of our being created in the image of God, sees our identity as male or female as permanent and profoundly significant, in fact absolute and eternal. After all, Jesus did not say there would not be male and female in the resurrection, only that there would be no marriage. Others make less of sexual differences. Bromiley says they are significant, but only relative and temporary.[1]

> Scripture makes it clear that oneness in marriage results from the union of two *different* people.

FOUR APPROACHES TO ROLES

One of the major questions surrounding male-female differences has to do with roles in marriage. Do men and women have different assignments on the basis of their sex?

Theoretically, there are four approaches to the roles of husband and wife. In the oldest structural type, called *enforced authority*, the wife is the property of the husband, who may bring her to obedience through beatings if he chooses. In the *traditional head-complement* arrangement the wife is submissive, she is supportive of her husband, and she is the homemaker. The *companionship* type allows the woman to pursue a career and the husband to be involved in domestic work. However, his career takes precedence over his wife's. Here the husband usually has the last word in decisions. The most recent to appear is the *egalitarian* form. Here both the husband and wife are free to have careers, share household duties, and have equal power in decision-making.

Historically, in North America the first type never appeared in pure form because it belonged mostly to medieval times. In the Colonies, religion promoted mutual love and respect that mellowed the husband-wife relationship. On the frontier, the rugged life of challenge and conquest led to a greater equality between the sexes. But the traditional arrangement prevailed in North America, particularly in Puritan New England and in the patriarchal South. By the time of the Civil War or mid-nineteenth-century America, the husband's headship was not a result of compulsion but of mutual love and respect.[2]

A companionship type of marriage was emerging in which the father's advice was authoritative, though his orders were not always obeyed.[3] Democracy had worked its way into the American family, even among the Christians, as the 1946 declaration of the American Lutheran church reveals:

> The husband is to be the head of the household, the wife to be submissive to her husband. Each of these relationships carries with it the overtone "as to the Lord," for the husband is not tyrant over his wife nor does the wife meekly grovel before her husband. The teaching emphasizes the importance of orderly human relations, in which for the sake of good order there must and can be only one head, the husband. The church has not taken a stand against "the democratic family," which does not imply indiscriminate equally divided authority.[4]

Today, however, some evangelicals maintain that equally divided authority is what the Bible teaches. Christians for Biblical Equality argue that the husband has no special authority in the family, but that husbands and wives are to mutually submit to one another, concluding that "In case of decision deadlock, they should seek resolution through biblical methods of conflict resolution rather than by one spouse imposing a decision upon the other."[5]

Egalitarian arguments against a special order in the home take three forms. First, the egalitarians assert that there is a mandate for equality among all Christians. Paul insists that "there is neither . . . male nor female, for you are all one in Christ Jesus" (Gal. 3:28). This equality, the egalitarians maintain, means equal power in a marriage. Equality precludes any difference in roles.

In the second argument it is asserted that all Old Testament references to submission-headship are a result of the fall of man, not the created order. Such references arise from chapter 3 of Genesis, not chapter 2. According to this view, many of the New Testament references to marriage come from the fallen order described in Genesis 3 and are now done away in Christ.

They insist, in the third place, that all of the New Testament references to headship can be explained as adaptation to the culture or holdovers of pre-Christian Jewish thought. In the case of Ephesians 5, where Paul declares that wives should submit to their husbands, egalitarians point to the revolutionary character of the passage. Paul calls for mutual submission of all believers in verse 21, thus nullifying any distinct submission of wives to their husbands. And Paul urges men to love their wives as Christ loves the church, which cancels out any ordained management order. In the case of 1 Corinthians 11:2–12, where the husband's and wife's roles are related to the differences between man and woman found in Genesis 2, Paul Jewett dismisses these thoughts as old rabbinical views still lodged in Paul's mind and thus not normative for Christians today.[6]

> There can be a God-given arrangement for marriage and still be equality between the partners

Those who hold to a companionship type of marriage, in which there are some differences between husband's and wife's roles, cite several references in Scripture pertaining to this type: 1 Corinthians 11:3–12; Ephesians 5:22–33; Titus 2:4; 1 Peter 3:1–7. Those arguing for this position insist that what is called for is not an order of privilege but of function. And that function is quite balanced. "At no time did this headship mean unlimited rule," a denominational statement points out. "At no time as a Christian could he dictate that his wife must do the work, while he enjoyed the wages. . . . At no time could he exercise violence upon her person. His wish is not to prevail in an arbitrary manner in the household."[7] Headship directed by Christlike love is drastically tempered. Calvin characterized it as being gentle and liberal.[8] It is recognized that even Peter's example of appropriate submission, Sarah, opposed Abraham and won her rights from him on several occasions.

That these principles are hangovers from rabbinic times, based on the Fall, or are concessions to culture is rejected by those who support role definitions. Paul gives theological root to the roles by appealing to Genesis 2, which covers the time prior to the Fall. Roles are based on the woman's derivation from the man and her being created for the man (1 Cor. 11:3–9). Had Paul been adopting the cultural views of his day, he would not have appealed to Scripture to support them. It is possible to see a consent to slavery in his writings, but he never offers theological support for the practice as he does for order in marriage. And to accept Jewett's explanation that Paul is presenting outmoded rabbinical ideas would place one outside evangelical principles of biblical interpretation and understanding of biblical authority.

That there can be a God-given arrangement for marriage and still be equality between the partners is also easily maintained. Peter urges husbands to consider their wives as "heirs together of the grace of life" (1 Peter 3:7 KJV), just as Paul acknowledges that there is equality in Christians' relationships with one another in Christ. But equality need not cancel difference and order. Even in the Trinity, where there is equality among the three persons in the Godhead, Christ is in functional subordination to the Father. Paul points to this as an example: "The head of every man is Christ, and the head of the woman is man, and the head of Christ is God" (1 Cor. 11:3).

While it seems clear that the New Testament describes some sort of headship/submission arrangement, it significantly qualifies what this means. A close reading of Paul shows that he is very careful not to suggest husbands "rule" their wives; the submission is to be rendered by the wives, not forced by their husbands. He avoids using the word obey, which he presses upon children (Eph. 6:1) and slaves (Eph. 6:5), and suggests instead that wives respect their husbands (Eph. 5:33).

That both headship and submission are to take place in a context of "mutual submission," also needs to be carefully considered. While there is a good exegetical case for concluding that the phrase "submitting to one another" in verse 21 may only apply to wives, children, and slaves, there is also much to be said for its being applied to husbands, parents, and masters as well.[9] While the word hupotasso is generally employed in a leader-follower type of relationship, it is possible that Paul is using it in a more general sense to refer to a "reciprocal subordination," where each gives to the other that which is proper to him. Certainly the fact that a husband is to love as Christ loves places him under a profound obligation to respond to his wife's needs, just as her submission is to do the same for him. No domination of one over the other is intended.

Yet even those who interpret the phrase to mean mutual submission are still left with the fact that Paul gives two distinct sets of instructions to the marriage partners. That he bases those distinctions on theological, not cultural, grounds makes it difficult to conclude they are not applicable today.[10]

MAINTAINING INDIVIDUAL IDENTITY

An issue in some families is codependency, a condition in which family members are unduly involved with one another. Although not limited to alcoholic families, the condition was first recognized by those studying alcoholic family systems. A codependent person is one who permits someone else to control his or her life. This

> Marriage is to be an amalgamation of two, not an annihilation of one.

occurs whenever someone in the family, say an alcoholic, loses control of his or her drinking. Other family members, to keep some semblance of order in their lives, try to control the addict. This being impossible, their lives are then controlled by the alcoholic's action. The alcoholic is controlled by drinking; family members are controlled by the alcoholic and therefore also by the alcohol;

thus the term codependent. Anyone seemingly out of control in a family can create such a system: a workaholic, an obsessed perfectionist, an angry or mentally ill person, and the like.

Even less-troubled persons can become too enmeshed with one another, particularly when they use marriage to overcome some personal defects. Marriage should not be used to complete one's personal development; ideally only fairly whole, mature persons should marry. Yet immature partners often use one another to compensate for some weakness. Persons with severe personality disorders are ripe candidates for getting into destructive, overdependent relationships.

Many American marriages, according to some psychiatrists, pair a compulsive male and a histrionic female. He is an achiever, always wanting to do things right; she is emotional, impulsive and passive. Because he seldom feels or expresses strong emotions, he enjoys the emotional response she arouses in him. She, on the other hand, being less stable emotionally, is attracted to his apparent stability. Being opposite of one another may be fulfilling for a while, but it will eventually lead to conflict or codependency. He will try to control his wife and she will soon be annoyed that he is too rigid and unfeeling. She gives into his domination, fostering his obsessive-compulsive behavior, and becomes codependent. Neither matures, each held back by the other.[11]

> We can even go so far as to rely on others to do for us what only God can do: give us peace, personal happiness, or significance.

"In marriage one-half plus one-half equals one," according to a well-known saying. Yet becoming one flesh does not mean that. Marriage is not a complete union, only a partial union. The Hebrew word *ahad* (one) denotes a unity in diversity. Oneness is more like two whole eggs in a nest, not two scrambled ones in a skillet.

Marriage is to be an amalgamation of two, not an annihilation of one. You may have heard the joke about the couple coming down the aisle after reciting their marriage vows. Someone says, "They are one, now; it's just a matter of time to determine which one they have become." Certainly there is a profound unity, with demanding, confining responsibilities. But, there is also a diversity; in marriage, partners should foster freedom for individuality, each maturing and developing as a person without too much reliance on or control by the other.

Avoiding Codependency

A certain amount of dependence on one another in the family is only normal. Certainly, we complement each other's weaknesses with our strengths. But when this goes too far, it becomes dysfunctional. This especially happens when we depend on someone else to do for us what we can only do for ourselves, like trusting someone else to give us personal discipline or keep us on our diet. We can even go so far as to rely on others to do for us what only God can do: give us peace, personal happiness, or significance.

Personal changes and accommodations will have to be made in a marriage as two people adjust to living together. However, it is problematic, even abusive, to demand conformity and change in personal areas that are not involved in the relationship. I have counseled wives whose husbands, in the name of leadership, forced dieting and exercising programs on them. In one case, a husband even limited his wife's use of the telephone. Whatever the role designations are designed to do, they are not intended to belittle or destroy either partner's individuality, initiative, and personhood.

Some of the excessive demanding that goes on in marriage is no doubt caused by one partner taking too much responsibility for the other. Spouses, for example, are not responsible for each other's spiritual lives. Certainly a husband and wife should be good examples and should support and encourage one another in their faith development. But that is not the same as feeling that my spouse's faith depends on me. The apostle Paul made it clear that even a believer and an unbeliever could live together successfully (1 Cor. 7:12–16).

We become codependent whenever we care too much. Sometimes this is a response to the mate's overdependence. "Stop me from eating desert at the banquet," she insists. Other times, it's the result of having grown up in a family where such caretaking became a way of life. This no doubt explains why so many daughters of alcoholic fathers marry alcoholics. They have confused caretaking with intimacy, their feelings of pity with love.

Love does care, but it does not care too much. The apostle Paul set the matter straight in Galatians 6. "Carry each other's burdens," he exhorts in verse 2. Yet, in seeming contradiction, he later says, "For each one should carry his own load" (v. 5). The confusion is cleared by an understanding of the original terms. We are to help each other bear each other's *bara*, a load like a large rock or tree stump. Yet, each must bear his own *phortion*, which is something like a backpack. Codependent persons needlessly carry each other's backpacks. This ends in stifling the growth of the one who should share his own load, and frustrating and even destroying the one who is trying to carry it for him.

"A hot-tempered man must pay the penalty," declares Proverbs 19:19. "If you rescue him, you will have to do it again." To avoid codependency we must stop trying to fix each other and believe that the only person we can change is ourselves. We do play a role in helping each other grow, but that consists of being a support, not a substitute for someone. That is called empowering.

Empowering in Marriage and Family

When we encourage individuals to discover their abilities and potential, we empower them. Acceptance is a key to making that happen. In marriage, partners must bring all they are to the relationship. In the family, a child's individual uniqueness should be honored and encouraged. Each must permit the other to assert himself. Family members should learn to see strengths in their differences and to capitalize on them, instead of allowing them to become the basis for competition. In love, they will avoid domination and manipulation.

One day recently in the kitchen, I listened to my wife quarrel with an automatic breadmaker we had borrowed from our neighbor. A part wouldn't fit into place and she was trying to talk it into doing so. As her frustration grew, the conversation growing longer and hotter, I was tempted to offer to rescue with the typical: "Here, let me try." This I would have done, readily and valiantly, in the past. But this concept of "empowerment," held me in check. Instead, I said, "Keep trying; you'll get it." And she did. She was pleased with herself for staying with it; I was proud of myself for staying out of it.

It is painful for me to recall some of the countless times I demeaned my wife's and my children's abilities to cope for themselves by insisting I do something for them instead of encouraging them to do it for themselves. By doing so, in marriage and family, we quench each other's confidence in our own abilities. Empowerment is doing just the opposite; it is "the power to act-each-other-into-well-being."[12]

> Family members should learn to see strengths in their differences and to capitalize on them, instead of allowing them to become the basis for competition.

The Balswicks rightly make "empowering" one of the major tenets of a theology of family, defining it carefully:

> Empowering can be defined as the attempt to establish power in another person. Empowering does not necessarily involve yielding to the wishes of another person or giving up one's own power to someone else. Rather, empowering is the active, intentional process of enabling another person to acquire power. The person who is empowered has gained power because of the encouraging behavior of the other.[13]

At times, the empowered will have to "live and let live," permitting others to fail and thereby learn to succeed for themselves.

Theologically, empowering is based on a number of ideas. I have already cited a few verses that stress how Christians should make people responsible for their behavior. The apostle Paul was very forceful: "If a man will not work, he shall not eat" (2 Thess. 3:10). In addition to that is all that the New Testament has to say about the fostering of individual talents and abilities.

Most of all, empowerment is based on Christian love defined as "concern for another's highest good." Love does not mean rescuing, helping, being

"Empowering" is one of the major tenets of a theology of family.

nice, etc., if that is going to debilitate a person. Sometimes love has to withhold, to stand by, to be tough, because it is better for someone else's welfare. Too often our attempts to help decrease the power of the other person and actually increase our power.[14]

Empowering focuses more attention on the means and the goals of the exercise of influence. The means used must be touched with grace, done with understanding and compassion so that, as in parenting, the child is not angered or depressed. The goal is to serve others, building them up so that they become less dependent upon our influence and more capable of self-control and self-determination.

SUMMARY

After we established the importance of family, our survey of the theology of family has focused on its basis (commitment) and nature (instrumental and expressive features). Marriage is a commitment to (1) possibly having children and, if so, responsibly raising them; (2) fulfilling the practical duties of family; (3) being an expressive partner, loving unselfishly, intimately, emotionally, and sexually; and (4) complementing and empowering one another. Besides this, the Bible prescribes special relationships and obligations of parents toward children, and extended kin toward one another.

These relationships are founded on what we know of God's creative plan for mankind. But, even more than this, they are rooted in the person of God, who is the source and model of commitment, intimacy, and love. Through redemption, God enables us to reach toward being Christlike children, fathers, mothers, husbands and wives, brothers and sisters. With this theology as the cornerstone, we will now propose a theory for local church family ministry.

NOTES

1. Geoffrey W. Bromiley, *God and Marriage* (Grand Rapids: Eerdmans, 1980), 59.
2. Herbert T. Mayer, "Family Relationships in North America," *Family Relationships in the Church* (St. Louis: Concordia, 1970), 126.
3. Arthur W. Calhoun, "Democracy in the American Family," *A Social History of the American Family* (New York: Barnes and Noble, 1917), quoted by Mayer, "Family Relations in North America," 126.
4. Research Summaries, unpublished report (1953), quoted by Mayer, "Family Relations in North America," 130.

5. "Men and Women under God: Hierarchy or Equality?" *Christianity Today* (November/December 1989): 46.

6. Paul K. Jewett, *Man As Male and Female* (Grand Rapids: Eerdmans, 1975), 112.

7. Mayer, *Family Relationships in the Church*, 30.

8. John Calvin, *Commentary on the First Book of Moses Called Genesis*, trans. John King (Grand Rapids: Eerdmans, 1948), 172.

9. Those who argue for *hupotasso* applying only to the first three groups contend that the word is a military term and that it involves following the orders of another. Therefore, persons in a situation where one ranks above the other cannot "mutually submit," since in a given situation, the leader's orders must be followed. For a complete discussion of this see John Piper and Wayne Grudem, *Recovering Biblical Manhood and Womanhood: A Response to Evangelical Feminism* (Wheaton, Ill.: Crossway Books, 1991).

10. Karl Barth, *Church Dogmatics* (Edinburg: T. & T. Clark, 1962), 3:312. Detailed exegesis of the major passages and exposition of the arguments can be found in the most comprehensive volume on the subject, Piper and Grudem, *Recovering Biblical Manhood and Womanhood*. Many other pairings have the same result.

11. Frank Minirth, Paul Meier, and Donald Ratcliffe, *Bruised and Broken: Understanding and Healing Psychological Problems* (Grand Rapids: Baker, 1992), 227. Many other pairings have the same result. Often one person controls, the other succumbs, to the detriment of both. In the appendix, there is a very helpful description of thirteen such pairs of people with personality disorders.

12. Andre Guindon, *The Sexual Creators: An Ethical Proposal for Concerned Christians* (New York: University Press of America, 1986), 30.

13. Jack O. Balswick and Judith K. Balswick, *The Family: A Christian Perspective on the Contemporary Home* (Grand Rapids: Baker, 1989), 28.

14. Ibid.

◆ *Part Three*

The Theory
of Family Ministry

The Subject Matter of Family Ministry

"Be exegetes of the Word and exegetes of the world." Punctuated with pauses and accents conveying robust conviction, this phrase was spoken often by a colleague of mine at Asian Theological Seminary. By these words he was saying that Christians can impact their respective countries when they grasp accurately both their message and their culture. Scripture must be integrated with life. We call this process "contextualization."

In Part Three, I want to propose a contextualized theory of family ministry. In Part One, I "exegeted" the contemporary family; then, in Part Two, the Word; now in Part Three, I will explain some principles to guide today's and, I hope, tomorrow's churches.

In the formulation of theory, two more basic ingredients will be added to the mix as we go along. First, I will be incorporating a theology of the church since that should be uppermost in shaping what our churches should be. And secondly I will try to keep in mind the reality of today's churches. Good theory must be practical; it must be in touch with the situation as it is, not just as it should be. An effective strategy of family ministry must work not only for large churches or for nontraditional ones; it should apply to churches of all sizes and types.

BE REALISTIC AND PRACTICAL

"When were you in our house?" strangers often say to me after they have heard me speak on marriage. I consider this the highest of compliments. They are telling me that I have addressed real life issues. And they assure me that is exactly what they need. First and foremost, the church must teach biblical truth about the family. To be effective, however, that teaching should be realistic and practical.

> An effective strategy of family ministry must work not only for large churches or for nontraditional ones; it should apply to churches of all sizes and types.

To minister to today's families, congregations will have to be like physicians. They must objectively recognize the pain, struggle, and suffering going on in homes. Because it is the church's mission to hold up the ideals of Scripture, however, it sometimes appears to be out of touch with the real condition of Christians.

The complaint that churches gloss over the suffering within a congregation is not new. Over a hundred years ago, a pastor said:

> The mass of suffering in a congregation hidden away behind the quiet faces in the pew is almost unbelievable. But, the average preacher seems not to be very sensitive to it, or to get dulled to it as the years go on; he can talk to people at their wits end while their souls cry why, and why and why? In a glib complacent, nonunderstanding way that does not help but maddens.[1]

To teach in a practical way requires us to give specific suggestions to people that they can take home and try out. Our analysis of the contemporary family has shown us that many people simply do not know how to live in the family, and that biblical advice is not always specific enough for every situation. The Scriptures, for example, teach us to practice patience. But parents of a teenage daughter who is not doing well at school may be hard pressed to know exactly how to exercise patience with her. Just how much should they pressure her? And how? Even Christians who know the Bible well will be perplexed in specific situations.

The first source of workable ideas is within the congregation itself. Many people have solutions they can offer to others if they are placed in positions where they can pass them on.

The first source of workable ideas is within the congregation itself. Many people have solutions they can offer to others if they are placed in positions where they can pass them on. Psychology, sociology, and related disciplines can also help us decipher the puzzles of the modern family and offer suggestions that make sense for today. Always, of course, the findings of science must be scrutinized in the light of Christian truth.

TRAIN FOR THE INSTRUMENTAL PART OF FAMILY LIFE

To meet the needs of modern people, the church will, in some instances, need to train people for the so-called instrumental duties of family life. Many adults from dysfunctional childhood families are not only emotionally injured but seriously unprepared to perform basic household tasks. People marry without being able to cook, manage finances, schedule time, or make decisions. They will have to learn elsewhere what they didn't learn in their homes. School and community family-life education courses will help many develop these instrumental skills. But the church should also help, since it is the church's business to teach its members to be mature Christians. Being able to function in these practical areas is a part of that maturity. The New Testament urges fathers to be providers and to teach and discipline their children, and wives to have children and to manage their homes. Paul suggested that such training was the church's concern when he urged older women to teach such things to the younger women (Titus 2:4–5).

Such skills can be taught in adult education courses. Elective courses could offer training in disciplining and teaching children in the home, managing finances, performing the roles of husbands and wives, cooking, and household management. But much of the training will be done with less formal methods. In small-group contexts and one-to-one ministries, both men and women will have ample opportunities to assist each other in practical family matters. In these more informal and intimate contacts, Christians will be helped when they confide to their mentors and other group members their inadequacies and struggles in the area of family.

Men will need to be taught to be responsible providers for their families. Abandoned single mothers are a major economic and social problem in our country. Granted, most of these so-called deadbeat dads will not be found in our churches, yet some may be. And the church can support programs to reach those who are not. A Detroit area pastor has developed a mentoring program for fathers who have abandoned their families. He trains disciplers who seek to build a relationship with such men, especially those just out of prison. After first supporting their rehabilitation from alcohol, drugs, crime, or other problems, the mentors try to help them spiritually. They move on to family issues, assisting them in dealing with their fears and inadequacies of being husbands and fathers. The goal is to eventually get them back into their homes and teach them family living skills.

The care of children in the family will continue to be a major concern of both church and society. The issue of providing adequate nurture of children has been particularly aggravated by large numbers of women working outside the home. Many churches conduct day care, preschool, and before- and after-school programs in order to help families where both parents work.

Even supposing the church could provide more quality care than community agencies, nonfamily day care of children is not very promising. A number of recent studies have raised serious concerns about the impact of full-time day care on the physical health, social development, and psychological well-being of young children. Research conducted by Jay Belsky at Penn State has found that infants placed in substitute care for twenty or more hours per week are more likely to establish weak and insecure bonds with their parents and more likely to exhibit problem behavior—serious aggression, social withdrawal, uncooperativeness, and intolerance of frustration—than children in maternal care.[2]

Findings from the social scientists combined with our theology of family should compel us to do everything we can to encourage parents to invest heavily in the socialization of their own children.

Practically, it does not seem to be enough to inspire mothers to stay out of the work force. In the first place, we must urge fathers, as well as mothers, to be involved in their child's nurture. And secondly, the economic trend has been away from one-income families. Many women, if not most, have to work to meet the family's financial needs.

The church can support creative solutions to the current problems of child care. As an alternative to a one-income home, some social scientists note the emergence of the symmetrical family, where both father and mother are employed part-time. If income is adequate, both parents are free to share household duties, possibly one babysitting while the other works. Such families are called "tag-team couples."[3] A national study revealed this practice is on the rise: in a three-year period from 1988 to 1991, more fathers cared for their children while the mother worked than ever before. From 1988 to 1991, the percentage of children of working mothers, age five and under, receiving day care from their fathers, rose from 15 percent to 20 percent.[4] Businesses are beginning to accommodate such arrangements with flexible work schedules and day care for children at the work place.

EMPHASIZE TRAINING FOR EXPRESSIVE SKILLS

Though these instrumental duties are important, the major emphasis of the church's family training needs to be directed toward expressive skills.

In the contemporary family, people want to be close to one another, and in the future that desire will increase. Love, affirmation, companionship, and intimacy—these are what people want out of family. And while God requires people to be faithful to the external tasks of marriage, Scripture also accents the expressive side of family. Love must go beyond providing, leading, doing housework, and the like. To apply Paul's words in 1 Corinthians 13 to family, behaving in loving ways toward one's spouse, without love, is "nothing"; a husband's saying the right things—even elegantly—without love is but a clanging cymbal to his wife; a wife who surrenders her body to her husband without love gains nothing. True love shows itself in warm, relational terms: it is kind and patient, not envious, rude, or easily angered, always trusts and hopes (1 Cor. 13:4–7).

> The major emphasis of the church's family training needs to be directed toward expressive skills.

Studies of "well" families reveal that love, intimacy, and empowerment dominate the list of the strengths of functional families. After studying 3000 such families, Nicholas Stinnett cataloged the six main qualities of strong families. Members are (1) committed to the family; (2) spend time together; (3) have good family communication; (4) express appreciation to each other; (5) have a spiritual commitment; and (6) are able to solve problems in a crisis.[5] As Stinnett describes each trait more fully, it becomes clear that the competency of strong families lies not so much in what they do, but in how they feel about and respect each other. They don't just spend time together; they *enjoy* being with each other. Theirs was "not a smothering type of togetherness."[6] Though family talk was not always on profound or deep topics, they listened to each other with respect and "shared their feelings with one another."[7]

Social trends suggest that people of the future will value the relational elements of family even more than they do today. Futurist Alan Sterling, as if writing in the year 2020, observes:

> The attraction of a committed, intimate relationship is most powerful. There seems to be no substitute for the security and satisfaction of having a reciprocal caring relationship with one primary individual. Even with all the flexibility available and essential in a space-age society, the most common form of intimate relationship remains monogamy. We expect this trend to continue well beyond 2020.[8]

Stable, satisfying marriages and families will more and more depend on people's capacity to be intimate and loving, not on their ability to perform household and economic tasks.

Studies of dysfunctional families, by contrast, suggest that they are more deficient in expressive terms—lacking in love, intimacy, and encouragement—than in instrumental aspects of home life. In an abusive family, for example, the wife may be very submissive and the husband a strong leader. The housework may be done with great efficiency and the husband's income may be very substantial. The children may be very compliant and even from time to time receive words of affirmation and encouragement. Yet the severe domination of the father (love deficiency), the beatings when he loses his temper (intimacy disorder), and the stifling of other family

> Stable, satisfying marriages and families will more and more depend on people's capacity to be intimate and loving, not on their ability to perform household and economic tasks.

members (inability to empower), create a tragic situation, even though the family looks healthy on the outside. Inadequacies in these three areas may also underlie individual personal psychological pathologies.

Sexual and social deviants know little of true love. Rapists, for example, use sex to dominate and hurt because they cannot express genuine love. Sociopaths feel little or no empathy for others. In other words, much mental and emotional illness is traced to insufficient and inadequate human contact.

Rene Spitz offered convincing scientific evidence that lack of intimacy causes personality disorders. More than four decades ago in a South American orphanage, this medical doctor observed and recorded what happened to ninety-seven children who were deprived of emotional and physical contact with others. Because of a lack of funds, there was not enough staff to adequately care for children three months to three years old. Nurses changed diapers, fed and bathed the children, but there was little time to hold, cuddle, and talk to them as a mother would. After three months many of them showed signs of abnormality. Besides a loss of appetite and inability to sleep well, many of the children lay with vacant expressions in their eyes. After five months, serious deterioration set in. They lay whimpering, with troubled and twisted faces. Often when a doctor or nurse would pick up an infant, it would scream in terror. Twenty-seven, almost one third, of the children died the first year. Not lacking food or health care, they perished because of a deficiency of intimate contact. For the same reason, seven more died the second year. Only twenty-one of the ninety-seven survived, most suffering serious psychological damage.[9]

Physical health, even immunity to disease, may be linked to the quality of one's relationships. Psychologist James J. Lynch has discovered a connection between weakened family ties and physical illness. He found that the amount of serious illness was significantly less among people who had deep relationships with other family members than among those whose relationships in the family were superficial. "Simply put," he concludes, "there is a biological basis for our need to form human relationships."[10]

At the heart of marital disorders is the inability to be intimate. In general, modern males are inept in knowing and expressing their own feelings. They reach out for closeness through sex, partly because they cannot be intimate in other ways. A wife feels used and frustrated because her husband satisfies his need for physical intimacy without offering her the emotional intimacy she desperately needs. Women, too, suffer from intimacy defects. They may be unable to be honest about—or incapable of turning loose—their sexual impulses. Low sexual desire or being inorgasmic are sometimes rooted in the broader problem of intimacy.

> **At the heart of marital disorders is the inability to be intimate.**

Inability or unwillingness to empower others is also characteristic of those with psychological problems. The immature and the neurotic usually enslave others, enmeshing them in stifling relationships. But, obsessed with a need to control, a man may stifle the self-expression of his wife and children. Unless he learns to affirm, encourage, and support, he cannot become the kind of man his wife and children need. As we noted earlier, families of the mentally ill, the addicted, and otherwise handicapped individuals often become codependent.

A CAUTIONARY CONCLUSION

Stressing the role of the expressive side of marriage and family, crucial as it is, may create a problem. It could foster dissatisfaction in people who desire an intensity of intimacy and love in their families but are slow to achieve it. Mary Pride, who argues for a more task-oriented view of family relationships, warns that many couples will use a lack of intimacy and romance as grounds for divorce.[11]

We need to address this issue, but not in the way Pride does. Her answer to marital difficulties is essentially: don't expect so much from marriage. She goes further than that, in effect saying: don't expect anything because that is being selfish.

> We cannot give up God's goals for marriage and family because we have trouble reaching them. Perfectly achieving God's ideal is not the basis for marriage. Commitment is.

Hers is a unique solution to the contemporary divorce problem: expect little and you'll be less disappointed. Hanging on to lofty goals leads to dashed hopes. To avoid nightmares, stop dreaming.

Because she has touched on the existing problem, we should heed Mary Pride's warning about this issue, but question her solution. We cannot give up God's goals for marriage and family because we have trouble reaching them. Rather, we must teach people to hang on to commitment to marriage as well as be devoted to the ideals of marriage. Perfectly achieving God's ideal is not the basis for marriage. Commitment is. People have to live within an imperfect marriage. That marriage may fall short is no grounds for falling out of it. Because some parts of marriage may be more difficult to achieve than others is no reason to drop them from our list of expectations. Marriage is a commitment to both the instrumental and the expressive. We will have to be patient with each other as we, together, reach toward God's ideal for both areas. Emerson said: "A man's reach should exceed his grasp." If couples expect little in marriage, they will achieve little, creating mediocre marriages that could end up being less stable than those in which partners expect more.

NOTES

1. Quoted in Halford E. Luccock, *In the Minister's Workshop* (Grand Rapids: Baker, 1980), 81–82.

2. Another study, done by Bryna Siegal of Stanford University, has concluded that children placed in day care at an early age tend to be more conformist and peer-dependent than other children. Studies show the differences found are still pronounced in later years. A good summary of the research of day care results is in *Family Policy*, a publication of the Family Research Council ("The Family-Friendly Corporation," 5:5 (November 1992): 7–8.

3. For a thorough description and discussion of this type of family see Patricia Voydanoff, "Changing Roles of Men and Women: The Emergence of Symmetrical Families," *The Changing Family*, ed. Stanley L. Saxton, Patricia Voydanoff, and Angela Ann Zukowski (Chicago: Loyola University Press, 1984), 125–38.

4. Karen Brandon, "Fathers Get More Child Care Duty," *Chicago Tribune* (Sept. 22, 1993), sec. 2, p. 1. The study was conducted by the Father Project and the results released Sep-

tember 22, 1993. Since during this three-year period the national economy was declining, it might be assumed that the increase in the number of fathers providing child care could be explained by that trend. But in past economically troubled times, such an increase did not take place. The study, however, did not seek to determine any noneconomic reasons for the changes.

5. Nicholas Stinnett, "Six Qualities That Make Families Strong," *Family Building: Six Qualities of a Strong Family*, ed. George Rekers (Ventura, Calif.: Regal Books, 1985), 38.

6. Ibid., 40.

7. Ibid., 42.

8. Alan Sterling, "2020 and Beyond," *Marriage and the Family in the Year 2020*, ed. Lester A. Kirkendall and Arthur E. Gravatt (New York: Prometheus Books, 1984), 293.

9. Rene Spitz, "Hospitalism: An Inquiry into the Genesis of Psychiatric Conditions of Early Childhood," *Psychoanalytic Study of the Child* 1 (1946): 53–74.

10. James J. Lynch, *The Broken Heart: The Medical Consequences of Loneliness* (New York: Basic Books, 1977), quoted in Lawrence Crabb, "The Family: Manipulation or Ministry," *Family Life Education* (Glen Ellyn, Ill.: Scripture Press Ministries, 1978), 9.

11. Mary Pride, *The Way Home* (Westchester, Ill.: Crossway, 1985), 18.

Methodology of Family Ministry

12

If family ministry were an atom, the nucleus would be made up of knowledge. The previous sections of this book, loaded with theology, have illustrated this viewpoint. Biblical and practical information—lots of it—will have to be conveyed. All of the local church's communication apparatus will need to be called into play, including traditional preaching and teaching. Add to these creative discussion techniques, films, audio and video tapes, books, etc. The following sentence expresses our theoretical guideline:

> Family ministry involves communicating to people of all ages, in as many ways as possible, the biblical and practical truths related to family living.

Being specific about effective methodologies would require a book-length discussion of Christian education and communication, which is impractical and unnecessary at this point. It is necessary, however, to explain why I believe knowledge is not enough and why our methods must do more than convey information.

FAMILY MINISTRY UTILIZES EXPERIENTIAL SKILL-BUILDING METHODS

Besides passing on relevant scientific and biblical information, we need to utilize skill-building methods designed to produce changes in people's attitudes, values, emotions, and spiritual perspective. Teaching and preaching will sometimes do that, but even scriptural knowledge does not always change a person's behavior. Right doctrine does not always produce right living. Thus James reminds us that it is possible to know the right thing to do, and not to do it (James 4:17).

> Scriptural knowledge does not always change a person's behavior. Right doctrine does not always produce right living.

Most people know that listening is important; however, many are very poor listeners. No doubt, when asked, the average parent could write out six guidelines for effective parenting. Yet many of them would confess they don't always practice them.

One of the greatest difficulties in family ministry is getting people to transfer what they know in their heads into what they do in their homes. A high school superintendent told this story: "Sometimes my daughter will ask, 'Dad, may I go out tonight?' It is then that I sift through what I learned in my adolescent psychology courses. After that, I run through the date from my secondary education classes. Then I dip into the resources of the management courses in my Ph.D. studies. After all this, I confidently reply: (long pause) 'Go ask your mother!'"

> One of the greatest difficulties in family ministry is getting people to transfer what they know in their heads into what they do in their homes.

This transfer of knowledge to action is especially difficult in the area of family, partly because family living is such an emotionally laden sphere—a sphere that involves the ongoing interplay of dynamics that are woven into the total fabric of our personalities. Training to be a competent mechanic or chemist is different from training to be a successful husband or wife. Training to be a family member requires in-depth personal changes and adjustments. Thus, the wisdom of courses and sermons has a tough time penetrating the front doors of our homes.

Because family living involves the whole person, family-living skills are best learned in the family rather than in the classroom. Our own childhood family or origin should prepare us for relating to our own spouses and children later on. But, if it did not, we carry this inadequacy into marriage.

Since, as explained before, dysfunctional families tend to produce dysfunctional families, it is difficult to provide training that will overcome the influence of the past.

For families to succeed, they must change—and individuals within them must change—not only in thought, but in action. Such changes are not easy.

> For families to succeed, they must change—and individuals within them must change—not only in thought, but in action. Such changes are not easy.

Many people who work closely with families are pessimistic about the church's ability to promote such changes. Christian psychologist Lawrence Crabb frets, "The unhappy truth is that people seem quite capable of enduring our well-researched, attractively packaged, and skillfully managed family-education programs without really changing very much."[1] We will need to employ methods that go beyond teaching concepts and try to develop those that train people in family living skills.[2]

Change is most likely whenever we use "experiential strategies." These will get people *doing* more than simply hearing what they should be doing. People who struggle with intimacy, for example, will be given opportunities to express their feelings in a safe context and in the process become more comfortable with intimacy.

GOALS OF FAMILY SKILL TRAINING

In the next chapter, I will show how the whole life of the church as a supporting, loving community will be the best training context. But our classes, seminars, club programs, small groups, and conferences can also be places that train through creative experiential techniques such as questionnaires, role playing, communication exercises, and simulation games. These strategies train people by aiming to achieve the following goals, all related to the transformation of lives.

To Create Awareness

A questionnaire, role play, or other experiential strategy causes people to evaluate themselves, helping them to overcome any denial about their shortcomings and needs. They may be more conscious of the need to change and open to suggestions on how to do it. A self-evaluation may also reveal to persons some strengths of which they were not aware. This may increase their confidence in what they are doing and inspire them to continue.

To Provide Practice

Getting into the habit of doing something takes practice. Role-playing exercises, games, group discussion, etc., can give people opportunities to practice good communication skills.

To Get Family Members Involved with Each Other

Mehods that get families to interact with each other may produce immediate improvement. An affirmation exercise, which prompts family members to say something positive to one another, may help a family become healthier.

To Create Understanding of What We Are Teaching

A role play or practice session can increase the depth of understanding of an idea we are trying to teach. Having couples role play discussing their marital problems, for example, can give them a better understanding of the idea of confrontation.

To Provide Support

Families and their individual members will receive encouragement from others whenever they participate in creative, educational experiences that they cannot get from listening to lectures.

Later sections of this book will include examples of experiential methods I have used, some designed by others as well as many I have invented myself. The positive results are very real. Even something so simple as having each couple do a twenty-minute communication exercise following my lecture has frequently produced comments like: "That's the best talk my husband and I have had for ten years." Some of the most dramatic and long-lasting changes I have seen in families have come from the use of these methods. Yet for some people and family situations, they are not enough.

FAMILY MINISTRY INCLUDES THERAPEUTIC STRATEGIES

To be effective for some people, family ministry will need to include strategies that are therapeutic in nature. By therapeutic I mean strategies that go beyond what we usually do in teaching and training in three ways. First, these strategies focus more on an individual's need or problem. This is usually done in one-to-one counseling situations, but can be done in group or whole-family therapy sessions. Second, therapy deals with a personal problem the person acknowledges in some way. The recipient of therapy may not be able to identify the real issue, but confusion, frustration, and struggle have prompted him or her to seek help. Third, the goals of therapy are personal, emotional, and behavioral change. While teachers and preachers may want to achieve the same goals—and sometimes do—therapeutic methods stand a better chance of doing so. Classroom sessions, no matter how creative, and sermons, no matter how good, will not produce needed change in some people. There are several reasons why this is true.

> To be effective for some people, family ministry will need to include strategies that are therapeutic in nature.

First, some people, particularly those with abusive or neglectful childhood backgrounds, have negative attitudes, habits, and emotions that need to be modified or "unlearned" if they are going to relate well. Such "unlearning" and changing is often so painful and difficult that individuals need regular support to achieve it.

Sometimes a person's emotional makeup thwarts any attempts at skill development so that even very practical training has little effect. Showing appreciation, for example, is one of the skills Nicholas Stinnett attempts to teach family members, since his research shows this is a major trait of strong families. However, learning to be appreciative will do little good for a parent with an uncontrolled temper who periodically angrily hurls verbal abuse at her children. Learning to say nice things in between the angry explosions may make that parent's actions even more distressing to a family exposed to such tragically contradictory behavior. Unless that person deals with her personal problem, she cannot solve her family problems. And she may need therapy to deal with herself.

Counselors who deal with insecure, immature people, particularly those raised by alcoholics or addicts, know how true this is. One of these counselors, Patricia Bassel, explains: "Parents eventually learn that 'you can't give away what you don't have,' and that reading parenting manuals and getting advice on child-rearing won't help in making the children of insecure parents feel secure. Parents with low self-esteem can't rear children with high self-esteem simply by trying hard to say and do all the right things."[3]

Another reason why skill training alone will fall short is that codependent people often misuse what they learn in skill training sessions. For example, codependent parents are usually involved in obsessive efforts to fix and train their children. Instead of focusing on their own need for spiritual and emotional recovery, they invest their energies in their children.

Bassel claims that we rarely understand the needs of codependent parents. Instead of focusing on their need for recovery, helpers (therapists, caseworkers, teachers) focus on the so-called "needs of the child." They press the parents to become more involved in directing their children's lives. In reality what such codependent parents need to do is to temporarily withdraw from a cycle of enmeshment. She describes the cycle that loops through a secession of stages: (a) over-involvement and overcontrolling; (b) failure to successfully direct and control the child's behavior; (c) guilt over the failure, anger, and withdrawal; and (d) returning to "square one"—renewed efforts to control the child, new failure experiences, and more anger and/or withdrawal, etc.[4]

In this case, to really help the family system, we need to encourage the parent to back off from the child for awhile and work on his or her own problem. This can hardly be done through a lesson or a sermon.

Family ministry will need to include ways to help family members understand themselves and deal with the reasons why they behave as they do in their homes. Perhaps we need fewer books on parenting and more books about parents.

> Family ministry will need to include ways to help family members understand themselves and deal with the reasons why they behave as they do.

At first, therapy in the church may sound like a complex and demanding task. Yet personal transformation has always been a major objective of the church. Encompassing the emotional and spiritual dimensions of life, church ministry is by its nature remedial. Scripture urges us to include exhortation, rebuke, reproof, and discussion in our preaching and teaching. In addition, it urges us to be creative in formulating means to produce Christlike living. "Let us consider how we may spur one another on toward love and good deeds" (Heb. 10:24). Therapy can take place in all types of situations: in a visit to a person's home, in a brief chat in the foyer of the church, or in a small group discussion. In reality, much of the therapeutic work will be accomplished in the ordinary interpersonal interactions of people within the life of the church.

Yet churches can offer specialized therapeutic approaches as well. Therapy usually requires a personal, individualized context found in one-to-one counseling, therapy groups, support groups, or seminars. Churches are often the setting for such activities, aimed at those who struggle with alcoholism, codependency, anger, overeating, or depression. Later chapters will explain how churches can develop these programs.

NOTES

1. Lawrence Crabb, "The Family: Manipulation or Ministry," *Family Life Education*, ed. Gil Peterson (Wheaton, Ill.: Scripture Press Ministries, 1978), 5.

2. Nick Stinnett has taken the lead in developing such training programs, geared to teaching families how to achieve the six family strengths he has uncovered from his research. (Stinnett, "Six Qualities That Make Families Strong," *Family Building: Six Qualities of a Strong Family*, ed. George Rekers [Ventura, Calif.: Regal Books, 1985], 38).

3. Patricia Bassel, "Passing Down the Heritage of Addictive Family Dynamics," *Focus on Family* (November/December 1986): 24–25, 36, 39.

4. Ibid.

Persons Emphasized in Family Ministry

13

In training families is there one family member we should especially target as a key to building the whole family? Some would immediately answer, "Yes—men." Producing strong husbands and fathers will eventually generate healthy families. Justification for this is lodged in Scripture, they say, both Old and New Testaments designating men the family's leader. They reason that if the head functions correctly, the home also will.

Yet our earlier discussion has shown that the man's headship position is not as clearly defined as this view supposes. And it is questionable whether men, by themselves, can have such an impact on their families. A better principle would be the following:

> Family ministry should involve all family members, but place emphasis on certain members.

Scripture suggests the rightness of this approach. In their letters, the Apostles included wives and children, not just men, when they dealt with family matters. Men cannot force their wives and children to act in responsible ways. They need the church to encourage them to do so, just as the wives and children need the church to prompt the men to be responsible. It almost goes without saying that all ages should be targeted and every family member addressed—grandparents, spouses, sons, daughters, brothers and sisters.

HIGHLIGHT TRAINING OF MEN

Though we should not deal exclusively with men, we should be certain to make their training a major part of our effort to influence families. There are some practical, if not theological, reasons for this.

Research shows that it is generally the woman who is most likely to try to improve the marriage and family and to seek counseling when the family is hurting. Speaking to couples at the beginning of a marriage seminar a friend of mine says: "I like to speak at these sessions because I know that at least half of you want to be here." And most everyone in the room knows which half

Family ministry should involve all family members, but place emphasis on certain members.

has insisted on attending. This truth is also borne out in the fact that women, not men, are the buyers of books about marriage and family. Books published for Christian men are bought by wives for their husbands. Publishers actually aim at women when marketing books written for men.

These facts would seem to suggest we aim family ministry at the women, since they are the most likely to respond. Yet the facts may be used to support the opposite: we should take special pains to reach men because they are the least involved.

> It is generally the woman who is most likely to try to improve the marriage and family and to seek counseling when the family is hurting.

After an extensive national study of men, Michael McGill concluded: "The average man is barely familiar with his family, let alone intimate with its members."[1] If not physically absent, many men are emotionally absent, rarely involved in their children's lives in affectionate ways. Often they communicate to the children through their wives, hardly ever speaking directly to their children.

The negative impact of this in the lives of children is becoming more and more apparent. Only recently have researchers begun to study fathers and what they are finding is of pivotal importance. The absence of fathers may be as damaging to the home as the absence of mothers. The physical absence of a father for as much as a year seems to be connected with the incidence of delinquency, low achievement, and other youth problems. Samuel Osherson maintains that men struggle with intimacy because they do not experience warm relationships with their fathers.[2] Though we lack clear-cut evidence for the cause of male homosexuality, one factor that seems to be important is that homosexual, more than heterosexual, men reported that their fathers were cold and detached.[3] All we are learning about human behavior emphasizes the importance of the physical presence and emotional accessability of both parents to the developing child.

Concurrent with the growing awareness of the crucial place of men in the family is a budding, yet substantial, men's movement. Linked with Billy Graham's organization, Here's Life America, and other prominent groups, these "Dad, the Family Shepherd" conferences are held throughout the U.S. and Canada. His dynamic sessions inspire men to dedicate themselves to their families and to form themselves into small groups to sustain one another in this effort. The National Institute

> Concurrent with the growing awareness of the crucial place of men in the family is a budding, yet substantial, men's movement.

of Fathering, led by Ken Canfield, and Christian Service Brigade are also prominent players in the men's movement.

Outside the church there are cues that, as one writer says, the nineties will be the decade of men. In poet Robert Bly's "Gathering of Men" seminars, men are meeting to talk frankly about their confusion of identify and their place in life. A growing number of periodicals are addressed exclusively to men, dealing seriously with their issues.

With a little effort even the smallest church can minister to men.

With a little effort even the smallest church can minister to men, if in no other way than by sending them to men's conferences and by organizing small groups for them where they can wrestle together with men's issues. Literature for men's groups is available; the momentum is building.

EMPHASIZE TRAINING MARRIED PARTNERS

Besides men, married couples should be high on our list of those to be trained. Marriage, you will have noticed, dominates the early discussion of the theology of family. This is not intended to diminish family, but to highlight the cardinal place of marriage in family. Strong families must be built on strong marriages. A popular statement to husbands makes this point: "The best thing you can do for your children is to love their mother."

Family systems theory, as well as theology, suggests that a sound family unit must distinguish and give prominence to the healthy sub-unit that is the married couple. Researchers argue that a satisfying marriage provides a stable basis for family functioning. Where the marriage is a good one, partners are better at parenting and solving problems. And all family members tend to be happier with family relationships whenever the marital sub-unit is healthy.[4]

Children, when present, will be caught up in the intimacy, love, and empowering practiced by their parents. Children cannot share in the benefits of these if they are not in their parents' marriage. Married persons must recognize that they are first of

Strong families must be built on strong marriages.

all husband and wife, and then father and mother. Otherwise, the boundaries of family members are not properly drawn, nor duties suitably assigned. Children then become mixed up in unhealthy ways with parents. They are sometimes desired and conceived to make up for the deficiencies of the marital relationship. Thereafter, the partners fill the emptiness of their relationship by devoting themselves to "family." In some cases, a son moves in to fill the vacuum left by his mother's love-starved marriage or children are wounded in the cross fire of their parents' perpetual conflict.

We should also acknowledge the significance of marriage apart from family. Childbearing is only one of the functions of marriage, particularly in modern times. With the popularization of birth control in the early part of this century, and awareness of the population explosion, families contain fewer children. This reduces the number of child-bearing and child-rearing years, giving couples many more years alone than was the case in the past. When we add to that the greater longevity of life, the average couple will have twice as many years of marriage without children in their home than with them. In the marriage drama, being parents occupies only one act out of three. A couple's success in family life depends on their playing well their roles for the other two acts of life.

> Special attention must also be given to people in the nontraditional types of families.

MINISTER TO SINGLES AND FAMILIES IN TRANSITION

Special attention must also be given to people in the nontraditional types of families. This may be difficult for some churches; it may require a change of attitude. Some churches are accustomed to thinking of families in traditional terms. For this reason, people from these families feel welcome while the never-married, widowed, divorced, remarried, single parents, blended families, and children of some of these often feel "left out." Authors Richard Olson and Joe Leonard have observed, "Churches that offer much to families in general become paralyzed when dealing with some of the newly evolving family types."[5] Undergoing serious transitions, members of these "families in flux" are not comfortable in many churches.

The first step toward ministering to these people is theological in nature. The local church will need to define its stance toward divorce, remarriage, and singlehood. It may help to see that families of various types were part of the first century congregations. Paul addressed married, widowed, deserted, single, and never-married people (1 Cor. 7).

The congregation can carefully monitor its language in every announcement, whether verbal or printed, being careful not to invite just "fam-

> A family-life conference can include—along with sessions for traditional families—workshops for the divorced, remarried, never-married singles, and widows.

ilies" to the church picnic or retreat. Using the word *household* instead will show awareness of the nontraditional families and singles present in the congregation.

It will be important to see that people from these assorted family types have family issues to deal with, some of them quite unique. It is not hard to see this in the case of blended families where the sensitive stepparent and stepchild relationships are only one of its several complications. Never-married singles must also deal with family issues. Family systems research has clearly shown us how the family of origin continues to cast its shadow over adults throughout their life span. Many singles are adult children of alcoholic or abusive parents and have family issues that were not resolved when they left home. A family-life conference can

> Singles of all kinds will be helped most by being integrated into the life of a close-knit congregation or small group.

include—along with sessions for traditional families—workshops, seminars, and the like for the divorced, remarried, never-married singles, and widows. The church can also provide special organizations and programs for them. As various family forms have become more prevalent in society, so have programs for them in the churches. Chapter 25 will describe these programs as well as introduce other ways to minister to them.

However, loading a church with highly specialized programs (which is impossible for some churches) is not the only way to minister to these people. The majority will be helped most by being integrated into the life of a close-knit congregation or small group. These offer them what they most need—the support and love of a spiritual extended family. Whenever they are asked, singles point to their need for fellowship. They want not only involvement, but close involvement. Chris Thomas saw this clearly through his survey of a large single's group in an evangelical Wisconsin church. Sixty percent said that their greatest need was to have fellowship with others, both single and married, within a Christian context.[6]

We should be careful not to view people who are not in traditional families as problems to be dealt with. Widows, singles, and those from "families in transition" often have a great deal to offer to the church body. Besides gifts, expertise and dedication, they often bring a great deal of wisdom drawn from life experiences, some traumatic. If we invite them, they can and will enrich the life of the church.

NOTES

1. Michael E. McGill, "Family Man Seldom Lives Up to His Name," *Chicago Tribune* (June 18, 1985), sec. 5, p. 4, quoting an excerpt from the book *The McGill Report on Male Intimacy* (New York: Perennial Library, 1986).

2. Samuel Osherson, *Finding Our Fathers: The Unfinished Business of Manhood* (New York: Free Press, 1986), 166.

3. A. Bell, M. Weinberg, and S. Hammersmith, *Sexual Preference: Its Development in Men and Women* (Bloomington, Ind.: Indiana University Press, 1981), reported in Jack O. Balswick and Judith K. Balswick, *The Family: A Christian Perspective on the Contemporary Home* (Grand Rapids: Baker, 1989), 188–89.

4. Elizabeth Vemer et al., "Marital Satisfaction in Remarriage: A Meta-analysis," *Journal of Marriage and the Family* 51 (August 1989): 713.

5. Richard Olson and Joe Leonard, *Ministry with Families in Flux: The Church and Changing Patterns of Life* (Louisville: Westminster/John Knox, 1990), 3.

6. Unpublished report, "An Approach to the Problems of Single Adults from a Positive Perspective" (1984), 5.

Some Overall Approaches

Many years ago I asked a Jewish man how many people attended his synagogue. His reply, "Over two hundred families," surprised me. I was used to thinking of the church as a group of individuals, not a group of families. Today, however, counting people as families is difficult in some churches that contain scores of single people who are not part of any family in the church. This creates a dilemma for churches because two groups of people need to be recognized: singles and families. Giving too much visibility to families offends singles, making them feel like a "fifth wheel." In making sure we don't leave singles out in our programs, announcements, etc., we can still give recognition to people in families. There is a need for this, as the following guideline indicates. It, along with the other two guidelines presented in this chapter, has to do with the church's overall approach to family ministry.

PURPOSES OF FAMILY APPROACH

Gives Identity to the Family

There are several reasons for giving identity to families. First, we need to encourage family members to be loyal to their families. Whenever the church treats us as family units, it reminds us of our responsibilities to our family. Second, family members need to feel they belong to their family. There are not many places in modern societies where people are identified with their families. Often schools and communities offer so little involvement and are so large that it doesn't take place there. Any public recognition the whole family unit receives in the church reinforces that feeling of belonging.[1] Third, the church needs to broadcast to its members and its community that family is important.

Finally, the church needs to be careful not to leave the family out when treating individuals in the church, particularly youth and children. Besides weakening family influence, we can get into trouble if we bypass the family and always deal directly with the individual. This happens when youth leaders teach youth about sex without consulting parents, or when we try to teach children in our Christian education programs and fail to enlist the cooperation of parents. Even when recruiting for positions in the church, we can foster respect for the family by urging people to consult with their family before deciding to accept. In all of its planning and programs, the church should "think family."

Giving visibility and identity to families requires more than including the word *family* in the church announcements. Priorities and values are communicated not just in what an organization says, but in what it does. The nonverbal messages sent by the church's activities and administration will need to say, "Family matters." If the church is obsessed with its numerical growth, demanding from its members so much time and energy that home life suffers, it will broadcast a negative message about the home that no Mother's Day sermon can overcome. Putting the family in proper perspective

> Putting the family in proper perspective includes selecting church leaders who, if they have families, give priority to them.

includes selecting church leaders who, if they have families, give priority to them; planning the church programs so they do not unduly compete with family life; and developing the evangelistic outreach in such a way that as far as possible whole families are reached, not split up. Our individualistic society tends to stress breaking out of family thinking; however, our theology and much of the psychological community are telling us to recognize the important place of family in our lives.

Nurtures Children Through Cooperation of Church and Home

One of the major theoretical issues in family ministry relates to Christian education: should we center our efforts to teach children in the home or in the church? Some argue for a strong family nurture approach, while others claim that the church, not the home, should be the center of Christian education.

Arguments for Church-Centered Christian Education

Though advocates of the church-centered Christian education recognize the influence of the home, they argue that it cannot, and should not, occupy center stage in the teaching of children. Supporting this view theologically are those, as we have already noted, who believe in a sacramental approach to the church's ministry. God dispenses grace through the church; therefore, the church should play the major role in spiritual formation. Even those who are not sacramentalists might appeal to Scripture for a church-centered Christian education. The "body" concept of the church suggests we can help one another with our responsibilities, including helping each other nurture our children in the faith. Viewed this way, Sunday school, club programs, youth groups, and other such programs would be a sort of parent cooperative. Parents conscientiously and responsibly share the task of Christian education. There is scriptural support for youth participating in the church life and thus being ministered to.

The concept of spiritual gifts is also offered as a basis for church ministry to children. God gives to the church gifted members who can minister to other people's children. Even though there are no children—and youth—

directed gifts mentioned in the New Testament, some people who have the gift of teaching or helping seem more effective with one age group than another.

But many of the arguments for placing Christian education of youth in the church are practical ones. Advocates point to the number of broken and troubled families, suggesting we can make little headway if we try to do most of the scriptural nurture of children in the home.[2] They also call attention to the success of the Christian education programs of the evangelical church, and the success of Sunday school, camping trips, youth groups, weekday clubs, children's church, and vacation Bible school in evangelism and teaching. To dismantle all this effective organization to center children's ministry in ailing families would be a costly mistake. Besides, they contend, these church-sponsored agencies have consistently won and taught youth from broken and non-Christian homes—those whom the home-centered program would neglect.

Arguments for Family-Based Christian Education

While the arguments for maintaining the present church-based strategy of Christian education are impressive, the reasons for a family-centered approach to nurture are also compelling. Advocates of home nurture argue that the plight of the families is no reason to abandon them as nurture centers; instead the church needs to build them up. If the church puts most of its efforts into replacing the family's spiritual influence, this will, by its neglect, contribute to family deterioration.

Besides this, the impact of the family is too significant to ignore. Studies of early childhood confirm that the child's first few years of life are a foundation for all later development.[3]

One of the most impressive reasons for getting families involved in the nurture of their children is the difficulty church programs have influencing children without the home's cooperation. Children and youth leaders increasingly complain about their inability to counteract the negative influence the home has on the youth they work with. Although the church has had notable success in discipling some children who have not had Christian parents, research shows that these are the exception. Any lasting influence on a child within the church program is usually coupled with the spiritual impact of a Christian parent.[4] The high percentage of youth (some studies show as much as 90 percent) who stay with the local church have parents who are also actively involved in the church. A study of 239 children done by Donald Joy led him to conclude forcefully: "It was perfectly clear that with middle elementary boys we are only kidding ourselves unless we get the family involved in their Christian nurture."[5]

Add to these practical arguments the biblical mandate given to parents to nurture their own children, and there is a strong case for the church helping them do it, instead of doing it for them.

End of Argument: Both Church and Home Should Nurture

All the arguments on both sides, however, seem to press on us one sensible conclusion: both church and home should be developed as agents of the spiritual formation of youth. The situation being what it is today, we can neither ignore nor idealize the family as a nurturing body.

> We can neither ignore nor idealize the family as a nurturing body. Our major task will be to integrate the spiritual nurture efforts of both church and home.

Our major task will be to integrate the spiritual nurture efforts of both church and home. In a sense, everything in this book is aimed at doing that, through building up families and bringing them together in the life of the church.

INCLUDES EFFORTS TO BRING POLITICAL AND SOCIAL CHANGE

We cannot attempt to help families in our church without giving some attention to the social and political context in which families must thrive.

Delores Curren explains how, in a very practical way, family life is tied to social life.

It is difficult for a family to eat dinner together if business schedules meetings, school holds marching band practice, junior leagues, etc., occur during the dinner hour. Four of the top ten everyday stressors named by parents in my recent research as the most stressful and disruptive of family life have to do with insufficient time and overscheduled calendars. Families often feel powerless in controlling the conditions that foster time pressures. Families don't create these stresses in our society; they inherit them from society. And if they fail to come up with resources adequate to overcoming these stressors effectively, they are subsequently blamed for failure. In this way, families become society's scapegoats. They are frequently blamed for poor discipline in the schools, crime in the streets, irresponsibility in the work place and disrespect for authority.[6]

Interwoven into the broader social fabric, families aren't going to become stronger all by themselves.[7] A long time defender of the family, Urie Bronfenbrenner claims, "The future of the family lies in the relationship between families and other institutions."[8] He makes a much needed correction in our thinking about the family:

In this country we have been taught that most of the problems experienced by families have their origin within the family and therefore ought to be solved by the individual family members primarily concerned. . . . We as a nation need to be reeducated about the necessary and sufficient conditions for making human beings human. We need to be reeducated not as parents, but as workers, neighbors and friends; as members of the organizations, committees, boards, and, especially the informal networks that control our social institutions and thereby determine the conditions of life for our families and their children.[9]

Social, educational, and political leaders often blame problems with the nation's children on the family. Parents, in turn, blame society. Society asks parents to keep their children from drugs; yet parents complain that society won't keep drugs away from their children.

The crux of the issue is whether our schools, community agencies, churches, business and political processes will foster or destroy family life. For example, how the federal government supports child care will either support or shatter families. Providing money solely for day care centers will promote the separation of children from their families. Instead, money could be directed in such a way that parents could benefit from caring for their children at home or at least pay relatives or friends to help them. A tax bill passed in 1990 did include a pro-family child care policy. Called the Young Child Tax Credit, it gave parents who care for their own children a tax benefit similar to those who use day care centers. The credit offers up to $355 in direct tax assistance to families with incomes below $21,000 if they have a child under age one.

The matter of day care provision is only one way that government and society can strengthen or weaken families. Another one includes the governmental actions that exclude or discourage parental involvement in decisions by their children to engage in activities that may be contrary to their health and well-being, and contrary to the values of the parents. Providing contraceptives for teens, or permitting abortions for teens

> Social, educational, and political leaders often blame problems with the nation's children on the family. Parents, in turn, blame society.

without parental consent, are just some of the issues in this category.

A few years ago, U.S. Sen. Jeremiah Denton said, "Now our governmental policies and programs are operating to erase the uniqueness of the family as an institution."[10] Should the government treat people (including children) as individuals or treat people in family units?

Moral issues are sometimes at stake. Whether the government and community encourages teens to abstain from sex or makes contraceptives available to them is a current instance of how politics impact morality.[11] Another example is found in laws that exclude parents from being notified when their minor daughters receive prescription birth control drugs or devices from federally funded family planning clinics. Yet the courts still insist that parents be consulted before anyone gives a child an aspirin tablet.

Should government publications and agencies send messages and offer counseling to children about drugs and other matters contrary to what the parents are teaching them? At issue here is whether parents stand in a position of authority between the state and their children, an issue that legislative bodies and the courts must address.

We would all agree that society should, in some cases, deal with a child as an individual, over against the child's family. Society has a responsibility, for example, to separate a physically abused child from abusive parents. But Senator Denton claims political leaders go too far, that some sectors of our society believe children must be "liberated" from the "captivity" of the family tradition. "Governmental policies no longer accept parental authority and responsibility for the education, health, safety and general well-being of their children," he claims. Government should not replace the family as the basic unit of society, but encourage and defend it as the major source of moral and spiritual strength.[12]

Some tax laws discriminate against the traditional family formation or drive women out of the home to seek careers out of financial necessity. The lack of increase in the dependent allowance for income tax deduction is a major case in point. Pro-family advocates charge that the decline in this personal exemption has been the largest single change in the income tax in the postwar era. When inflation is accounted for, the amount of the exemption should have increased from $600 at the end of the war to $5,600 in 1985. Instead it increased to only $1,000. Couples need money most as they start their families, yet these are the years when income will be lowest and when the relative tax burden is greatest.[13]

Other family issues cluster around how community and government services alleviate family problems such as divorce, teenage pregnancy, alcoholism and juvenile delinquency. Frequently, actions and policies promote the break-up of families by treating individuals without any attempt to involve their family in the treatment. When treating mental illness, the counselor could deal with the whole family, not just the individual, and more could be done to enlist parents' efforts to solve problems such as juvenile delinquency. Government funds allotted to communities could be tied to the condition that the parents be mobilized. Some experts advocate that the family would be better served if we followed the principle of getting state and local governments and family involved in solving problems, not the federal bureaucracy. Services are best rendered by agencies closest to the level of the problem.[14]

Economic policies in regard to the poor also impact the family. Forty percent of poor families are on welfare. It has been pointed out that this tends to decrease personal esteem and initiative of the family's men and this results in broken families. Only one out of four single mothers who deserve child support from estranged husbands are getting full support. Half of all children living with one parent are supported by Aid for Families of Dependent Children.[15] Better law enforcement can make fathers take more responsibility for their children.

WHAT'S A CHURCH TO DO?

The church can encourage Christians to support government and community leaders that have a pro-family stance on these and many other issues. In addition, churches themselves may have programs to deal with some of the social issues, such as being part of the "One church, one children" program of Father George Clement, which is responsible for a significant increase in the adoption of black children.[16] It can also encourage its members to be involved in community services, such as Meals on Wheels, that assist people who suffer from a lack of family care. As they are able, churches can provide services that deal with social problems: after-school child care for "latch key kids" who otherwise would have to wait for their parents in an empty house, and programs for military wives who must care for their children during long periods of their husband's absence, for example. Many examples of church-sponsored family social services can be found in black churches, which historically have been very active in this area.[17]

In addition, churches and individual Christians can have some impact through financially supporting the evangelical pro-family lobbying group, the Family Research Council, which is a division of James Dobson's Focus on the Family.[18] Gary Bauer, its president and chief spokesman, laments that the job is far from easy: "To be a pro-family activist in Washington is to confront the adversary culture head on. Many staff people and journalists here think of us as a phenomenon of the early Eighties (or Fifties), a temporary reaction to trends that have gone on anyway and are now irreversible."[19]

> To help families some churches may need to subtract, not add programs. It is more sensible to integrate teaching and training into the present ministry.

How can the church do all this, especially if it is small and resources meager? Adding more programs to some ailing churches is like throwing more cargo on a sinking ship to keep it afloat. To help families some churches may need to subtract, not add programs.

It is more sensible to integrate teaching and training into the present ministry. For example, without requiring people to attend additional sessions, special elective courses on family life could be added to the adult Sunday school. Fathering can be the topic of a men's breakfast meeting or annual retreat. Non-traditional families need not have specialized programs aimed at them. Singles, divorced, and widowed members can be discipled within the ongoing fellowship of the whole church body. In fact, it is within the community life of the church that the most effective work with families can be done. The next chapter describes the church as a community and explains why it is such a powerful force in people's lives.

NOTES

1. Granted, public recognition of a severely troubled or abusive family may embarrass and shame the members. But the answer to this problem is teaching individuals how to handle this reaction since people will be identified with their families whether we stress it in the church or not.

2. C. Ellis Nelson, *Where Faith Begins* (Atlanta: John Knox, 1971), 210.

3. Burton White, *The First Three Years of Life* (Englewood Cliffs, N.J.: Prentice-Hall, 1975), xi.

4. Samuel Hamilton, "International Conference on the Family" (1948), in *Helping Families Through the Church,* ed. Oscar Feucht (St. Louis: Concordia, 1957), 55.

5. Feucht, *Helping Families Through the Church,* 55.

6. Delores Curren, "How Community Leaders Can Develop Programs That Build Healthy Traits in Families," *Family Building: Six Qualities of a Strong Family,* ed. George Rekers, (Ventura, Calif.: Regal Books, 1985), 262–63.

7. Ibid.

8. Urie Bronfenbrenner, White House Conference on the Family, 1980.

9. Ibid.

10. Jeremiah A. Denton, Jr., "What National Leaders Can Do to Promote Family Well-Being," *Family Building,* ed. Rekers, 179–80.

11. See discussion of the Title XX program in *Washington Watch* 1:4 (January 1990).

12. Denton, "What National Leaders Can Do," 179–80.

13. Bruce Chapman, "Why Not 'Fairness' for Families?" *Family Building,* ed. Rekers, 198.

14. Dorcas Hardy, "How Government Can Serve Children and Families," *Family Building,* Rekers, 207.

15. Chapman, "Why Not 'Fairness' for Families?" 191–92.

16. Hardy, "How Government Can Serve Children and Families," 212.

17. For a survey of these programs, see Cleopatra Howard Caldwell, Angela Dungee Greene, and Andrew Billingsley, "Family Support Programs in Black Churches," in Sharon L. Kegan and Bernice Weissbourd, eds., *Putting Family First* (San Francisco: Jossey-Bass, 1994), 137–60.

18. Family Research Council, a Division of Focus on the Family, 700 Thirteenth St. NW, Suite 500, Washington, DC 20005.

19. Gary Bauer, "Taking Stock," *Washington Watch,* published by the Family Research Council, 12:2 (November 1990): 4.

A Family-like Church

The heart of family ministry is the nature of the church, not merely its work. For this reason, we must not think we can only help families through church-sponsored programs, conducting a seminar from time to time or putting family life topics into the Sunday school curriculum. The greater influence is embodied in the life of the congregation as a whole: the atmosphere that is felt, the way people relate, the kind of example the leaders show. This is summed up in this final principle: *Family ministry is best done in a church that is family-like.*

David Mace, along with other prominent family life specialists, is emphatic about this: "A Christian church should be at once an expanded version of a Christian family unit."[1] He contends that participation in the life of the church is the most promising way for people to learn what it means to be Christian in their families. People can best train for Christian family life in a church where relationships are patterned after a functional family. This is not difficult to understand; basketball players learn to play basketball best by playing basketball. Playing on a team that plays well will obviously improve anyone's game. Family members, too, can enhance their ability to live in families by participating in a family-like church.

To understand and employ this principle, two questions will need to be answered: "What is a family-like church?" and "How is one created?" In this chapter I will deal with the first; the second question will be dealt with in chapter 17.

WHAT IS A FAMILY?

To understand this principle we need to be precise about what we mean by a family-like church. In our society it is common to call all kinds of groups families, including churches. Players on a winning baseball or basketball club often say of their team: "We're family." I often hear people around me refer to our school as "The Trinity Family."

Saying the church should be family-like is not the same as saying the church should be a family. A baseball organization is not a family; it is a team. I keep saying to people who call my seminary a family, "We are not a family; we are a school." After all, there are more than 1,500 people in our institution. How can we call that many people a family?

One reason we call teams, schools, churches and other groups families is that the meaning of the term "family" has become vague in contemporary society, as George Barna discovered when he questioned people about the idea of family. A shift

> Family ministry is best done in a church that is family-like.

of people's thinking has come about in the last few decades. No longer does everyone describe family in terms of married people and relatives. Rather, the

One reason we call teams, schools, churches and other groups families is that the meaning of the term "family" has become vague in contemporary society.

term *family* is used of two or more people who really care about each other. The statement of one young adult is typical: "To me, family is more than just my parents and brothers. It's all the people I'm comfortable with, the ones I get along with."[2]

Another reason that we so easily apply the word *family* to groups is that we have not had much discussion about the differences between social groups and families. Even family systems experts have not explored the differences. In 1987 one of them pointed this out, criticizing the trend to quickly apply family systems theory to the church and other groups and making an initial attempt to distinguish families from groups.[3] He noted that they are different in the matter of choice and purpose. Groups are formed for a specific purpose and people join them based on it. Families, however, just are. For the most part, people do not choose to be part of a family. They do choose married partners; marriage, however, is not just the union of two persons, but the meeting of two families.

Also he observes another difference: families exist to help members separate from them, while groups exist because members unite around a common task. In short, family's ultimate task involves "going away," while the group's is "coming together."

A third difference relates to intimacy. While the major systems dynamic of families is intimacy, of groups, it is power. Because the primary task of the family is to "individuate" its members (help them be separate individuals), the family is primarily an intimate institution. In other words, members learn how to be separate together. If they don't, they are dysfunctionally enmeshed. Groups, however, may have a degree of intimacy, but the heart of their interaction is political (related to power).

When a group is large, it is especially different from a family system. Size affects operational procedure. Two hundred people, for example, cannot make a decision in exactly the same way three people might. Some special rules of formal discussion will guide the large group, while the smaller one can be much more informal and freewheeling. Processes related to intimacy will, in such cases, give way to processes associated with power.

Once we see that a church is not a family and cannot be a family, we are ready to be more precise about what it means for a church to be family-like.

FEATURES OF A FAMILY-LIKE CHURCH

While the church is not a family, it can be like a family; or at least it can foster family-like experiences. Social scientists refer to groups that are like the family as primary groups, the family itself being so classified, as contrasted with secondary groups. Primary groups are those where relationships are face-to-face, freewheeling, and intimate. Business and activities are carried on directly. Examples include groups that regularly lunch together, a group of close friends, a fellowship group, etc.

Secondary groups are larger and more formal groups such as businesses, lodges, and schools. They may have some face-to-face interaction, but the organization does not depend on intimate relationships, and business is conducted in an orderly, prescribed manner consistent with regulations and by-laws. For instance, when someone from a secondary group (a church) is hospitalized, there is an organized way of showing concern: the visitation pastor is notified and the appropriate committee sends flowers. Never mind that the pastor or the committee members have never even met the sick person; the organization's purposes are carried out in this "secondary" type of relating. Institutional contacts are secondary, rather than face-to-face. People learn about someone being sick by reading about it in the church bulletin. Instead of small group discussions, learning is done in large classes or audiences.

In a primary group, no committee would send flowers and no appointed person would visit. Since these group members are in regular, close touch with one another, they would know their friend has been admitted to a hospital and would simply drop by and offer their encouragement and support in various ways. This is because primary groups are fundamentally relationally oriented, one of their major distinctions. People who lunch together, or regularly meet for a coffee break, or have formed a fellowship group, as well as people in families, are in such groups for the purpose of relating to one another. In contrast, the purpose of secondary groups is for performing some task. People in task-oriented groups view relationships in the light of getting the job done. In secondary groups, relationships are as close as necessary to keep the institution running smoothly and fulfilling its task. Each person is valued for the role he or she plays in the corporate structure, not as a person to relate to. Therefore, it is important to formulate formal job descriptions so they each know their responsibility and that there be clear cut accountability (organizational charts) and that people function with limited conflict and discord (work management). Much attention is given to organization in a secondary group; a primary group requires little since it functions informally and intimately.

> While the church is not a family, it can be like a family; or at least it can foster family-like experiences.

Using these two models—primary and secondary—as lenses, we can see more clearly what it means for the church to be family-like. Too often churches have adopted almost exclusively the task-oriented secondary group model. Relationships are superficial, only regulated by doing the work of the church. Having myself been heavily committed to this model in the past, I am embarrassed by how I viewed Christian relationships in this institutional sense. More than once in a sermon or talk, I affirmed, "Love is the oil in the machinery of the church." I failed to perceive Christian love as an end in itself instead of a means to some end.

> An effective primary group is like a family; a secondary group is not.

For decades critics have chided churches where "the congregation remains a collection of individuals, determined to avoid conflict and maintain pleasant, but largely innocuous relationships."[4] And we have joked about them too: "The church is like a theater; the only difference is that in a theater you pay to get in, but in a church you pay to get out."

Even smaller groups, like Sunday school classes, can take the form of a secondary group. Teaching and learning is formal and there are infrequent personal contacts between class members. This affords little opportunity to observe the leader's behavior outside the formal context, and feelings and intimate thoughts are seldom shared.

In contrast to secondary groups, primary groups foster intimacy. Relationships are based on meeting individual, not corporate, needs. Effectiveness is not judged by corporate achievements but by the quality of group life. In short, an effective primary group is like a family; a secondary group is not. A church that fosters only secondary group relationships does not offer its members an opportunity to learn from those relationships how to function in their families.

A FUNCTIONAL FAMILY-LIKE CHURCH

One thing more is needed. Besides family-like relationships, the church must have *healthy* relationships. Both primary and secondary groups can operate in unhealthy ways, tainted with unresolved conflict and stifled by poor communication patterns. It is common today to dub institutions, as well as families, dysfunctional. If church life is going to train people for family life, the relationships within the church, by God's grace, will need to be governed by solid Christ-like principles.

My own experience in the church has shown me that this is not always true. As Director of Christian Education, I was once forced to replace an ineffective teacher of the single adult Sunday school class. I suggested to the Christian education board that we follow a principle I had learned in seminary classes a few years before. Instead of confronting the man about his inadequacies, risking hurting and possibly alienating him, we would move him to another position. In business-administrative parlance this is considered "kicking some-one upstairs." You promote the person out of the way. So I explained to him that he was needed more as a teacher of a Sunday evening elective course. Of course I didn't tell him that since people would choose his course, it would eliminate any complaints about his teaching, since malcontents could simply attend another course. This tactic worked quite well for awhile. But several months after his reassignment, he confronted me: "I heard why you asked me to leave the single's class." Then in tears, he pled, "Why weren't you honest with me?" I was ashamed. He left the church.

This manipulation of people, thought acceptable by some, we now recognize as dysfunctional. Sadly, some churches operate on the same misguided principles as dysfunctional families. They are governed by deceit, mistrust, bickering, secrecy, suppression of feeling, and compulsion to control. People from dysfunctional families fit right in, attracted to such churches like tall people to the game of basketball.

To be effective in family ministry, the church must operate on the kinds of rules that produce healthy families, those dictated by theology and validated by practice.

Nicholas Stinnett's research, mentioned earlier in this text, are one measure of a healthy family that we can apply to the church. He lists six qualities of a strong family: (1) Members would express a great deal of appreciation for one another. (2) They would spend a lot of time together, not because they have to but because they genuinely enjoy it. (3) They would have a high degree of commitment to one another. They would be "right there to help you if you got into trouble, if you landed in jail, or if some terrible tragedy happened to you." (4) Even though they fight once in a while, they have good communication patterns, each listening to the other with great respect. (5) There is a strong concern for their spiritual lives. (6) And finally, they handle crises in a positive way, uniting to deal with them instead of being fragmented by them.[5]

> This is what it means for the church to be family-like: to nurture functional primary group relationships instead of superficial unhealthy ones.

This list is only a start toward defining a healthy family, but at this point, it is ample enough to guide a church toward being family-like. That involves promoting attitudes of commitment, trust, acceptance, and affirmation. In addition, interaction should be intimate and honest. People should be encouraged to speak openly instead of being silenced by the dysfunctional family's unspoken rules: "don't feel" and "don't talk."

This, then, is what it means for the church to be family-like: to nurture functional primary group relationships instead of superficial unhealthy ones. In this context, Christian families will be bred. This is the principle. But is it biblically and theologically sound?

BIBLICAL ARGUMENTS FOR THE CHURCH AS A PRIMARY GROUP

Should churches be like primary or secondary groups? Theologians have scrambled for an answer to this question ever since the church renewal movement raised it several decades ago, contending the church had taken the form of a secondary institution.

Many leaders contested that the church should be a primary group and argued biblically for their position. However, their arguments were sometimes inadequate and unconvincing to those with more theological discernment. These shaky arguments need to be swept aside in order to see that there are some very solid theological reasons for shaping the church after a primary group model.

Not Because the Early Church Met in Homes

Some, for example, noted that the early church met in homes and concluded from this that these Christians intentionally designed churches to be family-like "house churches," thus, small primary groups. However, it is not certain that this was the purpose for the home-based meetings. There may have been simply no other place to meet. Meeting in homes does not necessarily mean that the groups were small since a large house would accommodate a rather large secondary type of group. Thus the fact that early Christians met in homes provides no basis for insisting that churches today must be small and intimate.

Not Because Church Is Called a Family

Some people have argued for the church to be family-like because it is called a family in the New Testament. As a glance in any theology text will show, family is clearly among the various metaphors (such as sheep, body, temple, etc.) used of the church.

Yet this argument is not as clear-cut as supposed because the family motif is seldom used and does not indicate a close primary group even when it is. Only once in the New Testament is the church actually termed a "family" (Eph. 3:15). Yet the reference there is not to the local, but to the universal, church. The family-related term used most frequently to designate church is *oikos*, "household," which is sometimes translated "family," but is not synonymous with our notion of the term. Sometimes the term *oikos*, translated household, designates a "temple," as in 1 Timothy 3:15 where Paul calls the church "God's household." Also the concept of *household* embraces all the residents in one house including servants, relatives, and others who may not be part of a nuclear family, making it wrong to read into these references the contemporary idea of a close-knit primary group.

Not Because Family-like Terms Are Used of Church Relationships

We do, however, come closer to our contemporary notion of family relationships in the other terms associated with the idea of *household*. Often

Christians are called "brothers and sisters." Still, even these terms may be quite limited in their meaning and inadequate as basis for arguing the local church be a primary group. Some scholars maintain that they are not direct references to family but rather to the Old Testament idea of Israel as a brotherhood.[6] Such references certainly dictate a special relationship between believers and a certain responsibility for each other's welfare. Yet this brotherhood motif does not portray the picture of the primary group we are trying to paint since it refers to a large group, a whole nation.

In fact, the familial picture of the church is even tied to these responsibilities, which are carried out in an orderly, institutional way found in a secondary group. An example is Paul's requirement that an elder be able to "manage his own family well" if he is to "take care of God's church" (1 Tim. 3:4–5). Both James and John stress our obligation to care for the needy brother or sister (James 2:15–16; 1 John 3:17). So also does Paul, in a passage intended to distinguish our duty to members of God's household from those to a mere neighbor. But even such commands need not require a primary group since in a large secondary group, members can donate funds to help needy members they do not know personally.

This is also true of certain other references to the family metaphor. Peter uses it to establish the idea of Christians submitting to God "as obedient children" (1 Peter 1:14); Paul and John employ it to urge obedience of leaders who are "fathers" (1 Cor. 4:15; 1 John 2:1).

All this data signals us to be cautious about jumping too quickly to the idea that the local church should be a primary group. Yet when the weak arguments are laid aside, those that remain are very solid and convincing.

Because Church Members Are Urged to Relate in Primary Ways

The image of the local church as a primary group does take shape in the New Testament. As we have already seen, family-like love is a constant theme. Consider the intensity of the love of Christ for the church in the bride-bridegroom simile in Ephesians 5, expressed in such tender, unselfish terms: "Just as Christ loved the church and gave himself up for her to make her holy, cleansing her by the washing with water through the word" (vv. 25–26). Phrases like *brotherly love* and *brotherly kindness* place warm family relationships within the local church context. Paul uses even the maternal image to describe his relationship with believers: "But we were gentle among you, like a mother caring for her little children. We loved you so much that we were delighted to share with you not only the gospel of God but our lives as well, because you had become so dear to us" (1 Thess. 2:7–8). All these passages suggest warm, close relationships, not a mere formal, institutional connection of members with one another and with their leaders.

But the most forceful argument for family-like relationships is lodged in the New Testament commands that are to regulate those relationships. The image of a primary group clearly emerges in these. Christians are urged to "speak truthfully" (Eph. 4:25) and "confess your sins to each other" (James 5:16), suggesting a depth of intimacy. "Carry each other's burdens," said Paul (Gal. 6:2), by which he meant helping each other with moral and spiritual failures. Christians are even to "greet one another with a holy kiss" (Rom. 16:16). Other commands are to "encourage the timid" and "help the weak" (1 Thess. 5:14), and "accept one another" as Christ accepted them (Rom. 15:7). While not all of these commands are tied to a familial metaphor, they are activities that demand some primary group interaction. Add to this the fact that descriptions of early church life depict Christians eating and fellowshiping together informally and intimately. In the face of these guidelines for believer's relationships, we are hard-pressed to defend a system of church life where members' involvement with each other is formal, shallow, and secondary.

> All of the deeper aspects of interpersonal relationships, such as in a family, are to be found within the church body.

In summary, gathering these bits and pieces of exegesis, we can construct some solid conclusions about the church as family. First, the church as family includes *order and corporate responsibility of the members for one another*. Being a family does not negate organization. In fact, the family is viewed as a managed organization itself. Loving as brothers and sisters can be less personal in its expression. For example, the collection gathered from the Gentile churches at the request of the apostle Paul was for believers in Jerusalem that these Gentiles had never met. Endeavors such as these are expressions of universal brotherly love of believers.

Second, a kindly, personal relating ought to characterize members' interaction with each other. All of the deeper aspects of interpersonal relationships, such as in a family, are to be found within the church body: cherishing, caring, encouraging, rebuking, confessing, repenting, confronting, forgiving, expressing kindness, and communicating honestly.

BENEFITS OF A FAMILY-LIKE CHURCH EXPERIENCE

When a local church attempts to foster such quality relationships, the benefits to the Christians and families are many.

Permits Modeling

First, the primary model of relationships offers families an effective relating style to copy; modeling can take place in a primary group. Adults need to be exposed to people with Christlike attitudes and effective communications skills. Even the children and youth of Christian parents need exposure to Christian adults other than their parents. Having good Christian parents does not seem to be enough for most children, particularly teenagers who tend to look outside the home for people to emulate.

Some provision for open, intimate relationships between the generations will need to be developed, and these should take place in a variety of experiences. "Children, youth, and adults together will need to be exposed to the whole range of human experiences," as Larry Richards so rightly asserts.[7] Church life will need to be constructed to allow for intergenerational learning, serving, playing, worshipping, struggling, praying, and living in as many ways as feasible.

Avoids Transferring Secondary Means of Relating to the Family

If church life is of a highly organized, formal nature Christians will have little opportunity to practice the kind of skills necessary for successful family living. In fact, families may begin to style their home life after the secondary life of the church. Fathers like the one in *Mary Poppins* try to run their homes like a bank or factory because it is the only way of relating they know. They stress the externals—duties, rules, regulations, and schedules—and are uncomfortable with warm, intimate ways of relating. People who come from dysfunctional families easily adopt such secondary means of relating. A church without primary group experiences provides little context for them to begin to value and learn these internal skills.

Training for Church Life Will Transfer to Home Life

The training of leaders in a secondary institution will not easily transfer to their home environment. Trained in formal, structured methods of teaching, pastors and church workers are not necessarily equipped to communicate Christian truth within informal, intimate exchanges in their own homes. For this same reason, successful corporate and military leaders are often inept spouses or parents. Returning home from work, they may drive around the block several times to summon the courage to face their families. It takes different skills to face a rebellious teenager in a dining room than a vice president in a board room. The executive cannot fire his son or otherwise enforce his executive power as he can at the office. If a church member or business person lives most or all of life in secondary groups, he or she may be hard pressed to adjust to the primary kinds of relationships the family requires.

Facilitates Christian Nurture of Children in the Home

When church-based Christian education programs foster primary relationships, the teaching in church can more easily be transferred to teaching at home. This is true because effective teaching at home is done informally, with truth conveyed across warm, intimate lines of communication. Church programs where relationships are shallow and teaching is formal contrast with this style of teaching, and according to noted Christian educator Larry Richards, are inferior. Treating Scripture as "classroom content" has left most believers unable to relate Scripture to their own feelings, attitudes and values.[8] Parents, then, can't relate God's Word to the daily life experiences of their children and are dependent on formal teaching even in the home.

Richards calls for both church and home to gain expertise in the socialization process of Christian education, which is more holistic than the church's usual formal approach, which he calls "schoolization."

By introducing the socialization process as a model for Christian education, Richards has raised an issue that is too crucial to be ignored here, but too large for us to fully explore.[9] No doubt there is a place for both formal and informal teaching in our churches, yet if only formal teaching takes place, the Christian education program is disabled. Life transformation cannot be done through educational systems that focus mainly on one human dimension, the belief system. "Whole person transformation takes place in the context of intimate, loving personal relationships and where living is modeled by maturing Christians," Richards asserts.[10] This requires openness in communication on multiple levels—sharing beliefs, personal knowledge, convictions and feelings. By mirroring each other, the church and the family will more adequately accomplish the nurture task that is the responsibility of both.

> By mirroring each other, the church and the family will more adequately accomplish the nurture task that is the responsibility of both.

Provides a Family for Those Who Have None

The people who have the most to gain when the church is like an extended family are those who are not part of a Christian family. Within the church community, single people, many of them separated from family for various reasons, will be able to experience some badly needed intimate fellowship with their peers as well as with people of other generations. Many of the children of the divorced and widowed badly need some close ties with other adults to make up for an absent parent.

Provides and Projects Acceptance for Individuals

A primary group can project acceptance much better than does a secondary context. In a formal setting, even if the people are gracious, the distance in the relationship and the reluctance for people to share their real struggles can convey an intolerance to people with problems. Yet if people are going to talk about their family problems and submit to training and repair of their behaviors, they will need a context that gives them permission to have such problems.

"I found a God who loves me at Overeater's Anonymous," a woman said to a group of us during a seminar for adult children from dysfunctional families. "The God of the church I attended many years ago was neither accepting or compassionate," she continued. "I would like to go back to church, but I am afraid to face the God I would find there."

Millions of hurting people have this same attitude toward the church. My friend, Paul, explains: "I can remember feeling that the church we were attending before coming here expected an awful lot: a problem-free Christian life." He admits that his attitude may have been more his than the church's: "I don't know if it was my particular sensitivities or if it was just that you weren't supposed to have any problems; there was something drastically wrong with you if you did. Even though I became a Christian years ago, I still based my relationship to God on how well I measured up." Not measuring up at home may be more shameful than anything. For this reason, people who are struggling there may need massive doses of acceptance before they will admit it to others. Paul explains how he finally came to that place:

> I just couldn't bring myself to give them a good look at how I really was. To be able to walk into a group of people who accepted without conditions and have the freedom to express my emotions, the anger, the hurt, the fears, all those things associated with growing up in an alcoholic family, was very healing for me. Acceptance and understanding by the others of the struggles I face is very important. It's a frightening thing to let your defenses down and be faced with yourself for the first time in your life. It was a scary process. While going through this process I had to have others' support and acceptance; I could not have done it alone.[11]

Our self-imposed privacy—an insistence that family problems should not be exposed outside the doors of the home—hinders people's growth. One counselor told me that more than half of his clients say, before disclosing their problems, "I'm sure you have never seen anyone with this problem before." "Yes," he smiles to himself, "only about ten people this week." People with secret problems often feel bizarre and peculiar, as if they are hiding some hideous monster in their bedroom closet. Filled with shame, they are convinced they would be laughed at or ostracized if found out. Secluded in lonely isolation, they are discouraged from seeking help. Once people learn their struggles are not so unique, they gain the courage to expose their problems, hurts, and failures, seeking help that leads to healing. An accepting atmosphere permits that to hap-

> Our self-imposed privacy hinders people's growth. Once people learn their struggles are not so unique, they gain the courage to expose their problems, hurts and failures, seeking help that leads to healing.

pen. A critical, disapproving one forces people into a social underground where the wounded suffer in agony and isolation, everyone pretending, through pretense and denial, that on the surface all is well.

Offers Support

Primary groups can offer support that is lacking in secondary institutions. In recent years, we have been discovering the immense power of primary groups to promote personal change. So-called support groups have become a major part of contemporary life. In the context of these groups, individuals are gaining freedom from drug addiction, alcoholism, overeating, and other powerful destructive compulsions. No one knows for sure why these groups have become so popular. That their rise coincides with the breakdown of families suggests that they provide the kind of support once supplied by families. One thing is certain: they are effective.[12]

According to the New Testament, the church should have the qualities of a support group. Many passages imply or explicitly state the powerful impact of interpersonal relationships. "Let us not give up meeting together . . . but let us encourage one another" (Heb. 10:24–25). "Encourage the timid, help the weak, be patient with everyone" (1 Thess. 5:14). The power of this impact is not, however, restricted to mere human forces. God is at work within a group of Christians who are open, honest and caring. The

> Preaching, teaching, and evangelism can function apart from intimate personal contact.

Holy Spirit works in and through these close intimate contacts. Paul linked Christian growth to honest interaction within the body of Christ: "Speaking the truth in love, we will in all things grow up into him who is the Head, that is, Christ. From him the whole body, joined and held together by every supporting ligament, grows and builds itself up in love, as each part does its work" (Eph. 4:15–16).

Certainly the Holy Spirit can, and apparently does, work in secondary institutions. Preaching, teaching, and evangelism can function apart from intimate personal contact. Yet much of the work of the Holy Spirit demands closer contact: confessing faults, encouraging, rebuking, bearing another's burden. Church without primary contacts limits the sanctifying operation of the Holy Spirit and the healing work of human support. Fostering in-depth relationships is no option for a church determined to enrich the lives of its members and families.

NOTES

1. David Mace and Vera Mace, *The Sacred Fire: Christian Marriage Through the Ages* (Nashville: Abingdon Press, 1986), 268. Also, Dennis Guernsey, "Prominent Family-life Education Also Stress Their Approach," *Family Ministry and Education: A Personal Journey*, Direction 19 (Spring 1990): 1.

2. George Barna, *The Future of the American Family* (Chicago: Moody Press, 1993), 26–27.

3. Daniel C. DeArment, "Families and Groups: Their Nature and Function from a Systems Perspective," *Journal of Pastoral Care* 41 (March 1987): 114.

4. George Webber, *The Congregation in Mission* (Nashville: Abingdon, 1946), 122.

5. Nick Stinnett, "Six Qualities That Make Families Strong," *Family Building: Six Qualities of a Strong Family*, ed. George Rekers (Ventura, Calif.: Regal Books, 1985), 35–50.

6. Hans Freiheer Von Soden, s.v. "adelphos," *Theological Dictionary of the New Testament*, ed. Gerhard Kittel and Gerhard Friedrich (Grand Rapids: Eerdmans, 1967).

7. Lawrence Richards, "Developing Family Life Ministries," *Family Life Education*, ed. Gil Peterson (Glen Ellyn, Ill.: Scripture Press Ministries, 1978), 41.

8. Ibid., 40.

9. Both of these church educational systems flourish today, and both are rooted in theology. Both hold promise, but pose problems as well. "Schoolization" is attractive because it fits well with the evangelicals' desire to transmit truth. The institution of the church can control the imparting of biblical concepts through a systematic, carefully designed program. The schoolization approach allows for modification of methodology to fit contemporary understanding of teaching and learning, but it does not require a radical change in the church's structure. But the schoolization approach also has a weakness. By-passing the family will continue to result in the neglect of it.

The socialization approach also has both strengths and weaknesses. Socialization is strong as an educational philosophy because it is grounded in some educational principles that have solid theological support. Also, the science of anthropology confirms the prominent place of the home and other primary groups in forming the life of an individual.

In socialization it is not the classroom or the teacher that needs to be modified, prepared, updated, and readied for the Christian development of the church's youth. Since the matrix of the process of Christian development is the combination of home life and church life, the quality of life in both of these must be overhauled. The chain of events goes like this: For children to be nurtured, the home life must be Christlike; for the home life to be Christlike, the church community life must be Christlike; for the church community life to be Christlike, the adults must be resocialized.

Of course, such an approach requires more than adult classes or sermons; it means a restructuring of Christian education as we know it. Socialization cannot appeal to a schoolization process to initiate the changes demanded. Thus the Achilles heel of the socialization approach, according to many, is the structural changes that would have to take place in the home and in the church.

The Christian education dilemma is so severe today because the choices to be made are so radical. Innovations no longer revolve around incorporating new agencies or installing new chalkboards or using expensive videotape equipment. The cost and effort go beyond the energy and time expended in drawing up a new organizational chart or inaugurating a new teacher-training program. Changes require the renewal of the church.

I get the impression that most of the evangelical churches that have wrestled with the questions of renewal have finally settled for both the structure and the nurture approaches that I am recommending in this book.

10. Richards, "Developing Family Life Ministries," 41–42.

11. From personal interview, published in Charles Sell, *Unfinished Business: Helping Adult Children Resolve Their Past* (Portland, Ore.: Multnomah Press, 1989).

12. A survey of the numerous studies of support groups can be found in Donelson R. Forsyth, *Group Dynamics* (Pacific Grove, Calif.: Brooks/Cole, 1990), 471–73.

◆ *Part Four*

Developing Family-like Relationships in the Church

Developing the Church as Family

A PAUSE FOR ORIENTATION

If family ministry were a house and this book about how to build it, we would now need a set of detailed blueprints. We've chosen a location—the modern family (Part One). The foundation—the theology of family life—is laid (Part Two). The overall design—the theory—is in view (Part Three). The rest of the book contains specific instructions for building a family ministry in a local church.

To continue the analogy, the model has five rooms. The first room, Part Four, explains how to create a church that is family-like. While it tells how to make the whole congregation more family-like, the major focus is on small groups and intergenerational events. The second room, Part Five, deals with marriage education. After explaining how the church can prepare people for marriage, the content and methodology of marriage enrichment are described. Part Six, the third room, will tell how to train parents. Part Seven, the fourth room, contains plans for specialized ministries. It will deal with ministry to those from dysfunctional families, to families in transition, and to singles. Plans for therapy and support group programs will be described. The final room, Part Eight, is about administration. It describes the practical steps a church can take to implement family ministry in its organization and life.

Now that we've glanced at the whole layout, we are ready to look closely at the blueprints for the first room: a family-like church. I begin here because I believe that this is the most crucial element of family ministry.

MAKING THE OVERALL CHURCH MORE LIKE A FAMILY

To make the church more family-like, we can start by fostering more accepting, open, and honest relating in the congregation as a whole. When people don't feel close to one another in a church, the problem often lies in the size and the formality of the Sunday morning services. In my experience, unfriendly churches are not always filled with unfriendly people. Rather, the stuffy and cold atmosphere engulfs people in a thick emotional climate where reaching out to talk to someone is difficult, if not threatening.

There are ways, despite the size of a church, to modify this atmosphere. A family-like church will broadcast the message of grace: "If you are in trouble, we understand and will try to help." The church climate will tell the visitor that he is among struggling "Publicans," not self-righteous "Pharisees."

The key to achieving this is wrapped up in the term *identification*. Support groups like Alcoholics Anonymous that know how to project acceptance instruct newcomers to "identify," instead of "compare." By this, they urge people to perceive in others the same human predicament they themselves are in. In the church we sometimes miss doing this because we focus so much on what we are trying to be, that we fail to admit where we are. We feel threatened to admit we do not measure up. Yet such an admission should be easier in church than anywhere else; it's the only institution that requires people to publicly confess they are sinners in order to join.

> To make the church more family-like, we can start by fostering more accepting, open, and honest relating in the congregation as a whole.

The message of grace can be communicated from the pulpit and in the classrooms with compassion and empathy. Rebukes and reproofs can sound more like the rebuke of a father than the censure of a prophet. Pastors and teachers can admit their own struggles and shortcomings in order to identify with people. Empathy for struggling people is communicated in this way at Willow Creek Community Church, the largest church in the United States. Though pastor Bill Hybels preaches a high degree of commitment to Christ, he does it with a touch of grace. After visiting a support group for sex addicts that met in their church, he publicly cited the courage of those who would attend such a group, showing he understood the ferocity of their personal battle. The very mention of such a group sends a message to Christians that it is all right to have problems and encourages them to face them.

When a church sponsors such support groups or allows groups to use their facilities, it telegraphs concern for and acceptance of people in distress. So do seminars, retreats, and courses that deal with problems Christians face. Many of these are family related: a support group for adults with troubled teens or adult children of alcoholics; a retreat for those with marital problems; a divorce recovery workshop, etc.

The large group can even be a setting for intimate contact between people, though that contact may be limited in depth. A brief moment for greeting one another during a worship service or Sunday school class can break down some of the stiff formality that obstructs interaction. Space for informal contacts before and after church meetings is crucial. Architects suggest a large foyer for this purpose, particularly for churches where the climate does not permit lingering outside. If the foyer is inadequate for this, refreshments can attract people to a fellowship hall between Sunday morning church services. To save building expenses, churches are constructing large "multi-purpose" rooms that can be used for this purpose as well as for worship, recreation, and other fellowship events.

Sunday mealtime can be used to create opportunities for people to connect with one another. A large Chinese church in Houston, Texas, facilitates warm personal contact between people by serving over 800 meals each Sunday at noon. People of all ages meet, staying till mid-afternoon when classes, youth group, choir practices, and special meetings begin.

Providing Primary Relationships Through Small Groups

Despite what we do to make the large church family-like, our efforts may fall short simply because of size. A group would have to be fairly small to have the intimate caring a family has. For this reason, some church leaders advocate keeping churches small, the size of house churches. Yet there are reasons why this is not a workable solution. Many Christians, still immature, will not be willing to make the commitment necessary for the level of personal involvement that being in a house church requires. They will be attracted to large church gatherings where they can choose their own level of closeness to people. In these anonymous contexts, by hearing God's word these Christians may progress to a higher stage of commitment to Christ.

> There is an effective way to provide New Testament-type primary group experiences for people while preserving all the benefits of a large church: developing small groups.

There are many other reasons why, when it comes to churches, bigger is better: they are more evangelistic, they provide better Christian education programs for children and youth, and they can offer more specialized ministries. Many church growth experts are predicating that the churches that will function best in the future will be large "meta" or "mega" churches. Whether true of not, it is unrealistic to believe all churches can remain small in order to provide the kinds of interaction described in the New Testament.

There is an effective way to provide New Testament-type primary group experiences for people while preserving all the benefits of a large church: developing small groups. Through his books and seminars, church growth specialist Carl George has created renewed interest in the small-group movement that began about thirty years ago. He claims that churches have not placed enough priority on small groups of ten Christians (the cell), instead putting their energy into the large group meeting (celebration), and the medium group of thirty or so (Sunday school classes and the like, called congregation). George argues that churches would revolutionize their ministry by focusing their leadership and resources more on developing the cell groups and less on the congregation-size groups. He predicts that this offers churches a local model capable of growing to tens and even hundreds of thousands.[1]

Whether Carl George turns out to be right or not, he and other church growth experts have shown that a group must be quite small to be a primary group. Turning an average-sized congregation into a family is virtually impossible. It can only be done if the church is quite small, with perhaps seventy people or less. Church growth experts call these groups "cells." Whenever they get above seventy people, they become "stretched cells." People know about everyone, but it is not always face to face: "If Mrs. Crenshaw's son is bringing a girl home for Christmas, in a single-cell congregation Mrs. Torres would hear about it from Mrs. Crenshaw, but in a stretched cell congregation she might hear the news from Mrs. Boyer, but hear about it she would. It is still a one social cell, but it has been stretched by additional members to a point where it is difficult to grow and still remain a kind of unitary cell. This brings anxiety."[2]

Churches often make the mistake of believing they can remain a one-celled church with more than seventy people. A simple formula demonstrates why they cannot. The number of one-to-one relationships in a group can be calculated by multiplying the number of people times that number, subtracting the number and then dividing by two. For example if there are three people in a group, there are three one-to-one relationships ($3 \times 3 = 9 - 3 = 6$ divided by $2 = 3$). Notice what happens when you increase the size of the group by two, turning it into five members. Using the formula, the number of one-to-one relationships is now ten ($5 \times 5 = 25 - 5 = 20$ divided by $2 = 10$). The group now has ten relationships to develop even though it has only two more members.

As people are added, the number of relationships increases at a drastic rate. In a group of only one hundred people, there are 4,950 relationships. This shows how difficult it is for all of those relationships to become intimate. Suppose, for example, in an effort to do so, you could force everyone in a church of two hundred to sit beside a different person and talk to them for five minutes each Sunday morning. It would take three-and-a-half years for everyone to meet everyone else, and that for only 300 seconds of conversation.

After hearing this, a pastor's wife in one of my classes was struck with the futility of her scheme to get every member in her church to know everyone else. She would regularly invite six members to her home for dinner. Using the above formula, we predicted how long it would take her to reach her goal by having monthly dinners. In a church of 150, it would take slightly over sixty-two years. Dinners once a week would reduce the time to slightly over fourteen years. Figuring about three dollars per meal, it would take about $13,500 from her food budget.

Continuing to add small groups will not only produce primary relationships; it will also promote church growth. Cal S. Dudley claims you can only

> In today's churches, the two models most like an extended family
> are "support groups" and "growth groups."

stretch a single cell so far. Unless more cells are added, the church will not grow. A new cell can be formed by having a few people in the original cell start a new group (Sunday school class, home Bible study, etc.) that will absorb new members. A multi-celled large church will keep growing by constantly starting new groups.

The First Evangelical Free Church of Fullerton, California, formerly pastored by Charles Swindoll, is one of many churches that has capitalized on the advantages of a large church while reaping the benefits of the small groups.

After describing the exciting multiple services each Sunday, Swindoll tells where the "real" ministry of his church takes place:

> The "real" ministry—the part that touches people by bringing the gospel up close—occurs behind the scenes, on the ragged-edge of people's needs. We have support groups for virtually every need a person wrestles with: single parents; the handicapped; the unemployed; those struggling with alcoholism and drugs; incest victims; the aged (to name only a few)—plus opportunities for folks to meet in small groups during the week for mutual encouragement and prayer.[3]

Though all types of small groups are in vogue in today's churches, the two models most like an extended family are "support groups" and "growth groups." Details about support groups for dysfunctional family members will be given in chapter 26.

We'll give attention here to "growth groups" because this small-group style is having such an impact on church life.

Developing Growth Groups

Growth groups are unlike other small groups primarily because of their broad purpose. Small groups usually stress one activity: study, prayer, evangelism, or service. If a study group studies a Bible passage, it has achieved its goal. Growth groups, on the other hand, are rather revolutionary because their goal is personal growth. To do this, they include many different activities. In fact they are sometimes called "mini-churches" because they do almost everything a church does: worship, study, fellowship, and serve. Yet they do not replace the larger church body that they supplement. Concerned about serving those inside and outside the group, they also devote themselves to evangelism. Combining Bible study with in-depth relationships, they provide the kind of support and accountability to one another that foster change and growth.

George Whitfield, John Wesley's colleague, confirmed the emotional and spiritual benefits of the small group:

> My brethren . . . let us plainly and freely tell one another what God has done for our souls. To this end you would do well, as others have done, to form yourselves into little companies of four or five each, and meet once a week to tell each other what is in your hearts; that you may pray for and comfort one another as need may require. . . . None, I think, that truly loves his own soul and his brethren as himself, will be shy of opening his heart in order to have their advice, reproof, admonition and prayer, as occasions require. A sincere person will esteem it one of the greatest blessings.

Though nurturing personal growth will be the small group's greatest contribution to the family, these groups will contribute in a more direct way as well. A couple's own relationship will be strengthened by their participation in the group's in-depth interaction. A report from Latin America about small groups, called "base communities," confirms this:

> The experience in many such groups is that when couples participate together they find new things which unite them. Their idealism, tarnished so easily in a skeptical world, is supported in the community (group) relationships. Where intimacy is fostered, people generally emerge the winners. Many couples in base communities speak of having fallen in love once more and those outside the community note it . . . the base community seems to encourage couples to develop more intimacy in their marriage.[4]

At times a group may focus directly on family themes, studying together, for example, a book on marriage or one dealing with parenting. No matter what Scripture is open to them, the application will automatically drift to family matters. The group's love and intimacy will prompt members to share personal struggles in order to receive help and support to cope with them. A growth group my wife and I were part of provides a typical example of the sorts of problems people bring to the group in one year: one couple was dealing with a single daughter who was pregnant; a wife of one couple had a seriously ill father; a single man in his thirties was trying to learn better how to relate to women; a woman whose husband, not a Christian, provided no leadership in the home, talked often of the turmoil in the family caused by her son's problem drinking.

Growth groups can at times bring whole families together. Groups often begin without children, but it is a simple matter to bring the children into the warm circle of relationships after it has been nurtured among the adults. Most important, as I stated in the last chapter, the small groups will most help families by practicing the same kind of skills people need in family life.

Administering Growth Groups

In the thirty years since the growth group movement began, countless churches have experimented with growth groups. Not all of them have been successful. Yet enough of them have succeeded to confirm growth groups as a viable ministry as well as show us how to make them effective. The guesswork of the earlier experimental stages is no longer necessary. The following are tested guidelines for forming and maintaining small groups in the church context.[5]

Intentional Balance

The key to growth groups is the inclusion of four elements: nurture (study, discussion); community (open sharing, love, caring); worship (prayer, praise, celebration, etc.); and mission (evangelism, service projects, etc.).

Groups easily slip into stressing one or two of these to the exclusion of the others. Leaders will have to be alert to keep all four elements in the group's meetings. The size of the group will have to be small enough to permit "community" to happen. Anywhere from six to twelve is usually considered an ideal size for a group that meets weekly. Yet because of the possibility of absences, groups should have several more members or they sometimes may not have enough present to have an effective meeting.

High Priority

Growth groups won't be effective if they merely increase the number of church programs people are expected to attend; however, adding groups doesn't necessarily require dropping other programs that some people are loyal to. Instead, a church can use the "add-on" technique for bringing about change in the church program. Make small groups an option to other adult programs instead of pressuring adults to attend all meetings. Some churches, for example, continue to have the traditional mid-week prayer meeting for those who want to attend, while other adults are meeting in small groups in homes. I know of churches that have even urged adults to skip the Sunday evening service in order to meet with their group. This "add-on" technique permits people to decide which program best meets their needs. Eventually, if the great majority of adults choose one option over others, then programs can be dropped accordingly.

Commitment of Staff and Resources

Leadership training, provision of literature, and administration of the program will require time and money. To provide this, the pastor and church board will need to have a vision for small groups.

People Made Aware and Leaders Made Ready

Attempting to launch a growth group ministry, a church immediately faces a major problem: most people will not know what you are asking them to join. While adults have participated in discussions, worked on committees, and studied in classes, few of them have ever been a part of an intimate group of people dedicated to changing each other's lives. And not everyone understands just what a growth group is.

Clear explanations and announcements will help, as will handouts that describe growth-group goals and features. Yet because the concept is so new to them, most people will be confused or may think they are merely joining another Bible study.

The only way to be reasonably sure that the groups will have all the dimensions of a growth group is for the leaders to be properly selected and trained. One church discovered this many years ago when they first launched their neighborhood groups. After holding a twelve-week class for leaders, they simultaneously launched fifty groups. At the end of a year or so, nearly half of them had stopped meeting, and not all of those that remained were the kind of groups they had envisioned. Some of them were like some adult Sunday school classes, a lecture followed by a prayer and some refreshments. One group ended up being little more than a doctrine debating society that they continued for many years. In their assessment, the church leaders decided that because the growth group concept was so novel, their training program did not adequately convey the concept to their leaders.

Other churches have made the mistake of placing their elders or deacons in charge of small groups, convinced that board members are also undershepherds. Theoretically, it sounds like a good idea; however, board members don't always make good small-group leaders since they are not chosen for that role. It would be better to assign board members to different groups—as members, not leaders—so that through each of them the board can keep in touch with the congregation.

If there are no potential leaders with growth group experience in the congregation, you will most likely succeed if you train them in an actual growth group, not in a class. This means you will have a modest beginning, with only seven or eight possible leaders meeting for a year or so in a growth group. After that, they can be taught group theory and leadership skills. In this way, you may have at least three or four model groups the second year. From these you can select leadership people who know what a growth group is.

> The only way to be reasonably sure that the groups will have all the dimensions of a growth group is for the leaders to be properly selected and trained.

A Proper Strategy to Begin

Starting small with one group of leaders and slowly expanding is probably the best way to launch a growth-group program; however, there are other possibilities. For a congregation that is wary of growth groups, you could introduce them as a temporary, short-term program. For example, substitute small-group meetings in homes for four consecutive Sunday evening services, or for one Sunday evening service each month. Or, to give people a taste of a growth group, you could schedule one or two of them in the elective program of the Sunday school.

Continual Leadership Development

In-service training of current group leadership will continually enrich the groups. Elmbrook Church in Waukesha, Wischonsin, trains its current leaders by having sessions about every two months. Leaders are encouraged to place someone else in charge of their group the week they attend their training session. This not only saves the leader's time, but also provides a chance for a substitute to practice leading. At the leadership training meetings, leaders swap ideas with each other, assist each other in solving group problems, and celebrate the good things that are happening. They also brainstorm together creative methods for each of the group's elements: study, worship, service, mission.

> Leaders should be trained to guide the group in being responsible for itself. They alone cannot make the group work.

In addition to training, the church should supply leaders with resources. Some churches have a curriculum lab. Leaders go there to examine books, courses, and study guides they might use in their group.

Once a number of effective groups are meeting, a church can enlist new leaders from these groups. Present leaders should be alerted to watch for potential leaders in their own groups. They can "disciple" these people by having them occasionally lead a group activity (a small one at first). Once the leader judges that the person qualifies for leadership, he can inform those in charge of the small-group ministry. Elmbrook's potential leaders are interviewed and, if qualified, are then placed in a special growth group for leaders. They also attend a leadership training class to learn the theory and practice of growth groups.

Group Ownership

Small groups function best whenever they make their own decisions. Yet since the church is responsible for them, this creates a major dilemma. Fearing the groups will teach the wrong doctrine or otherwise betray the church's standards, some churches will not encourage small groups. Others try to control them by prescribing a program for them. Leaders are given an outline of the meeting they are to follow. This, however, tends to thwart the group's development, since commitment and cohesiveness tend to soar whenever members make their own decisions.

The best answer to this predicament is to select carefully the group leaders and arrange for them to have some—but not total—control of the group. Choose mature individuals who can be trusted to uphold the church's purposes and values. Leaders should be trained to guide the group in being responsible for itself. They should not be pressured by the feeling that they alone must create exciting meetings and make the group work. They should expect that the group's vitality will spring primarily from the life and interaction of the group. The leader must resist making decisions for the group, instead guiding the group to exert its own will. He or she will call the group to account whenever its decisions begin to deviate from the church's stated policies, exerting influence sufficient to keep the group in line with the church's expectations.

New Groups Constantly Formed

Churches start additonal groups in different ways. Some of them reorganize all their groups each fall, allowing members to remain in the same group for just one year. When reorganizing, they expand their number of groups. Others permit existing groups to continue indefinitely, occasionally adding new groups. Some do this by training a leader, designating a host couple, and then requesting that people sign on. Others more carefully place members in groups they judge would be best for them.

A popular way of starting new groups is through new members' classes. Instead of having prospective members meet in a church office or classroom to study church doctrine, they move the class to a home and expand the time to allow for fellowship and worship. At the end of the new-member preparation, the class members are asked to continue as a growth group. Since they are usually new Christians or people new in the community who are eager to build relationships, they are glad to do so.

Attention Given to Stages and Termination

After polling 225 churches, Charles Olden reported that 70 percent of them said they observed a definite life cycle of a group and that understanding that cycle is a key to administering growth groups.[6] The stages are described by people in different ways. One church listed them as curiosity, anxiety, resolution, despair, and anticipation. Olden lists them as discovery, romance, struggle, and investment.[7]

It is crucial for a leader to realize that groups tend to go through a let-down stage some time after they are started. At first people are anxious, but quite expectant. When they begin to get closer to each other, there is a sort of honeymoon stage when they are excited by the prospects of getting beyond superficial relationships. Some call this the "enchantment" phase. But at some point the excitement wears off, and they begin to see that it's not so easy to get close and that the group is not so electrifying. At this point a "disenchantment" sets in. It is only after they continue to be open with one another and really care about real life issues that they enter the next stage: "deep love." This is truly satisfying, but it is costly since it requires an investment in one another's welfare.

A leader unaware of such a "despairing" stage in the life of a group is like a parent who is not informed of the "terrible two" stage of childhood. He or she may panic, get discouraged, or try too hard to keep the members enchanted by entertaining them. Refusing to be solely responsible for the group's happiness, the wise leader permits the group to struggle through the difficult time so it can progress to the next stage.

Another critical period of group life is at its end. Eventually group interest may begin to wane. Though some groups continue for years, most small groups seem destined to end before that. Knowing this, leaders should not be disappointed when the size and zeal of a group starts to decline. At this point, church leaders should intervene. Realizing that permitting groups to just fizzle out will dampen the church's enthusiasm for groups, they will put them to rest properly. Olden recommends a final, festive evening of celebration. Former members can be invited back, even those who have moved out of town. Testimonies, sharing of memories, praise, and prayer help people to look positively at their group's life, instead of merely regretting that it is over.

Using Small Groups with Children and Youth

For many years churches have been using the growth group format in their youth ministries. Many Sunday schools break down the larger group into smaller ones for at least a portion of the Sunday school hour. Weekday clubs afford opportunities for youth to build brother-sister relationships with other youths and to have closer contact with mature adults.

> Now many children's workers are using small-group techniques to create "cell groups" instead of classes.

Most promising is a recent movement to foster closer relationships among the children in our church programs. Christian educators have always advocated getting children to talk and play together in Sunday school, clubs, and other children's programs. Yet they have not always believed that children could develop in-depth relationships in these contexts. Considered too competitive, immature, or shy, children were not thought to be as open and emotionally supportive of one another in a small group as adults could be. Now many children's workers have changed their minds. Encouraged by the creation of peer support groups in the public schools, they are using small-group techniques in the church's children's division to create "cell groups" instead of classes.[8] The atmosphere is warm and accepting. Leaders describe the mood as like "talking with a good friend," or "being honest with the kids." Being open with each other, children learn that others have problems like their own. Understanding fully the pressure they are under, they can, under adult supervision, give each other good support and counsel. The adult group leader creatively teaches Scripture within this context. Serious, frank, give and take is encouraged and conflict is dealt with openly in a climate of security and concern for others. Everything is done to make the interaction like that of a healthy family.[9]

Limitations and Failure of Small Groups

Those who work with small groups should keep in mind the group's great potential for failure as well as for success. Because they consist mostly of informal relating, they are not subject to the same control as more highly organized formal programs. Some groups will not function well no matter what the leader does. In fact, groups that are mediocre and superficial will just not last. Herein lies the strength of small groups. They will exist only as long as they are doing something significant for the participants. This is not something we can always say for other church programs, that often continue long after they have lost their impact. Though we should do everything we can to assure a group's success, we should not be troubled over those that falter and eventually collapse. We will anticipate this and teach others to do the same. We will glory in those small groups of Christians who move to a deep level of intimate, supporting, and challenging fellowship. When that happens—John Whitfield described it well: "None but they who have experienced it can tell the unspeakable advantage of such union and communion of souls."

> Herein lies the strength of small groups. They will exist only as long as they are doing something significant for the participants.

SUGGESTED RESOURCES

Coleman, Lyman. *Serendipity: Small Groups Training Manual*. Littleton, Colo.: Serendipity House, 1991. • By one of the experts in the field of small groups.

Egan, Gerald. *The Skilled Helper: A Systematic Approach to Effective Helping*. Pacific Grove, Calif.: Brooks/Cole, 1990. •A book, not about small groups, but actually for counselor training. Egan is an expert in relational skills and treats the subject profoundly here. A valuable resource for those who train small-group leaders.

Gorman, Julie. *Community That Is Christian*. Wheaton, Ill.: Victor Books, 1993. •Deep insights on in-depth relationships in the church.

Hamlin, Judy. *The Small Group Leaders Training Course: Trainer's Manual*. Colorado Springs: Nav-Press, 1992. •A good step-by-step guide.

_____. *The Small Group Leaders Training Course: Participant's Manual*. Colorado Springs: Nav-Press, 1992. •Together with the trainer's manual provides a package for training small-group leaders.

_____. *The Curriculum and Small Group Resource Guide*. Colorado Springs: NavPress, 1991.
  •An expensive but valuable guide to curriculum materials for small groups. It lists and evaluates just about everything available. Put this in a place where your group leaders have access to it.

The Lifestyle Small Group Series. Individual titles such as *Career, Stressed-Out, Family, Success, Transitions, Money*. Littleton, Colo.: Serendipity House. •Serendipity also offers Bible study guides. There is also the Serendipity Bible for Groups, NIV translation with guidelines for discussion of passages of Scripture. All Serendipity materials are designed to build relationships and relate to life. Write P.O. Box 1012, Littleton, CO 80160, or call 800-525-9563 ext. 300.

Nichols, Ron, et al. *Good Things Come in Small Groups*. Downers Grove, Ill.: InterVarsity Press, 1985. •A very practical book full of specific ideas on all facets of growth groups: learning, worshiping, relating, and serving together.

McBride, Neal F. *How to Lead Small Groups*. Colorado Springs: NavPress, 1992. •The essentials of leading a discussion.

Meier, Paul, et al. *Filling the Holes in Our Souls: Caring Groups That Build Lasting Relationships*. Chicago: Moody Press, 1992. •From a team of psychologists, a good guide for leaders of growth and support groups.

Price, Richard, and Pat Springle. *Rapha's Handbook for Group Leaders*. Rev. ed. Houston: Rapha Publishing, 1992. •Another good book for support group leaders.

Williams, Dan. *Seven Myths About Small Groups: How to Keep From Falling Into Common Traps*. Downers Grove, Ill.: InterVarsity Press, 1991. •A reality check for small groups.

NOTES

1. *Prepare Your Church for the Future* (Tarrytown, N. Y.: Revell, 1991), 22–23.

2. George G. Hunter III, "Helping the Small Church Grow," in *Church Growth Strategies That Work*, ed. Donald P. McGavran and George G. Hunter III (Nashville: Abingdon, 1980), 82–85.

3. Charles Swindoll, *Living on the Ragged Edge* (Waco, Tex.: Word Books, 1985), 11.

4. Thomas G. Bissonnette, "Communidades Ecclesiales De Base: Some Contemporary Attempts to Build Ecclesial Koinonia," *The Jurist* 26 (Winter/Spring 1976): 37.

5. These principles are based on my observations of a number of significant churches and interviews with their leaders as well as on the research done by Charles M. Olden, reported in his book *Cultivating Religious Growth Groups* (Philadelphia: Westminster, 1984).

While these guidelines apply particularly to a special form of a group, we should keep in mind that any small group has the potential of having elements of a growth group. Administrative boards and committee meetings as well as Sunday school classes, can include a time of sharing and prayer in their meetings, where they support one another in facing the struggles and challenges they face as Christians. In addition to their regular meetings, they can gather informally for recreation, fellowship, or service, from time to time. At these times, they might include spouses and children in the circle of family that they are developing.

6. Ibid., 31–34.

7. Ibid., 49.

8. For a recent, complete discussion of this concept, see chapter 12 of Ralph Neighbor, Jr., *Where Do We Go from Here: A Guidebook for the Cell Group Church* (Houston: Torch Publications, 1990), 267–96. This chapter is based on the groundbreaking dissertation of Lorna Jenkins, completed at Columbia Biblical Seminary and Graduate School of Missions.

9. Ibid., 270.

17 Intergenerational and Family Unit Ministries

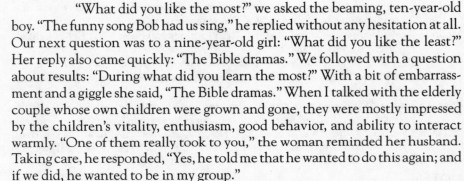

"What did you like the most?" we asked the beaming, ten-year-old boy. "The funny song Bob had us sing," he replied without any hesitation at all. Our next question was to a nine-year-old girl: "What did you like the least?" Her reply also came quickly: "The Bible dramas." We followed with a question about results: "During what did you learn the most?" With a bit of embarrassment and a giggle she said, "The Bible dramas." When I talked with the elderly couple whose own children were grown and gone, they were mostly impressed by the children's vitality, enthusiasm, good behavior, and ability to interact warmly. "One of them really took to you," the woman reminded her husband. Taking care, he responded, "Yes, he told me that he wanted to do this again; and if we did, he wanted to be in my group."

These are the varied comments of people who had just participated in their first intergenerational learning experience, a novel way to foster meaningful contact between people of different ages.

Traditionally, churches provide all sorts of events and activities that bring the generations together: eating meals, work days where volunteers clean or improve church facilities, service projects, parent-child banquets, family recreation nights at the church, picnics, etc. Today there are new, promising approaches for keeping the family units together as well as fostering intergenerational contact.

Since the sixties, North American churches have been gaining expertise in planning multi-generational learning activities. Prompted in part by the anxiety and disappointment resulting from the generation gap and in part by the desire to discover unique individuals around us, this type of experience satisfies many needs of contemporary individuals, even the needs of singles. Sometimes intergenerational activities involve all generations over a considerable period of time, perhaps an evening or a whole weekend devoted to playing and learning together. Often a multi-generational activity may be brief and less complex: an impromptu rhythm band from the children in the congregation to accompany congregational singing in a Sunday morning worship service; or five people, each representing a different age group, leading the congregation in prayer.

INTERGENERATIONAL MINISTRIES

As is true of any novel learning venture, however, the usual hazards and confusions are companion to the introduction of intergenerational education. One basic confusion is over the precise meaning of intergenerational education. It should be singled out of the many possible intergenerational experiences or ministries, which include recreation, worship, field trips, and other special activities. Intergenerational education does include learning, not just experiencing. An early starter in this field, George Koehler, distinguishes intergenerational ministry from intergenerational education, defining the latter as "a planned opportunity for nurture, discovery, or training."[1] Thus, it is planned learning.

> Today there are new, promising approaches for keeping the family units together as well as fostering intergenerational contact.

To make the experience intergenerational, it must include two or more generations; but the term *generation* is by no means easily defined. The way graduate students fail to understand undergrads, a Supreme Court justice half-seriously concluded, we have a generation every four years. However, for purposes of definition, intergenerational ministry refers to two or more generations out of five different age groups: children (from birth to twelve), youth (thirteen to twenty-four), young adults (twenty-five to thirty-nine), middle adult (forty to retirement age), and older adult (retirement and upward).

And there is a third distinction: these learning events should include interaction. If several generations view a film, they are not really participating in an intergenerational event. But if discussion follows the film, the activity would be an intergenerational one.

The Goals

Intergenerational education has some basic objectives that are similar to those of other learning contexts. Sometimes the learning may be specifically *content* centered, such as learning about biblical concepts of death. If the learning is in the *affective* domain, the goal might be to shape values and attitudes. For example: the goal might be to instill a Christian attitude toward death. Training, too, can be a goal since interpersonal skills, creative Bible study, and serving can be effectively developed in the intergenerational context. At times the goals may be family oriented—when dealing with intimate communication or handling problems or conflict. But learning goals will not always be family related.

The value of intergenerational education is located in the process itself, which becomes both the means of learning and the occasion of gaining certain learning by-products. Of course, the novel aspect of the process is the intermingling of generations.

Since discussion of the value of intergenerational education may prove to be too abstract without a more complete description of the process, let's look at a typical intergenerational event.

A Typical Intergenerational Event

You arrive in the evening at Trinity Evangelical Divinity School with a bit of apprehension, because all you know are the directions to the campus and the fact that you volunteered for an intergenerational learning experience. A friendly man greets you at the door and warmly converses with you as he takes you to a table, at which some children and adults are making something from construction paper. You, too, are asked to make a name tag with your name on it and also to write on it or cut it out to display a favorite animal or interest. While you are printing your name, someone explains he is pinning a picture of an animal on your back as part of a mixer game. You are to ask questions that require merely a yes or no answer in an attempt to discover your animal. As you wander around, you ask questions and are asked questions. The children's excitement is contagious, you think; but you also notice some apprehension on some of the adults' faces.

You also observe that the room is a bit different than you had expected for a "learning" experience. The walls of the carpeted room are decorated with posters. Only a few chairs and a couple of tables around the edge occupy the room, along with four leaders and the participants. These include eight or so children, a couple of teenagers, one bearded college student, eight or so adults of mixed ages, and a couple of "seasoned citizens." Someone calls you to the center of the room, inviting everyone to sit on the floor and form a large circle while he strums on a ukulele.

After he encourages you to relax and enjoy yourself, he leads you in a ridiculous rendition of "When the Saints Go Marching In." It is obviously for fun, and especially the children know that; everyone enters in.

Another man leads all of you in an old game that you may know as "Zip and Zap." Inside the center of the circle the one who is "it" points to someone, says "right" or "left," and counts rapidly to five while the surprised person attempts to blurt out the newly learned name of the person to his immediate right or left. If "it" says "scramble," everyone moves to another position. You are pleased to find that after ten minutes of this you have talked to a dozen or more of the thirty people and that you remember the names of quite a few. And a number of children now seem to remember your name easily. When the nine-year-old girl with cerebral palsy becomes "it" and struggles to stand in the center of the floor with the assistance of her father, there are numerous sympathetic smiles, and you feel a warmth stealing into your heart.

Another fun song immediately follows the game; this time it is an eleven-year-old boy leading rather effectively in a nonsense-syllable song, "Enimenedesiminy, ohwallawallowmeni." So far it's been a fast-moving, lively evening, and you feel caught up and involved with the group.

The theme of the evening is introduced by the song leader as "Christian Joy," and he leads you in two brief songs about it. "Now it's time to get to know each other a little better," another man announces. After you and the others form two concentric circles, you march in different directions while the ukulele player is singing a Jewish song of joy. When he stops singing, all of you in the circles stop marching; you happen to face off with a six-year-old girl and you tell each other what the leader suggests—one food that each of you most dislikes. Her answer comes quickly: "Spinach." The music starts and you're off again; you stop when it does, this time to share the most joyful time of the past week with a pleasant-looking woman who is the mother of four of the children. Before it is over, you have shared with four other persons, but the exchanges with the children linger most in your mind.

All of you form one circle again—this time for instructions about the evening's main event. You will be divided into three groups, each producing a drama of a biblical event that portrays joy. Your aim is to share with each other what the Bible describes as Christian joy. Each of the three groups is given a passage of Scripture and two tasks: one task is to produce a drama describing joy, and the other is to make a banner that colorfully shows what joy is. Your group is working on the imprisonment of Paul and Silas, who sang hymns at midnight. You don't yet know that the other two groups are working on the discovery of Christ's resurrection at the tomb and the reuniting of Joseph with his brothers and father.

When all groups are ready for the drama, and when the banners have been created with large, white sheets of paper and felt-tip pens, each group in turn presents their drama and tapes their banner to the wall. Your group has created a prison from a clever stacking of folding chairs. One folding chair falls away when the earthquake occurs, leaving an open door. You're a bit surprised by the creative way all of the groups perform, each having had only fifteen minutes to read the passage, decide on the approach, and plan the drama. Some discussion follows each drama, and the groups' energetic actions and words reveal that they are having a lot of fun learning about joy.

Now your smaller group is split into two, as are the other groups, so that there are six small intergenerational groups. A large empty punch bowl is brought into the center of the room while each group receives a large can of juice with a blank label on the can. Each group is asked to write on the label one ingredient of Christian joy, attempting to answer the question "How can Christians rejoice always?" Someone holds up a large sign that says, "Rejoice in the Lord always" (Phil. 4:4). After some discussion one of the children in your group prints "PRAY" on your can of juice while one of the men writes on the wall under the word "RECIPE" what is on each label. When each can of differently colored juice has been poured into the punch bowl, it is full of the "joy drink."

But before you drink any of it, you are part of a large circle again, this time holding hands. You sing with the others, "The Joy of the Lord Is Our Strength." Then the leader asks your group (one of three who performed the dramas) to step into the center of the circle. You hold hands while the others sing to your group, "The Joy of the Lord Is Your Strength." The song is sung in this manner two more times, one time each for the other two groups.

You form one circle again for closing prayers. The prayers begin with "God, I thank you for. . ."; "God, I praise you for. . ."; or "God, I feel good about. . . ." The first to pray is a boy about eleven: "I really feel good about the joy we had tonight and that we all could get together and learn about you, Jesus." You learn later that the adults were surprised how quickly the children prayed in this circle. Adults also prayed.

All are now invited to surround the huge tray of cookies being brought in to be eaten along with the "joy drink" all of you have created. You and the others linger together for twenty to thirty minutes, reluctant to leave the warm and cheerful atmosphere.

Benefits of Intergenerational Education

What, then, are the benefits of intergenerational education? Learning? Certainly. But not in a traditional classroom manner. Nor is the learning always cognitive, that is, the learning of a new idea or concept. Sometimes there is a new awareness of a doctrine or a new sense of a value, and this is learning in the affective domain. Or the learning is concomitant, that is, the attitudes, ideas, and behaviors acquired are sometimes distinct from the actual subject discussed. Adults often say, "I didn't learn anything new." Then they go on to say that they did "learn" something about a particular child, or that they were surprised to see that children would pray so readily or participate so eagerly. While the learning of "content" is also happening in these settings, it is the new awareness, understanding, empathy, and ability to relate to other generations that is most prominent.

Real cognitive learning can also be present, though the method and source of learning are often different from those of normal cognitive learning. Sometimes there are inductive studies or brief lectures, but the teaching-learning

> Real cognitive learning can be present, though the method and source of learning are often different from those of normal cognitive learning.

is not always directly done from open Bibles. Biblical and practical truth is released from within the individuals, who by their knowledge of the Scriptures and by their Spirit-filled lives are themselves the source of knowledge and wisdom. Learning in the form of nurture is carried on through exposure to adult models.

And what are some other benefits of intergenerational education?

Affirmation. The acceptance of individuals across the generations is a rewarding outcome. Children are seen as persons to be talked *with* and not merely *to*. The activities themselves provide avenues of support and caring for all present, including the elderly and singles. At the conclusion, the prayer of thanksgiving I have heard most often is "Thank you, God, for each other."

Development of family ties. Whether a particular subject of an intergenerational experience is related to the family or not, the relationships for family participants are strengthened. For one thing, the whole experience is done as a model family. Sensitivity, joy, sharing, and caring all characterize the group in a way that makes us want to practice these qualities in our own families. And individual families within the group have opportunities for meaningful interaction during the sessions that spills over into their home lives.

Understanding. The discovery of one another in the intergenerational setting produces new understanding of the needs, desires, traits, feelings, and anxieties of other generations. Participants usually come away with a new awareness of the extent to which they have been segregated from those outside their own age brackets. Certainly the differences become more apparent, but also less threatening and mysterious.

Joy. Initial enjoyment seems to come from the fact that intergenerational learning is different from cognitive learning; this learning offers a change of pace. But joy also results from the variety of discoveries that occurs as well as from the new dimension of relationships that develops. Spontaneous expressions, kidding, and individual antics mixed with the gleeful responses of the children make it a time of great fun. And the worship and praise that result produce a time of great joy.

We don't have information about these benefits from scientific study of the intergenerational movement since that kind of research has not been done yet. However, the benefits are real, as those of us who have been involved have experienced and have seen. And on this basis we can testify that the enthusiasm level is high. Koehler has even seen a "new sense of life and unity in the whole congregation" as a by-product of intergenerational education.[2]

But some have concluded that intergenerational experiences require too much effort to initiate or to continue. Difficulties may arise from both the traits of the program and the nature of the participants. It is true that these events take some specialized and extensive planning. Most of the format and methodology has to be developed by those familiar with the discovery educational process. But with the growing reservoir of plans and programs for intergenerational learning, these difficulties will be a less formidable barrier than they have been up to now.

Hazards of Intergenerational Education

Adults may not understand the process. In evangelical churches, understanding the process of learning in intergenerational education may be the greatest hurdle, since learning is usually viewed as receiving truth or insights in a transmissive manner. Adults may be impatient when the biblical input is not always heavy and direct; but this problem can be overcome by giving them assurances that this is only one form of Christian education. Adults soon discover for themselves that there are different dimensions and methods of learning.

One generation may dominate the discussion. At times the adults may dominate by thoughtlessly speaking over the heads of the children. Or else the adults may feel the children's presence too keenly and thus speak down to them, condescendingly. Often adults have not learned to talk with children. But healthy, meaningful intergenerational communication is a goal of these sessions, not actually a prerequisite. Therefore, the example and guidance of the leaders soon overcome these initial inadequacies. Without a doubt, the most exciting byproduct of intergenerational education is contributing to bridging the generation gaps in both church and home.

> Intergenerational learning is not intended to replace age-level education.

The wide range of needs may not be met. The strength of the intergenerational experiences—the generation differences—is also its weakness. Formulating a curriculum that appeals to the wide range of interests, knowledge, needs, and behaviors is quite a challenge. In this situation it is easy to slip into planning too narrowly for one age group and thus miss those in other age groups. Perhaps the only solution to this weakness is to be found in limiting the use of these experiences in the total church ministry. Intergenerational learning is not intended to replace age-level education, but these experiences can fit into the larger church ministry in a number of ways.

Programming Intergenerational Education

In the most comprehensive and detailed guide to intergenerational learning yet written, Koehler recommends primarily short-term and voluntary settings. He warns against making this an ongoing educational effort because that is better left to age-level programs. Ninety percent of intergenerational education takes place in elective, short-term situations. For example, an elective, six-week Sunday morning class or a special four weeks of Sunday evening sessions can be offered to those interested. Sometimes only two generations might be involved, as in a parent-teen Sunday school class in which a book of Scripture or a family-related subject such as communication is studied. Imagine, too, the benefits for parents and elementary school children who volunteer for a ten-week intergenerational Sunday school class.

Inserting intergenerational learning into the regular existing programs of the church on a short-term basis is also a feasible option. I know of several churches that have divided the whole Sunday school into intergenerational learning groups for one month. The same could be done for just two generations of youth and parents or children and parents. Making some of the holiday sessions times of intergenerational celebrations is becoming a common practice. Easter, Thanksgiving, and Christmas intergenerational curriculum is becoming readily available.

After gaining some experience in intergenerational education, a church could build a regular option into its total program. Koehler mentions a weekly, Wednesday evening supper meeting that includes learning and fellowship for all ages as one example, and a monthly Sunday evening fellowship as another.

Devising an Intergenerational Event

As in other educational ministries, there are three options open to the planner: select and use a ready-made event from among available printed resources, select a program and adapt it to your situation, or devise your own. The more personalized element of the last two offers more certainty of being relevant to your situation. But they also call for more creativity and experience than the first option does. Drawing on some resources, an inexperienced person can succeed by applying some principles and following the planning steps.

Determine the goals. Because goals give birth to theme and methods, the formulation of objectives must be first. Naturally you begin with the formulation of general goals for the series of sessions. These goals are based on the needs of your congregation in general and the individuals to be involved in the intergenerational experiences. For example, an overall goal might be to produce more understanding between adults and teens. Or it might be a family-related goal—to develop communication skills between family members. The goal might be content oriented; for example, it might be to understand the nature of the church as a family.

Individual sessions have two types of goals. The first is the primary goal of the session, which is related to the main event. This goal is primary in the sense that it is the main announced intention of the session. For example, it might be to become more aware of the sovereignty of God in life, or to understand more fully the concept of grace (both cognitive goals), or else to improve our ability to affirm others (affective goal).

Most sessions include more than one objective. Particularly relevant to intergenerational events is a secondary goal, which is related to the anticipated concomitant learning. Along with the primary goal, for example, which is to understand the sovereignty of God in life, the occasion may have this outcome to consider in planning: that the teens and adults understand each other's viewpoints. Another secondary goal could be that the participants get to know each other in more depth, or that the group experiences worship.

Incorporating the possible objectives in both of these categories, the list of objectives for the "Joy" session described earlier provides a sample. The goals for the participants in this session are the following:

1. Be able to state elements of Christian joy and to describe ways to maintain it (primary learning aim).

2. Be able to describe some others in the group and state their names.

3. Have an enjoyable time so that the particpants will say so when they are asked.

4. Feel a closeness to some others from other generations and manifest this in statement or action.

5. Realize that the relationships and the closeness to God and others are conditions of joy.

6. Gain understanding of the thinking and actions of other generations so that they will articulate and use this understanding later.

7. Better understand intergenerational experiences so that they can state some of their purposes.

Select the methods. Keeping in mind the two types of goals, plan first for the methods related to the primary goals. Certain principles dominate the selection. Methods should (1) provide for intergenerational interaction, (2) allow nonreaders to participate, (3) challenge adult thinking, (4) provide for physical movement between approximately ten-minute segments, (5) offer variety, (6) creatively involve the various senses, (7) make the experience enjoyable, (8) stimulate in-depth relationships, and (9) provoke interaction with God and His truth.

The dramatization we chose for the main event in our "Joy" session was one kind of drama form, one category among many. The drama category also includes role playing, skits, play reading, and pantomime. Discussion methods are another category, which include buzz groups, conversation, pair discussions, panel discussions, etc. Discussion techniques can be attached to some transmissive methods such as films, filmstrips, slides, cassettes, puppets, records, videocassettes, storytelling, or illustrated lecture. For intergenerational learning, discovery forms are best, embracing a whole range of creative activities: paraphrasing, drawing, making posters or banners, producing a puppet show, writing poetry or songs, playing a simulation game, or making collages.

Secondary goals are accomplished, in part, during the main event of the intergenerational experience. Our participants came to know more about each other, for example, when they were formulating their drama about joy. But activities can also be planned with concomitant goals in mind. When a person tried to guess what the picture of the animal pinned on his back was, it facilitated the knowing of others, intergenerational contact, and having fun. The musical circles game was also intended to provoke productive relationships, as was the "Zip and Zap" mixer. These techniques can be planned to take place either before or after the main event and can usually be related to the main theme as well. Some activities are related to developing the Godward relationship: singing, choral reading, praying, poetry writing, and sharing praise verbally or in writing or in art form (posters or banners). Strategies that relate the individuals and the generations to each other consist of such methods as one-to-one sharing, small-group sharing, interviewing, using questionnaires, using agree-or-disagree statements, completing sentences, doing circular response, name-tag making, eating together, wishing and dreaming, making and sharing of gifts, verbally completing sentences, and verbally sharing feelings, personal experiences, and concerns.

Keep in mind that normally the intergenerational session should involve people as they arrive so that there is no time for inactive boredom or awkwardness. A schedule for an event might look like this plan for a three-hour-long Thanksgiving celebration devised by Trudy Vander Haar:

Name-tag making (trace hands and turn over for turkey)

Games

Fun, action-oriented songs such as "I Wiggle My Thumbs Like This"

Bible study dramatizations: Small groups prepare and perform dramatizations of "Ten Lepers" (Luke 17:11–19) and "The Feast of Booths" (Lev. 23:33–44; Neh. 8:13–18; and Deut. 16:13–15)

Brief discussion of gratitude

Midafternoon break

Making of Thanksgiving collages (family groups, singles, and mixed groups)

Sharing of collages

Sandwich supper

Spontaneous sharing (what each is thankful for) listed on newsprint

Singing of "For the Beauty of the Earth" as related to list of items

Carry-over activity: Removed name tags become a "helping hand" symbol.[3]

Evaluate the session. The final step, evaluation, is somewhat different for intergenerational events than it is for most other events since some of the children are not able to write. Other forms of expression than writing may be called for, such as having participants draw a smiling or an unhappy face to express their feelings. Leaders may circulate among the group afterward to get verbal responses to prepared questions. Keep in mind, too, that children may not be able to respond to general questions and may need some specific help. Specific questions are needed to test for achievement of the primary objective, such as these: "What did you learn?" or "Can you finish this statement: 'Joy is. . .' and give three different answers?" or "From what activity did you learn the most?" The concomitant learning can be tested by specific inquiries as well: "What did you enjoy the most?" or "Name one person you came to know," or "How did you feel about the others in the group?" or "What would you change in the program and why?"

FAMILY CLUSTERS

Another program that involves whole-family participation is called "Family Clusters." Developed by Margaret Sawin, the program amounts to forming artificial extended families as a way to solve the problems of the isolated nuclear family. Sawin rightly holds out clustering as a unique approach, defining a cluster as

> The family cluster program amounts to forming artificial extended families as a way to solve the problems of the isolated nuclear family.

"a group of four or five complete family units who contract to meet together periodically over an extended period of time for shared learning experiences related to the questions, concerns, and problems of their lives."[4]

While family clustering is intergenerational, it is also markedly distinct from mere intergenerational learning. One major difference is that family clustering requires whole family units, though the unit may be a whole nuclear family, a one-parent family, a single person, or a couple without children. All who are living together in a home are invited to the sessions as a unit, including infants or resident aunts or uncles. Family clustering requires a much more specialized approach than intergenerational experiences. Themes and goals arise out of the life of these units rather than from some specified biblical or practical curriculum. The substance of the clustering sessions is the stuff of the family life of those who attend.

Goals of Family Cluster

Like the intergenerational groups, family clusters also have learning goals, but these goals are more closely related to the family units in family clusters than in intergenerational groups. *Support* and *mutuality* of the individual participants is a major objective, providing individuals with a broader base of people intimately concerned for them than is true in intergenerational groups. Members of the cluster are encouraged to help each other achieve individual goals. Intervention into the family system is also intended. "One family may say, 'Help us help each other feel good about ourselves,'" Sawin explains. "So after a particular exercise the others in the group may say, 'You're not helping so-and-so feel good about himself; you're putting him down.'" In this way the group offers outside feedback and gives support to family members to help them carry out what they say they want to do.[5]

Facilitating intergenerational relationships is another major objective of family clusters. Interaction is such that children can relate easily to adults, and adults to children. A statement often heard is this one: "We've enjoyed seeing relationships build between our children and other adults."

Another objective is to provide models. Families can model for each other aspects of their family systems in decision making, disciplining, interrelating, problem solving, etc. The implications of this goal are quite powerful, considering how such exposure to one another as families is almost completely absent in our society. We see what happens in the contrived family television shows while knowing almost nothing about what goes on in the homes immediately to the right or the left of us. One participant confessed, "Cluster gives us a chance to compare our style of living with other styles; we have become more confident as parents. I can see who I used to be and where I have grown."

Family clustering also proposes to develop perspective. Parents can gain perspective about their children through contact with other children and also through observing other adults' perception of their children; likewise children can gain perspective about their parents. "Teenagers felt cluster provided an opportunity for them to realize in what ways their parents are unique; thereby allowing for more tolerance in the acceptance of parents' mores," reports Sawin.[6] Singles who are cut off from their nuclear families can gain new insights into their past family lives as well as clearer concepts of reality in regard to family life.

Sharing and discovery are not lacking. Through the joint experiences of clustering, youths and adults can share their concerns regarding the meaning of life amid a time of rapid social change and straying from aberration of traditional values. "Children can deal existentially with their real world experiences, using the group as a place to check out their experiences amid the group's support and value system."[7]

Contracting in Family Clusters

Clustering is usually a weekly event that requires several hours of an evening; the event includes a potluck supper before the learning activities begin.

Clusters meet for about twelve weeks, after which they may decide to continue for another period of time. Contracting marks off family clusters from other intergenerational experiences. In a private session with the leader, each family unit agrees to sign a contract committing the members of the family to active, regular, and quality participation in the cluster.

Family clustering draws from the current educational philosophy known as *experiential education*. Members of the group reflect on experiences they are having as families or on structured events contrived by the cluster leader. Group members are taught to look back on their experiences to gain perspective and insight from what they have gone through. This reflection is the key to *experiential education*.

Since family clustering is so close to family therapy, it requires trained and experienced leadership. Margaret Sawin has been conducting workshops for this purpose throughout North America. Now that she is retired, it remains to be seen what the future holds for this helpful form of ministry.

FAMILY CAMPING

Much intergenerational interaction occurs at family camps, though not all programs that use the term qualify for the designation "family" or "camp." Housed in motel-like accommodations, eating meals in a large dining-room setting, and meeting in large speaker-centered sessions, the people are in a conference more than a camp. On the other end of the spectrum are those family camps whose leaders engage in carefully planned and supervised living-learning experiences designed for marriage and family enrichment. In these camps relationships plumb depths far beyond what is afforded by the superficial recreational contact in other camps.

Whatever the form, family camping contributes to the contemporary family something not readily available in other settings.

Unique Values of Family Camping

Two distinct dimensions of camping make their mark in a powerful way, sometimes transforming enthusiasts for the movement into downright fanatics. The dimensions are wrapped up in this simple definition: "Camping is simply outdoor living."[8] First, camping offers natural surroundings for people caught up in a fast-paced, complex, concrete, steel-belted existence. In the out-of-doors most people shift gears; they downshift. Attitudes change with the slower pace. Perceptions are sharpened so that one sees and hears novel and welcome sights and sounds.

In that setting the second dimension makes a major spiritual impact. Family camping is a total living together, unlike the partial exposure we have to each other in our churches and homes. The outside environment moves us back to basics, to simple existence. Israel knew this experience during the Feast of Tabernacles. Though the Israelites didn't dwell in a metropolis, God moved them once a year into a simple living style in lean-tos for a week. In that setting the people related to God and to others unencumbered by life's routine, day-to-day pressures.

The church, too, can be strengthened by family camping. Christ-like relational patterns learned at camp carry over to the church. The intergenerational and interfamily contacts build the unity of the whole church body. This is happening for those churches that regularly sponsor their own family camps. It is also a reality for churches that regularly have eight or ten families attending their area's independent or denominational camp.[9]

> Family camping contributes to the contemporary family something not readily available in other settings.

In its relational dimension, family camping is an expression of the meaning of Christ's church. John Rozenboom describes what happens in a camp setting:

> Just as the needs of every member of the immediate family become the needs of the entire family, so the needs of all the families in a camp setting become the needs of each family and each individual. The members of each family become in reality members one of another, and can experience ministering and being ministered to. They can witness to their belief, and in witnessing, belief and commitment become part of being.[10]

Evangelism in family camps is not uncommon. Some report significant outreach in their family camps, often accomplished through low-key, personal contacts with noncommitted family members brought along by their families. The joyful Christian atmosphere and the sharing of God's Word combine so that the one who witnesses communicates the gospel effectively.[11]

Clifford Gustafson maintains that the church denomination has much to gain through its family camps. The Lake Retreat Baptist Camp in Washington has become a center for all types of contact within the Baptist General Conference Northwest District. Families meet other Baptist families, reinforcing ties and broadening awareness. Denominational leaders interact with church families at camp, occasioning nonformal communication about denominational matters and issues. In fact, the objectives of their camp include being a "rallying point for the denomination."[12]

Family camping is not always an easy ministry to maintain. Bob Hilts of Hume Lake Christian Camps in California states: "When you try to minister to all age levels at one time you find that you hit one age level here, another one there, and the rest are kind of missed."[13] Some camp leaders also equate family camps with red ink since charges must be minimal in order to make camping affordable for families. But many others are enthusiastic, seeing family camps as a ministry with benefit to the whole camp program.[14] For one thing, family camping offers some firsthand communication between camp leaders and parents of campers who attend the youth weeks. Those contacts increase the bond between camp leaders and youth as well as between parents and youth. Furthermore, the family camp weeks have promotional value; kids attend the youth weeks as a result of exposure to the camp during family camp. And adults who learn firsthand about the camp during family camp sometimes become financial contributors to the camp. They also become supporters in other ways, often joining work crews and offering profitable suggestions. In fact, Gustafson's camp has a family work week, when families attend without cost in exchange for their daily work in the maintenance of buildings and grounds.

Types of Family Camping

A description of the contemporary patterns show us how rich and exciting family camping can be.

Resident-Centralized Family Camp

Though this kind of camp is the more traditional type, many of the family camps that fall into this category have vital, ongoing programs. Conference grounds like Camp of the Woods in Speculator, New York, are usually filled to capacity. Lake Retreat Baptist Camp in Washington cannot accommodate all who want to register.

Essentially, the spiritual program revolves around platform speaking sessions. Families live together in tents, campers, or camp facilities. Some recreation is planned: talent nights, sports competition, and special events such as sand-castle building and kite-constructing contests. Families fare for themselves but can use the waterfront, the crafts room, and the sporting and natural facilities of the site. Little or no place is made for contrived learning experiences or skill-development exercises, let alone any cluster or small-group involvement. Meals and programs are provided for families, who, the planners assume, don't want to be hassled on their "vacation with a purpose."

Personal care is sometimes given to the family in some camps that try to help the family as a unit. At Timber-Lee in Wisconsin, a staff counselor assigned to each family orients them to the program and grounds and relates to them, observing them as a family. The counselor may get a chance to help them with their family relationships. Timber-Lee also gives the family high profile through a family parade that has family floats, through discussion of family-related films, and through family projects like "plant a family tree."

But generally the goals of these camps and conferences are individualized. Speakers center on evangelistic and Christian-growth themes, usually offering exposition of Scripture. Sometimes family living is a central theme.

Generally, the major obstacle in the pathway toward this kind of camp is facilities. Youth-oriented camps rarely have enough rooms to handle many family units. Separating the families into men's and women's cabins and dorms is unworkable, except for a weekend—when it may be tolerated but not enjoyed. The recent popularity of trailer and recreational-vehicle camping has given many camps a rather easy solution to the problem of lack of facilities and has done much to increase dramatically the number of family camps. The installation of electrical and even sewage hook-ups at camping spots has been a major trend. Special family-camp waterfronts, nature trails, and sporting facilities are also being installed.

Though this type of camp fails to use the more dynamic educational strategies, it is not sterile of dynamic results. Camp leaders and family members attest to the dramatic changes that occur during family-camp weeks. The growing popularity of these camps indicates that something substantial is happening at them.

Resident-Eclectic Family Camp

Drawn by contemporary family-life educational approaches, some camps are modifying their centralized camps. California's Mount Hermon attempts to put the family back together at camp. Though the program is carefully scheduled and planned for the campers, the family is generally the central unit for experiences. Dads, trained in special classes, lead the family devotions at breakfast. Families are involved in the projects and contests, such as the annual sand-building competition. In the evening sessions there are experiments with family clusters and intergenerational events. There families participate as families and not as individual spectators. A welcome change to the more traditional family camp, this type could easily be instituted at other camps with the assistance of some family-life educators.

Family-Enrichment Camping

A full-blown, family-enrichment program is now being offered at some camps. A campsite is an ideal setting for some of the marriage and family-enrichment programs discussed earlier in this book. Ed Branch, Jr., writes of the experience of the University of Alberta's Family Studies Department. Their family camp is designed around out-of-doors experiences and experiential education, particularly the Minnesota Couples Communication Program. His chapter in *Marriage and Family Enrichment* contains a complete description of the schedule and particulars.[15] Families are able to participate because the leaders use a long weekend. Beginning on a Friday evening, the sessions continue through the following Wednesday, making it necessary for family members to miss only a few days of work. As with other enrichment programs, we have yet to see evangelicals substantially committed to this kind of camp. But weekend marriage-encounter and family-enrichment programs are increasingly offered at evangelical campsites.

Family-Camporama Camping

"Camporama is for fellowship. Camporama is a rally of families, a weekend outing for families, with fun and enthusiasm." This is John Rozeboom's description of a camporama, a major type of camp, in his booklet, *Family Camping: Five Designs for Your Church.*[16] A camporama can take place at a church resident campsite or a park, anyplace where a large group of families can camp together, usually for a weekend.

> The camporama is a popular idea in churches today, since it cultivates annually the total relationships the church body is trying to achieve on a daily basis.

I concur with Rozeboom's assessment that "many churches are finding this one of the most exciting activities in their year's schedule."[17] The program is centralized; there is a campfire or a meeting, replete with speaker or film. Usually families camp at their own sites, cooking meals for themselves. An adaptation can be made for a conference setting, in which families stay in cabins, and meals are served in a central dining hall. I have seen camps where both conditions occurred; cabins and dining room were there for those who wanted them, while some family units set up their own campsites.

Small-group activities for learning, discovery, fellowship, and work are sometimes added to the program along with nature-oriented activities: nature hikes, bird-watching, ecology sessions, etc. These activities usually end up being intergenerational and thus contribute to the relational dimension.

When the camporama is carried over to Sunday, there can be a worship service to which all households are welcome. This possibility is making the camporama a popular idea in churches today, since it cultivates annually the total relationships the church body is trying to achieve on a daily basis.

Family-Cluster Camping

Cluster camping is distinguished from the camporama by size. A cluster camp includes only ten family units. But it differs from the camporama in other respects as well. In a cluster camp the group establishes its own objectives, schedule, and program with the help of a *lead family.* Thus the schedule tends to be much more free and relaxed than in any of the previous designs. Families are free to follow their own wishes at times, but it is generally agreed that the entire cluster of families will be involved together. A common meal, a trip to a nearby point of interest, a nature hike, a game, or a project might bring them all together. These decisions are made in whole-camp meetings early in the week or by delegated representatives of each family.[18]

Naturally, some decisions are made prior to the camp regarding the supply of camping equipment, provision of meals, etc. Sometimes the church can help with the renting or borrowing of equipment. The lead family needs some training ahead of time, and a skeletal schedule of activities needs to be announced.

A church might have four or five family-cluster camps in its annual schedule. Bill Dinkelman, Christian education director in a church of about three hundred in Illinois, started with one such camp one year and ended up with enough demand to hold three the next. The families stayed at the campsite through Sunday afternoon and held their own worship service, thus missing the one at their home church; this was something that was optional according to the local church's convictions, and caused no friction.

Family-Colony Camping

If we were to cross the camporama and the cluster camp, the result would be something called the "family colony." Though the clusters are smaller than in a cluster camp, with about sixteen people (or three or four families) in each cluster, it acts as a unit and those in the unit plan activities together. But the units, or clusters, attend an occasional experience that is planned for the entire camp. The program is described in *Family Camping: Five Designs* as focusing "on the activities of the three or four families as they study, experience, work, play, and explore nature skills, campcraft skills, and conservation."[19]

This design calls for more attention to out-of-doors living than the other designs do. It adds a dimension missed by the others, since in the family colony the families are actually forced into a living-together situation in which they share responsibilities for campcraft, cooking, and program planning. This small-group camping offers some true-life experiences of cooperation and even of conflict. Coupling this living arrangement with sessions on interpersonal relations during the entire-camp meetings creates a powerful educational and fellowship setting. The key to the success of this sensitive kind of camping is the lead family of each colony. Rozeboom maintains that the lead families should be selected wisely and trained carefully, preferably in a special lead-family training weekend, that he describes in detail.[20]

Family Caravan Camping

As the name suggests, caravan camping links camping with travel. Families make excursions together, stopping at designated parks and campgrounds for evenings of study, sharing, and recreation. Caravan camping, like cluster camping, has sometimes been a threat to the local church. The regular

> Camping is not an escape from life; it provides an enrichment of life.

weekend departure of a sizable number of church families to travel and camp together or on their own has caused serious problems in some churches. Not only does this keep them from Sunday worship in their home church, but it may also produce cliques in the church. And these, in turn, may cause division.

One leader says the church should face this threat by organizing caravan experiences under church auspices. Though there are problems, the values are worth the risk, he says.[21] Some creative programming can add a spiritual-growth dimension to the trip. Combining the family-caravan idea with a trip to some mission project or site can give the travel an additional purpose. Because caravan camping involves travel, some special precautions and particular long-range plans have to be made. *Family Camping: Five Designs* offers complete guidelines.

Camping is not an escape from life; it provides an enrichment of life. Camping is as inexpensive or as uncomplicated as many of our activities. It is a back-to-basics movement—back to God's Word and to creation, to the true body of Christ, and to the family.

CONCLUSION

Churches have not been quick to develop intergenerational and family unit programs despite their obvious value. Because they are so novel, people have not been willing to give them a try and church leaders have not known how to concoct successful programs.

The availability of appropriate literature is changing that. Two major books on intergenerational ministries have recently appeared. Both *Intergenerational Religious Education*[22] and *Families Growing Together*[23] are complete and practical guides for this type of ministry. There is a growing body of curriculum material as well. *Families Growing Together* has an up-to-date listing of the resources available for launching and sustaining exciting and meaningful intergenerational events.

The need for these is great, even urgent, according to one of today's most informed experts on American families, Urie Bronfenbrenner. We are seeing daily the effects of isolation of the generations from one another that he warned us about in 1973. If the institutions of society continue to remove parents and other adults from our children, he claimed: "We can anticipate increased alienation, indifference, antagonism, and violence on the part of the younger generation in all segments of our society—middle-class children as well as the disadvantaged."[24]

SUGGESTED RESOURCES

Koehler, George E. *Learning Together: A Guide for Intergenerational Education in the Church School.* Nashville: Abingdon Press, 1976. •Not a curriculum, but the best guide for developing your own intergenerational events, particularly those designed for learning.

Miles, M. Scott. *Families Growing Together: Church Programs for Family Learning.* Wheaton, Ill.: Victor Books, 1990. •The best overall guidebook for getting families together in church.

White, James W. *Intergenerational Religious Education.* Birmingham, Ala.: Religious Education Press, 1988. •A comprehensive volume that offers the most thorough discussion of the nature and purpose of intergenerational ministry.

Any curriculum for Sunday school can be adapted for intergenerational learning sessions. Modify any of the lessons for children from third grade through sixth. Use your denominational materials or other curricula such as David C. Cook, Gospel Light Publications, Scripture Press, or Standard Press.

NOTES

1. George Koehler, *Learning Together: A Guide for Intergenerational Education in the Church* (Nashville: Discipleship Resources, 1977), 14.

2. Ibid., 15.

3. Trudy Vander Haar, *Generations Learning Together in the Congregation* (Orange City, Ia.: Office of Family Life, General Program Council, Reformed Church in America, 1976), 2–4.

4. Margaret Sawin, "An Over-All View of the Family Cluster Experience: Historically, Leadership-wise, Family-wise," *Religious Education* (March-April, 1974): 184. See also Scott Miles, *Families Growing Together: Church Programs for Family Learning* (Wheaton, Ill.: Victor Books, 1990).

5. Sawin, "Over-All View of the Family," 188–89.

6. Ibid., 188.

7. Ibid., 185.

8. Werner Graendorf, "Camping Purpose," *Introduction to Christian Camping*, eds. Werner C. Graendorf and Lloyd D. Mattson (Chicago: Moody, 1979), 18.

9. Clifford Gustafson, "Philosophy and Styles of Family Camping," cassette recording of a workshop at the International Camping Convention, Christian Camping International (Baniff National Park, Alberta, Canada, 1977).

10. John Rozeboom, *Family Camping: Five Designs for Your Church* (Nashville: Board of Discipleship of the United Methodist Church, 1973), 4.

11. Gustafson, "Philosophy and Styles."

12. Ibid.

13. Personal correspondence between the author and Bob Hilts, March 23, 1977.

14. Gustafson, "Philosophy and Styles."

15. Ed Branch, Jr., "The Family Camp: An Extended Family Enrichment Experience," *Marriage and Family Enrichment*, ed. Herbert A. Otto (Nashville: Abingdon, 1976), 51.

16. Rozeboom, *Family Camping*, 39.

17. Ibid.

18. Ibid., 29.

19. Ibid., 33.

20. Ibid., 12–15.

21. Ibid., 43.

22. James W. White, *Intergenerational Religious Education* (Birmingham, Ala.: Religious Education Press, 1988).

23. Miles, *Families Growing Together*, 1990).

24. Urie Bronfenbrenner, *Two Worlds of Childhood* (New York: Simon and Schuster, 1973), 116.

◆ *Part Five*

Marriage Education

Preparation for Marriage

The haphazard way we often go about choosing a life partner may underlie the problem we have living with the ones we choose. If a person's selector is bad, his adjuster had better be good. One counselor put it bluntly: "The problem with American marriage is American courtship."[1]

If this is true, preventing marital breakdown will need to include teaching youth how to select a mate as well as how to live with the one they select. This education has to begin with children who have not yet reached puberty, since children of all ages need information about relating to the opposite sex.

SEX EDUCATION IN THE HOME

Until recent times, sex education was ignored or else relegated to sharing biological facts through books or through showing the child the sexual habits of pets and other animals. Freud uncovered childhood sexuality, making it clear that the attitudes and inner feelings toward sex are framed early in the child's experiences. Sex education begins when the mother first holds her newborn infant. In the warmth and comfort of the mother's arms the child experiences human love through touching, which provides the basis for later exchanges of sexual affection. Should those early sensate experiences be excluded or be negative, the child's sexual capacities and outlook may be greatly harmed.

Sex education is far more than just transmitting facts. It includes the ways the child is cared for, talked to, and held and touched by both parents. It also includes the way sex-related concepts are discussed in those early years. Parents' attitudes are conveyed unconsciously in a myriad of verbal and non-verbal interchanges. Any parental embarrassment connected with repeating words like *penis, vagina,* or *intercourse* helps to build an unfavorable inner attitude toward sex in the child. The parent's comfort with his or her own body as well as with the child's body and its functions will favorably influence the child's view of, and acceptance of, sex.

The child's attitude toward sex is also developed through exposure to the parents' love relationship between themselves. Howard and Jeanne Hendricks have said it well: "Parents are stamping a permanent tattoo on their children in terms of marriage readiness."[2] Though the child never really witnesses the explicit sexual relationship of his parents, he will nonetheless see and hear much to color his image of sex in marriage. The child will catch their warm glances directed

> "The problem with American marriage is American courtship."

at one another; their casual, lingering touches; the occasional hug; and the excited, passionate kiss and embrace at the airport or doorway celebrating the return of a loved one. The absence of such visible manifestations of love may distort the child's attitude, contributing to his or her being a very passive, unaffectionate mate later on. The impact of these informal channels of love makes the right sexual training of parents a prerequisite to the right sexual education of their children. Biblical concepts of sex must first shape adult minds, hearts, and practices before parents can teach these concepts to their children.

Parents can also be intentional in their sex education. They can deliberately make use of everyday experiences as well as special experiences. The arrival of a new baby in the home or the neighborhood can be used to teach the anatomy of the human body and the reproduction process. Exposing children to animals is a proven sex-education experience, but it is not a substitute for frank talk about human sexuality. Parents can respond to television scenes in a way that conveys a positive stance to the beautiful aspects of sexuality while affirming the reality of high morals and biblical guidelines in this area. The same is true of parental response to sex words the child brings home. By the parent's explanation and emotional reaction the child will learn to distinguish between an unacceptable word and a perfectly acceptable act or part of the body. An imprudent parent may denounce something good when deploring a bad word.

> Sex education is especially the task of the church and the home because at heart sex education is substantially a matter of morals and attitudes, not biological facts.

Another guideline that reflects common sense for mothers and fathers is for them to respond honestly to their children's sex-related questions. The answers should be true and simply given, including whatever is necessary to satisfy the child's curiosity. Words used to describe the body and the sex act should be factual and acceptable. Speaking in general terms to avoid specific instruction will only make the child suspicious, cautious, and curious. It is better to answer, "The baby comes into the world through the vagina, an opening in the mother's body," than to merely respond, "God brings babies into the world." While stating that the father's sperm enters the mother's body during intercourse, it can also be explained that this occurs during a very private, loving, and pleasurable experience that married people enjoy.

Sometime before puberty some explicit instruction should be imparted to children. James Dobson says that sex education should be over by the age of twelve. Prior to puberty the child is much more objective about such intimate matters than he or she is later and is able to discuss them without embarrassment with the parents. After puberty the subject becomes emotionally laden.

Parents can take the emotional edge off the explicit discussion through the use of a good book for preadolescents. Reading it aloud together and discussing matters in depth as they arise is probably the least threatening way for child and parent to handle the subject. Perhaps the parent who is more comfortable in taking this task should be the one to do so, while the other stands by to respond to questions so that communication lines are open with both parents.

If books on sex were used earlier than the age of eleven and twelve, it would make this special prepuberty training easier. For this reason a number of good sets of books have been prepared, supplying information to children at the various stages of childhood. An effective method is to assign books for reading. One parent can then administer a simple, multiple-choice or true-false test to the child, and the testing period can be turned into an occasion of discussion.

The method for conveying information should conform to the fact that children need to see that their parents are willing to talk about these things. Merely purchasing a book and giving it to the child without any plan for discussion may show a concern on the part of the parent, but it also may reveal the parent's reluctance to talk with the child. Besides, if the parent doesn't discuss the book, he or she will not have assurance that the book was read, let alone understood.

SEX EDUCATION IN THE CHURCH

It is obvious that the most important role of the church in sex education is the training of parents. Marriage enrichment programs will help the most. Special courses on parenting and sex education will also contribute. But should the church also teach directly to the children and youth?

How and what the church teaches children and youth about sex is an issue subject to debate. Some parents object to explicit sex teaching in the Sunday school or in club programs, particularly since it may be handled by persons untrained for the task. Yet the church program can legitimately include sex education and marriage preparation for youth. Pastors can deal with this subject in the normal course of biblical exposition, since the Bible frequently touches on this area. Special sermons and lectures can focus on Christian values and practices related to sex.

Pastors and church leaders can build bridgeheads to youth during special Sunday school talks or youth gatherings. A special series will open communication lines as well as convey the biblical stance. Theologians and other visiting lecturers could be enlisted to speak to children and youth at special times. This might be especially appropriate during a family life conference.

Sex education is especially the task of the church and the home because at heart sex education is substantially a matter of morals and attitudes, not biological facts. If it is left to public-school classrooms and peer conversations, deviance from Christian values and principles is likely to occur.

TEACHING ABOUT COURTSHIP

Sex education is just one part of the whole fabric of teaching about courtship and marriage. Subjects like friendship with the opposite sex, interpersonal relationships, and dating can be taught to children and youth from the point of view of their role in selecting a mate. We should try to make young people see how guidelines for sex and personal relationships are part of a total process of choosing someone to marry, which is one of their major life tasks.

Teaching about courtship isn't simple, in part because courtship practices in the West are neither clear nor standardized. In fact, though the term *courtship* has an old-fashioned ring to it, no modern term has replaced it.

Scripture offers some guidelines for courtship but does not give precise patterns. In both Old and New Testament times parents chose mates for their children. To impose this on Christians living in the West would be unwise and probably impossible. It would be better to integrate the following biblical tenets with what we know about modern practices of mate selection:

1. A person should seek a husband or wife—the process is not to be left to chance (Gen. 2:24; 1 Cor. 7:2).

2. A Christian should seek God's will, deciding whom to marry based on sound reasons as well as circumstances and feelings (1 Cor. 7:24).

3. The Christian should marry only another Christian (1 Cor. 7:39; 2 Cor. 6:14).

4. A sound reason to get married is to have sexual satisfaction (1 Cor. 7:1–7).

5. Romantic love is possible before marriage, as in the case of Jacob (Gen. 29:20), but it is not always present before marriage, as in the case of Isaac (Gen. 24:67).

6. Love can and should be developed after marriage. True love is something under a person's control; it is not merely something that controls us (Eph. 5:25; Titus 2:4).

7. Persons should get their parents' advice and consent before marriage, though they are not always subject to parents when they are adults (Gen. 24:67; Eph. 5:28; Titus 2:4).

Courtship instruction might be organized around the idea of four stages, each more narrow than the previous one.[3]

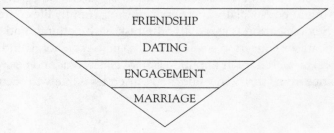

FRIENDSHIP

DATING

ENGAGEMENT

MARRIAGE

Once goals are attached to each stage, teenagers can see that dating is not regulated by arbitrary parental or biblical rules but by a sensible approach to selecting a mate. This selection process begins during the *friendship stage*, which includes several goals. First, young people should seek to cultivate many friendships with those of the other sex; in this way they get a chance to learn about themselves and the characteristics of others. Social contacts with a number of persons can help a young person realize there are a variety of personalities available. Another goal for the friendship stage is to develop quality relationships. Such relationships will help the person more easily be a friend to one's future wife or husband. He or she will also learn appropriate ways of relating to the opposite sex outside marriage. Unwholesome and flirtatious relating may harm the person after marriage as well as hinder the success of the selection process. An old saying reminds us, "Everybody's sweetheart is nobody's wife."

> Scripture offers some guidelines for courtship but does not give precise patterns.

Goals should be kept in mind also during the *dating stage*. It is most advisable to date widely and selectively, as this will give the same benefits as in the friendship stage. In addition, one will have a greater certainty about the final choice if he or she has known many possible partners. This is the stage to formulate and confirm moral standards in regard to male-female relationships. It is also a time for a person to formulate a list of qualities he or she desires in a future mate. One will wrestle with the answers to three questions: What do I need? What do I want? What can I get? The answers are not always the same. Somewhere a compromise, and then a decision, will need to be made.

Dating may often include a sub-stage called "going steady," where the couple exclusively dates one another, a step above "just dating" and below engagement. Other forms of commitment may also be sandwiched between these two stages, depending on one's subculture. Among college youth "pinning" may be a definite preengagement stage. And as mentioned previously, some, betraying Christian norms, include a stage of "living in" prior to marriage.

Dating is a process with considerable risk. People can exploit one another brutally as in "date rape." Less severe, but still damaging, a couple can be harmed when one of the partners wants to move toward a sexual relationship before deciding on marriage.

A substitute or supplement to dating is called "getting together." Facilitating, but not unduly emphasizing the relationship with the opposite sex, "getting together" refers to groups of men and women sharing in a party or activity. More casual and less threatening than a one-to-one relationship of dating, "getting together" has many advantages over dating as a courtship process. It is common for churches to provide these kinds of activities for their youth to have informal contact with others from their own, as well as other, churches.

The *engagement stage* has some crucial objectives:

(1) Intimacy. That the relationship should become more intimate than it was previously is usually accepted. Just how intimate is quite a controversial subject. Premarital intercourse is obviously forbidden, though in Scripture it is not dealt with as harshly as adultery is. Though many psychologists advocate it as practically advisable, the weight of research and judgment falls on abstaining. Going too far in intimacy creates many problems, since this stage is not the final one. Engagements are often broken. Estimates of the proportion of engagements broken run as high as 50 percent.[4] Physical intimacy prior to marriage can make an advisable separation difficult and painful to carry out and leave the participants guilt-ridden. Sometimes people carry their guilt feelings into marriage, causing sexual dysfunction. Mistrust can be fostered when one partner is suspicious of a mate who has broken moral standards prior to marriage.

(2) Learning. The engagement period is a ripe time for learning about intimate relationships and marriage. Through reading and group or private premarital counseling, couples can arm themselves with information.

(3) Communicating. Communication before marriage should be easier than afterwards, when the pressures increase. Engagement offers a chance for developing and testing the couple's communication skills.

(4) Deciding. Once the couple is engaged, others will look on them differently than before. The vantage point from which each views the other will also change. Out of this unique perspective the final decision will emerge. In *The Dating Game*, Herbert J. Miles offers the best summary of the basis for that decision from a Christian perspective. When one or both are in doubt, the most favorable ally is time. Sometimes postponement of the marriage will eventually bring the needed confirmation, but many times the relationship will fade and eventually be terminated.

PREMARITAL COUNSELING

That church leaders are usually involved in the marrying of people puts them in an excellent position for preventing family problems, providing an occasion for premarital counseling. "This is a ministry for which I have no regrets," says one marriage expert. "I cannot say that about many things, but I have never wasted an hour in this form of ministry."[5]

This ministry has been given a number of different names, perhaps reflecting some question about its precise function. Called *premarital education* by some, they place the emphasis on the preparation aspect. With the term *premarital counseling*, the stress is put on helping couples solve problems related to their premarriage experience, such as making the final decision or overcoming barriers in communication. The term *premarital conversations* portrays the informal nature of the sessions. Whatever the experience is called, it includes both counseling and education. It centers around the interpersonal relationship of a man and woman considering marriage, helping them evaluate their relationship and their expectations for their approaching marriage. This counseling also acquaints them with practical advice for building a happy marriage. It includes past, present, and future orientation.

To do any good, premarital education has to employ the right methods and aim at certain goals.

Many counselors are enthusiastic about the benefit of premarital counseling, yet research has not shown conclusively that it is effective. Some past surveys have been positive. A 1977 study of the premarital counseling programs of one thousand churches revealed that 90 percent of the couples responded positively to their sessions and even encouraged their friends to get premarriage counseling.[6] A number of other studies showed positive results immediately and after six months.[7]

Yet other studies don't support this upbeat view of the value of premarital education, particularly when viewed long range. In one experiment, couples were trained for marriage, then evaluated twice following the wedding: after six months, then after three years. Compared to the control group of couples who received no training, the trained couples' marriages looked better. But the difference between them and the control group was not maintained at the three-year follow-up check.[8]

Although research can't confirm conclusively that premarital education helps couples have more success in marriage, it does make one thing clear: to do any good, premarital education has to employ the right methods and aim at certain goals.

Employing Interactive Methods

Correct methods include those that get couples to talk about their relationship and prompt them to practice good communication skills. Sessions that consist primarily of giving information through talks and films do little good. Engaged partners must be made to encounter one another and talk about themselves. Methods for doing this are plentiful and will be described later.

Attempting Several Goals

Effective sessions will seek to achieve a number of goals. A major one is to make the couples face any problems, present or potential, in their relationship. Before marriage, men and women are often in such a state of "bliss"—emotionally detached from reality—that they aren't very teachable. They just aren't ready to learn how to solve problems they don't really expect to have. The counselor must seek to break through this blind idealism and help them prepare for crises by uncovering and making them face the issues in their relationship. Improved communication and ability to handle conflicts are considered two of the most crucial outcomes of successful premarital training.[9] Unlike the wedding, which should be pleasant, warm, and festive, successful premarriage sessions will at times be touchy and disagreeable.

Some counselors believe improved relational skills to be so crucial that they belittle other goals and functions of premarital counseling, particularly the attempt to teach the couple new information about marriage. Yet lack of such knowledge can be a hindrance to marital success. Research confirms that marital quality does depend, for one thing, on the couple's understanding and agreeing on the proper roles of husband and wife.[10] But whether research confirms it or not, the Christian counselor will be convinced that having a biblical understanding of marriage is crucial and should be part of premarital training.

> Many people marry for insufficient or wrong reasons. Efforts to help teens and young adults select a mate require helping them understand their needs and expectations.

Many couples will need to learn techniques of financial management, particularly since money problems are a major cause of marital unhappiness. They will also need information about marital sex, at least an adequate working vocabulary for talking about their sex lives. Husbands may be reluctant to discuss these issues because they are embarrassed to use the four-letter words that are the extent of their sexual lexicon.

Building rapport with the couple is another essential purpose of premarital counseling. Initiating counseling before marriage will swing the door wide open for marriage counseling if it is needed later. During premarital counseling, couples get accustomed to discussing their relationship with a third party, paving the way for their having less hesitancy to seek future counseling.

Unfortunately, many people marry for insufficient or wrong reasons. Losing much of their good judgment during courtship, they may marry because society expects them to, to improve their status, or because parents have pressured them. Sometimes an unconscious desire to improve themselves, or to reach out for something they didn't get from father or mother, will make them say "I do" prematurely.

Efforts to help teens and young adults select a mate require helping them understand their needs and expectations. Those who come from dysfunctional family backgrounds or are immature for other reasons will benefit from understanding how they may seek to use marriage to overcome certain "deficits" in their own personalities. For example, if they have lacked love from their parents, they may endeavor to use marriage to overcome an enormous hunger for affirmation. Or they may have been smothered by a parent or otherwise become codependent.

As a result they may be unconsciously looking for a parent. As one person described it: "We are truly a culture of dissatisfied consumers of each other." We learn to look to others to do for us what we have failed to do for ourselves. We often carry this type of consumerism into marriage. Instead, we need to say to our spouses and those we pledge to marry: "The quest for love, self-esteem, and happiness is my problem and my challenge, not yours. These are attainable only through my own growth and development." As long as people expect marriage partners to do for them what they can only do for themselves, they will foster an unhealthy dependence on them. And when their partners don't continue to make them happy, they interpret this to mean they are no longer loved. This leads to greater unhappiness for both the partners and the marriage.

Ideally, a person should resolve personal issues with his or her family of origin before marrying. This "differentiation" from parents involves an individual's development of a personal identity after a healthy psychological separation from them, something usually more difficult for those who have come from dysfunctional families.

Since approximately half of engagements are broken, the possibility of using premarital counseling to prevent a poor match is a realistic one. In some cases the counselor will help the couple solve problems they might have failed to resolve on their own, thus preventing an unnecessary breakup. At other times postponement of marriage might be suggested until the couple feels more certain about the relationship. And, of course, the premarital testing and interaction may enable either the couple or the counselor to decide that the relationship should be broken. Not always pleasant work, premarital counseling nevertheless deserves its reputation for being crisis counseling.

Premarriage sessions are a good opportunity to explore the engaged partners' families of origin. There may be unhealthy emotional ties to parents that may need to be broken in order for a person to successfully "leave father and mother and cleave unto his spouse."[11] The pastor can point out what it means to be properly disengaged from parents and help individuals start dealing with unresolved issues that either may have with their parents. If serious symptoms of a personality disorder appears in either, the counselor may suggest postponing the wedding to offer time for personal healing, unencumbered by marital adjustment. Above all, they should be led to comprehend how each one's background may impact their marital relationship. Forewarned, they may be prepared for expected complications of their adjustment to each other as well as predictable entanglements with in-laws.

Evaluating the couple's parents' marriage will also help the counselor judge just how much difficulty the couple will have in their own marital adjustment. Two researchers found that the quality of parents' marriages affected the quality of a person's own marriage. If parents were good marital role models, the quality would most likely be high; if not, success in marriage would be more difficult to obtain.[12]

Promoting the Sessions

The potential of such a program means that it should become a regular part of the church's life. For this to happen, the pastor will need to do more than make premarital counseling a requirement for those who plan marriage. The awareness level of the whole congregation needs to be raised. Otherwise, couples will be coming to be married at the last minute, making it difficult or impossible to plan for the necessary four or five sessions. Without advanced awareness of what the pastor's requirements are in this matter, couples from the congregation will have a difficult time graciously accepting the pastor's refusal to preside at their weddings. Getting the backing of the church board is the place to begin. Then the pastor can communicate regularly through oral and printed announcements. Both youth and adults will come to understand the necessity of notifying the pastor of wedding plans months ahead of the date.

After a time, the best promoters of the sessions will be the enthusiastic couples who have benefited from them. But there are additional ways to advertise. Some pastors conduct personal interviews with the youth of the congregation regularly, during which, among other things, the pastor informs the young people of the premarital counseling he offers. Sometimes pastors become involved in the pre-engagement stage of the couple's life. By assisting them in the engagement decision, the pastor establishes rapport early in the relationship.

Promotional contact can also be made during annual lectures and discussions in the youth group or in Sunday school classes. By scheduling three or four sessions to discuss dating and marriage, the pastor can include mention of his counseling. By making the program and policies known, the pastor can anticipate that people will know (1) that premarital counseling is an essential prerequisite to marriage under his pastorate and (2) that his consent to give premarital counseling to a couple is no guarantee that he will perform the wedding, since making the decision of whether or not to marry will be one of the objectives of the counseling.

Guidelines for Effective Premarital Counseling Sessions

We turn now to the actual sessions themselves. It is wise for the counselor to tailor a program best fitted to him or her and follow some guidelines or principles. I will share what I consider to be essential guidelines for premarital counseling and then discuss briefly some of the more recent developments, such as group premarital counseling.

Whatever the actual program, premarital counseling should be premarital conversation. The objectives require discussion. Trained in the art of homiletics to communicate to many, pastors are sometimes unable to talk with a few. One may find two-way interaction threatening and difficult to initiate. In my first feeble attempt at premarital counseling I was anxious and unable to elicit conversation from the couple. Introducing the topic of sex relations, I asked if they had read any books on the subject. The young man said yes and the girl nodded slightly in agreement. When I scanned my mental computer for a question to approach the subject, I found nothing but a useless question: "Do you have any questions about sex you would like to ask?" Needless to say, after that clumsy, fear-ridden approach, they didn't.

Premarital counseling should be premarital conversation.

Since then I have discovered some effective tools to get beyond the couple's reticence and turn these sessions into dynamic times of interaction while still covering all the bases. *Prepare/Enrich*, one of the most widely used instruments for determining actual and potential problems in a couple's relationship, is an invaluable aid. The scored test is used to diagnose the relationships of someone who is married or about to be married. Couples are asked to evaluate themselves in ten areas that research determined were the most important factors in good marriages. Scored by computer, a printout flags needed areas of discussion, making it easy for the counselor to use.[13]

Using this test, the counselor can easily discuss discrepancies in expectations and the areas in which they will need to make adjustments. In addition, the written information can become a basis for determining compatibility and marriage readiness. Scripture and theological insights can often be inserted into a critical area of discussion, not as short, isolated, formal homilies, but as relevant messages from God. The counselor is only a postage stamp away from scores of helpful interaction tools, some that will be discussed later, and many that are listed at the end of this chapter. Armed with these discussional, evaluative, and educational tests and inventories, the pastor or counselor need not fear having a tense, pressure-cabin atmosphere or lecture-prone sessions.

Along with discussion, the premarital counseling should include content. Some counselors tend to downplay the informational aspect, and seem to emphasize the relational aspects of the counseling. But as the counseling is both spiritual and practical, it should be characterized by substantial information.

Two components of premarital counseling make it a choice educational opportunity. The anxiety level of the couple is one feature. Marriage failure being what it is today, we can expect that reality for couples entering marriage includes fear and uncertainty. And anxiety over the decision to wed is often accompanied by guilt about the past. In such cases the couple is ripe for learning about criteria for choosing a mate and about biblical passages related to decision making. Sometimes anxiety is related to the unknown, which can range from confusion about managing finances to ignorance about sexual matters. Information is needed and usually wanted.

Another motivating factor is their idealism. We can capitalize on this, urging them to prepare for the best, not the mediocre. I have always found couples to be in a state of readiness to learn in some, if not all, marriage areas.

To make the most of this learning moment, the counselor will include three features: (1) providing assignments, (2) utilizing tests, and (3) devising a plan.

Giving the couple assignments will give the counselor some assurance that all important information will be provided, though not necessarily within the sessions themselves. In addition, if it is known both of them have completed the necessary study and reading, the counselor will be able to proceed in a conversational way and not feel compelled to lecture. Assignments are either given in a prepared handout at the beginning of the premarital counseling series or presented at the end of each session as preparation for the next session. The form of assignments may vary, but usually they include (1) reading or listening to recorded material, (2) inductive Bible study, and (3) conversation-provoking exercises or inventories.

Recommended texts usually cover the areas of communication, such as H. Norman Wright's *Communication: Key to Your Marriage*. For ready reference on sexual matters the couple could not have a better book than *Intended for Pleasure*, written by Ed and Gaye Wheat, a Christian doctor and his wife who approach sex in a relational as well as a detailed, technical fashion. Their cassettes cover the same material and provide a good alternative for couples who are not used to reading or who need some variety in assignments. Scores of other books are available, any combination of which will be chosen according to the counselor's viewpoint and the couple's needs.

Apart from reading material, assignments can take the form of study guides. Designed to guide the couple through appropriate biblical passages, some guides can be handed out by single pages prior to the appropriate session. Some study guides are oriented to other reading, to analysis of the individual, or to the relationship of the couple. Self-study can be most simply stimulated by including the *Handbook for Engaged Couples* as part of the program. Published by Inter-Varsity Fellowship, this guide can provide the basis for any discussion of the aspects of marriage. For couples who are not very familiar with biblical passages related to marriage, I commend the workbook entitled *Before You Say "I Do."*

The information function of premarital education also requires the use of a plan. Even though several sessions of random, unstructured conversation amounts to quite a bit of time, that is not enough. Assurance that all the basics will be touched, even if only lightly at times, should be built into the program. Such a plan calls for determining the number of sessions to be held and the actual procedure to be used in each. In Wright's comprehensive book, *Premarital Counseling*, he recommends five sessions.[14] Following the recommended program of Howard Hendricks, I have used four sessions prior to the marriage, with a fifth session some time after marriage. The number of sessions is not as important as their comprehensiveness. The counselor will want to devise his or her own schedule.

Helping the couple develop the skills needed for a good marriage should be a notable mark of premarital counseling. Aaron Rutledge regards the development of skills as being both crucial and possible. He includes skills in two of the counselor's goals listed: "In summary, the counselor's goals with the engaged couple are (1) to test the growth and growth potential of each personality, (2) to develop skills in and to stimulate spontaneous communication, and (3) to expose areas of stress, and develop problem-solving skills.[15]

> The sessions should be filled with communication, problem-solving, and even conflict resolution.

Note, too, that when "marriageability" traits are mentioned by Wright, skills dominate the list: adaptability and flexibility, empathy, ability to work through problems, ability to give and receive love, emotional stability, similarities in family backgrounds, similarities between the two individuals, and communication.[16] Though such skills as problem-solving, adaptability, and communication are acquired during childhood and adolescence and are, in part, the measure of the person's maturity, you can still seek to foster their development and improvement during the sessions.

For this reason the sessions should be filled with communication, solving of problems, and even conflict resolution. I have often been in some very uncomfortable sessions with couples who were grappling with present problems of adjustment. These issues can be worked through with the couple in order to promote their personal and joint maturity. Testing that exposes problems and areas of disagreement, tension, or needed adjustment is a great help in improving living skills under the counselor's guidance. Even the skills involved in praying together and in reading and studying the Bible and other helpful books can be enhanced.

The final ingredient of premarital counseling is perhaps the most difficult to accomplish—evaluation. Sometimes, when the couple is uncertain, the sessions are necessary to enable the two to come to a decision. At other times, when the decision to marry has been made, it is a matter of their evaluating themselves and their relationship in order to expose strengths as well as expected areas of conflict. All of the activities of the sessions will be called upon for the evaluation: the counselor's observations and insight, the couple's growing self-knowledge, their feelings, their developing skills, and their growing knowledge of biblical truth as it relates to the will of God for them.

Even if one is not a professional counselor, he or she can utilize tests, questionnaires, and inventories to make the evaluation objective. I have listed several of these in the last part of this chapter. I have found two to be especially precise and revealing.

For a comprehensive look at the marriage, which results in a graph of all the relationships, you can use the *Premarital Inventory*, by Bess Associates. When it is completed, the couple and the counselor will hold in their hands a chart showing where the couple agrees with one another in the major areas of marital adjustment: interests and activities, personal adjustment, children, religion and philosophy, interpersonal communication, finances, in-laws, sexuality, and role adjustment. In addition to scores in these areas, a score for general marriage readiness is included, which immediately can alert the counselor to possible problems in the future.

To test for temperament compatibility, *The Taylor-Johnson Temperament Analysis* is a highly recommended and reliable device. Although it is designed to be used by professional counselors, clergy can qualify to use it by attending a one-day seminar. The *TJTA* breaks temperament down into nine traits that are measured by means of a brief questionnaire of eighty-two questions that is easily scored. The *TJTA* is neither designed to be a thorough analysis nor adequate for diagnosing severe personality disorders. The results, however, can be used to assist a pastor in understanding extremes in behavior patterns of individuals and in foreseeing possible problem areas due to clashes in temperaments.

For example, one area explored is that of attitude toward social life. At one end of the scale the person rates as being socially active; at the other end he or she rates as being quiet and socially inactive. Johnson reported from his experience that there was greater marital stability present when scores in the area of activity were moderate rather than extreme or when the couple scored approximately the same. While these test scores may not call for terminating plans to be married, they may initiate intensive discussion about the decision or even cause postponement of the marriage. They provide a basis for counseling couples concerning their differences in temperament and the extent to which the divergent temperaments might influence the marriage.

Variations in Premarital Counseling Procedures

Improvements in and modifications of premarital counseling procedures continue to appear as counselors in growing numbers seize the opportunity to improve or modify their programs. Some modifications are in the interest of saving the counselor's or pastor's time while the quality of counseling is maintained. Some are aimed at raising the quality of the counseling.

Group premarital counseling is an attempt both to save time and to enrich the experience. Providing a series of sessions for groups of five or six couples at a time adds a valuable dimension: couples can discuss their relationships, problems, and questions with peers facing the same experiences. In addition, outside people with particular skills can more easily be involved in the sessions. A doctor can lecture and answer questions regarding sex, a business person can deal with budgets and finances, and a professor or church staff member can share in the area of biblical interpretation.

The utilization of other people is another current trend. While this procedure sometimes is related only to group sessions, it need not be. The

> Even though premarital counseling is beneficial, there is one type of marital training that outshines it: post-marital sessions.

pastor may enlist the cooperation of a trusted physician in order to integrate his session on sexuality with his or her own. The same can be done for other areas of expertise, such as finances. Having an engaged couple interact with a well-adjusted married couple of the congregation during the sessions can also add a dimension: after the young couple's marriage, when they need support or information, they can consult with the other couple that was in the sessions.

A new and growing trend is the use of audio-visual communication. I know of pastors who are videotaping some of their lectures, requiring the couples to view and listen to them in the church library as part of the assignment package. Though the video cassette offers a lecture only, it does provide a background for ample discussion in the couple's face-to-face sessions with the pastor. It also gives some assurance of information input for those not inclined to read.

Post-Marital Sessions

Even though premarital counseling is beneficial enough to make it a wise investment of a pastor's time, studies show there is one type of marital training that outshines it: post-marital sessions. A major four-year study completed at the University of Toronto tested this assertion. Two dynamic programs were provided for a group of couples, one premarital and the other six months after the wedding. The couples involved in the study were individually interviewed three times: before the wedding, six months later, and one year later. While it was found that the premarital program did provide some help, it was the program offered six months later that was really effective.[17] It seemed to take couples six months of marriage to see themselves in realistic terms and be ready for help. Most conceded they needed help before the wedding but that their idealistic attitude prevented them from receiving it.

This suggests that the first year of marriage is the most likely time to help a couple build their relationship. In fact, the time is critical since research shows that during that first year, patterns in the relationship are formed that continue year after year. Helping couples adjust during their first twelve months may be the most crucial thing anyone can do for them. Some carefully planned post-marital sessions provide a context for doing just that.

Prior to the wedding, some post-marital sessions should be scheduled, usually one six months, and another one year, after the wedding. In a large church, where a number of weddings may have occurred at the same time, it might be well to have some group sessions at these times as well. One pastor calls these the "Ten-Thousand Mile" and "Thirty-Thousand Mile" check-ups. However, meeting informally with the couple alone sometime after the wedding is powerfully effective. The key to their success is the kind of relationship the counselor forms with the couple before the wedding. If it is warm and genuine, it will build the kind of trust and confidence that will persuade a couple to commit themselves to post-wedding sessions.

The method for these sessions is relatively simple, since they are not intended to be lectures or discussions of any previously determined content. Rather the strength of the sessions comes from their being an evaluation and discussion of what has taken place during their months of initial marital relationship. The interaction can be easily facilitated by having each of them fill out a form or take a test. *Prepare/Enrich*, having been used during the pre-marital sessions, can be taken again. Test results after the marriage can be compared with those taken before to locate and affirm their strengths and to ferret out and deal with the difficulties.

CONCLUSION

In our complex society people are not always properly prepared for marriage. Broken homes and inadequate parent models often leave individuals without any guidelines or skills for making the right decision concerning marriage or for adjusting after marriage. People spend years preparing for a vocation and sometimes hundreds of hours preparing for an athletic contest; four or five sessions along with study seems little to demand as preparation for such an important and valuable relationship as marriage. Premarital education makes sense.

SUGGESTED RESOURCES

Besides the *Taylor-Johnson Temperament Analysis* and the *Prepare Enrich* inventory mentioned in this chapter, there are some other helps for premarital education, as follows. Also consult resources on marriage at the end of chapter 19.

Eyrich, Howard. *Three to Get Ready*. Grand Rapids: Baker, 1991. •An explanation of the content and methodology of premarital learning sessions.

Fryling, Robert, and Alice Fryling. *Handbook for Engaged Couples*. Downers Grove, Ill.: InterVarsity Press, 1978. •Guidebook for Bible study and thinking about marriage; especially good for more educated Christians.

Muzzy, Ruth, and R. Kent Hughes. *The Christian Wedding Planner*. Wheaton, Ill.: Tyndale House, 1991. •Thorough and practical advice, full of specifics from why to have a "Christian wedding service" to how to make "the garter."

Wheat, Ed, and Gaye Wheat. *Intended for Pleasure*. Old Tappan, N.J.: Fleming H. Revell, 1981. •The best basic first sex manual for couples.

Wright, Norman. *Premarital Counseling.* Chicago: Moody Press, 1977. ● A solid approach.
Wright, Norman, and Wes Roberts. *Before You Say I Do: Study Manual.* Eugene, Oreg.: Harvest House, 1978. ● A choice workbook with Bible study as well as communication and relational exercises.

NOTES

1. Some parts of this chapter are adapted from Charles Sell, *Transitions Through Adult Life* (Grand Rapids: Zondervan, 1991), 61–72.

2. "Preparing Young People for Christian Marriage," in *Adult Education in the Church,* ed. Roy Zuck and Gene A. Getz (Chicago: Moody Press, 1970), 279.

3. These stages and goals follow class notes from the course "The Christian Home," by Howard Hendricks, Dallas Theological Seminary. The courtship process and steps are described in numerous texts on marriage and family such as David Knox, *Choices in Relationships: An Introduction to Marriage and the Family,* 2d ed. (New York: West Publishing, 1990).

4. Knox, *Choices in Relationships,* 200.

5. Howard Hendricks, "Practical Process of Premarital Counseling," transcript of cassette, (Dallas).

6. H. Norman Wright, *Premarital Counseling* (Chicago: Moody Press, 1977), 40.

7. Carl Ridley et al., "Conflict Management: A Premarital Training Program in Mutual Problem Solving," *American Journal of Family Therapy* 9:4 (1981): 23–32.

8. Dennis A. Bagarozzi et al. "Premarital Education and Training Sequence (PETS): A 3-Year Follow-up of an Experimental Study," *Journal of Counseling and Development* 63:2 (1984): 91–100.

9. Michael Klassen, "Counseling for Quality: Some Considerations for Premarital Counseling in the Church," *Journal of Pastoral Counseling* 17:1 (Spring/Summer 1983): 73–80.

10. Ibid., 73–80.

11. Kenneth R. Mitchell and Herbert Anderson, "You Must Leave Before You Can Cleave: A Family Systems Approach to Premarital Pastoral Work," *Pastoral Psychology* 30:1 (Winter 1981): 71–78. See also an excellent book by John Patton and Brian H. Childs, *Christian Marriage and Family: Caring for Our Generations* (New York: Abingdon, 1988), for a family systems perspective on pastoral premarital counseling.

12. R. Spainier and G. Lewis, "Theorizing About the Quality and Stability of Marriage," in *Contemporary Theories About the Family: Research-Based Theories,* eds. Wesley R. Burr et al., 1 (New York: Free Press, 1979).

13. Available from Prepare/Enrich, P.O. Box 190, Minneapolis, MN 55458-0190. Phone (800) 331-1661.

14. Wright, *Premarital Counseling,* 41.

15. Aaron Rutledge, *Premarital Counseling* (Cambridge, Mass.: Schenkman, 1966), 22.

16. Wright, *Premarital Counseling,* 28.

17. Edward Bader's research done at the University of Toronto, reported in an unpublished paper by David Mace, "How Effective Is Premarital Counseling?": 2.

19 Marriage Education Themes

There are scores of novel marriage-enrichment seminars, secular and religious, available today. They all have a common goal—to enrich the marriage and, through it, the family experience. And they often make a mark, even on couples who have been together a long time. Results are expressed in comments like these: "This is the first time in twenty-three years of marriage that my husband has opened up to me,"[1] and "Since that weekend we have felt closer to each other and to God than we have at any time in all the thirty-one years of our marriage."[2]

THE ISSUE OF TOPICS FOR MARRIAGE ENRICHMENT

Marriage enrichment seeks to impart the basic truths and skills. Experts aren't agreed on exactly what these should be. For many years, training in communication has had center stage. However, a follow-up study of couples taking part in enrichment programs confirms that a good marriage requires more than good communication. A Relationship Enhancement Program, which aided couples in many other areas of marital life, proved much more effective in immediate and long-term effects than the Minnesota Couple Communication Program, which stressed communication skills.[3]

The subjects that are described in this chapter are based on the theology and theory of this book's part 2. The guiding force will be a Christian view of marriage; the emphasis will be on developing the expressive side of marriage. In the next chapter, I will sketch in detail

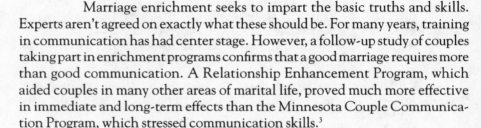

The guiding force in marriage enrichment will be a Christian view of marriage; the emphasis will be on developing the expressive side of marriage.

some creative methods for marriage enrichment programs as well as guidelines for administering them. Taken together, these two chapters should enable any pastor or teacher to conduct an effective, ten-week course or weekend seminar.

Topics for Marriage Enrichment

Building on Commitment

Teaching about commitment is essential since it is the foundation on which marriages are built. First, couples should study the nature of marriage as a personal contract as described earlier in part 2. Then they can be helped to see the practical implications that arise from this truth. They will need to understand that they cannot build a marriage on feelings. Feelings often drive couples into marriage; if the feeling leaves, the basis for their union is shaken. Maintaining a romantic relationship is a goal of marriage, but by itself is not a solid foundation.

Commitment calls for being realistic; romantic love is idealistic. "I married an ideal, I got an ordeal, and I want a new deal," said one woman to her divorce attorney. Part of the cause of the ordeal was the ideals she brought into marriage. People emotionally in love see things through the proverbial "rose-colored glasses," overlooking, or at least underestimating, their partners' faults and differences. As someone once said, "In engagement we sleep, in marriage we awake." We must learn to accept our partners for what they are, not what we supposed they were.

> Teaching about commitment is essential since it is the foundation on which marriages are built. Commitment calls for being realistic; romantic love is idealistic.

Understanding the biblical concept of commitment fosters this acceptance, beautifully described by Gibson Winter:

> Acceptance in marriage is the power to love someone and receive him in the very moment that we realize how far he falls short of our hopes. It is love between two people who see clearly that they do not measure up to one another's dreams. Acceptance is loving the real person to whom one is married. Acceptance is giving up dreams for reality.[4]

Another difference between commitment and romantic love is this: commitment provides stability while romantic love does not. By its nature, romantic love is a fluctuating feeling. It fades, only to return later, then to wane again. "I hate you for what you did today," the wife's note said. "Love, Jane." It's the "love" in "Love, Jane" that embodies the sacrificial, committed side of love that enables couples to cope with the whimsical day-to-day emotions they have for one another.

Romance may bring a couple to marriage, but it is commitment that keeps them together. Couples who think feeling is the foundation of their relationship often panic when it begins to fade. Instead, they need to see that they must build their feelings on their commitment and not base their commitment on their feelings.

Playing Marital Roles

The balanced tenor of biblical data and the confusing tone of contemporary life suggest we should avoid two extremes when teaching about roles. We would do well to resist making too little of roles, including the temptation to be silent because of possible controversy. Role guidelines, stated generally in

Scripture, can provide stability even though their application in modern society is not always immediately clear. We will continue to need realistic dialogue between individuals and couples to satisfactorily work out the biblical arrangements today.

Along with the biblical issues, a number of practical issues will also have to be faced. Caution should make us place strong emphasis on the husband's duty to love his wife as Christ loved the church. Otherwise, women will be oppressed by men who see headship as a right to dominate. Research seems to show that wife abusers tend to harbor this attitude. Egalitarians claim that the way to combat this is by denying the leadership role to the husbands. Traditionalists insist that we properly define the husband's leadership as a responsibility, not a privilege, and that it is to be exercised unselfishly, in love.

Related to the issue of the oppression of women is that of codependency. Women more often than men assume the role of enablers. Nine out of ten women with alcoholic husbands stay with them; only one out of ten men, however, stay with their alcoholic wives. This difference may be caused by the fact that women, assuming the submissive role, take it upon themselves to help their husband needlessly, to his detriment as well as hers and the children's.

We might be careful not to overstate the place of traditional roles in a successful marriage. Family members are to relate to one another as persons, not as parts in an organization.

Whatever theory of roles a couple adopts, they will probably need some help in determining how to work it out on a practical day-to-day basis. I have used agree-disagree statements to help them decide how each will function. Or else lists of duties and obligations can prompt them to work through their respective job descriptions and attitudes. Issues revolve around: providing, shopping, doing housework, caring for the children, planning meals, doing long-range planning, managing finances, handling conflict, making joint decisions, etc.

We might also be careful not to overstate the place of traditional roles in a successful marriage. To suggest that legalistic compliance with a specific gender role in marriage is the final answer to all family adjustments and conflicts is unbiblical and too simplistic. Family members are to relate to one another as persons, not as parts in an organization. Patience, understanding, forbearance, unselfishness—these are to be the final words in family relationships. The bottom line of the New Testament is love, not compliance (1 Cor. 12:31–14:1).

Not much research has been conducted to compare the success of traditional over egalitarian marriages. Some have suggested that there is a higher divorce rate among those couples who both pursue their careers in an egalitarian way. Yet research done by others doesn't confirm that either the traditional or egalitarian practice determines marital success. Both seemed to work well as long as both spouses liked it that way.[5]

Sharing Feelings

The sharing of inner feelings is essential to good communication as well as to in-depth intimacy, two of the major ingredients of marriage. Vulnerability, openness, and transparency are terms used to describe this willingness to self-disclose. Because there are a variety of concepts related to these terms, self disclosure needs careful definition. Equating it with psychological nakedness is a mistake; honesty does not require our sharing every thought or feeling or secret about ourselves. A good guideline for what we should say is suggested by the apostle Paul. We should ask ourselves whether or not it will build "others up according to their needs" (Eph. 4:29). Lawrence Crabb wisely advises husbands and wives to sometimes keep their feelings to themselves:

> Self-disclosure also should not be confused with impulsiveness. To be honest and authentic does not require saying everything we think or feel.

> If we asked people to define an intimate relationship, most in our feeling-oriented culture would suggest that an intimate relationship is one in which they can share everything they feel. . . . There are times in relationships built around mutual ministry in which one partner will choose *not* to share certain feelings . . . because holding in his feelings furthers the purposes of God. . . . A depressed husband should simply push his depression on the back burner when his wife is boiling from the pressure of three kids and a dirty house.[6]

Self-disclosure also should not be confused with impulsiveness. Couples must avoid quickly blurting out whatever they feel, going from the lung to the tongue. To be honest and authentic does not require saying everything we think or feel.

Scripture encourages true self-disclosure. Paul commands believers to be "speaking the truth in love," and to "put off falsehood" (Eph. 4:15, 25). Sharing one's true feelings plays many roles in a marriage. Self-disclosure is essential to solving conflicts between people since so much of what has to be dealt with lies below the surface of ourselves, in our feelings and inner thoughts.

Self-disclosure is a crucial means of being intimate. The marital intimacy described in the Song of Songs is replete with expressions of feelings and self-disclosure. "You have stolen my heart with one glance of your eyes," he says of his beloved (4:9). Sometimes, feelings are described in similes or metaphors, a regular practice of people in ancient times. Describing his lover's hair as "a flock of goats descending from Mount Gilead" may be a way of saying how he feels when he looks at her. By this comparison, he tells her he feels refreshed and restful, similar to how he feels when looking at the flock of goats at the end of a day.

Self-disclosure is also a profound expression of love, since the essence of love is giving and receiving. What is more loving than entrusting and accepting the most personal gift a person has to offer or receive, the inner self.

Understanding

Honest talk is half the process of communicating; good listening is the other. Understanding each other is essential. "Be considerate as you live with your wives," wrote the apostle Peter (1 Peter 3:7). Other texts stress the importance of sympathy and empathy. "Be sympathetic, love as brothers, be compassionate and humble" (1 Peter 3:8). James seems to suggest that listening is an alternative to too much talking or anger (James 1:19). The book of Proverbs claims that it's foolish not to listen. "A fool finds no pleasure in understanding but delights in airing his own opinions" (Prov. 18:2). Understanding requires patiently listening to a person until they have expressed themselves fully. It involves grasping what is being felt as well as said and then conveying to the speaker that you have heard. There's a great deal of love, concern, and affirmation expressed in the phrase, "Oh, I hear you," when it is actually true.

Communication experts usually suggest three steps to improving a person's ability to understand others. First, deal with the difficulties they have in understanding each other. Couples in my marriage seminars usually list the following when I ask them about difficulties: failure to listen; different backgrounds that make them and their messages confusing; being too busy to take time to understand; anger that makes them unwilling to understand; differences between men and women in how they think and how they perceive things; talking instead of listening; pride that makes them feel the other person is not worth understanding; thinking they already know what the other person is thinking when they really don't; being afraid to really understand because it will hurt them or because they may have to do something about it; impatience; indifference; and self-centeredness.

> Honest talk is half the process of communicating; good listening is the other.

Bringing to light these barriers can help couples become aware of their own problems and cope with them. It can also help them see that understanding isn't easy for any couple and that to achieve it will take some effort.

Second, each partner should be asked to come to grips with any bad listening habits he or she might have. Many people have learned what the experts call "non-listening": responses that keep them from hearing what someone is saying. Any number of these could be deeply entrenched in a person's behavior: always changing the subject; thinking of what to say in response; mind wandering; always making jokes; giving an opinion instead of listening to the whole story; making quick judgments; fidgeting with things; not looking directly at the speaker; etc. Often, these habits are practiced unconsciously. Once persons become aware of them, they must make the effort to break them. Step three will help them do that because it will give them some specific things to put in their place.

The third step involves teaching couples good listening responses. The good listener listens with his body and his mouth as well as his ears. Proper posture involves leaning forward and looking at the person who is talking, giving clues that the person has your attention. Responses from the mouth may simply be nonverbal sounds like *umm*, *ahh*, *hmm*, and *oh*, that signal that you are tracking what is being said. Then the good listener asks questions to probe deeper and explore alternatives and issues. Giving opinions, sharing ideas, and making judgments are also appropriate as long as they aren't offered when a person doesn't really want them. Sometimes a man or woman merely need to be heard, not answered.

A technique for good listening that seems to be universally accepted by those in the field of communication is paraphrasing. Sometimes called *reflective listening,* it involves repeating, in your own words, what has just been said to you. For example, a husband, driving home from a visit with his mother-in-law, says to his wife, "Sometimes I get so upset by the subtle criticisms of me in what your mother says." To paraphrase this the wife would say something like, "You mean you get angry when you feel my mom tries to put you down without coming right out and saying so." Such reflective listening contributes a great deal to the process of communication. First, the wife will show she understands. Otherwise, her immediate response might have been to give her opinion or defend her mother by denying what he is saying without really showing that she fully understood. Secondly, she will have given her husband a chance to release some of his anger by talking about it. After her statement he is then free to say more about his emotions if he chooses to, and his wife may offer her opinion. Paraphrasing is not equal to agreeing. It is a technique to employ when someone merely wants to be listened to or else has something very important or even complicated to get across.

Handling Conflict

Conflict results from building oneness out of two. It is to be expected and is not always the result of sin. Marriage is like two individual streams of water cascading gleefully down the mountainside, now joining in a frenzied, noisy, bubbling, swirling current. Conflict can be avoided by the two persons withdrawing

> **Conflict can be avoided by the two persons withdrawing from each other, but it cannot be successfully solved that way.**

from each other, but it cannot be successfully solved that way. And the closer the two get, the more potential there is for conflict.

Someone has said marriage is like two porcupines sleeping together. In fact, communication is relatively easy when there is little conflict. For this reason engaged couples are lulled into thinking they have no communication problems. But the true test of communicating is exercising it when in conflict. Resolving the conflicts openly will deepen the relationship. Leaving them unresolved or using manipulative maneuvers only separate people.

Conflict management will require some restraint. Avoid the negative ways of handling conflicts. Instead of facing the issue at hand, many couples allow nagging, blaming, and criticizing to become habitual. Public sarcasm and joking often result from inner feelings about undiscussed conflicts. Instead of using these methods, Jesus calls for open confrontation between Christians in such situations. "Go and show him his fault, just between the two of you," he urges (Matt. 18:15). Obstacles within the relationship should be discussed with sensitivity and openness. Since we would rather "flee than fight," according to Erich Fromm, open discussion is not easily achieved.

Once discussion takes place, the couple will discover that there are a number of options for solving the issue. Sometimes one person submits to the other. But not always. At times, acceptance of bothersome behavior will be the final decision. Tolerance and forbearance sometimes have to be substituted for the other's changing the habit or personality trait. Sometimes the couple can compromise in a fashion that shows mutual respect.

Dealing with "Hard-to-Handle Feelings"

If we flee from conflict we may ignore feelings of hostility. Yet a negative surge of feeling that is built up through months and years may finally create a relational explosion. The sensible approach to a problem is to recognize that it may arouse various "hard-to-handle feelings"—anger, jealousy, bitterness and the like. Admitting to ourselves and to our spouse or children is the place to start. But, it is precisely at this point many of us fail.

In the name of being a good Christian or a good spouse, we can easily deny that we really are angry or jealous. "Good wives don't get jealous," the Christian woman says to herself. This denial can lead to repression, whereby the feeling may build up in the subconscious. Repressed, unrecognized, unresolved anger results in millions of marital fights—and thousands of murders—each year.

The honest, confessional spirit of the New Testament forbids our fooling ourselves about ourselves. When angry or jealous, a Christian, above all, should be able to face himself and admit that whatever is going on inside him is really there. Once the feeling is recognized, he should seek to analyze it to identify its nature and to uncover its cause. Not being used to doing this, many of us will find this difficult to do.

It's tough at times to know whether one is angry, jealous, or just disappointed. But to know the exact feelings in a certain situation may be very important. If a wife refused her husband's sexual advances, it will be crucial both to him and her to know what he is feeling at the moment. This search for one's feelings is not a surrender to them. It's just the opposite. Ignoring one's feelings may be the easiest way to succumb to their influence.

The recognition of a particular feeling will make possible the next step—control. In part, the New Testament answer to hostile feelings is the control of the indwelling Holy Spirit (Eph. 4:30–31). There are times when he will keep the feeling from occurring; but apparently he also works to control the negative actions, even though the hostility is not curbed. Thus Paul says, "In your anger do not sin" (Eph. 4:26).

> It's tough at times to know whether one is angry, jealous, or just disappointed. But to know the exact feelings in a certain situation may be very important.

The third step is crucial: verbalizing feelings. Admitting feelings honestly to one's partner as well as to himself or herself is a healthy route to dealing with both the feeling and whatever caused it. Once this is done, they can work together on managing the feeling and solving the problem. When my wife said recently, "Chuck, I'm angry with you," I actually responded with excitement: "That's wonderful, let's sit down and discuss it." For us, this directness was a sign of the maturing of our relationship.

Marital Sex

Following our theological cues, we will teach that the couple's sexual relationship is more than physical since human encounter is not the same as sexual encounter. The entanglement of bodies without the intermingling of souls constitutes the major misuse of sex. Sex between strangers betrays the true meaning of sex.

Psychologically speaking, sex is a medium; it cannot be reduced to mere pleasure or passion. The human being is capable of giving meaning to sexual expression. It can be a vehicle for human emotions and intentions. A man, for example, can express anger and dominance by acts of violent sex.[7]

One psychologist declares exactly what we have stated theologically: "The search for meaning is central to our understanding of the role of sexuality in our existence."[8] Because of this, I have discovered that the best way to deal with the topic of marital sex is to draw inferences from the purposes of sex drawn from Scripture. These purposes are as follows:

Procreating

Sex derives a great deal of its significance from its purpose of bearing children. That God creates persons in his own image through the sensual act of intercourse ought, first of all, to condone sex as something good. "Sex is okay," Billy Graham has said. "Without it, none of us would be here."

Also, the fact that sex is related to childbearing should remind us that it is a biological—that is, a physical—process. On the sixth day, I like to explain, "God created hormones." Couples need to be warned about how their physical condition affect a person's love life. For example, there are physical causes of impotency, including poor blood circulation, that can be treated by medicine or surgery. A man or woman's desire for sex can be curbed by certain medicines, sickness or chronic illnesses. It's not fair to simply say to a spouse: "You don't want me, therefore you don't love me." When there are sexual problems, a couple might well face them first by consulting a physician.

Achieving Intimacy

Becoming one flesh in the sexual embrace is a powerful form of communication, as Elton and Pauline Trueblood described so well:

> One of the most significant things to say about sexual intercourse is that it provides husbands and wives with a language which cannot be matched by words or by any other act whatsoever. Love needs language for its adequate expressions and sex has its own syntax.[9]

Couples will be advised to ask themselves what they are communicating. A positive experience can contain all sorts of nonverbal messages: "I love you; I need you; I like you; I enjoy revealing myself to you; I thrill over your revealing yourself to me; I like all of you." Sex, when less than satisfying, will contain a negative message, even when unintended: "I don't like you; I don't respect you; I take you for granted; I think you are strange." Out of the sexual experience either a poisonous brew of ill feeling or a refreshing stream of new life can flow steadily into the marital reservoir. Improving the couple's sex life will enrich their intimate life.

Fostering Identity

A good sex life in marriage will also fortify a person's identity. That our being male or female is a significant part of our personal identity is confirmed in the first two chapters of Genesis. Gender is not the most important aspect of our sense of self; being a child of God is. Yet within marriage, the way we relate as man and woman will enhance or weaken our sense of who we are. Healthy sexual interaction will help us feel good about being a man or a woman.

Married persons should be urged to maintain an unconditional acceptance of each other's different outlooks, likes and dislikes in the area of sex and gender. Rejecting harshly what a partner may want to initiate in foreplay or during intercourse may hurt him or her deeply. Also, jokes, criticisms, and sarcastic remarks about the opposite sex can make the partner feel badly about himself or herself.

Asserting one's own sexuality is another way to strengthen each other's personal identity. Being assertive, a characteristic commonly associated with men, may make his wife feel more "womanly"; the opposite is also true. Couples should seek to learn what their partners think being a man or woman means. Then they each, as far as possible, should try to be that. Because men often focus on the physical aspects of sex, a wife may need to learn to be a more erotic and playful sex partner. Women, on the other hand, often look for companionship through sex. To be manly in her terms, a man needs to be tender, intimate, and romantic.

Giving Pleasure

Since pleasure is one of the purposes of sex, couples can be taught to maintain their enjoyment in a number of ways. Boredom can be avoided and excitement stimulated by changing the surroundings. Periodic weekends away, as well as different occasions or places at home, can enhance the variety. Variety in technique will also prevent the expression of sex from becoming matter-of-fact. In sex manuals, like the ones listed at the end of this chapter, Christian authors confirm the rightness of agreed-upon variations in marital sex that are not harmful, such as mutual fondling and oral-genital expression. Having diversity in the total set of circumstances can also be rewarding: reading love poems or listen to music, for example.

Preventing Immorality

A good sex life in marriage plays a part in helping partners maintain their sexual purity. Therefore, they should offer themselves freely to one another. Sex is not a favor to withhold, a weapon to dominate, or a reward for good behavior. When partners have different sexual desires, it can be quite difficult for the one with the greater appetite. Couples with an imbalance can manage their differences in loving accommodation, the nonaroused one providing release for the other from time to time in various ways.

Developing Romance

Cultivating the romantic side of marriage can be a major means of enriching it. Our theology calls for married couples' loving each other with feeling. And those who do, tend to have more satisfying marriages and are deliriously content with their spouses.

A common myth is that romantic love diminishes as the years of marriage increase, according to prominent sociologist, Andrew Greeley. Yet he claims studies show that many couples keep it alive.[10] Foremost, we need to teach the theology behind this and help couples see romance as a possibility.

Those that will be able to do so will need to know what romance is. First, we should try to explain that being romantic includes more than creating peak, sensational moments. Couples too often limit romance to going out to dinner, or going off to a motel for a weekend. In his fine book on romance, H. Norman Wright

> Couples need to understand that romance doesn't just happen; they make it happen—in marriage, we "make love."

reminds us that there are many daily expressions of romance through meeting needs, being tender, being sensitive and thoughtful toward one another.[11] A husband once told me that one of the most romantic things he can do is to help his wife with cooking.

Secondly, we can break down the facets of romance and make suggestions for making those things happen. A description of romantic love is given in Part Two of this book. It is based on the idea that our concepts and feelings of romance spring from the experience of falling in love, which can be broken down into various components. A couple can provoke these feelings by activities that recreate some of these. They can, for example, pamper each other, which is something new lovers do (serve a husband breakfast in bed, or draw a bubble bath for a wife and take care of the kids while she enjoys it). They can create: *surprise* (calling a wife on Tuesday to ask for a date for Saturday without telling her where they're going, or a wife's greeting her husband in the evening dressed seductively with a surprise party planned for just the two of them, or abandoned sexual experimentation); *intimacy* (writing love notes, going off to a hotel for a weekend together, slowly undressing one another or showering together); *unselfish giving* (doing a partner's chore for them, giving a gift when there is no special occasion); *enjoyment in just being together* (taking a walk in the rain, watching a sunset, playing a game); *being idealistic* (seeing the best in a partner and affirming him or her, dreaming together of the future, being ecstatic about the possibilities of marriage).

Specific suggestions can enable couples to understand that romance doesn't just happen; they make it happen—in marriage, we "make love."

Planning

Christian psychologist Jack Pease maintains that planning is the major route to Christian growth. This is particularly true in the area of family life, where it may be used least. A prominent feature of his family-life course is that it includes several sessions on how to plan. He suggests that couples have a weekend together away from home several times a year.

The skills used in good planning are basic to business administration. After evaluation, the husband and wife determine their objectives, then seek means to put these into their routine schedule. In addition, they plan ahead of time for special events like conferences, study programs, vacations, etc. Monthly and weekly planning sessions will also be necessary in order to put principles of Scripture into practice. Otherwise, strong family-life teaching can produce an unbearable guilt; or else the teaching prompts people to reject suggestions as being idealistic and unworkable.

Managing Finances

Larry Burkett states that in over 70 percent of the marriages that fail, the primary symptom of failure is finances.[12] This is overstatement, perhaps, but counselors agree that in our credit-ridden and materialistic economy the love of money is indeed the root of much marital evil. A nationwide survey disclosed that when it comes to the cause of fighting between husbands and wives, nothing else even comes close to money. It may not be enough to preach and teach Christian values if our Christian education programs do not help people relate those values to practical financial matters. We Christians need faith to give some of our income to God but wisdom to know how to handle the rest. This wisdom includes analyzing one's spending habits and discovering the basic problem behind the symptom of failure in the handling of money; sometimes the problem is ignorance in budgeting, at other times it is sheer covetousness.

> Planning is the major route to Christian growth. This is particularly true in the area of family life, where it may be used least.

Couples should be helped to explore and deal with the psychological reasons behind their spending patterns. Personal inadequacies often cause financial difficulties. The financial troubles are like the top layer of the "ball of wax" we've gotten into. Underneath the top layer may be greed. Strip away the layer of greed and another problem is likely to show up. For example, wanting too much can be caused by a lack of self-esteem. A person wraps things around himself to cover his inferiority complex.

Dr. Raymond Pendleton, a clinical psychologist, observes that different people have different reasons for spending more money than they have. Emotional causes rank high. "Impulsivity is one reason," he explains. "People think, 'If I don't grab everything now, I'm going to lose it.'" Plus, "There is tremendous pressure in our society to be like everyone else. This means buying a new car, new clothes, going out to eat three times a week. Once the personal problems cause the financial ones, the financial struggle stretches the relationship to the breaking point."[13]

> Good analysis will uncover the one who has the problem. "Owning another's problem" is as wrong as it is frustrating.

Many of these financial problems can be averted by teaching couples skills of money management, including determining their financial needs, planning financial goals, and budgeting.

Handling Problems and Crises

Somehow problems and crises hit us on the blind side. Life seems to bring those for which we are least prepared. We feel this way because we can never be fully prepared for novel experiences. But family-life education can provide some preventive education, along with remedial counseling and support when they are necessary. Scripture can be brought to bear on life's crises in the regular Christian education program. In addition, special teaching and training can be offered in preparing family members to face death, accidents, divorce, and other crises.

Inability to handle problems causes severe stress. Too often the Christian family delays action, hoping the problem will dissolve itself. Even prayer can become a form of delay and denial, a substitute for needed action. First of all, then, families need to be encouraged to face the problem or crisis head-on. Emotionally stunned, the immature person spends precious time asking, "How could this happen to me?" instead of asking, "How can I handle it?" Guilt also worms its way in with an insidious inner voice saying, "This shouldn't have happened to me." The temptation to deny the existence of a problem instead of admitting to its reality is destructively forceful, lulling a person into inactivity when activity is most needed.

Analysis of the problem should include not only seeking its cause but also its present consequences. Fallout from the problem affects different family members in different ways. Measures are needed to deal with the way a death or birth is affecting each family member, including the children. Good analysis will also uncover the one who has the problem. "Owning another's problem" is as wrong as it is frustrating. A wife needs to know that she cannot force her husband to quit drinking, and that her efforts to do this will fail. It is his problem. Parents should not accept for themselves the child's struggle with math. Both youth and adults are often only too happy to give the responsibility for solving their problems to someone else. That is part of the difficulty. People must help the problem bearer to see that the challenge to solve the problem belongs to him or her. Once that is established, other people can offer help when it is asked for and give support when it is needed. Parents of young children, for example, can create conditions for the child's success in math, but the parents cannot succeed for the child. Intense emotional outbursts and inner disappointment accompany any attempt to own someone else's problem.

Having analyzed the problem, the individual can be encouraged to see possible solutions. This calls for creative thinking. A course of action can be prayerfully chosen and attempted. Though trusting God in the situation, the individual is still prepared for the possible failure of his approach, knowing that the Lord will enable him to discover other solutions. He knows he must not be afraid to fail. Praise and thanksgiving to God will follow success, with the knowledge that it is He who saves us from all troubles (Ps. 34:6).

Fostering Spiritual Oneness

Experience confirms that how couples relate spiritually plays a major role in their marriage. Concluding his analysis of a broad-based national survey of marriages, Andrew Greeley writes: "According to our respondents, 32

> Given our theological basis for spiritual oneness in marriage, helping couples achieve it should be a major goal of our marriage-enrichment sessions.

percent of American husbands and wives pray together often. Whether they pray often together or not is a very powerful correlate of marital happiness, the most powerful we have yet discovered."[14] This obviously does not mean that simply praying together will make a happy marriage since the study does not prove that the former causes the latter. Nor does it mean that couples who have no religious compatibility cannot have a good marriage. Scripture urges people who are married to non-Christians to remain with them (1 Cor. 7:12–14). They can work at making their marriages strong in areas apart from the spiritual.

Yet, given our theological basis for spiritual oneness in marriage, helping couples achieve it should be a major goal of our marriage-enrichment sessions. Besides urging couples to make this a priority, I ask them to work at overcoming what prevents them from doing spiritual things together. Usually, they cite busyness or fatigue. But they should consider other matters. Many of them just don't know exactly how to relate spiritually.

They can be given guidelines and specific suggestions, such as taking advantage of informal times to be spiritually linked; for example, pausing to praise God after watching a brilliant sunset or after hearing good news. Much more could be included here, but I will not go further here since what is contained in chapter 23 on the family's spiritual life is applicable to couples.

CONCLUSION

The topics explored in this chapter deal with the must crucial areas of marriage life and are suitable for all couples. Though fundamental to any marriage, they are not the only topics for a church's marriage education curriculum. Programs that include other themes will be needed to address the many types of marital situations. Courses, with appropriate topics, could be held for people of different ages. Newly married couples will have issues related to their first year together that differ from those who are in their fortieth. Special workshops could be offered to wives alone or to husbands, working through issues common to their gender. Approaches can also be geared to those who are in their second marriage, who may also be heading a blended family. Couples like these are not always satisfied with a basic, generic marriage seminar. Then, too, there are the couples whose marriages are in trouble. Sometimes they will be willing to attend sessions, as a couple or alone, that confront the issues they are facing. A catalog of such topics might include: Facing Your Childhood Family; Dealing with Addiction in Marriage; Rediscovering Love in Marriage; Dealing with Anger; Building Your Mate's Self-Esteem; etc.

Curriculum materials for all sorts of marriage education ventures are available, many of them listed in the resource section that follows this chapter. Courses and seminars can also be built around one or more of the books cited there.

SUGGESTED RESOURCES

Augsburger, David. *Caring Enough to Confront*. Scottdale, Pa.: Herald Press, 1980. •Best book on the subject.

Beauchamp, Gary, and Donna Beauchamp. *The Religiously Mixed Marriage*. Abilene, Tex.: Quality Publications, 1981. •Practical, sympathetic approach to the subject.

Hendricks, Howard, ed. *Husbands and Wives*. Wheaton, Ill.: Victor Books, 1991. •A large but very worthwhile volume with short articles on scores of marriages subjects by contemporary Christian authors.

Mason, Mike. *The Mystery of Marriage*. Portland, Oreg.: Multnomah Press, 1985. •Delightful in-depth look at marriage.

Penner, Clifford, and Joyce Penner. *The Gift of Sex: A Christian Guide to Sexual Fulfillment*. Waco, Tex.: Word Books, 1982. •A bit gourmet, best for those who have been married a while.

Quigley, Pat. *Making It Through the Night: How Couples Can Survive a Crisis Together*. Berkeley, Calif.: Conari Press, 1992. •An important book in the light of the research that shows how crises tend to divide couples; a psychological approach.

Rosberg, Gary. *Choosing to Love Again: Restoring Broken Relationships*. Colorado Springs: Focus on the Family, 1992. •A book that, dealing with forgiveness and handling conflict in any relationship, will save some marriages.

Rosenau, Douglas. *A Celebration of Sex*. Nashville: Thomas Nelson, 1994. •Frank, specific, and theological, the best sex handbook available.

Smalley, Gary. *Hidden Keys of a Loving, Lasting Marriage*. Grand Rapids: Zondervan, 1988. •A reissue of some of Smalley's previous books, and very practical.

Wright, H. Norman. *Communication: Key to Your Marriage*. Glendale, Calif.: Regal, 1974. •Simply written, with insightful guidelines.

_____ . *Holding On to Romance: Keep Your Marriage Alive and Passionate After the Honeymoon Years Are Over*. Ventura, Calif.: Regal, 1992. •Packed full of specific suggestions.

Wright, H. Norman, and Gary J. Oliver. *How to Change Your Spouse (Without Ruining Your Marriage)*. Ann Arbor, Mich.: Servant Publications, 1994. •A book many people have been waiting for, containing good suggestions.

NOTES

1. Susan Middaugh, "Marriage Encounter: Is It for Everyone?" *Sign* 55, 4 (December 1975/January 1976): 10.

2. Antoinette Bosco, *Marriage Encounter* (St. Meinrad, Ind.: Abbey, 1972), 11.

3. Gregory W. Brock and Harvey Joanning, "A Comparison of the Relationship Enhancement Program and the Minnesota Couple Communication Program," *Journal of Marital and Family Therapy* 9:4 (1983): 413–21.

4. *Love and Conflict*, quoted in Helen Kooiman Hosier, *The Other Side of Divorce* (New York: Hawthorne, 1975), 141.

5. *Prepare/Enrich Newsletter* 4:1 (Winter 1989): 1.

6. "Manipulation or Ministry," *Family Life Education*, ed. Gil Peterson (Glen Ellyn, Ill.: Scripture Press Ministries, 1978): 14.

7. John F. Crosby, *Illusion and Disillusion: The Self in Love and Marriage*, 4th ed. (Belmont, Calif.: Wadsworth, 1985), 189.

8. Ibid., 189.

9. Elton and Pauline Trueblood, *The Recovery of Family Life* (New York: Harper, 1953), 59.

10. Andrew Greeley, *Faithful Attraction* (New York: Tom Doherty Associates, 1991), 122–38.

11. H. Norman Wright, *Holding On to Romance* (Ventura, Calif.: Regal Books, 1992), 35.

12. Larry Burkett, *What Wives Wish Their Husbands Knew About Money* (Wheaton, Ill.: Victor Books, 1979), 6.

13. Quoted in Ann Rogers, "Hard Times," *Eternity* (April 1980): 30.

14. Greeley, *Faithful Attraction*, 189.

20 Marriage Education Programs

The church can use many settings to foster marriage enrichment: a special weekend conference, a retreat, an elective Sunday school class, a weekly small group for couples, or a one day or evening seminar. Often these are led by speakers brought in from outside the local church. Many pastors are conducting these in their own churches or else enlisting knowledgeable laymen from their own congregation. In this chapter, I will describe the goals, methods, and principles for some marriage enrichment sessions. This, along with the data on topics in the last chapter, should enable any gifted teacher to guide couples through some life-changing sessions.

GOALS FOR MARRIAGE ENRICHMENT PROGRAMS

From a Christian point of view one of the foremost goals of marriage education is to teach relevant biblical truths. In addition, we can aim at some of the broad range of goals suggested by specialists in this field. First, programs should be as holistic as possible. By this, they caution that we should not merely focus on the couples, but consider also the individual, the church, the world community, and God. This goal works its way out in too many ways to mention here. But, for example, it demands that we see marriage not just as a sphere of satisfaction to be sought, but as a means of service and influence in the world and for the Lord.

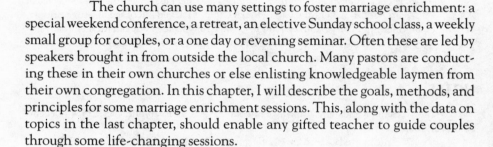

One of the foremost goals of marriage education is to teach relevant biblical truths.

Second, programs should provoke self-understanding. Sessions should be crafted to make persons see realistically themselves and their marriages, since such awareness is essential for change to take place. This requires providing the time and techniques for evaluation and reflection. A third goal is the renewed discovery of one's spouse. Probably the most effective, yet simple, method of achieving this is used in the popular Marriage Encounter retreats. After creating an accepting, loving setting, leaders ask married partners to write long self-revealing notes that they then read to one another. For some couples, the breakthrough into each other's lives is revolutionary.

Finally, helping couples develop their spiritual oneness should be another major objective. They will come to see that loving and communicating are spiritual matters. In addition, through Bible study, worship, and prayer their ability to relate to God together can be enhanced.

METHODS FOR MARRIAGE ENRICHMENT PROGRAMS

Though the methods of achieving these goals will accent personal "discovery," traditional methods are also used. Lectures, films, or videos on various marriage themes are in order and should provide a biblical pattern for guidelines. A lecture on intimacy, for example, can provide a solid basis for a sharing exercise that follows. Second, having one or two "lead" couples share their personal experiences can be a catalyst for sharing between couples and increased awareness of one for the other. The lead couple can explain practical guidelines for developing intimacy as well as share their struggles and experiences. Third, learning methods can include the distribution of brief essays, of chapters from books, of a one-page definition, or other forms of direct content input. Couples can read together or separately and then discuss. Sometimes that discussion can be done in groups. Most distinct and central to marriage enrichment is the fourth methodology—couple-discovery experiences, including tests, exercises, questionnaires, nonverbal interaction, etc.

While the first three of the above methodologies are important, the fourth is crucial for accomplishing the highly personalized goals of the program. And because discovery is the key, discovery techniques are essential.

Sometimes the discovery techniques lead to knowledge: a husband learns about his wife's dreams or ideas of marriage. These techniques usually also facilitate experiencing; for example, the couple learns to experience what it is like to share feelings they had never before expressed verbally. Thus, they will actually experience affirmation, acceptance, sharing, intimacy, and love. In past marriage education we have talked about these, but the new marriage programs emphasize actually experiencing them.

EXPERIMENTAL EXERCISES AND ASSIGNMENTS

Following is an extensive list of recommended possible creative exercises that can be used to get husbands and wives to interact with their partners and work on various aspects of their marriages. From among these it would not be difficult to construct a marriage-enrichment weekend, a ten-week course, or a few evening sessions.

Sharing backgrounds. Those who stress this technique do so on the basis that "knowingness" is important to understanding and accepting. Enjoyable games are used to establish rapport between the couples when group interaction is important to the success of the sessions. Or else couples participate in communication games with each other. Games involve sharing things like a memory from age six, the greatest event that happened in the sixth grade, a religious experience of the teen years, or the time when one felt he or she had become a man or a woman.

Sharing feelings. Sharing of significant meaning and feelings is one of the deepest forms of intimacy. It is the touching of the innermost selves of two human beings that Charlotte and Howard Clinebell maintain is the "foundation of all other forms of intimacy."[1] The leaders of Marriage Encounter prompt this sharing through their "ten-and-ten" approach. For ten minutes the husband and wife individually write an answer to a question. Then for another ten minutes they read their answers and discuss them. The questions in this approach can relate to personal life, such as "When do you feel the most secure?" or to the couple's relationship, such as "When do you feel the most secure in your relationship?" Questions can cover the range of human emotions, such as "How do you feel when you are rejected?" "How do you react when you fail?" and "What feeling is most difficult to talk about?" A list of open-ended statements can prompt openness in sharing feelings.

- I usually handle frustration by . . .
- When I feel rejected, I . . .
- Right now I am feeling . . .
- When I meet new people, I feel . . .
- The situation that makes me feel anxious is . . .
- I need support of others most when I feel . . . (For a more intimate version of this, use this statement: I need your support most when I feel . . .)
- At a social gathering I feel most uncomfortable when . . .
- I feel very comfortable when . . .
- When I am alone, I feel . . .
- When I don't like myself, I feel . . .
- What I am most afraid to talk about is . . .
- The feeling I find most difficult to talk about is . . .
- Right now I feel . . .

Sharing desires and wishes. Ability to tell the other person what one hopes for in the relationship is basic to communication. Yet because of fear of rejection, it is difficult to share one's desires. Unstated wants and needs in a relationship form a divisive dynamic. Based on a systems view of marriage, Bud and Bea Van Eck foster one's "being intentional."[2] If couples do not tell one another what their needs and wants are, they may resort to nonverbal means of expression; those expressions, in turn, are often overlooked or misunderstood by the other partner. Bringing these desires into the open facilitates the function of the marital give-and-take system. To discover their patterns of communication, as well as their needs in this area, the couples can first list five nonverbal behaviors they have observed in their spouses. These behaviors are then shared by a husband or wife with his or her partner by acting them out or by stating them. Then there follows a discussion of the power and the place of these actions in their relationship, as well as of the need or the desire being expressed. After this, each partner can write down and then communicate to the spouse three or four wants.

A simple tool for achieving this is a wish list. Wives and husbands write down what they wish their mates would do and would not do. The latter are told that they are not necessarily bound to comply with their spouse's wishes but that an open and trusting relationship should include such sharing. According to one leader who uses this approach, the wishes are sometimes quite simple: "I wish you would stay at the table until I finish eating" or "I wish you would do more just for yourself."

> If couples do not tell one another what their needs and wants are, they may resort to nonverbal means of expression; those expressions, in turn, are often overlooked or misunderstood by the other partner.

Sharing images of love. Closely related to the sharing of desires is the sharing of forms of love. Often mates are unaware of the way they are saying "I love you" to each other. Their different backgrounds and personalities have endowed them with varying concepts of love's expressions, out of which two things result. One partner may miss the other's signals of love because they are not in his or her terms. For example, he may value gift-giving as a major expression of love, while she may not. Irrelevant expression of love is the other result of partners having different concepts of love's expressions. Not understanding why his message fails to get through, the husband continues to offer his irrelevant expressions while accusing his wife of not understanding how much he loves her.

To share knowledge about ways of expressing love, couples are asked to formulate two lists. The first list is "Five ways I express love to my spouse." The items are numbered according to importance. "Five ways I believe my spouse is saying 'I love you' to me" comprises the second list, the items being numbered according to frequency of occurrence or perceived importance. Ideas are compared and dialogue follows. Knowing each other's concepts can help bring expressions of love into line with each partner's expectations, as well as provide newer appreciation of one another's acts of love.

Sharing ideas about sexuality. The confirming of one's sexual identity, which is basic to marriage, takes two forms—accepting and asserting. He accepts her femininity while asserting his masculinity. She makes him feel like a man by accepting his maleness as well as by asserting her femaleness.

Crucial to such accepting and asserting is one's concept of sexuality. If a husband believes vulnerability is not masculine, he will try to maintain that posture with his wife, rarely revealing any of his weaknesses. This can cause trouble if her concept of maleness involves his sharing areas of weakness where she can help and support. Dissatisfaction is generated because each is accepting and asserting on his or her own terms of masculinity and femininity.

Discussing such terms can help immensely. Formulating and comparing lists is a simple means of getting at this subject. Each is asked to list five concepts of true manhood and five of true womanhood. Comparison of the lists may bring surprises that will merit discussion and change.

Affirming each other. Focusing on positive relationships is usually done early in the enrichment sessions. A "revolving dialogue" is used by Herman Green.[3] Each person is asked to write down what he or she loves about his or her mate in terms of behavior, looks, and being. The "revolving dialogue"

> The modern stress on feelings in the marriage relationship should not be misunderstood as a surrender to emotion. Rather, the opposite is intended. Currents of emotion need to be understood and identified lest they carry us off in the wrong direction.

that follows is an attempt to prompt thorough understanding. The first person makes a statement. The second person either agrees with the impression or clarifies the statement and then expresses his or her feelings about the statement. Couples are encouraged to sit with knee-to-knee, hand-to-hand, and eye-to-eye contact during the exchange.

Affirmation can be centered on events or expectations related to the past, present, or future. Telling each other about the three most meaningful experiences together fosters appreciation of one another. Frequent opportunities for affirmation can be created by open-ended statements, such as "I want to tell you I love you in a very special way because . . ."

Looking at their integration. In order to provide more appreciation for and understanding of their relationship, couples can be encouraged to see the way they look together as a unit. They concentrate on seeing the way they have integrated and what they have become as a couple. This is particularly urged by those who see marriage as a system, the understanding of which creates better functioning. A verbal integration exercise can make a husband and wife think about themselves as a couple. After each person writes down five characteristics about himself or herself, the couples are asked to combine the two sets. Or else they are asked to give a nonverbal expression of their marriage, perhaps by doing a living sculpture or drawing a picture. If these things are done in a group, other couples can react to the sculpture or picture, giving each performing couple knowledge of the way he and she are perceived as a couple.

Evaluating and building trust. Expressions of and feelings of mistrust greatly interfere with closeness. Wayne Oates suggests that trusting is more important to each mate than verbal expressions of love. Healthy couples can be encouraged to explore their trust levels though leaders should be aware of the sensitive nature of this process. A nonverbal expression, "the trust walk," has been used for many years with groups and couples. A blindfolded person is led by his partner on a five-minute walk. The roles are then reversed for another walk. Afterward, the spouses discuss (1) when each trusts the other and why; (2) when one of them mistrusts the other and why; and (3) what each can do to improve the feeling and expressions of trust. Or else trust can be explored through a series of statements. For example:

- I feel you trust me most when . . .
- I feel you trust me least when . . .
- When you trust me, I feel . . .
- Whenever I think you don't trust me, I feel . . .
- Some reasons behind our mistrust are . . .
- You communicate mistrust by . . .
- I think I can improve your trust of me by . . .
- I think you can improve my trust of you by . . .

Evaluating and understanding intimacy. Besides biblical exposition related to intimacy, couples can be helped to think about ideals in this area through dialogue. The Clinebells dimensions of intimacy can be distributed as a guide to the couples' discussion. These authors describe the following as constituting the many strings of the instrument of intimacy: sexual intimacy, emotional intimacy, intellectual intimacy, aesthetic intimacy, creative intimacy, work intimacy, crisis intimacy, commitment intimacy, and spiritual intimacy.[4]

Sharing negative feelings. A backlog of undiscussed conflicts and ill feelings, the proverbial sleeping dogs, destroys intimacy. Carefully developed maneuvers and manipulation replace honesty and understanding. Skills related to verbalizing hostile feelings can be taught. After the leader explains that negative feelings should be stated accurately by the mate while he or she is in control, and without judgment, couples are asked to identify from a list accurate statements of feeling. For example:

- I feel bad when you tear me apart like that.
- I feel you are always putting me down.
- You have all the right answers, don't you?
- Well, I'm sorry I'm not a superperson, too.
- I feel rejected when you say that.

The last expression is the best since it is an honest expression of one's feeling without putting the other person on the defensive. None of the expressions but the first and the last even state what the feeling is; the rest are judgmental remarks that arise from the feeling. A complete exercise can be found in David Johnson's book, *Reaching Out.*[5]

Another popular approach to the development of this skill is used by family-enrichment programs based on transactional analysis. The use of *I* and *you* statements in order to communicate the feelings that are going on beneath the surface is encouraged. Instead of saying, "You are inconsiderate," the partner is taught to say "I feel left out when you act like that."

Identifying feelings. The modern stress on feelings in the marriage relationship should not be misunderstood as a surrender to emotion. Rather, the opposite is intended. Currents of emotion need to be understood and identified lest they carry us off in the wrong direction. Therefore, each of the partners needs to learn to understand his or her own feelings, as well as their spouse's feelings. Worksheets, in which a partner practices identifying the feeling behind one or more statements of his or her spouse, can help in this process.

For example, a worksheet for wives might include a statement by the husband such as the following: "Why do you say it's my fault? You didn't do anything to help!" One of the statements of the wife on a worksheet for husband might be: "Sure, just roll over and go to sleep as if nothing had happened!" Behind each statement on their spouse's worksheet the husbands and wives write what, in their opinion, their mate is feeling when he or she makes this statement.[6]

Handling conflict. Some enrichment programs avoid dealing directly with conflict; instead, they prompt positive expressions of intimacy and allow conflict to arise naturally. Some programs encourage couples to grapple with conflict but always within a loving, positive context. For instance, after a half hour of exercises containing open-ended statements that share positive feelings, a statement can be used to prompt discussion of conflict: "There is something about our marriage that has been bothering me for a long time; it's. . . ." Of course, conflict exercises are sensitive and should be preceded by teaching about biblical conflict management.

Exercises should focus on helping the couple to understand the ways they have been handling conflict and the ways they might improve their handling of it. They can often identify their past patterns from a list like this:

- I always yield.
- I always fight to win.
- I nag.
- I avoid discussing it.
- I simmer in silence.
- I always seek to compromise.
- I make public statements of sarcasm or insult.

A list of "fight guidelines" can be distributed to help couples establish their own pattern for dealing with conflicts that arise.

- Don't harbor ill feelings for more than a day without discussing them. "Do not let the sun go down while you are still angry" (Eph. 4:26).
- Stick to the subject. Don't bring up other problems.
- Don't misuse a third party, getting this person to side with you and confiding in him or her and not in your spouse.
- Don't bring up the past; deal in the present.
- Avoid name-calling and insults.
- Share feelings without judging the other person.
- Hold hands while quarreling.
- Talk about the problem behind your "outbursts" later, when you are in control of your emotions.

Planning together. Planning experiences are easily formulated and can be patterned after a management process, which begins with evaluation. Evaluation exercises include any of those mentioned previously. Also, questionnaires and tests can be devised to review the marriage relationship.

The second step involves goal setting. A guide for goal setting should include answering questions like the following:

1. What areas of your relationship are most in need of improvement?
2. What area is of the highest priority right now?
3. What area can be improved easily?
4. What area will take the most time to be improved?
5. What areas of improvement would you establish as being short-range goals (taking several months)?
6. What areas of improvement would you establish as being long-range goals (taking a year or more)?

Developing a specific improvement program, the last step in planning, can be facilitated by the following suggested guidelines.

1. Choose the most important long-range goal: state it in terms of the place you would like to be in your relationship a year or two from now.
2. Determine what things you would need to do to reach that goal (reading, getting counseling, practicing, experiencing, discussing, deciding, etc.).
3. Determine the actual order of the steps it will take to reach your goal. For example:

   a. First, read a book together on the subject.
   b. Take a course related to the subject.
   c. Begin to discuss weekly how to improve in this area.

4. Determine which of these steps or activities can be put into your regular schedule—such as scheduling Tuesday evenings to go out together to work on a certain area.

5. Determine which of these steps will need special, monthly, or annual scheduling.

Sharing differences. Consciously looking at differences can enable partners to better understand themselves, their mates, and the ways each relates to the other. Actual tests like the *Taylor-Johnson Temperament Analysis* can help couples come to grips with their dissimilarities of temperament more objectively and understand how these differences affect their relationship.[7] Though it would require personal counseling for each couple, it is possible to use this approach at a retreat or within a seminar or course.

> As is true in other areas of marriage, each couple will be unique in their abilities and problems in the matter of relating jointly to God.

A more simplified approach is to ask couples to write about and discuss the perceived differences of their personalities and the differences they make.

Evaluating Communication. While all of the above exercises promote communication, some are designed specifically to evaluate and improve this dynamic. A questionnaire called the Marital Communication Inventory is a useful educational tool.[8] Or you may use communication games. For example, using building blocks or Tinker toys, spouses sit back to back on the floor. One leads by building something and verbally communicates directions to the other, who builds a model according to instruction. The one following the instructions must be silent. This rule makes the exercise a hilarious test of the ability to give and receive verbal messages.

A foursome dialogue is used by Del and Trudy Vander Haar. Two couples decide to participate in this together. The first husband and wife to converse select a real issue that faces them. They discuss it together for five minutes while the other couple observes the interaction of the first couple. The observing couple then gives feedback on various aspects: who initiates conversation; who checks out what he or she thought he or she heard; who looks for alternate solutions, etc. The process is then reversed and repeated.[9]

Sharing spiritually. As is true in other areas of marriage, each couple will be unique in their abilities and problems in the matter of relating jointly to God. Imbalance in spiritual maturity is a major contributing factor to problems at this point. But other factors are influential, communication ability being one of them. Some individuals are unable to pray aloud with a spouse, though they are able to pray individually. Part of the problem of such individuals is the inability to be vulnerable before someone else. Therefore, exercises in spiritual sharing could help couples with problems in other areas. A simple pattern for those unaccustomed to relating to God together is to ask them to share ideas on a problem and then, while they face each other and hold hands, pray silently about the matter. They then do the same with another issue, and then another, until every issue has been dealt with.

Exercises in inductive study of Scripture can be distributed for private use. Such exercises can induce questions to be asked related to discovering the meaning and applying of Scripture. For example, after studying the subject of the fruit of the Spirit, the partners may be asked to share what fruit of the Spirit they see most prominently in each other. Then, what quality each would like to see more of in himself or herself.

Thanksgiving and praise exercises can lend a positive note: to ask "What was the greatest evidence of God's presence in your life today?" prompts an answer that becomes a prelude to prayer. Praying between the reading of verses from a psalm prompts expressions of worship that otherwise might not so easily come to mind.

PRINCIPLES AND HAZARDS
OF MARRIAGE-ENRICHMENT PROGRAMS

Those familiar with the helpfulness of marriage-enrichment programs are also aware of the hazards. Such programs use teaching methods that can be misunderstood. And such programs aim at in-depth spiritual and personal changes that can prompt resistance and resentment. But the implementation of these programs can have a powerful, positive effect if established guidelines are followed.

Promote marriage-enrichment programs on a voluntary basis. Whereas sermons and teaching on marriage and the family can be included in any church program, in-depth marriage encounters should not be forced on couples. Such experiences can be incorporated into the church program as special events—a special weekend, a course, or an evening just for couples who really want to do something different. A Sunday evening or the Sunday school hour can be used for a participatory exercise if there is enough flexibility so that couples can choose the level of communication that fits them best.

Generally, experts have advised that marriage enrichment should be directed toward couples whose marriages are fairly good, emphasizing that their goal is growth, not correction. People with serious marriage problems might expect too much from the experience and their relationship might be damaged by their participation in exercises that demand they talk openly with one another. However, researchers have now found that people who attend non-church marriage enrichment programs tend to be people who are less satisfied with their marriages. Moderate marital stress seems to motivate them to invest the time in such enrichment activities.[10]

They also discovered that marriage enrichment programs tend to have greater results among distressed couples. Those conducting the study concluded: "These findings appear to challenge the belief that enrichment 'works' only with normal, healthy, nondistressed populations."

However, when promoting marriage education programs, care should be taken to make it clear that couples that attend such activities are not signaling by their participation that they are having severe marital discord. Often, announcements state that the sessions are for "couples with good marriages that they want to make better."

> The body of Christ, by its biblical message and positive marital programs, can be the foremost destroyer of these myths.

Promotion should also aim at dispelling notions that produce threat or opposition. A pioneer in family development, David Mace, counsels that we must deal with resistance. He writes: "The sober truth is that married couples desperately want to have loving relationships but fanatically resist attempts to enable them to get what they want."[11]

In our culture certain roadblocks to loving relationships exist in the form of myths. The first one is the myth of naturalism—that by following one's instincts, anyone can make a marriage work. Mace characterizes this myth as an "unexplained prejudice that persists in the face of all evidence to the contrary."[12]

The second roadblock is "privatism." It says, "Marriage is a very private, very personal matter. Whatever you do, don't ever talk to anyone else about what goes on inside your marriage." When kept within reasonable bounds, this approach makes sense. But it also constitutes a marital taboo that does much harm. It shuts married couples up in little boxes, where in their fumbling ignorance they destroy the very things they most desire. It prevents their obtaining the help they badly need.

Cynicism is the third roadblock. Boisterous jokes and snide remarks pervade many discussions of marriage. Despite our prizing the concept of a happy marriage, this lack of serious discussion about marriage makes people feel that it is an overrated institution.

The body of Christ, by its biblical message and positive marital programs, can be the foremost destroyer of these myths.

Plan for biblical and God-centered experiences. Many of the marriage-encounter and marriage-enrichment programs have a secular or a nonevangelical base. But the evangelical can allow God and His Word to dominate a program even if a sizable percentage of its sessions are experiential. Lectures relating the Bible to current issues, presentations and testimonies about a personal relationship to Christ, inductive study of Scripture, and group Bible study can inject God's truth into the program. And throughout the sessions the theological basis of the family can be laid so that it is said clearly that one must be open to the Savior and his love.

Use groups wisely. While some marriage development programs use group encounter, most do not. Close and intimate group interaction usually requires professional leadership. Because many are suspicious of sensitivity groups and because of the strong sense of "privatism" in regard to marriage, group experiences should avoid in-depth sharing of family problems. Certain feedback activities, by which the group helps the partners understand each other, might be employed, but these activities must be handled carefully. Some opportunity for insight into other couples' relationships might also help couples admit that there are problem areas in their own relationship. Positive sharing can be encouraged, as well as a general discussion of struggles. A warm, enthusiastic group context should be built as a support for each couple's own encounter, not as a substitute for it.

Utilize couples as leaders or contributors. Modeling is a prominent feature of many groups. Lead couples may share their struggles and successes in areas under discussion. This sharing can be part of a lecture on an aspect of marriage or it can follow such a lecture. Before husbands and wives are sent to complete an exercise or answer a question, a couple can demonstrate the process. Their candor before the group can have a dramatic effect, not only clarifying the exercise but also stimulating openness between the partners.

Be realistic. One of the most frequent criticisms of a marriage encounter is that its leaders tend to exaggerate. Hyperbole easily replaces realistic statements about the joys of intimacy. Susan Middaugh noted this tendency in her encounter experience:

> I got the same feeling [about exaggeration] the next day, when Sal and Rita [lead couple] told how desolate and lonely they felt one afternoon at home. Sal was working on business; Rita was cleaning. They were together but separated by responsibilities. To me, this scene is a part of everyday life. But Sal and Rita made it sound extraordinary. If hyperbole is used so casually, what words are left over to distinguish those rare moments of grief and joy from the mundane?[13]

Caution against exclusiveness. In a desire to promote future sessions, we often send people home to tell others what they have missed. This too easily separates people into the haves and the have-nots. For this reason some leaders are warning that Marriage Encounter is becoming an "exclusive club."[14] Couples who have not participated are made to feel that their marriages are inferior, that they could not possibly in any other way gain what is available at the retreat or through the course.

Produce some follow-up approaches. As a movement, Marriage Encounter has a twofold follow-up. A monthly group meeting for those who "encountered" is one form of follow-up. Here concepts previously given at the weekend retreat are reviewed; then discussion between partners and between couples is fostered. For couples at home there is the ten-and-ten tool mentioned earlier. This method gets both spouses to express their feelings on a chosen theme in a written note (ten minutes of writing), which is then exchanged and shared as the take-off point for their daily dialogue (ten minutes of talking).

Advanced courses and retreats are also part of a follow-up approach. Thus Bud and Bea Van Eck have developed their Phase II Marriage Enrichment Lab.[15]

However the follow-up is handled, some carry-over exercises, suggestions, or programs can help the couple build and develop what was initiated at the retreat.

Beware of legalistic approaches. Closely related to the danger mentioned above is the danger of legalism. Effective, man-made methodology too easily becomes a set of absolutes. The ten-and-ten method advocated by the New York branch of the Marriage Encounter movement has generated a wave of controversy. When presenting this daily exercise, these leaders insist that it is not optional—a couple must agree to commit themselves to the daily assignment, or they are not really "making" the encounter. When asked if there are other ways for maintaining intimate communication, a leader explains: "The main source of strength for the couple is the dialogue. The writings technique is the only way a couple can be sure of setting aside some time each day for dialogue. The ten-and-ten is compulsory; it is absolutely not negotiable."[16]

> An institutional marriage, in which an emotional union is ignored and which is held together by rules and roles, fits neither modern times nor biblical tenets.

An enthusiastic reaction by couples to the novel approaches of the movement can stimulate leaders to place all of their trust in a proven methodology rather than in the Holy Spirit. But when the trust is not misplaced and the objectives are biblical, the marriage enrichment techniques merit widespread use among evangelicals. Perhaps this movement will be a temporary one, as so many North American remedial and educational movements have been. Yet it has been caused by the changes that have taken place in marriage—smaller families, the separation of sexual intercourse from procreation made possible by contraceptives, and the tripling of the life expectancy of both men and women. The result of these changes has been an inevitable revolution in the way in which people attempt to cope with life.[17] An institutional marriage, in which an emotional union is ignored and which is held together by rules and roles, fits neither modern times nor biblical tenets. It is a necessity that marriage be marked by multifaceted intimacy and by satisfaction. Marital enrichment programs are in the middle of this revolution, helping couples emerge out of their traditional, cool, contractual entrapments into fresh, warm, personal relationships.

SUGGESTED RESOURCES

Garland, Diana, and Diane Pancoast. *The Church's Ministry With Families*. Waco, Tex.: Word Books, 1990.

Guernsey, Dennis. *A New Design for Family Ministry*. Elgin, Ill.: David C. Cook, 1982. • A very worthwhile look at the needs of families at various developmental stages.

Kehrwald, Leif. *Caring That Enables: A Manual for Developing Parish Family Ministry*. Mahwah, N.J.: Paulist Press, 1991.

Larson, Jim. *A Church Guide for Strengthening Families*. Minneapolis: Augsburg, 1984.

NOTES

1. Charlotte H. Clinebell and Howard J. Clinebell, *The Intimate Marriage* (New York: Harper, 1970), 29.

2. Bud Van Eck and Bea Van Eck, "The Phase II Marriage Enrichment Lab," in *Marriage and Family Enrichment*, ed. Herbert Otto (New York: Abingdon, 1976), 15.

3. Herman Green, Jr., "A Christian Marriage Enrichment Retreat," in *Marriage and Family Enrichment*, ed. Otto, 91.

4. Clinebell and Clinebell, *The Intimate Marriage*, 29–32.

5. David Johnson, *Reaching Out* (Englewood Cliffs, N.J.: Prentice-Hall, 1972).

6. See a complete worksheet in Del Vander Haar and Trudy Vander Haar, "The Marriage Enrichment Program—Phase I," in *Marriage and Family Enrichment*, ed. Otto, 209.

7. Robert Taylor, *Taylor-Johnson Temperament Analysis* (Los Angeles: Psychological Publications, 1967).

8. Millard J. Bienvenu, Sr., "Marital Communication Inventory" (Saluda, N.C.: Family Life Publications, 1969).

9. Vander Haar and Vander Haar, "The Marriage Enrichment Program—Phase 1," 194.

10. Gleam S. Powell and Karen Smith Wampler, "Marriage Enrichment Participants: Level of Marital Satisfaction," *Family Relations* 31:3 (1982): 392.

11. David Mace, "We Call It ACME," in *Marriage and Family Enrichment*, ed. Otto, 171.

12. Ibid.

13. Susan Middaugh, "Marriage Encounter, Is It for Everyone?" *Sign* 55, no. 4 (December 1975–January 1976): 10.

14. Antoinette Bosco, *Marriage Encounter* (St. Meinrad, Ind.: Abbey, 1972), 98

15. Van Eck and Van Eck, "The Phase II Marriage Enrichment Lab," 217–26.

16. Bosco, *Marriage Encounter*, 102.

17. Ibid.

◆ *Part Six*

Parent Education

Parent Education Principles

Mention children, and many parents will think of Psalm 127:3: "Children are a gift of the Lord." Still others may think of trouble and feel pain. Catherine Brown states the case realistically: "As all parents and non-parents know, life with children can be hell."[1] Because of this, some parents wish they had had no children.

Many parents feel guilty and uncertain. Haim Ginott notes this as a special feature of today's parents: "Whatever grandfather did was done with authority; whatever we do is done with hesitation. Even when in error, grandfather acted with certainty. Even when in the right, we act with doubt."[2] Parents badly need assurance about their parenting practices. Giving them that assurance may be the greatest contribution that parent training can offer. Speaking of participants in these courses, Brown observes, "The change that excites them most is that they no longer spend so much time vacillating between suicide and murder. They find themselves able to love, even enjoy, both their kids and themselves."[3]

But experts in the field often don't provide the needed confidence. And personal feelings of being a failure as a parent himself often render a pastor reluctant to speak with conviction about parenting principles. A lecturer once gave a talk entitled "Ten Commandments for Parents." But after having his first child, so the story goes, he changed the title to "Seven Principles for Parents." After having two more children, he modified his speech again, entitling the talk "Three Suggestions for Parents." And when his children were in their teens, he quit lecturing altogether.

Modern controversy surrounding modes of parenting also erodes the confidence of parents. Sometimes the credibility of a researcher or a teacher who is confident of his or her own viewpoint is destroyed because of the contradictions of other researchers or teachers. Even Christian experts are not unified on basic issues, such as spanking. One book seems to say that all parents need to do is love their child, while in the same year another book appears calling for a more rigid discipline.

Inconclusiveness in theory is producing contradictions in practical application. Theorists are not yet agreed on explanations regarding the forces that shape a child. And evangelicals do not agree on a sound theology of child rearing. This confusion results in the spreading of a variety of

> Parents badly need assurance about their parenting practices. Giving them that assurance may be the greatest contribution that parent training can offer.

ideas on parenting in a given church or community. Closest friends will not always agree on what is best. Their judgment will depend on their church affiliation, their own parents' practices, or the wisdom they have gained from the latest seminar they attended.

Our task is to search for some common biblical and practical guidelines that will make parents more comfortable with their role. We will start with a summary of parent and family themes and then describe a suggested model for parent training.

PARENTING CONCEPTS

Scanning the fields of learning theory, developmental psychology, and parenting, we see that there is surprising agreement about many things. By integrating these concepts with biblical principles, we can lay out some foundational guidelines for contemporary Christian parenting.

Good Parenting Does Not Require Perfection

A parent can assume that he can be a responsible, successful parent without being perfect. Faith in Christ strikes at the root of the problems of being a parent because forgiveness and love, not obedience and perfection, constitute faith's bottom line. Realistically, the home will sometimes be a place of conflict, sadness, tension, hurt, and sinfulness. Parents will have to deal with chronic, trivial problems without the benefit of the wisdom of Solomon. Parents will face reluctance to do homework, sibling fights, bad table manners, disobedience, communication breakdowns, etc. Parents will be distressed—sometimes shouting, or criticizing, or exploding, or wondering how they can manage their child's sinfulness without being able to control their own. Continually repenting of their failures, they will go from one crisis to another, uncertain about their ability to cope.

> The Christian parent understands that the dynamics of Christian relationships are built around forgiveness, grace, forbearance, understanding, and love. These dynamics work.

The Christian parent understands that the dynamics of Christian relationships are built around forgiveness, grace, forbearance, understanding, and love. These dynamics work. A parent or a child may explode from time to time, but the parent can ask for forgiveness or offer it. An example for these dynamics of parenting is not to be found in a psychology book. Rather, such an example is discovered in the biblical picture of God the Father, the ultimate parental model. The dynamics that God exemplifies to us are these: caring, responding, disciplining, respecting, knowing, and forgiving.[4]

The nonrequirement of perfection offers the parent hope that he or she can somehow manage what sometimes looks like an impossible task. Awareness of this lends realism to the task, too, since parents often think they are the only ones who struggle and worry so much, and it should make them more comfortable with their role. They believe that ultimately their success will not depend on any particular skill or management technique but on their own personal growth and development in God's grace.

Good Parental Power Is Limited

Parents are responsible for their children's behavior, but the influence of parents is limited. Virtually all authorities are agreed on this. Some parenting experts see the child as being basically good, but not as independent. Parents can't divorce their child. They must face the parenting task.

The necessity of managing one's children is so clearly stated in Scripture that the principle does not require much exposition. Yet the implications of this responsibility can be too strongly stated. Proverbs 22:6, which reads, "Train a child in the way he should go, and when he is old he will not depart from it," has received a variety of interpretations. This verse is even used as a text to confirm treating a child according to his nature and personality since the phrase "in the way he should go" can be translated accurately as "in his own way." But this proverb, like other proverbs, is a general statement of truth, not an absolute promise in every individual case. This verse does not teach environmental determinism, as if no other force can undermine parental training. If no other force could work against it, parents could be held responsible for their grown children's sins. Even the Old Testament law recognized the possible rebellion of youth, despite parental effort; and the rebellious youth, not the parents, was stoned to death (Deut. 21:18–21).

> Parents are responsible for their children's behavior, but the influence of parents is limited.

Overemphasizing the influence of parents has led to the indiscriminate heaping of guilt on their heads. In sermon and in print the weeping David is blamed for Absalom's political revolution, despite the fact that God vindicated David through Absalom's judgment and defeat. The prevailing idea that parents are always the major cause for their grown offspring's behavior has created an insensitivity to the grieving parent's plight, and we have handed them blame when they needed our support.

Good Parenting Is Good Relating

Good parenting requires the building of warm relationships. The leaders of most parent workshops would agree with William Glasser's idea that the home should include warm, honest, affectionate relationships. Some see these relationships as an end; Glasser views them as a means to an end. Any helping relationship needs to be warm, honest, and affectionate, he maintains.[5] And parenting is a helping relationship. That discipline and love are not mutually exclusive is obvious from the biblical viewpoint: "The Lord disciplines those he loves" (Heb. 12:6). God's love, as a model, is not expressed in stern, cool, authoritarian discipline; his relationship with his children is expressed warmly, intimately, and forgivingly.

Good Parenting Produces a Healthy Self-Concept

Good parenting will result in the child's feeling of worth. What the child ultimately thinks about himself is a basic concern of the parenting process. All modern theorists agree with this statement. As a child grows into adulthood, a good feeling about himself becomes a basis for good action. William Glasser stresses this truth in a program called Parent Involvement Program (PIP). Parents too often ignore or punish children when the children have failed and are upset with themselves. Glasser thinks that the feeling of failure is a cause of a child's misbehavior. Therefore, to improve his or her conduct, the child's self-concept must improve. Even behaviorists emphasize that their techniques should help children feel good about life and themselves. Behaviorist techniques are not manipulative devices to get the child to conform to the parent's arbitrary wishes but should help the child be comfortable with himself or herself. As believers in the Bible, we should have no quarrel with this statement. Basic to all of people's conduct with others is the fact that all are made in the image of God and that all are of great worth. Parents should avoid cursing their children as well as any other person made in the image of God (James 3:9). The tenderness and kindhearted approach of the Christian in general should be the approach of the parent in particular (Eph. 4:31–32). Love believes in and hopes for another (1 Cor. 13:7). Paul speaks even more directly to this point in his instructions to parents. He warns parents to consider the inner life of their children when nurturing them. Do not drive the child to anger (Eph. 6:4) nor to exasperation (Col. 3:21), he cautions. Measures that push a child to anger or depression ignore the inner life, the sense of personal worth, and the right to life. Parenting should impart self-respect to the child.

Good Parenting Produces Self-Discipline

Good parenting should result in inner control. While there is some difference of opinion over the use of outer constraints, there is none when the matter of inner control is concerned. The child is to be handled so that eventually he will become responsibly independent of the parents and be able to function in society on his own. For this to be accomplished, parents must build development and self-control into the disciplining process. They will need to attach certain consequences to certain kinds of behavior in order to shape the child. But they will also need to make the child aware of the fact that improper behavior produces negative consequences for others as well as for the child. The more the punishment and reward conform to real life punishment and reward, the easier the

> The test for good parenting is not merely to control by any means. Methods used to control children should be in conformity to God's methods and to ethical principles, not merely to the arbitrary whims of the parents.

transition from the dependent to the independent life will be. Misbehavior will be seen by the child as more than merely a matter between self and parents; behavior will be viewed as being related to others, to God, and to the child's own well-being. Thus, a prominent national program like Parent Effectiveness Training (PET) is geared to teaching children to solve their own problems with a view to making them independent. Glasser's PIP program also proposes to cause children to see the results of their behavior.

The test for good parenting is not merely to control by any means. Methods used to control children should be in conformity to God's methods and to ethical principles, not merely to the arbitrary whims of the parents. Otherwise, the necessary ingredients for later self-discipline will be lacking.

Good Parenting Develops Sensitivity

Good parenting should lead to the development of empathy in the child's personality. A large measure of internal self-discipline results from learning to respect others. This demands awareness of the way one's behavior affects others, along with an understanding of personal rights. Teaching children that they have no rights will give them little basis for understanding about the rights of others. Brutally forcing children to comply may make them ethically irresponsible. Glasser has been commended by Christians for his strong emphasis on human responsibility. He insists that we avoid a Freudian approach to delinquency, by which a child's misbehavior is blamed on early childhood experiences over which the child had no control. Delinquents should be made to feel responsible for their actions, Glasser demands. Thomas Gordon, with his Parent Effectiveness Training, seeks to train parents to share their feelings with their children in order to help the children know how their behavior affects others internally. This is an important parental function. Telling children that their loud talking is making you feel nervous helps build their awareness of others and responsibility to them.

That we have biblical warrant for this training seems clear enough from our Lord's view of ethics. Certainly he viewed one's love of God as a major means of control of conduct. But love for one's neighbor as oneself also regulates one's actions. Children should be guided to see this fact.

Good Parenting Includes Power

Parents possess a certain power. Parental power is basic to all of the major national parent programs. William Glasser works toward equalizing the power between parent and child; the child, with the parent's backing and assistance, evaluates and changes her or his own behavior. But Glasser does affirm parental power. Rudolph Dreikurs's parent-training program, based on the book *Children: The Challenge*, stresses power as a fact of life, a drive we are born with. Of course the parent must use this power to direct the child's behavior into socially useful channels.[6] Behavior modification advocates build on the use of authority. Thomas Gordon radically departs from the others, believing that a parent can and should give up the use of power. In his Parent Effectiveness Training (PET) he teaches that power is destructive and that in any situation, through conversation and compromise, everyone can win.

> Parental power is to be exercised toward biblical ends and is to be harnessed by kindness and love.

For this reason the biblical approach is distinct from that of PET. While growing up, the child is to be taught to respect parental authority within God's order (Eph. 6:1). This parental power, however, is limited and governed by the framework of God's values and standards. Thus, parents are reminded to bring up children according to Christian nurture, not according to their own whims. Behavior modification approaches lack standards. Mastering the techniques of these approaches gives a parent unusual power over the child without any protective guidelines for its exercise. For the Christian, parental power is to be exercised toward biblical ends and is to be harnessed by kindness and love. Thus the Christian can more easily validate parental power as being part of God's order because that power is protected from misuse.

Good Parenting Utilizes Behavioral Modification

Parenting through using certain consequences for certain behavior is effective. One does not have to be a behaviorist to know that the results of an action will influence whether or not the action will be repeated. This idea was around long before B. F. Skinner's animal research demonstrated it to be so. One critic of Skinner put it well: he said that Skinner had spent millions of dollars on research to tell us what we already knew—that if you pay a man to work, he will, and if you stop paying him, he'll stop working.

The role of consequences in shaping behavior is well grounded in scriptural teaching. Numerous proverbs speak of regulating behavior through punishment (Prov. 13:24; 19:18; 23:13). The New Testament confirms God's use of consequences to guide us (Heb. 12:5–7). But there are differences between scriptural learning theory and behaviorism. The Christian parent can use the guidelines of behaviorism, but not exclusively.

Good Parenting Requires, When Possible, Both Parents

Included in today's family trends is a new awareness of the crucial role of the father as parent. We now talk about the "new father" image, which differs from older images in several key respects: he is present at the birth; he is involved with his children as infants, not just when they are older; he participates in the day-to-day work of child care, not just play; he is involved with his daughters as much as his sons.[7] This new awareness is generating new father training designs. Foremost among them is one based on the Personal Fathering Profile.[8] After massive research to discover what makes strong fathers, the researchers designed a test to show a man the weaknesses and strengths of his own fathering style. The results are then used by men in small group settings to invoke change where necessary.

The areas stressed in father training are: involvement, defined as playing or working with the child, tending to daily routines or just spending unstructured time with them; consistency, being predictable; awareness, understanding children and their world; and nurturance, showing affection and intimacy for one another in spontaneous, unself-conscious ways. Other aspects of nurturance in fathers include activities to support, protect, comfort, heal, and gratify the needs of family members.

Good Parenting Considers the Nature of the Child

It is over the matter of the nature of the child that the Christian clashes most with current parent-training programs. Thomas Gordon and other humanists believe that the child really wants to do the right thing. The child misbehaves only because he is legitimately trying to satisfy personal needs. In doing so, however, the child comes into conflict with others who are only trying to satisfy their needs as well. The child who arrives late to dinner is catering to his own needs while, at the same time, hindering the fulfillment of other people's needs. Thus, Gordon recommends discussing this clash and coming to some compromise. Glasser places more stress on human responsibility than does Gordon but still sees self-fulfillment as man's basic drive.

Behaviorists take a neutral attitude toward man's nature, refusing to define acts as being either morally good or bad. Since they deny human will, they view all action as being conditioned by outer circumstances. Thus, for example, being a good driver is not to be classified as morally good behavior since the driver was only conditioned to be so, something he or she is not responsible for.

Christians identify misbehavior as a result of sin within the individual and society. Humanists see man as being basically good and ignore evil as it is presented in Scripture.

UNDERSTANDING MISBEHAVIOR

Saying that misbehavior is sin is theologically correct, but it is also too general. It does not deal with the actual reason for misbehavior specifically enough to be used as a base for nurturing practices.

Dealing with misbehavior requires careful understanding of its cause. Psychologists are not agreed on its cause but they offer some insight. Gordon says that misbehavior results when a person tries to meet his own needs and, in the process, his actions constitute an obstacle to someone else meeting his desires. Parents also call such actions misbehavior. When a child's screaming disturbs the parents' reading, for instance, it is misconduct. But PET advocates tell parents to discard the word *misbehavior* since it is only motivated behavior. PET is relativistic; according to its doctrine, conduct is forged out of legitimate individual expression in a democratic context.

In Glasser's system, conduct is considered misconduct when it is neither helpful for society nor for the individual. Rather, the conduct is prompted by the desire to succeed. "People who engage in *irresponsible behavior*, Glasser's catch-all term for everything from schizophrenia to neglect of chores, see themselves as failures," notes Catherine Brown.[9] Dreikurs views misbehavior in terms of goals that children are seeking to achieve in relation to their parents. When children want attention, power, respect, or a sense of adequacy, they may misbehave. Because of Dreikurs's Freudian base, he does not believe children ever misbehave for reasons unrelated to their parents.[10]

> Dealing with misbehavior requires careful understanding of its cause.

If we think our way through the above descriptions, it is by no means clear that these explanations of misbehavior are entirely unbiblical simply because the authors refuse to use the word *sin*. Two matters are in question.

The first matter has to do with the definition of sin. To understand naughtiness, we must first understand the nature of sin. What is the evil tendency that causes children to misbehave? But there is another issue: Is misbehavior sin? Is it a sin not to eat green beans?

In regard to the first matter, conservative scholars have never been fully agreed. Is sin equal to selfishness, as Augustus Strong suggests? Or is Calvin right in calling sin pride? Or is the heart of sin rebellion, as some biblical words suggest? Take Gordon's explanation of misbehavior. All people, including children, are pursuing the satisfaction of their needs. This is legitimate, he maintains. However, when this pursuit brings one into conflict with someone else, it is termed misbehavior. Thus, when a child who is talking loudly (fulfilling his need to enjoy excitement) interferes with a parent's reading (fulfilling the need for some diversion), the child is being naughty in parental terms.

We can agree with Gordon, at least in part. The quest to satisfy one's needs is not always wrong. Sometimes parents need to talk with the child and negotiate a conflicting situation. Speaking biblically though, the quest to satisfy one's needs is not always right either. Sometimes a person is extremely self-centered in trying to reach his goals, disregarding others. Also people seek satisfaction for their needs from the wrong source and in the wrong way. Thus, in a clash between persons, not everyone can have his own way. Gordon wants us to teach the child to align himself with others, using only conversation and compromise in the process. But Christian parents seek to train the child to comply with God's Word, and this calls for discipline. Therefore, Gordon's analysis is partly true and helpful, but it is also misleading.

Glasser's approach may also be instructive. People misbehave because they are made to feel like failures, he asserts. When other people begin to have confidence in them, they will begin to improve their behavior and their self-concept. Glasser's approach can explain man's sinfulness. In this case it is the social nature of sin that is obvious. The self-centered lack of respect for others prompts misbehavior. At times the individual seeks recognition in the wrong way. The motivation for self-fulfillment need not be seen as wrong per se, but the means of attaining it are sometimes perverted and wrong. Also, society itself is sinful, often preventing the self-fulfillment of people and condemning them needlessly as failures.

The theological problem of the nature of man revolves around two facts about man: Humans are created in the image of God and yet are corrupted by sin. However, total depravity does not cancel entirely the creative work of God in nature (James 3:9). Thus, it is not always immediately clear whether an act is motivated by the created impulse or the sinful perversion. Is seeking to fulfill one's needs sin? Or is the manner of seeking their fulfillment wrong? Is self-fulfillment wrong? Or does sin lie in the direction self-fulfillment takes?

Whatever form a Christian system of psychology takes, we are sure enough of some matters that we can construct a view of child training that includes the concept of sin. First, self-fulfillment or satisfaction of one's needs is basic to human life and should not be considered the essence of sinfulness. Jesus promised abundant living for believers, and Paul said that God would supply all of the believer's needs. God is not opposed to life; he created it. Therefore, we can assume that some of the acts of children are expressions of creativeness even though they come in conflict with the parent's desires. The two-year-old who wipes his peanut-butter-and-jelly-laden fingers across the kitchen wall may merely be expressing his created self, not the sinful Adam, even though he had been warned against doing so. A preschool child learns about the world through touch. His impulse is legitimate.

But the Christian also knows that a child will at times act in a self-centered way or in a manner that is morally and ethically wrong. And the child may also have a tendency to rebel against God and his or her parents. Concerning this biblical understanding, Christian psychologist James Dobson strongly warns parents to make certain that the young child is not allowed to control the parent.[11]

The Christian parent should approach an instance of misbehavior with a number of questions in mind. Is the misbehavior contrary to God's revealed standards and values? Parents who tend to see all misconduct as being sin may jump too quickly to this conclusion. Much naughtiness and resistance from children constitute conflict with other people's wishes, but not sin. When a child forgets momentarily, and noisily and spontaneously bursts into a room, he or she may not be rebelling or sinning. It may be true that the child has broken the parent's command not to run in the house, but the running may not be a manifestation of a rebellious nature, just a childish one.

Is the misbehavior a quest for legitimate fulfillment? At the time the behavior may bother the parent, but it should be handled with respect for the child's right to live. When a child is talking loudly in the kitchen while the mother is talking on the phone, the situation should be handled so that the child is not exasperated. By explaining that excited talking is not bad in itself and by explaining how it is conflicting with the parent's right to talk on the phone, the mother can suggest that the child continue his conversation in his own room. Thomas Gordon's suggestions at this point are quite good, since they convey a proper respect for the child.

Is the misbehavior sometimes possibly a result of the parent's sinful reactions? Psychologists who study discipline are discovering how misconduct is linked to a pattern of interaction with others. Sometimes the teacher or the parent can contribute to the problem. Parents, too, are sinful. Not all misbehavior is entirely the fault of the child. A parent might prompt sassy remarks from the child by giving disrespectful orders to the child.

A parent, in his or her view of childhood conduct, will need some specific answers to these questions about the nature of children. It is not enough to build a philosophy of discipline on some general statement about the sinfulness of man.

USE OF PUNISHMENT IN PARENTING

Experts also do not agree on the role of punishment in discipline. The advocates of PET present a thoroughly positive approach, believing that problems can be handled by talking them through, except in emergencies. (When the toddler is headed for a busy street, for instance, there is no time to talk.) Glasser recommends praise, not punishment, since punishment will cause physical and mental pain, which will interfere with the parent's helping relationship to the child. But Glasser does suggest the use of reasonable negative consequences, such as withholding privileges. Behavior modification experts do recommend some forms of punishment. Yet they usually refrain from endorsing spanking.

Sometimes, according to Scripture, spanking is an effective means of discipline: "The rod of correction imparts wisdom" (Prov. 29:15). Wisdom comes from the rod the same way it comes from other forms of correction: it shows that wrong acts produce negative results. Physical correction is loving: "He who spares the rod hates his son, but he who loves him is careful to discipline him" (Prov. 13:24).

Since child abuse is so prevalent, however, some Christians have argued that Scripture does not sanction spanking. Some argue that it is an Old Testament practice not germane for those who live by the New Testament. The Balswicks dismiss proof texts for spanking by claiming the word *rod* used in Proverbs refers to a shepherd's crook, used not to hit but to rescue.[12]

Attempts to undermine biblical support for spanking are no doubt rightly motivated. We should shun any measure of discipline that borders on abuse. Spanking is illegal in Sweden because authorities there sensed that it too often lead to harsh abuse of children. Yet the danger of child abuse should not press us to discard Scripture so easily. In the first place, the rod is repeatedly linked to physical punishment in Proverbs (Prov. 10:13; 23:13, 14). And the New Testament grants some warrant to spanking by suggesting that God himself practices it on his children. "The Lord disciplines those he loves, and he punishes everyone he accepts as a son" (Heb. 12:6).[13]

> Immature children need encouragement. And it may take many positive remarks to overcome a few impulsive, critical ones.

But these biblical occurrences do not call for a stern, authoritarian, punitive control that lacks warmth and kindness. Studies show that children subjected to such an atmosphere have emotional problems. Exclusive use of punishment, particularly in a cool or negative atmosphere, is the wrong manifestation of parental power. Parents in our society may tend to be punishment-oriented; it is part of our culture. This may result in negative forms of punishment, particularly psychological whippings and dressing-downs, prompted by a parent's outburst of anger.[14] We get trapped in negatives. We maintain control, but the environment is neither warm nor pleasant.

The occasional use of physical punishment is no substitute for positive words or acts. In the struggle of immature children to grow up, they need encouragement. And it may take many positive remarks to overcome a few impulsive, critical ones. Thus the positive, reinforcing approach of the behaviorists can prove to be beneficial for Christian parents. Good long-range results come from the use of praise. Encouragement can build the child's self-esteem while improving his behavior. Most parents find it difficult to praise a child for doing only a little better than previously or for only partially complying with an order. After a seminar on behavior modification, one parent said, "I found it hard to praise a child for small decreases in behavior you think should never occur at all, partly because it sounds so silly. But I am learning to say, 'Gee, Dan, I don't think you've bitten Michael in two whole days—that's great,' and 'Look at that: you asked for an apple and you ate almost half of it all up!'"[15] Such remarks are not out of keeping with a biblical understanding of childhood.

BUILDING THE CHILD'S AWARENESS OF GOD IN PARENTING

Parenting includes building the child's awareness of God. This proposition introduces us to the greatest difference between secular and Christian systems of child education. Though some of the secular-based programs operate in churches, they are not concerned with orienting a child to God. Yet they do not interfere with the parents passing on values, including religious ones, to their children.

The moral and ethical system of the Christian faith is based on man's relationship to God. Christian nurture should call attention to that fact. "Bring them up in the training and instruction of the Lord," says Paul (Eph. 6:4). Teaching, counseling, and reproving should be God-related. Humanistically based programs are built around human relationship.

As alluded to earlier, however, this God-orientation does not exclude human relationships. Humanistic parent training programs have some worthwhile suggestions for training children, even though God is not part of the systems. Children need to learn how to respect the feelings of others, something that is emphasized by PET. PET also teaches the skills of listening and problem solving—skills that orient children to loving their neighbor as themselves. William Glasser's responsibility-based approach is also helpful here. Parents are in a position to help children see the consequences of their behavior for themselves and for others. Certainly Christians add God to the nurturing process, but we must not ignore the good ideas of others who do not reckon with God in their systems.

SUGGESTED RESOURCES

Arp, Claudia, and Linda Dillow. *The Big Book of Family Fun*. Nashville: Thomas Nelson, 1994.
    • All kinds of activities to keep a family busy, happy, and together.
Bly, Stephen, and Janet Bly. *How to Be a Good Grandparent*. Chicago: Moody Press, 1990. • Highly recommended.
Canfield, Ken. *Seven Secrets of Effective Fathers*. Wheaton, Ill.: Tyndale House, 1992. • A book that will make a difference, from a careful researcher and good communicator.

Clarke, Jean Ilsley, and Connie Dawson. *Growing Up Again: Parenting Ourselves, Parenting Our Children*. San Francisco: HarperCollins, 1989. •A much-needed book for understanding how our upbringing relates to our parenting and what to do about it.

O'Gorman, Patricia, and Philip Oliver-Diaz. *Breaking the Cycle of Addiction*. Pompano Beach, Fla.: Health Communications, 1987.•How one's own dysfunctional family childhood might affect one's parenting, and how to change.

Dobson, James. *Discipline With Love*. Wheaton, Ill.: Tyndale House, 1986. •Much wisdom.

_____. *Raising Teenagers Right*. Wheaton, Ill.: Tyndale House, 1988. •Guidance parents need.

Dockrey, Karen. *When a Hug Won't Fix the Hurt: Walking With Your Child Through Crisis*. Wheaton, Ill.: Victor Books, 1993. •What a crisis means to children and how parents can support them.

Frydenger, Tom, and Adrienne Frydenger. *The Blended Family*. Old Tappan, N.J.: Fleming H. Revell, 1984. •Insightful and practical.

Kesler, Jay, ed. *Parents and Children*. Wheaton, Ill.: Victor Books, 1986; and *Parents and Teenagers*. Wheaton, Ill.: Victor Books, 1984. •Large, encyclopedic-like volumes in which prominent evangelicals write about the issues.

Lewis, Margie M., and Gregg Lewis. *The Hurting Parent*. Rev. ed. Grand Rapids: Zondervan, 1988. •Sympathetic support for parents whose teens are in trouble or causing it.

Papernow, Patricia. *Bonds Without Blood: Stages of Development in Remarried Families*. New York: Gardner, 1987. •A thorough book on helping family members understand what blending is all about.

Strommen, Merton P., and Irene A. Strommen. *Five Cries of Parents*. San Francisco: Harper & Row, 1985. •A book based on research of parents of teens, with lots of savvy.

NOTES

1. Catherine Brown, "It Changed My Life," *Psychology Today* (November 1976): 47.
2. Haim Ginott, *Between Parent and Child* (New York: Macmillan, 1965), 91.
3. Brown, "It Changed My Life," 3.
4. Myron R. Chartier, "Parenting: A Theological Model," *Journal of Psychology and Theology* (Winter 1978): 54–61.
5. William Glasser, *Reality Therapy* (New York: Harper, 1965), 21–41.
6. Brown, "It Changed My Life," 57.
7. C. Darling-Fisher and L. Tiedje, "The Impact of Maternal Employment Characteristics on Fathers' Participation in Child Care," *Family Relations* 39 (1990): 20–26.
8. For leader's guide and test information, write to the National Center for Fathering, 217 Southwind Place, Manhattan, KS 66502.
9. Brown, "It Changed My Life," 53.
10. Ibid., 109.
11. James Dobson, *Dare to Discipline* (Wheaton, Ill.: Tyndale, 1970).
12. Jack O. Balswick and Judith K. Balswick, *The Family: A Christian Perspective of the Contemporary Home* (Grand Rapids: Baker, 1989), 98.
13. The apostle Paul uses the Greek word *paideio* in Ephesians 6:4 to refer to discipline. In Hebrews 12:6 the verb *paideuo* is used for discipline. While both words refer to the broad idea of discipline, they do include the idea of whipping.
14. Brown, "It Changed My Life," 57.
15. Ibid.

22

A Parent Training Model

In the last twenty years the number of parent training programs has grown by leaps and bounds. The variety of philosophies and methods they contain creates difficult choices for church leaders. The best option may be for the church to create its own parent training program. Local church seminars and courses can provide the necessary time to consider subjects in depth as well as to practice skills and experience group support.

FEATURES OF PARENT TRAINING

We will take for granted that an evangelical program should be biblical. Certainly not all programs will take the same approach, yet the training model will include grappling with biblical texts and raising theological questions. Merely bringing into the church contemporary pyschological principles without scriptural references does not constitute an effective evangelical approach to preparing parents.

A second feature will be comprehensiveness. Too often the parenting task is reduced to following a few simple ideas or using a couple of clever techniques. Forcing the complex personalities, relationships, and problems in the home to yield to several simple principles or methods creates frustration. How often we hear words like these: "If you will only pray together"; "If the father will just lead"; "If you will praise the child"; or "If everyone will love."

Any one of these suggestions may be helpful for stable families, but for others who need more help, the insistence on such a simplistic approach can drive them to guilt and exasperation.

> Biblical methods are best formulated in the light of biblical goals. What are parents really trying to do for their children?

Third, parent training will need to include actual training. Neither lectures nor discussions will be enough. Old habits will not easily give way to new patterns without some tolls for evaluation and practice.

The following model for parent training attempts to bring all of these features together. It covers the range of parental skills needed as well as provides suggestions for the development of those skills.

BIBLICAL OBJECTIVES FOR CHILD REARING

We begin with parenting objectives. Biblical methods are best formulated in the light of biblical goals. What are parents really trying to do for their children? Keeping peace in the home and holding the family together are not sufficient as goals. Goals must be related to the child. When we look at goals this way, three biblical goals of child rearing become clear.

Reverence for God is the first. "Bring them up in the training and instruction of the Lord" is the most significant New Testament injunction regarding this goal (Eph. 6:4). The purpose of child rearing, like the purpose of the Ten Commandments, is to develop love for God.

Second, parenting should produce respect for self in the child. Paul guards against severe or improper modes of discipline by urging parents to be careful of the child's inner attitude. Overbearing parenting may "provoke the child to wrath," (Eph. 6:4) including perhaps self-hatred, or make the child "lose heart" (Col. 3:21 NRSV), stifling self-expression and creating depression. It is significant that Paul worries about the psychological welfare of the child when speaking to parents.

Prominent parent trainers H. Stephen Glen and Jane Nelson teach parents to foster the following crucial self-perceptions in the child: strong perceptions of personal capabilities ("I am capable"); strong perceptions of personal power or influence over life ("I can influence what happens to me"); strong perceptions of significance in primary relationships ("I contribute in meaningful ways and I am genuinely needed").[1]

Since the first objective relates to God, and the second to self, the third is quite obviously respect for others. Loving one's neighbor as oneself is part of the substance of the Old Testament and New Testament ethic. Built on regard for God's Word, morals and values training are also oriented around regard for others.

Any system that leaves out one of these objectives is inadequate and even damaging. It is possible to develop persons who are oriented to God but who hate themselves and have little regard for others. Also, an unbalanced person can relate to others but have little respect for God.[2]

Parent Power

A parent training program will be constructed around the avenues of influence a parent possesses. Calling this influence "parent power" is not a bad idea, since it calls attention to the fact that the parent does have something of substance to work with. This power can be broken down into five basic forms: modeling, control, communication, interaction, and experiences. All of these together comprise the sum total of the parent-child relationship, which is the realm in which the parent operates.

Modeling

Parental example is a major force in the child's life. Since learning theorists have documented the power of adult models, we now have some new information about this old idea of being an example.[3]

First, modeling does not call for perfection. A parent may project an unreal picture of himself in an effort to be a perfect example, thus hiding personal struggles and even marital conflicts. This projects an unrealistic and hypocritical example, which can cause disrespect or even rejection on the part of the child. Parents are to be maturing examples, not perfect ones. They should be real, modeling the dynamics of confession and humility so that the child will understand the way that imperfect Christians can live with respect for each other and with a forgiven relationship with God.

Second, a close, revealing relationship is best. Modeling is more effective when inner thoughts and feelings are shared than when they are kept to oneself. A child will learn morality and standards from parents who talk about their views of life and themselves.

Third, modeling requires, above all, personal development. It is not a dramatic show to be put on; it is a real-life demonstration that is often very subtle in its influence. The unsuspecting parent screams, "Don't yell in the house," not thinking about the essential ingredient needed to stop the child's shouting, which is that the parent must stop shouting.

A fourth observation is simply this: modeling may not be enough. Values engineer Sidney Simon warns that parental models are insufficient of themselves, since modern children are exposed to so many other influential examples.[4] Parenting will require developing the child's internal knowledge and value structure in other ways. Also, children will need to be exposed in some depth to other Christian adults.

> Parental example is a major force in the child's life.

Control

Though not all parents exercise control, they do have an authority to control bestowed on them by society. Though there is considerably more discussion about and defense of children's rights today than previously, our culture supports parental rule. Also, the Scriptures urge parents to exercise control with care (Prov. 22:15; Eph. 6:4). This control is especially needed during the child's early years.

We are now discovering, though, that parents are not always able to exercise this control well. Their training will need to include both the understanding and the practice of the several ways to achieve this objective.

Control by consistent action. Actual physical control may need to accompany the parent's words when he or she deals with the very young child. Parents who depend on verbal control alone will soon recognize the powerlessness of the human voice. Parental discipline often fails at this point.

> The Scriptures urge parents to exercise control with care. Their training will need to include both the understanding and the practice of the several ways to achieve this objective.

The mother nicely asks the toddler to put away his toys and then leaves without making certain he does so. He continues watching TV, ignoring her request. She returns to discover this disobedience and changes her tone. "Put your toys away," she commands a second time, now more sternly. But returning again, the mother discovers her child has not complied. Overflowing with frustration, she angrily shouts the child into submission, but the emotional scene is not good for either mother or child. In effect, the mother has taught the child to respond only to shouting because she did not insist on obedience when she first spoke.

Control by natural consequences. The various writers of Proverbs maintain that one of the major ways to get wisdom is by learning through negative consequences. An ill-tempered man will learn to control his anger whenever his anger gets him into enough trouble to make him want to do something about it. Therefore people should not rescue him, but let him face consequences of his actions (Prov. 19:19). Permitting the results of behavior to shape a child is a legitimate, biblical form of parental power. Though protecting a child from serious harm is sometimes necessary, parents should be cautious not to unduly shield a child whenever the natural results of his conduct will be a powerful teacher. Parents can even permit a child to behave in a way they know will bring such results. For example, they might permit a child to buy a cheap toy, if she insists. Later when it breaks, the parent can stand by—without ridiculing or blaming—and permit the child to learn from her choices.

Sometimes, however, permitting natural consequences to teach will not work, for example when the consequences of an action could be severe (such as being injured by running out into the street) or long range (failing in school). Also, a child can't always detect the connection between an act and what follows (eating foods that limit energy). Parents will then need to produce some consequences for the child, either good ones to encourage good behavior or bad ones to discourage wrongdoing. The following are useful ways to do this.

Control by negative consequences. The behavior modification process includes various forms of appropriate negative correction: deprivation (no rollerblading today); banishment (two minutes alone in the bathroom); and overcorrection (the child who spits on the floor scrubs the whole floor). Each of these must be used carefully, keeping in mind concern for the child's emotional well-being.

The authors of *Systematic Training for Effective Parenting* (STEP) suggest financial payment as an example of negative consequences. After children have failed to make their beds or to perform certain chores, they are required to pay a small sum (ten or twenty cents) to the family member who does the chore for them.[5] The good feature of this approach is that it is lifelike. As the child grows up, if he fails in his responsibility, someone else will have to bear it. Because the core ingredient of responsibility is recognizing the way one's actions affect others, this approach makes the child see that his failure causes extra work for others. When he must pay money for shirking work as a child, just as he would have to do in real life later, the consequences of shirking, which otherwise would be hidden from him, are made visible. Note, however, that the money is not subtracted from the child's allowance. If this is done, this is punishment rather than a payment, and this has a different impact on the child.

Control by physical punishment. Since spanking can so easily turn into or be linked to child abuse, spanking should be approached cautiously. Consider these guidelines: (1) Spank carefully; it must not injure. (2) Use spanking sparingly. Use it as a last resort and only when other means cannot be used or other means have failed. We must avoid teaching children that the use of force is the only way or major way of resolving conflict. (3) Spank only after an explanation. Remember, good discipline looks to the future, aiming to teach a lesson, not to get even. (4) Use it against moral wrongs, not mistakes. A child should not be punished for acts that flow from his immaturity, like knocking over a glass of juice or coming home late because he forgot the time. Parents should discipline especially when the child defies them. When a child flagrantly refuses to obey, hits the parent, shouts, or shows other signs of mutiny, a parent should come out on the top of the situation. (5) Spank only in private. (6) Spank only when you are in control of yourself. Count to ten and always use the same paddle (and not your hand), which forces you to think and allows you to calm down while you are going to get it. A parent who is the type of person who typically uses force to solve problems, or is hot-tempered, may be well advised to forgo using spanking at all and use other forms of discipline. (7) Consider what is socially acceptable. Practicing a form of discipline that creates undue social embarrassment is going to be counter-productive. Spanking teenagers or those close to this age, for example, would be emotionally painful and damaging to them. (8) Consider the child's temperament. Spanking does not seem to be effective with some children. A child that is loved and consistently getting wiser will probably require less stringent discipline. "A rebuke impresses a man of discernment more than a hundred lashes a fool" (Prov. 17:10).

Control by verbal reproof. Loving rebuke is a scripturally sanctioned process. But care should be taken to reprove the child for misbehavior without damaging the child's sense of self-worth.

Control by reinforcement. Behaviorists such as Richard R. Abidin have constructed courses to teach behavior modification, built largely around encouraging remarks and other reinforcers.[6] Behavior modification would be unwise if it were used exclusively, but if it is used with other types of control and communication, it can be very effective, particularly with young children. It involves the following steps:

First, identify the behavior to be changed. Behavior is best changed in small bits and steps. Thus, we should be as specific as possible about the misconduct. Behavior modification calls for a specific goal—for example, getting the child to go to bed on time instead of getting the child to be on time in general.

Second, identify the positive behavior you wish to see. Usually we focus on the misconduct, getting the child to stop doing something. Rather, we are told to concentrate on what we want the child to do that is the opposite of the misbehavior. In other words, concentrate on getting the child to arrive on time for supper rather than focus on stopping his being late.

Third, ignore the undesirable conduct. This is the toughest principle of all to carry out since most of us feel compelled to scold every time the child comes up short. But ignoring the specific misbehavior paves the way for the effectiveness of the next steps.

Fourth, catch the child being good. The proper behavior must be present sometime if it is to be developed. This will mean giving attention to the child, for example, when he or she arrives on time for supper.

Finally, reinforce the desired behavior. A reinforcement is anything that will delight the child or give the child a good, confident feeling. "Because you came to supper on time, you can choose your favorite game for the family to play tonight."

Reinforcements can be given even if the child has only partially achieved: "Well, great, you were only two minutes late tonight," or "You are really improving; you were on time four out of seven nights this week." Such statements communicate to the child that you don't consider his lateness a sinful pattern of rebellion, but an expression of immaturity he is overcoming.

Reinforcements in the form of pleasant activities can be promised for the purpose of promoting and developing a certain practice: "Make your bed first; then you can go outside." This is called the *Premack principle*, named for the man who stated it, or the *Grandma principle*, for the person who always seemed to practice it.

Some may criticize behavior modification for its use of praise that appeals to the child's ego. Yet a distinction should be made between pride-producing statements and confidence-building ones. Producers of the STEP parent-training sessions make this clear distinction and attempt to train parents to use the latter.[7] The commendation, "You played perfectly at the concert tonight; I'm proud of you," is a reinforcement, but it builds on the wrong base.

It appeals to the child's pride, making him compare himself favorably with others. In addition, it will suggest that the parents' pride depends on perfection in the child, linking acceptance to excellence; such a commendation builds unrealistic standards within the child.

Instead, encouragement can be based on values that are not competitive—values that center on the child's contribution to others. The statement, "I really enjoyed hearing you play tonight; I know the others did too," puts the orientation in the right place. It focuses on others and gives the child a wholesome view of himself. To say, "I know God was pleased by your expression of kindness," relates our Lord to the reinforcement.

Praise comments are contrasted with confidence-building ones in the following ways. Praise statements emphasize external control, while confidence-building ones stress inner control; for example, "I think you are a great kid for winning that match" (praise) rather than "I know you really felt good about trying so hard" (confidence building). Praise statements provoke confidence in one's image while confidence-building ones inculcate satisfaction in one's actions. "I think you are a great pianist" (praise) instead of "You really seem to enjoy playing for yourself and others" (confidence building). By using confidence-building statements, Christian parents are emphasizing the values of cooperating, contributing, and living life as God intended. They avoid encouraging unhealthy competitive motivation that is based on pride.

Control with support. Attitude, not technique, is the most important ingredient of control. Studies show that being too permissive or overly restrictive cause the most damage. In a recent project, researchers related each type of discipline to a child's self-respect and behavior. They concluded that the most effective pattern was the authoritative one.[8] The authoritative parent is compared with three other types: neglectful, permissive, and authoritarian. These four styles were measured in two areas: control and support.

The neglectful pattern offers little or no control or support. For example, "Work it out yourself, I'm busy." The permissive style is low in control but strong in support: "Well, you can stay up this time. . . . I know you like this program." Also less effective than the authoritative style was the authoritarian type that consists of high control and low support: "Rules are rules. You're late to dinner. To bed without eating!" Most effective of the four, the authoritative manner offers both control and support: "You're late again to dinner, tiger. . . . How can we work this out?"

Dennis Guernsey has written a simple test for parents to examine their own style of parenting.[9]

Communication

While the section on control includes communication, this process deserves distinct treatment as an aspect of parental power.

Communicating feelings. Just as in the marriage union, self-disclosure is important in parent-child relationships. When parents share their feelings at appropriate moments, they are accomplishing a number of things.

First, parents help the child see the consequences of his or her actions. If the child's actions irritate the parent, the child needs to know that. When parents disclose their feelings of annoyance, children learn the result of their actions. Second, self-disclosure builds the parent's relationship with the child. Sharing inner feelings is a way of cementing a relationship. Saying, "I really feel good about being with you," draws parent and child together. Third, self-disclosure teaches the child about the real world. A parent who keeps all inward struggles to himself will hide from the child some important knowledge. The child will assume that dad and mom never had the same doubts, temptations, and dreams. Knowing others have these same experiences will fortify the child's self-confidence. The child also benefits by learning to share his or her feelings, which is important for personal growth.

> Just as in the marriage union, self-disclosure is important in parent-child relationships.

Simple guidelines and exercises can help parents learn to verbalize feelings. Some of these are recommended for couples in the chapter on marriage enrichment. One simple guideline is to replace "you" statements with "I" statements. Instead of "You stop shouting, or I don't know what I'll do to you," the parent says, "I feel very nervous when you shout like that." An example is furnished by Kenneth G. Prunty, who has developed a training program for Church of God people patterned after Parent Effectiveness Training:

> Friends come over for a visit. Your two small children are playing in the kitchen and dining areas as they frequently do, but their joy, laughter, and loudness in playing make it difficult for you and your friends to visit. Follow these steps in formulating and sending an "I" message.
>
> Step 1: What I see and hear the children doing: They are playing and talking loudly and joyfully.
>
> Step 2. The real effect: We cannot hear, and it is hard for us to carry on a conversation.
>
> Step 3: The feeling: We want to be able to hear and talk, and are feeling upset because we cannot.[10]

Completing open-ended statements can also help establish the habit of exploring and expressing feelings. Parents can practice with one another with statements such as these:

- Whenever I feel frustrated, I . . .
- When I am alone, I feel . . .
- Something that makes me afraid is . . .
- Whenever I am upset, I feel like this inside . . .
- When someone disobeys me, I feel . . .
- Whenever someone disappoints me, I feel . . .

If the group includes both parents and children, adults could pair off with children for a twenty-minute sharing time, using a list like this. Exercises for sharing feelings, both positive and negative, are plentiful. Lyman Coleman's *Serendipity Books* are a major source of such exercises.[11] And *Reaching Out* by David Johnson can be adopted for family training.[12]

Communicate interest by listening. Listening is a form of power. If the parent fails to listen, it amounts to a damaging rejection. The parent's good listening prompts the child to think for himself and builds self-respect and self-control. Thomas Gordon, founder of PET, teaches reflective listening. This form of listening helps children think through an issue for themselves. It is patterned after the nondirective counseling of Carl Rogers, who calls it paraphrasing.

Listening is a form of power.

In reflective listening a parent avoids a thoughtless reaction to the superficial aspects of a child's statement. When the child complains, "I don't know why Mrs. Craig gave me a *D* on that paper," the parent is often tempted to scold the child for complaining or to rise up in defense of the fairness of American education. PET teaches the parent to repeat the child's statement, in other words, to paraphrase it: "You don't see what Mrs. Craig saw about your paper that made her give you a *D?*" This shows a willingness to hear what the child has to say. In addition, the simple reflective statement gives the child a chance to think it through out loud. Gordon says the child will usually end up giving himself or herself the advice the parent was about to give in the first place.

Certainly the Christian parent is entitled to offer some rebuke and some advice from time to time. But a very wise man once advised people first to listen: "He who answers before listening—that is his folly and his shame" (Prov. 18:13). Most parents will need a lot of practice in reflective listening before it is internalized.

Communicating God's Word. This is a prime aspect of parental influence, one that is most commended by Scripture. It is so central that part 6 in this book is devoted to this practice of family nurture. Preparing parents for this takes more than an annual sermon on family devotions. It demands some solid connections between church and home.

Interaction

Though the term *interaction* includes modeling, communication, and controlling, it embraces the total give-and-take in the household.

It refers, first of all, to the general atmosphere and life of the home. Dorothy Law Nolte describes in verse what takes place:

> If a child lives with conflict, he learns to fight.
> If a child lives with fear, he learns to be apprehensive.
> If a child lives with pity, he learns to feel sorry for himself.
> If a child lives with ridicule, he learns to be shy.
> If a child lives with shame, he learns to feel guilty.
> If a child lives with encouragement, he learns to be confident.
> If a child lives with tolerance, he learns to be patient.
> If a child lives with praise, he learns to be appreciated.
> If a child lives with acceptance, he learns to love.[13]

Home interaction is so broad in scope that it requires no less than the personal development of the parents—their growth in grace and in the knowledge of our Lord. Thus the whole adult ministry is closely related to family ministry. But there are some areas of interaction in which parental training can be more specific.

> While it is biblical to teach children to live under authority, it is also right to teach them how to live in a democracy.

Interact with understanding. The findings of developmental psychology should be made available to parents through library books and courses because home interaction should be based on understanding. An unknowing mother can stifle the child's zest for life by uninformed, unfair treatment. When a five-year-old boy lifts the skirt of another child, he is usually not displaying his sinful nature but rather his curious nature. The parents' reaction at such times are very important to the three goals of child rearing—the child's respect for himself or herself, for others, and for God.

Interact democratically in decision making. While it is biblical to teach children to live under authority, it is also right to teach them how to live in a democracy. Contemporary life demands that we be able to think through issues for ourselves and gain the moral and cooperative skills for successful living in a democratic society. Certainly life includes submission to Christ as Master, but not all issues are settled from a direct statement of Scripture.

For the answers to questions like "Shall we play Monopoly or Pay Day tonight?" and "Shall we endorse nuclear electric power?" the child must learn the process of give-and-take, giving due consideration to biblical principles and to other people. The child can't learn *that* in a home where all the answers are handed down by the father and mother. In fact, not allowing children to hammer out rules and ethics in debate and interaction with others stifles their ability to think morally, according to developmentalist Jean Piaget.

Thus, parents can have some of their interaction on a democratic basis. A family council or meeting can serve the family well. A weekly or a periodic meeting of the family is called. There the family discusses matters such as vacations, recreation, relationships, home rules, standards, chores, etc. Care is taken not to permit problems to dominate these meetings, creating distasteful times of scolding and reproof. Decisions are made in a warm, businesslike manner that allows for arguing and free expression.

> If children are not allowed to solve some of their problems alone, they are made unnecessarily and unhealthily dependent on the parents' authority instead of God's.

Interact in solving problems. Going through an acceptable approach to problems contributes to the child's later ability to manage. PET's problem-solving approach is quite commendable. When a Christian adds to this approach suggestions on how to know the will of God and insight on how to trust God's Spirit, the process is a solid one. There are five steps in this approach to solving problems.

First, identify the problem. Sometimes Christians retreat from problems instead of facing them squarely.

Second, analyze the problem prayerfully. We are justified in praying for insight, not just release. Problems are not dissolved by prayer; they are faced with prayer. God doesn't promise to take the challenge away. "With any trial he will give you a way out of it and the strength to *bear* it" (1 Cor. 10:13 JB, italics mine).

Insight in the case of family problems can be gained from asking this question: "Who 'owns' the problem?" If any family member takes another's problem for himself, successful overcoming of it will be hindered. Since a child's problem may cause problems for the parents, distinguishing between the child's and the parent's problem is important. If a child is failing a subject in school, that is the child's problem. The parent's difficulty is knowing how to live with and work with a child who is failing math. If the parent tries to "pass" the math course for the child, the parent becomes frustrated and the child becomes dependent.

The parental task is to help and support the child in solving his or her problems and not to own the problem for the child. Families can be taught how to do this by giving them a case study and then analyzing it. In some situations the role of the parent may be to do nothing but stand by and pray; and the child is led to understand and accept this. In that case the parent is there to help, but only if requested and only if the help is not in the form of solving the problem for the child.

Third, list all possible solutions. This requires some creative thinking.

Fourth, imagine all the possible consequences of each solution. This requires one to imagine the future on a cause-effect basis. Younger children do not have this ability; therefore, when the parent helps the child think through possible courses of action and their results, the parent is aiding the child to develop his or her rational powers.

Finally, choose the best solution. This step requires some understanding of the ways that God leads us, such as through scriptural principles and circumstances. Inner feelings of peace regarding a course of action should also fit into place. Selecting the best solution demands adjustment to values and morals, since one's decision will affect others as well as oneself.

Leading a child through the problem-solving process need not exclude an order of authority in the home, where parents' decisions are final; but even when the parent hands down a decision, he or she should reveal to the child the process that led to the decision. The problems that are the child's alone to solve will provide many occasions for training in decision making for his or her future welfare. If children are not allowed to solve some of their problems alone, they are made unnecessarily and unhealthily dependent on the parents' authority instead of God's. Later, such children may be dangerously susceptible to blind dependence on some misguided political or religious leader.

Interact through recreation. Fun times of interacting can make their mark on children. Besides developing respect for their own mental health, recreation can build their relationships with the family. Recreation also induces communication by generating small talk that can lead to significant conversations.

Spending fun time together is not optional. Training in this area could include practical helps in planning wholesome family recreation and exposing parents to good books on recreation. The church can communicate recreational ideas during its church-sponsored intergenerational recreation and camping.

Creating Experiences

The fifth form of parental influence is the power to control the child's world of experiences. The parent's control here is not total, but it is substantial. Since so much learning results from interacting with life, the quality and type of experience will make a great impact. The parent can guide the child into situations both inside and outside the home. For example, reading missionary biographies can infect the child with hope and love for other people, and music lessons or sports participation can develop self-confidence. Such activities will shape the child's values, attitudes, and moral stance.

We can help parents be more systematic in directing the child's experiences. From my exposure to parents in training situations, I have found that they are often unaware of the way to do this. It will take, first, an awareness for the values we wish to instill in the child.

One workshop guide to values training lists eight basic character traits and abilities related to maturity. These are: *affection*—the ability to love and care; *respect*—including both self-respect and the ability to respect others; *enlightenment*—the skill of learning from others and from experience; *skill*—discovering and developing one's talents; *power*—participating in the making of decisions; *wealth*—awareness of money as an instrument that should be respected and handled well; *well-being*—the attainment and maintenance of mental and physical health; and *rectitude*—an abiding sense of responsibility for one's attitudes and behavior.[14]

Drawing from Scripture, we can produce a list of Christian virtues that can be used in conjunction with these basic societal values. The list in 2 Peter 1:5–7 lends itself to this:

- Faith—trust in God
- Goodness—respect for virtue
- Knowledge—desiring to have wisdom and truth
- Self-control—self-discipline and the legitimacy of society's control
- Perseverance—enduring, finishing the job
- Godliness—being serious about God
- Brotherly kindness—respect and affection for others
- Love—sacrificing for others

Once parents are aware of the precise values they want to inculcate, they can explore the possible means of doing so. Listing the categories of life's experiences will reveal the many alternatives that are open to the parent:

- Exposure to examples
- In-depth relationships
- Reading
- Activities with nature and created life
- Large-group activities
- Small-group activities
- Leadership experiences
- Serving experiences
- Decision-making experiences
- Responsibility-related experiences
- Skill-developing experiences
- Hobbies, sports, music, recreation, etc.

Parenting will require matching the child's experience to some value to be learned. Parents should understand that values are not taught by mere repetition of words or nagging rebukes. Rather they are developed—that is, forged—through interaction with life and interaction with other people.

For example, a couple might like to establish or develop rectitude, or responsibility, in their children. The parents would first define this value. They might define rectitude as follows: an abiding sense of responsibility for one's own attitudes and behavior. This quality would manifest itself in a dedication to truth, honesty, justice, fairness, and compassion. The parents could then plan together how to develop this value in their children. There are many areas that could be chosen for developing such responsibility. Here are some:

> Parents should understand that values are not taught by mere repetition of words or nagging rebukes. Rather they are developed—that is, forged—through interaction with life and interaction with other people.

- Children are expected to obey rules that have been established and discussed in the home.
- Children are encouraged to establish their own rules and standards beyond those of the parents.
- Each family member is expected to do his or her chores or duties, and these must be done consistently.
- Children can participate in family discussions of standards and rules and the reasons behind them.
- Children can participate in democratic family discussions of family practices.
- Children can be involved in programs and intergenerational events at church that give them in-depth exposure to adult models who practice responsible behavior.
- Children can be encouraged to read biographies and stories that show the value of acting responsibly.
- Children can be encouraged to participate in camping, sports, and other activities that show the need for personal discipline and cooperation with others.
- Children can be given the responsibility of caring for a pet or be encouraged to develop another hobby that builds responsibility.
- Children can be allowed to work out conflicts and thereby learn the importance of give and take, without the constant interference of an outside authority to settle disputes.
- Children can be involved in special occasions such as family get-togethers on holidays, dinner guests and parties in the home, etc., and thereby learn the importance of and practice of social skills and graces.

The above list is given for the purpose of developing one value. Parents can be taught to formulate lists of experiences for each of the values mentioned earlier in this section. Specific parent training sessions can be devoted to this, and the values developed can be discussed in other adult-education sessions.

THE BLAME-TRAIN OPTION

In our society, notes Thomas Gordon, parents are blamed, not trained. The church is in a strategic place to do something about this dilemma. The above model of parent training shows that we have plenty of agreement on some of the basics. And we have within our grasp some effective training tools to accomplish the job.

One of the most exciting aspects of this ministry is that it will benefit so many. Not only will children and future generations be helped, but present-day parental life will be enriched. Parenting skills are closely related to Christian living skills. When learning how to communicate, to handle feelings, and to exercise parental influence, parents are learning how to be mature Christians. Parental development is personal development. For that reason the task is as all-encompassing as it is imperative.

SUGGESTED RESOURCES

Chartier, Jan, and Myron Chartier. *Nurturing Faith in the Family*. Valley Forge, Pa.: Judson Press, 1986. •Five fine videos on basic aspects of parenting from a Christian viewpoint; not enough for a whole parenting program, but a good supplement to one.

Dinkmeyer, Don. *Systematic Training for Effective Parenting: Parent's Handbook*. Circle Pines, Minn.: American Guidance Service, 1976. •Based on STEP, a nationally known parent training program; not Christian, but reflecting many Christian values. Parent's manual and leader's guide available. An excellent program for teaching parenting skills if the trainers help evaluate guidelines from a Christian perspective.

Gardner, Freda. *Active Parenting Today in the Faith Community*. Atlanta: Active Parenting Today, 1993. •An attempt by the Family Ministries Committee of the Presbyterian Church (USA) to integrate Christian concepts into the Active Parenting Today parent training program. Democratic in its approach to discipline.

Popkin, Michael H. *Active Parenting Today*. Atlanta: Active Parenting Today, 1993. •Parent's guide also available. A program like the STEP program, but incorporates interactive video. Especially good for teaching basic skills to parents.

Ward, Ted. *Values Begin at Home*. •See under suggested resources for chapter 23.

NOTES

1. H. Stephen Glenn and Jane Nelson, *Raising Self-Reliant Children in a Self-Indulgent World: Seven Building Blocks for Developing Capable Young People* (Rocklin, Calif.: Prima Publishing, 1989), 49–50.

2. Catherine Caldwell Brown, "It Changed My Life," *Psychology Today* (November 1976): 47.

3. A. Bandura, "Influences of Model's Reinforcement Contingencies on the Acquisition of Imitative Responses," *Journal of Personality and Social Psychology* (1965): 589–95.

4. Sidney Simon, Leland W. Howe, and Howard Kirschenbaum, *Values Clarification* (New York: Hart, 1972), 17–18.

5. Don Dinkmeyer and Gary McKay, *Systematic Training for Effective Parenting* (Circle Pines, Minn.: American Guidance Services, 1976).

6. Richard R. Abidin, *Parenting Skills* (New York: Human Sciences Press, 1976).

7. Dinkmeyer and McKay, *Systematic Training*.

8. Dennis Guernsey, "What Kind of Parent Are You?" *Family Life Today* (January 1978): 29–30.

9. Ibid.

10. Kenneth G. Prunty, "The Care-Lab: A Family Enrichment Program," in *Marriage and Family Enrichment,* ed. Herbert Otto (New York: Abingdon, 1976), 68.

11. Lyman Coleman, *Serendipity Books* (Waco, Tex.: Word Books, 1972).

12. David Johnson, *Reaching Out* (Englewood Cliffs, N.J.: Prentice-Hall, 1972).

13. Dorothy Law Nolte, "Children Learn What They Live," from the L. A. American Institute of Family Relations, quoted in Barbara Bolton, *Ways to Help Them Learn: Grades 1–6* (Glendale, Calif.: Regal Books, 1971), 29–30.

14. Herbert Brayer and Zella W. Cleary, *Valuing in the Family: A Workshop Guide for Parents* (San Diego: Pennant, 1972).

23

Training Parents for Spiritual Nurture in the Home

Having a special section on the spiritual nurture of children in the home may convey that spiritual training is distinct and separate from the nurturing process described in the last chapter. On the contrary, I believe that God is to be part of all of life and that spiritual life should not be compartmentalized. Everything in the life of the child is related to the spiritual, and everything a parent does will either help or hinder a child's moral values, self-discipline, interpersonal relationship skills, etc., all of which are spiritual. All aspects of "parent power"—modeling, controlling, communicating, interacting, and creating experiences—relate to the process of spiritual formation. It is the church's business, as I have tried to make clear, to teach couple and parent skills because that will affect the spiritual lives of both children and adults. Because of this, family ministry is spiritual ministry.

But this chapter on spiritual formation is necessary for two reasons. First, there are some special methods, materials, and guidelines for parents to utilize in communicating Christian faith. Though parents cannot and should not try to force a child's spiritual development, they can intentionally and systematically assist it.[1] Second, the subject of the spiritual formation of children and youth in the home needs to be integrated in a unique way with the church's Christian education program.

> **Family ministry is spiritual ministry.**

Where the church and the home most converge is around the matter of Christian faith. Therefore this chapter will focus on how the church can help parents contribute to a child's faith nurture and how church and home can cooperate together in that nurture process.

PREPARING PARENTS FOR INFORMAL TEACHING

Parents should be alerted to the fact that the best approach to aiding their child's faith development is not formal, but informal, instruction. The interjecting of biblical truth and values into routine everyday life is something the family is best suited to do. It is as biblical as it is powerful: "Talk about them when you sit at home and when you walk along the road, when you lie down and when you get up. Tie them as symbols on your hands and bind them on your foreheads. Write them on the doorframes of your houses and on your gates" (Deut. 6:7b–9). Sunday school teachers and club leaders seldom have a chance to do this, but parents do.

> The best approach to aiding their child's faith development is not formal, but informal, instruction.

Informal teaching is the best approach to what educators consider the most effective type of instruction: need-oriented education. The biggest problem in teaching is to get pupils interested in what you have to teach. But in the home, scriptural truth can be injected into the mainstream of life as a response to curiosity or events; it need not be dragged in irrelevantly. In the context of life, the child's motivation to learn is already present.

Parents also have an opportunity, during informal moments, to deal with the child's misunderstanding of Christian concepts. By asking questions and answering them, they can try to discover what their children believe and correct them when necessary. Developmental psychologists propose that children are not capable of understanding many of the abstract and figurative concepts of Scripture until later in life.[2] When they reach the level of "formal operations," at about age twelve or so, most can understand the meaning of ideas like "light of the world," and "fishers of men." Talk to younger children about building your house on the rock and they don't get the message that they should ground their lives on Christ's word; rather they think they just got some advice about constructing a building. Since children are used to hearing adults talk about things they don't understand, they usually just let it go by them. And when they do misunderstand, their misconceptions are sometimes funny: "Draw a knife on God and he will draw a knife on you," is the way one child understood the King James Version of James 4:8: "Draw nigh to God, and he will draw nigh to you."

But some misunderstandings can confuse and hurt a child. What pictures of God are etched early into a child's mind? What view of salvation do they really have? One of my students looked into some of these views, asking children to draw a picture that defined salvation. Few of the children under age six showed they understood. Most often, being saved was construed as being rescued from some danger in this life. Explaining her picture, a little girl said: "This is a pasture with a goat; the goat is going to run into this little girl. However, God made it rain and she was saved." Unless we explain in more concrete terms the many metaphors and symbols of Scripture, children may easily miss the message we are trying to convey. Through close, informal conversations with their children, parents can explain these portraits of God, balancing them with illustrations of God's love and grace.

There are ways we can prepare them to do this.

We can help parents, first, to watch for the child's questions. The Old Testament pattern capitalized on children's curiosity in order to have truth passed on to the next generation: "In the future, when your son asks you, 'What is the meaning of the stipulations, decrees and laws the LORD our God has commanded you?' tell him . . ." (Deut. 6:20–21). Parents might easily overlook opportunities to teach, since children's questions are often posed at the wrong time. The wise mother later goes back to the question her impulsive young son asked her just as she was sliding the hot chicken from the pan to the platter. Wise parents make it a pattern to go to the shelf for the Bible as they do for the encyclopedia when children are searching for answers.

The Christian parent, too, can become skillful at asking questions of the children. This is particularly important because the home is the proper setting for correcting children's misconceptions. At the right moment during conversations the father or mother can ask questions like these: "What is your idea of God?" "What is faith?" "How do you explain the word *forgive*?" During play parents can encourage the concepts. Discussing the child's picture about forgiveness, for example, can be an occasion of honest exchange of feelings and ideas related to Christian faith and life.

> Parents who understand the informal process of instruction can capitalize on life's momentous occasions, turning them into joyful times of celebration, teaching, and worship.

Parents who understand the informal process of instruction can also capitalize on life's momentous occasions, turning them into joyful times of celebration, teaching, and worship. Events surrounding a birth can evoke thoughts about the gift and meaning of life. Parents and children bowing over the newly arrived family member and offering their simple words of thanks to life's Creator constitute a sincere and emotional liturgy unmatched by any church service. To celebrate requires the ability to do three things. First, it demands that we know how to live—to act, to experience, to love. Next, it requires awareness—thinking back over an experience, assessing it, judging it, evaluating it. The third requirement is the foremost one—the ability to share, or to turn private reflections into public awareness of them. And so we ask each family member, "What does having a new baby in the house mean to you?" We give the adult or child time to meditate, to search heart and mind; then we ask him or her to share. And in that sharing of life and awareness and response, we celebrate the gifts and presence of God. In that celebration the Word and the person of God are integrated into our living.

That integration can take place during the negative experiences of life as well, during the crises we endure and the pain we suffer. Our Lord is present in such experiences also, and we speak of him at such times with dignity and gratitude. We interpret our feelings for ourselves and for each other in the light shed from his truth. Such a perspective offers an occasion for celebration when we suffer, for he always offers hope and light, even when it seems hopelessly dark.

Parents can also do things to prompt the child to ask questions—something Jewish ceremonies were intended to do. During the home-centered Passover celebration parents were to be ready to explain whenever the children would ask, "What does this ceremony mean to you?" (Exod. 12:26). Joshua built a monument at Gilgal from twelve stones taken from the Jordan River and then told the Israelites, "In the future when your descendants ask their fathers, 'What do these stones mean?' tell them, 'Israel crossed the Jordan on dry ground'" (Josh. 4:21–22).

Both the church programs and the family will constantly be provoking children to ask questions. Parents can be taught to do so intentionally in many ways: inviting a missionary to the dinner table, watching TV or a video, reading stories, sharing their own experiences, etc.

One of the most powerful educational tools, as well as a question producer, is ritualizing. Ritualizing embraces for spiritual formation something every family already has: family rituals. These are the ordinary patterns of doing things—how we say goodnight to one another, pass food at the table, celebrate birthdays, Christmas, etc. We become so accustomed to these practices that no one in the family has to ask who is going to do what or what's going to come next. Rituals ensure that our lives are ordered, not chaotic.[3]

Prominent Christian educator Lewis J. Sherrill has maintained that the best way to keep faith alive is to build rituals that will cause children to ask, "What does this mean?"[4] In our parent training classes, we can encourage parents to creatively develop rituals that best fit their family background and temperament. We can suggest activities such as reading a Bible story or Christian storybook at bedtime, praying with a child before he leaves for school, having a special prayer time for the child whose birthday we are celebrating. Rituals that include God and the Bible in holidays of Thanksgiving, Easter, and Christmas can be meaningful to all family members; such practices often continue through families for many generations.

FORMAL TEACHING

Some Christian leaders resist encouraging parents to use more formalized methods of teaching in their homes. Having family devotions to intentionally teach children Christian truths too readily produces in the child an intellectual faith that is unrelated to life, they contend. The child is saturated with words about Christianity before he or she has had an opportunity to understand those words experientially.[5] An informal situation, such as answering a child's question while taking a walk, is less likely to occasion such intellectualizing. When parents respond to a child's question in ordinary conversation, there is less possibility that the answer will be too bookish or unrelated to life. Forcing a child to concentrate on the intellectual content of the Christian faith may give children a distaste for God, they say. Others observe that formal methods don't fit well into modern home life. Parents and children are not accustomed to having teaching-learning situations in the home setting.

But developing some formalized Christian instruction in the home makes sense biblically as well as educationally. Teaching the Scriptures to children at home is well grounded in Scripture (Deut. 6:7). Two important considerations make clear God's reason for instructing us to do this. First, the accumulation of vocabulary is important while the child is interpreting experience and framing it into a total worldview. While it is true that the child is confronted with words beyond his experience, he learns words that explain it. If the child is living with the biblical realities of hope, trust, forgiveness, etc., the teaching confirms and explains the nature of and reasons for those realities. The teaching also provides some basis for discussing these things with others. While this teaching can possibly be done within the regular conversations of the home, it is too important to be left to that alone.

Second, important questions about God and the Christian faith need to be raised. Contemporary life does not always prompt the kinds of questions the Bible addresses. A walk through an airport will prompt all kinds of questions from a fascinated child, but the tour will hardly raise questions about God. Our secular, materialistic, plastic world protects and separates us from some of the major issues of life and death. We cannot be sure that teachings about God will automatically occur in the nonformal processes of the Christian family even if parents are prepared to communicate those teachings. We need to alert and prepare parents for both approaches—the nonformal and the formal—because each contributes to the other. Questions asked during the intentionally planned learning time prompts questions and observations during the informal moments. And informal times provide some of the grist for the formalized instructional moments.

> Developing some formalized Christian instruction in the home makes sense biblically as well as educationally.

Family Devotions and Family Worship

One of the sacred cows of the evangelical subculture is the *family altar*. In our thinking, it has stood as the norm for a healthy Christian family.

Some historical evidence seems to point to the fact that regular family devotions were once a part of Christian family life in America. During the times before the American Revolution the family altar was the means of giving Christian nurture to the children. Most families had and used the Bible.[6] Many evangelical pastors continue to insist on using the so-called altar. Those who have found it useful speak of it in glowing, dramatic, emotional tones, often making claims unsupported by biblical or practical evidence. "The altar has been a focal point of religious experience since time began," one writer generalizes and then misleadingly confuses family devotions with Israel's bloody altar. "In Old Testament times the Israelites met God at the altar. When the altar lay in ruin, Israel's life was at a low ebb."[7] Central to the problem of the family altar has been the unexamined acceptance of it in theory, while the nonpracticing silent majority "listen with respect, feeling a bit guilty at this hiatus in the family life."[8]

What research we have for its actual practice is not very encouraging. A survey done by the Family Altar League of America revealed that only 5 percent of professing Christian families have any kind of regular, meaningful family worship.[9] And a check of family worship practices in the homes of professional Christian educators was rather disappointing also. A majority of the two hundred youth directors and Christian education directors who responded to a questionnaire reported that they did not have prayer and Bible study with their families more than three times a week. The rest had less than this. And half of these model leaders said that they did not have sufficient time for their families.[10]

Lacking extensive reliable research, we must turn to some theoretical debate on the matter. The editors of *Eternity* magazine once invited some evangelical authors to face the issue squarely, asking them, "Should we have daily family devotions?" The three different replies were "Yes," "Not necessarily," and "No, not if. . . ." Two of the authors mentioned the problem of Christians' guilt feelings over the matter of daily family devotions, which is a subcultural tradition, not a biblical mandate. The author in favor of the family altar never mentioned guilt; he laid it on:

> We need family worship so badly. Parents will then have the opportunity to tell their children about God's saving love revealed in Jesus Christ. If you really believe on the Lord Jesus Christ, how can you fail to make opportunities within your family to tell your children about Him?[11]

To justify such an extreme statement, we must establish whether or not regular family devotions is a biblically sanctioned practice. That is the first issue. Joel Nederhood assures us that the practice is absolutely biblical, citing Psalm 78:3–7, a passage that states there is in Israel a law commanding fathers to communicate God's truth to the next generation. But he fails to produce a specific Old Testament or New Testament text that identifies the so-called family altar as the place for that transfer of truth to take place. Enos Sjogren is thus correct when he asserts that it is not a practice that is expressly commanded in Scripture. In fact, in Scripture the emphasis falls not on some twenty-minute period but on the whole day.[12] And that is the major concern of Harold H. Hess, who is most outspoken in pointing out the weakness of family devotions, maintaining that the practice utterly fails to catch the spirit of the approach in Deuteronomy 6. He objects to the formalized, structured, and compartmentalized approach of family devotions, which is a substitute for the rich, nonformal communication available in the home.[13]

The practical results of family devotions are taken for granted as much as the supposed biblical base is. But the results are not all positive. At this point research does not help us much. We have a great deal of individual testimony about their value from parents and their children. Yet we don't have solid evidence concerning the factors that influence children in Christian homes, particularly because the whole matter of these factors is so complicated and mostly because research is so expensive. However, we do have clear testimony about the negative results of the family altar.

Many young people have been turned off and "case hardened" by this daily routine. In part, this is true because it's tough to keep such a day-to-day ritual from becoming boring. Occasional dinner guests may enliven it from time to time, but it too often is a dull affair from which children are only too glad to escape when they leave home. Certainly this is not true of all of them, but that it certainly is true of some. This may be particularly true in homes where the parents have little gift for reading out loud or for creative planning, and are primarily prompted by the nagging guilt that if they don't force the family through this daily practice, they surely will fail to communicate Christ to their dearly loved children. A sour and negative attitude soon dominates such a household at the very announcement of the family altar.

As for the suspicion that children who are not exposed to this ritual will not be exposed to Christ, such a suspicion remains just that—a suspicion. It is refreshing to hear a word of testimony from the writer on the other side. Enos Sjogren writes:

> I had the great fortune to be brought up in a Christian home. We never had a family altar, yet the presence of Christ was pervasive. Both children accepted Christ as personal Savior when teenagers, after passing through the normal period of rebellion. Both have been active in Christian work ever since, at home and overseas. Neither of the two homes have family altars. There are seven grandchildren. All are well adjusted children who have professed Christ and who remain active in evangelical youth movements.[14]

Neither the biblical nor the pragmatic evidence supports the contention that one cannot build a Christian home without a daily family altar. I side with Sjogren in answer to this question: Should we have daily family devotions? Not necessarily.

That we can recommend family devotions in certain church situations and for certain people is
fine. But the practice is at best
an inferior substitute for a
more totally integrated plan
for church and home that we
will consider later.

> Rather than push parents to conform to a certain procedure, we do better to help them personalize their approach to the family altar.

Those who do recommend having family devotions will need to do more than preach and teach about it. Few parents seem to be able to take the verbal instructions and then carry them out successfully in their home settings. A pastor who invites families into his home and has sample devotions with them has a workable approach. And parents might profit from some practical guidelines.

Make the devotional period personal. Recently a dedicated Christian father told a group of pastors I was with that his family had consistently read the Bible and had sung together early in the morning for over twenty years. In fact, the parents and children had memorized all the hymns in a large hymnal. The temptation to copy such successful parents pressed upon all of us who heard the story. But not all parents are capable of accomplishing such an achievement, particularly a father who sings in a monotone or is not musically inclined. Rather than push parents to conform to a certain procedure, we do better to help them personalize their approach to the family altar, offering various options to them.

Make family devotions regular. To be sure, a regular time and place is necessary for this practice. Individual families should be encouraged to give thought to determine what is the best time of day for them. And while the parents need to apply discipline and leadership, they should be instructed to avoid heaping oppressive guilt on themselves if they miss devotions from time to time.

Make family devotions simple. Simplicity is the key; otherwise, the day-to-day demand for creativity will make it impractical to maintain daily devotions. But simplicity does not preclude planning. Someone will need to decide what Bible storybook to read, what cassette to play, or what Bible passage to choose for the weeks to come. Otherwise, too much time will be absorbed in deciding on the spot what to do.

Make family devotions short. This may be the one principle that keeps the experience away from the city limits of "Dullsville." Sharing God's Word and experiencing worship together is the heart of the matter; the length of time spent will not replace the quality of the devotional sharing.

Allow for participation. Though it sounds simple, this principle is not easily applied. It may be great to keep seven-year-old George's interest level up by having him read the passage, but it will do little for his teenage brother's attention if he has to listen to his young brother stumble along.

Also, a mistake can be made in demanding the wrong kind of participation from an individual. Asking questions of kids, for example, is generally a good practice. But if the answers don't come freely to questions that are too tough, the child ends up being embarrassed, and thus sacrificed on the family altar.

Permit spontaneity. Granted, it is not easy to be spontaneous during a routine event. Spontaneity means we do something when we feel like it, when we have inner inspiration. And rarely does the inner state seem to cooperate with the outer schedule. But we can provoke some personal thoughts and sharing. After reading about the fruit of the Spirit, we might ask, "Which characteristics do we most see in each other's lives?" We can start with mom: Does she most exemplify love, joy, peace, long-suffering, etc.? Then we can do the same with each member of the family circle, lovingly affirming each one in this way. At times the Bible reading might be replaced by a question: "Shall we each share what we've been thinking about that relates to God?"

Following such principles could qualify daily family devotions for a major role in family nurture. But we can't be certain. Beset by difficulties lurking in modern family life and lacking solid biblical sanction, family devotions can hardly constitute the backbone of family nurture.

Use of Books and Other Media

A few minutes in a Christian bookstore will alert anyone to the many creative audio and video cassettes, books, and even games that aim at a child's spiritual and character development. The church can help parents use these materials with their children by informing parents about them. Better yet, they can promote them in a church bookstore (or simple book rack) and provide them in the church lending library and resource center. We can continually remind parents not to lose sight of the power of the simplest of all educational methods: reading to children.

An Integrated Approach

The most promising system for family nurture is one that interfaces Christian education in the church with that of the home. Besides equipping parents to effectively nurture their children in the home, the ideal program would include the following: (1) a weekly Bible study session for parents that deals with the same lesson their children would study in the child's class; (2) creatively-taught weekly children's classes; and (3) learning activities related to the weekly sessions for children and parents to do together during the week.

> We can continually remind parents not to lose sight of the power of the simplest of all educational methods: reading to children.

Such programs have proven very effective for families with children up to the early teen years. No curriculum is available for such a system, but churches are adapting published Sunday school literature for this purpose.

A church need not press all parents to be part of such an integrated program to make it successful. Inviting volunteers to form a parents' class to center their session around the content being taught to their children is a simple way to initiate such a program. Just being aware of the concepts being communicated to their children will stimulate conversation during the week and help parents be alert to opportunities to apply that truth to all family members' lives.

Curriculum such as that published by David C. Cook is readily adapted to integrated church and family Christian education since it uses a topical approach to all age groups. Each week parents, children, and youth will be studying the same subject, though not the same passage of Scripture. Home interaction is then stimulated through a guide that offers creative activities for parents to do with their children between the Sunday sessions.

Some churches have encouraged parents to try teaching their children what they themselves have heard in the Sunday morning worship session. Each week parents are given a one page handout that offers creative suggestions for parent-child interaction centered around the sermon topic.

However it is done,

> The most promising system for family nurture is one that interfaces Christian education in the church with that of the home.

making the home a nurture center requires relating activities of church and home. In some churches the only educational system that is active is the church-oriented one. Sometimes both home and church systems are operating, but they don't connect with one another. Parents are involved in a round of church activities that do little to support their home-nurturing attempts. Even though attempts at such integration have not been widely used, their results have been extremely satisfying and powerful.[15]

SUGGESTED RESOURCES

Covenant Keeping: Sharing the Family Story. Grand Rapids: CRC Publications, 1986. • An entire—and effective—course on the Christian family, with the purpose of teaching parents how to pass faith on to their children. Videotapes, workbooks, and leader's guide available for each of the seven sessions. Videos can be borrowed. Contact CRC Publications, 2850 Kalamazoo Avenue SE, Grand Rapids, MI 49560, or call 800-968-7221.

Chartier, Jan, and Chartier, Myron. *Nurturing Faith in the Family*. • See under suggested resources for chapter 22.

Richards, Lawrence O. *A Theology of Children's Ministry*. Grand Rapids: Zondervan, 1982. • The best theory anyone has offered for integrating church and home nurture of children.

Ward, Ted. *Values Begin at Home*. Wheaton, Ill.: Victor Books, 1981. •A simply written book on understanding how parents can pass on values to children.

NOTES

1. A fine discussion of the definition and process of the spiritual formation of children in the home has been written by Craig Williford. See "Spiritual Formation in the Home," *Christian Education: Foundations for the Future*, ed. Robert E. Clark, Lin Johnson and Allyn K. Sloat (Chicago: Moody Press, 1991), 583–96.

2. For an overview of the child's cognitive thinking stages related to thinking about spiritual matters, see James Fowler, *Stages of Faith: The Psychology of Human Development and the Quest for Meaning* (San Francisco: Harper & Row, 1981).

3. Lewis J. Sherrill, *Covenant Keeping: Sharing the Family Story* (Grand Rapids: CRC Publications, 1986), 23.

4. Ibid.

5. Ronald Goldman, *Religious Thinking from Childhood to Adolescence* (London: Routledge and Kegan Paul, 1964).

6. Herbert T. Mayer, "Family Relations in North America," in *Family Relationships and the Church*, ed. Oscar E. Feucht (St. Louis: Concordia, 1970).

7. Joel Nederhood, "Should We Have Daily Family Devotions: Yes," *Eternity* (March 1971): 15.

8. Enos Sjogren, "Should We Have Daily Family Devotions: Not Necessarily," *Eternity* (March 1971): 15.

9. T. C. Van Kooten, *Building the Family Altar* (Grand Rapids: Baker, 1969), 15.

10. H. Norman Wright, "The Church Building Christian Families—Myth and Possibilities" (report at Talbot Theological Seminary, Los Angeles, n.d.).

11. Nederhood, "Should We Have Daily Family Devotions: Yes," 15.

12. Sjogren, "Should We Have Daily Family Devotions: Not Necessarily," 15.

13. Harold H. Hess, "Should We Have Daily Family Devotions: No," *Eternity* (March 1971): 15.

14. Sjogren, "Should We Have Daily Family Devotions: Not Necessarily," 15.

15. The system developed by Larry Richards, called Sunday School Plus, was the most thorough attempt to interface church and home in the nurturing of children. In the first edition of this book, I described this approach in detail. However, since that edition was published, the curriculum ceased to be printed. Launched by some special financial grants, the literature was used by more than a thousand churches and was hailed by these churches as extremely effective. However, the publishers were unable to make the venture self-supporting, and it ceased.

◆ *Part Seven*

Specialized Family Ministries

Educational Approaches Toward Dysfunctional Families

24

In 1965, Andrew Blackwood put it clearly: "Yesterday's actions produce results today. Today's actions will produce results tomorrow. Each generation carries a crushing load of unfinished business from the past."[1] Until recent research enlightened us, we weren't quite sure how much of this unfinished business children carried with them into adulthood. Apparently they carry a lot, judging by the trend described in chapter 4: dysfunctional families are reproducing themselves.

Scriptures tell us of this multi-generational influence in passages like Exodus 20:5: "I, the LORD your God, am a jealous God, punishing the children for the sin of the fathers to the third and fourth generation of those who hate me." That this text is not claiming that God actually unjustly punishes children for parent's sin is made clear by Deuteronomy 24:16. Also, Ezekiel 18:20 states, "The son will not share the guilt of the father, nor will the father share the guilt of the son." What the Exodus text does affirm is that children are so often like their parents. While Ezekiel established that individuals were responsible for their own actions, he tried to point out that his generation was sinning like the former generations. "Like mother, like daughter," he said (Ezek. 16:44).

Other Scriptures make it clear that parents profoundly shape their children: "Train a child in the way he should go, and when he is old he will not turn from it" (Prov. 22:6). Though this is speaking of positive influence, might not negative parenting

> Helping one another to face ourselves and calling each other to repentance are important facets of church life.

also have some lasting effects? Because he knew this to be true, the apostle Paul warned fathers not to "exasperate" their children or "embitter" them so that they "become discouraged" (Eph. 6:4; Col. 3:21).

The church can do a great deal to help people who have been or are in a dysfunctional family. Most important perhaps is confirming that dysfunctional families have a negative impact on family members and that it may be quite substantial. People tend to deny this because it is painful and shameful to label one's family dysfunctional. This, then, becomes the greatest obstacle to their recovery and growth. But helping one another to face ourselves and calling each other to repentance are obviously important facets of church life.

TEACHING ABOUT THE IMPACT OF DYSFUNCTIONAL FAMILIES

Research establishing the long-term effects of troubled families on their members is quite impressive. For example, a recent study of those who grew up in violent homes focused on people who, though not physically abused themselves, watched one parent strike the other. Testing showed they were clearly more anxious than those who came from homes where no such acts of violence took place. Women in the study who had viewed marital violence were more aggressive and depressed than other women.[2] Another study dealt with 181 adults who were physically abused in childhood. Seven out of ten of them mistreated their own children.[3]

Granted, such studies do not absolutely confirm that family violence causes depression or aggression. Just because X trait shows up in a person from Y kind of home still doesn't absolutely prove Y produced X. We can note these two facts, but we can't actually observe the connection. Thus we can't say positively that research proves that witnessing abuse in childhood has a certain lasting effect on adults. But research like this does seem to suggest a link.

Some persons barely escape harsh childhoods. In the case of incest victims, research shows that only 23 percent of the victims survived without any adverse effects.[4] The closer the relationship and the longer the victimization continues over time, the greater the psychological problems in later life.

Those from alcoholic or abusive homes face more than the threat of becoming alcoholics or abusers. Going beyond the observations of counselors, Black, Bucky, and Wilder-Padilla compared 409 adults raised in alcoholic homes with 179 adults raised in nonalcoholic homes by having them fill out a questionnaire. Four major problem areas cropped up in the Adult Children of Alcoholics (ACoAs): problems with trusting people, handling feelings, being depressed, and being over-responsible. The researchers remind us that though convincing, their study is not conclusive. Its major limitation is that it dealt with what people said about themselves, instead of confirming the results through other means: asking others about them or using tests for depression, etc. But the study clearly shows that whenever they are asked, adult children of alcoholics say they are somewhat different from those who grew up in nonalcoholic homes.[5]

> ACoAs have more than average difficulty trusting God and extending forgiveness to others.

The most believable proof of the impact of the childhood family on adults comes from a researcher who studied 129 evangelicals. She compared two groups of evangelical adults: those who were children in alcoholic families and those who were not. Instead of merely asking them to fill in a questionnaire, she actually examined them with proven tests. Sandra Wilson reports that the findings were decisive: Evangelical ACoAs "appear to be significantly more depressed, guilt-prone, anxious, approval-seeking, and unable to trust others."[6] In their spiritual lives, ACoAs were also different, the research reveals. They have more than average difficulty trusting God and extending forgiveness to others.

The catalog of the traits of adult children from dysfunctional families is quite long. They guess at what normal behavior is, feeling they are different from other people. They judge themselves without mercy, have difficulty having fun, or following a project through from beginning to end. Finding it as easy to lie as to tell the truth, ACoAs constantly seek approval and affirmation. Either super responsible or irresponsible, ACoAs take themselves very seriously and overreact to changes over which they have no control. They are extremely loyal, even in the face of evidence that loyalty is undeserved. They also tend to be compulsive about many things. Claims one expert: "They get into 'overs.' They overachieve, overeat, overwork, overexercise, and overspend. They develop addictions of different types: to sex, pain, eating, religion, power, money, and spending."[7] Emotional problems plague them; they exhibit a tendency to have above-average feelings of depression, guilt, anxiety, fear, anger, and shame.

> Knowing how people were entrapped in the dysfunctional family system is necessary to helping them out of it.

The children of dysfunctional families are not the only ones affected. Friends and other relatives, particularly the spouses of these people, are also impacted in an unhealthy family system.

Getting some insight into the dysfunctional family system is a key to dealing with these families. Knowing how they were entrapped in the system is necessary to helping them out of it. In various family ministry programs, we can teach people about these processes.

TEACHING ABOUT THE PROCESSES OF FAMILY INFLUENCE

No one knows for sure exactly how our families influence us. There are as many theories about this as there are psychological theories about human behavior. Out of all of these, there are three that seem to make the most sense in analyzing dysfunctional families: codependency, identification, and learned coping mechanisms.

Codependency

Families with the compulsive behaviors we've mentioned tend to impart these addictive traits in their children through the family system. When some behavior is compulsive, it is out of control; when out of control, it dominates the individual's life. As a result, the addicted person's family life is centered around the alcoholism, workaholism, uncontrolled anger, or whatever. A family can even become oriented around a mother's obsessive care for a chronically ill or mentally retarded child. A daughter of such a woman explains: "I can really relate to my friends who grew up in alcoholic homes. Talk about guilt and shame. My sister, who is mentally retarded, lived at home and I never wanted to bring school friends by. . . . My mother took care of her around the clock and my father, brother, and I got very little of her attention. Poor martyred woman, she didn't have any energy left after looking after Ginnie. . . . All of our lives centered around Ginnie's condition."[8]

Within this codependent system, family members yield to the compulsive member who has forfeited control to his or her addiction. There is an ironic twist at work: the irresponsible, unpredictable, obsessed person is in charge of the family. Family activities and plans are torn to pieces. Picnics are canceled and holidays ruined when the compulsion dictates plans, such as when a workaholic dad has to work or an alcoholic mom is too sick because of her drinking. A fight between the parents or an angry outburst of a mentally unbalanced parent can wreak havoc on the family plans for a weekend camping trip. The personal life of family members is also upset. The third grader's plans to do homework after school may be shattered by the fighting between his mom and dad or the demands of a baby brother he is forced to watch because of a drunken mother.

The child of the dysfunctional family soon learns that life is regulated by the condition of the parent: is he or she drunk, angry, sick, or is he or she going to sexually shame me tonight? The response is codependency. One is controlled not for one's good, but for the sake of the other.

Some experts call this condition "learned helplessness," claiming that the dysfunctional family unconsciously teaches it to the child from birth.[9] Day by day the child is made dependent on something or someone beyond him or herself. Dependency alone is not the problem, since it is a natural part of childhood. Yet in a healthy dependency situation, the parent fosters the child's personal development and gradually encourages the formation of the child's individual self. A codependent system, to the contrary, hinders personal development. Individual needs are not fulfilled directly. This leads to a lack of independent action, as the person or the activity on which the dependency is centered becomes the focus of the majority of the individual's emotional energy and time, in lieu of directly taking care of himself or herself. The resultant lack of a sense of personal selfhood increases the likelihood of compulsive dependent behavior: developing crippling, dependent relationships; overeating; etc.[10]

Simply put, the codependent person gets hooked on things external to himself. In a family where a behavior is rewarded one time and punished the next, children learn to be dependent on cues from their environment in order to know how to act. They are often not taught to follow their feelings, but rather to follow the actions of another—to react as opposed to act.

They learn that feeling good can only come from a source outside of themselves. Betsy says, "It's taken me a long time to realize that my compulsive overworking and binge shopping filled a false need to be satisfied from the outside."

Something else is going on that helps explain why the codependent child gets so externally oriented. The codependent person never fully develops a sense of true self. The child's personal development is in control of the addict and is stifled; emotions are not expressed or adequately dealt with.[11]

Situations of overt child abuse graphically illustrate this tragic process of inhibiting a child's personal development. Sexual and physical abuse is such an intense violation of the person that a growing child's psyche is eclipsed by the domination of another. The youth is left with little self-respect or self-concept that is not related to the one who is violating him or her. Consequently their sense of self becomes tied to what others think about them. This can explain why a man or woman who was sexually abused may become promiscuous, even to the point of sexual addiction. For instance, a woman continues to get some sense of self from the men she sleeps with, as if without them she would be nothing.

These compulsions lead to a vicious cycle. In order to defend oneself from the emptiness and pain of being nothing, he or she finds some way—eating, drinking, working, etc.—to be somebody. However, the way that is chosen is usually demeaning or impossible. Compulsive sex doesn't satisfy or make one feel respectful; the workaholic is never really satisfied. Compulsive behavior leads to shame that then increases the compulsion because the person has chosen destructive or impossible means toward fulfillment. Alcohol, sex, work, even religious practices—all these means are idolatrous since God is the only source that satisfies our thirst for existential meeting.

The idea of identification is another useful way of explaining how adults have been impacted by their dysfunctional family background. When growing up, children identify with various persons, seeking to be like them. Usually they identify with their parents simply because when they are young they bond with them or are otherwise attracted to them. Even though children are not conscious of the influence, or even when they resist it, these role models shape children's behavior.

One of the exercises used with Adult Children of Dysfunctional Families (ACDFs) instructs them to compile a list of their father's worst traits (reminding them to sometimes do the same for his good qualities, as well). Afterward, they ask themselves how many of these traits they also have. Most of them are amazed at the results, often surprised that they are behavioral and emotional carbon copies of their parents.

Learned Coping Mechanisms

Another plausible theory for explaining the process of family influence is embodied in a theory of learning. Children learn their emotions and behaviors by reacting to the family situation. Think of the family as a boat. The dysfunctional family member is always rocking it, threatening danger for everyone on board. Unable to keep the person from shaking the ship, the people in it have to do whatever they can to keep it steady.

> A whole family can adopt certain rules that stabilize the situation but only worsen the condition.

A person who lives or has lived in such a home needs to ask two questions: "When the boat was rocking, what did I do?" and "When things were upsetting, how did I feel?" Essentially, the adult's present personality traits contain the past coping behaviors.

One of the reactions of the whole family is to adopt certain rules that stabilize the situation but only worsen the condition. "Don't feel, don't talk, and don't trust," become their unwritten mottoes in order to cover up and somewhat ignore the shame and pain of their situation.

Individual coping strategies may be as diverse as rebelling against the family or trying to save it. Some members become superachievers in an attempt to overcome the family's shame and protect the family's name. Others withdraw from people, resulting in their becoming compulsive masturbators or awkward recluses who hunger for intimacy.

TEACHING ABOUT THE RECOVERY PROCESS

Whatever explanation of how the family of origin influences us, the emotions and behaviors of those who come from dysfunctional families usually block their efforts to establish successful homes. Thus the abused child grows up angry with his/her parents and plight. Often unaware of that anger, the person displaces it, exploding at the spouse or lashing out at the children. The abusive family reproduces itself, as do other types of dysfunctional families.

It seems that there is little hope for change unless people deal with what has happened to them in their family of origin. Those who work closely with Adult Children from Dysfunctional Families are continuing to understand just what that recovery process entails.

Phases of recovery now advocated for ACDFs include:

1. *Reviewing their background to determine its effects upon them.* Many ACDFs have dealt with their childhood experiences by forgetting them.

Because of this they are unaware of their impact upon them, unable or unwilling to deal with family issues they don't really see are there. Because the past was so traumatic for many of them, they should not be encouraged to dig up the past without some support from a counselor, a close friend, or support group.

2. *Dealing with unresolved issues with parents, whether those parents are living or not.* Some are still needlessly influenced and attached to parents through negative emotions like anger and bitterness. Others are attached in a codependent fashion by ties of guilt or feelings of responsibility. Adult children need to learn how to forgive and to cut their emotional ties to their parents. They also must begin to master new, healthy skills in relating to their parents, breaking free from codependent behaviors.

3. *Handling emotional and behavioral problems that were derived from their childhood experiences.* Some individuals need to break free from addictions to substances or to processes. Others will gain a new perspective on their depression, guilt, anxieties, etc., that will enable them to achieve new levels of emotional well-being.

4. *Proceeding through a grief process.* Facing and suffering the losses of their childhood seems to be a major process in the ACDFs recovery. Often in the initial stages of recovery, when they first concentrate on facing the past, depression sets in. They are finally entering the tunnel of grief that they had tried to escape. Lamenting and finally accepting their past brings release that has eluded some of them for decades.

5. *Relying on spiritual resources.* Most encouraging in the recovery movement is the fact that most leaders and support group strategies admit that personal recovery is not possible without reliance upon some spiritual power. While we could hope that many more would turn to Christ, we can at least be heartened by this admission of spiritual need. Many evangelical publications are available to direct ACDFs to Christian concepts that relate to their recovery.

> There is little hope for change unless people deal with what has happened to them in their family of origin.

Specific programs have emerged to help churches aid ACDFs in the recovery process. First of all, educational strategies can be employed; an evening lecture or a Saturday seminar can make people aware of how their family has influenced them. Inter-Varsity Christian Fellowship distributes a video, *Ripped Down the Middle*, that is a first-rate introduction to the subject of dysfunctional families. Secondly, churches can either offer counseling and sponsor support groups or else send members into the community for help in recovery. "New Hope," an evangelical support group program of the First Evangelical Free Church of Fullerton, California, is an outstanding model that can be transferred to any church situation.[12]

GRANTING PERMISSION FOR RECOVERY

One of the most important functions of churches and their pastors is the granting of permission for its ACDFs to enter into some recovery processes. Many of them are embarrassed by their family backgrounds, or else they feel that their Christian experience has been a failure if they have to deal with issues they hoped were behind them. They need a Christian who will virtually say to them: "It's okay to have problems." After I told of my own efforts to overcome my childhood alcoholic family background, a seminary student said to me: "I couldn't accept the idea that the past was what made me like I was. As a Christian, I guess I thought I was beyond the past's influence. I thought my problems were merely caused by my personal sin and failure to obey God. However, when you told me about your struggles, I felt free to accept the fact that mine might also be due to the past. You gave me permission to look into it."

NEW HOPE

Frankly, when I wrote the first edition of this book years ago, I was dismayed by what I had learned about dysfunctional families. When I wrote: "Dysfunctional families are producing dysfunctional families," I was not really sure what could be done to stop this dreadful, depressing cycle. The new movement to help Adult Children of Dysfunctional Families has given me a reason for hope. These adult children are in such a crucial place within the family structure. Many of them now as parents are the middle link between their abusive or neglectful parents and their own children. If their lives change, families will change in unprecedented ways. This movement may, by God's grace, be what breaks the generational cycle of dysfunction that binds so many.

SUGGESTED RESOURCES

Major resources . There are many resources to choose from, but three major sources are the following. Write or call for catalogs.

Hazelden. 15251 Pleasant Valley Road, P.O. Box 176, Center City, MN 55012-1076. Call 800-328-9000.

Health Communications, Inc. 3101 S.W. 15th Street, Deerfield Beach, FL 33442-8109.

Recovery Publications, Inc. 1201 Knoxville Street, San Diego, CA 92110-3718. Call 800-873-8384.

Books on various issues:

Carnes, Patrick. *Out of the Shadows: Understanding Sexual Addiction.* Minneapolis: Compcare Publications, 1983. •The most important book on the subject, written for the addict.

Carder, Dave, et al. *Secrets of Your Family Tree.* Chicago: Moody Press, 1990. •Outstanding discussion of adult children issues, especially the chapters on codependency.

Minirth, Frank, and Paul Meier. *Love Hunger: Recovery From Food Addiction.* Nashville: Thomas Nelson, 1990. •Problems of binge eating from a Christian viewpoint.

Ross, Ron. *When I Grow Up, I Want to Be an Adult.* San Diego: Tools for Recovery, 1991. •Insights into growing up in a dysfunctional home, including group and individual exercises within a plan for recovery.

Sell, Charles M. *Unfinished Business: Helping Adult Children Resolve Their Past*. Portland, Oreg.: Multnomah Press, 1989. ●Biblical and psychological data integrated to explain the issues and provide answers.

Springle, Pat. *Codependency: A Christian Perspective*. Dallas: Rapha/Word Books, 1991. The major book on the subject.

The Twelve Steps: A Spiritual Journey: A Working Guide for Adult Children From Addictive and Other Dysfunctional Families. San Diego: Recovery Publications, 1989. ●An effective workbook that provides biblical support for the twelve steps as well as exercises to deal with recovery issues.

The Twelve Steps for Christians. San Diego: Recovery Publications, 1991. ●A brief, biblically based explanation of the twelve steps, useful for people in support groups.

The 12 Steps for Adult Children. San Diego: Recovery Publications, 1989. ●The twelve steps related to adults from dysfunctional families.

NOTES

1. Andrew Blackwood, *Ezekiel: Prophecy of Hope* (Grand Rapids: Baker, 1965), 18.

2. Barbara Forsstrom-Cohen and Alan Rosenbaum, "The Effect of Parental Marital Violence on Young Adults: An Exploratory Investigation," *Journal of Marriage and the Family* (May 1985): 467.

3. Bryon Egeland, Deborah Jacobvitz, and Kathleen Papatola, "Intergenerational Continuity of Abuse," *Child Abuse and Neglect: Biosocial Dimensions*, ed. Richard J. Gelles and Jane B. Lancaster (New York: Aldine de Gruyter, 1987), 270. Note, however, that not all the abused children became adult child abusers; 30 percent did not. Likewise, not all children of alcoholics become alcoholics nor all from divorced homes end up divorced. Our family is not the only force in our lives. In the case of the abused, those who didn't mistreat their children received love and support from one parent and had a spouse who helped rear the children.

4. Richard H. Price and Steven J. Lynn, *Abnormal Psychology in the Human Context* (Homewood, Ill.: Dorsey Press, 1981), 369.

5. C. S. Black, S. Bucky, and S. Wilder-Padilla, "The Interpersonal and Emotional Consequences of Being an Adult Child of an Alcoholic," *International Journal of the Addictions* 21:2 (1986): 213–31.

6. Sandra D. Wilson, "A Comparison of Evangelical Christian Adult Children of Alcoholics and Non-Alcoholics on Selected Personality and Religious Variables." Doctoral diss., Union Graduate School of the Union for Experimenting Colleges and Universities (1988), 69.

7. Sara Hines Martin, *Healing for Adult Children of Alcoholics* (Nashville: Broadman, 1988), 14.

8. Emily Marlin, *Hope: New Choices and Recovery Strategies for Adult Children of Alcoholics* (New York: Harper & Row, 1987), 5–6.

9. James Leehan, *Pastoral Care for Survivors of Family Abuse* (Louisville: Westminster/John Knox, 1989), 45–46.

10. Patricia O'Gorman and Philip Oliver-Diaz, *Breaking the Cycle of Addiction: A Parent's Guide to Raising Healthy Kids* (Pompano Beach, Fla.: Health Communications, 1987), 31.

11. Charles L. Whitfield, *Healing the Child Within: Discovery and Recovery for Adult Children of Dysfunctional Families* (Pompano Beach, Fla.: Health Communications, 1987), 30.

12. Write to the First Evangelical Free Church, "New Hope" ministry, to receive a packet of materials providing a step-by-step procedure for church's starting a group.

25 Developing Therapeutic and Support Ministries

In chapter 13, I made a case for churches to have a therapeutic ministry, claiming that for many people change requires more than information gleaned from sermons, books, and classes. They also need and want personal care, emotional support, and counseling. Leaders of the North Atlanta Church of Christ learned this through a survey of 729 of the congregation's adults. When asked what services they most wanted the church to offer, therapy received the highest number of votes, over forty percent asking for personal or family counseling. In response the church created the "Genesis Center for Christian Counseling," staffed by full- and part-time therapists.[1]

What is true of this Atlanta church seems to be true everywhere. When pastors get together their talk soon turns to demands on them for counseling. Confused and disturbed, people more than ever are looking for someone to talk with about their unresolved problems. Church historian Martin Marty claims the demand is overwhelming: "The need for human care is so vast that professionals in religion and medicine cannot begin to meet it."[2]

Offering this care is something that can be done by the whole church, laypersons and pastors alike, with the church functioning as a sort of therapeutic community. This fits into the church's spiritual mission since solving psychological problems becomes an occasion for spiritual awakening or growth as a person probes the deeper issues of life and soul. A large number of mental problems have religious ramifications that are better met by religiously-oriented counseling than by psychological counseling alone. Besides, churches that offer this therapeutic care are growing ones, according to church growth research.[3] They are doing so in a variety of ways.

> Offering care can be done by the whole church, laypersons and pastors alike, with the church functioning as a sort of therapeutic community.

Instead of standing by while troubled families suffer, there are techniques for comforting them so that they will have to face their problems. Such interventions, however, must be based on an understanding of the nature of many of these troubled families if they are going to work.

RESPONDING TO CODEPENDENT, ADDICTIVE FAMILIES

Often, people enmeshed in a dysfunctional family feel trapped; every solution they apply fails them. Often too, the counsel they get from others, even from church leaders, doesn't seem to work. These family systems are so different from other families that typical attempts to solve their problems are largely in vain; their abnormal condition calls for unusual remedies. Close scrutiny of codependent and addictive family systems gives us some clues as to why this is true.

Loss of Control

The major trait of the addicted is loss of control. Not only is an alcoholic seemingly unable to stop drinking, but he or she cannot predict what will happen after taking the first drink. The same seems to be true for people who lose their temper or who cannot cease being compulsive about work, overeating, or whatever. Such persons may say they have no problem, but all the while, they will be undergoing a colossal battle to control themselves. Though they keep on losing that struggle, they still believe that they can manage themselves. Deceived about their inability to stop, they keep making promises that they will. People who don't understand the extent of their lack of self-control often suggest solutions that work for others, but don't work for them.

For example, it's sensible to council a wife to forgive a husband's angry outburst, if it is the first flagrant one in six years of marriage, if it is explained by the stress of his recent layoff from work, and if it is followed by a repentant attitude. Yet if the husband is an alcoholic or an abusive husband, the advice to quickly forgive may compound the problem and foster continued abuse.

Since apparent sorrow and repentance is common for abusers and addicts following their bizarre behavior, they will predictably do it again. For such people, we will need to be careful to define what the word repentance means. It must include recognizing that they have lost control and doing something drastic about it, not just saying that they won't do it again. We must teach their loved ones to withhold their forgiveness until an authentic resolve to change is made.

Passing the Blame

Besides pushing people toward too quick and easy forgiveness, another mistake is often made with these families. Too often, we urge family members to share the blame for their loved one's addiction or compulsive behavior. This is quite proper in other kinds of problems, but when we do this in cases of alcoholism or abuse we comply with the family's dysfunction.

These families are usually not conscious of the nature of their problem. Even though a wife may be frequently treated for injuries inflicted by her husband, she may still not understand that the source of the problem is her husband, instead believing she is to blame. She reasons that she is not being submissive enough or that she can't keep the kids from making him angry.

Addicted or abusive people usually cause this attitude because they typically blame someone else for their problem. "Why do you drink too much?" asks the wife. "Because you yell at me," he replies. "Why do you yell?" he asks. "Because you drink too much," she says. Filled with guilt and shame, unwilling to face their inability to control their compulsion, obsessed persons accuse everyone and everything but themselves. And they tend to convince others they are right.

This projection of blame is often behind a family's seeking help. Typically, it's not the addict's or abuser's problem that takes them to the counselor; rather, it's a teen who is caught stealing, a wife who is depressed, or a child who is wetting the bed. These presenting problems are merely symptoms, persons acting out because of the compulsive person's behavior. Unaware of this, counselors can be trapped into treating the wrong person, a rather common practice. Studies have shown, for example, that in some clinics, counselors missed discovering alcoholism in the family as much as 70% of the time.

Counselors must be careful to avoid blaming the wrong persons, as well. Otherwise, pastors and counselors will urge kids to be more compliant or spouses to stop yelling, joining the abuser's game of projecting blame onto others.

Covering Up

Yet it's not only the compulsive person who makes it difficult to diagnose the family's problem; all members of dysfunctional families tend to hide what's going on in their homes.

Part of this cover-up is due to their affinity for denial. It takes many forms: minimizing (Mother says, "It's okay, kids, Dad only broke my arm this time"); comparison ("Our family isn't as bad as others we know"); delaying ("Someday we need to deal with this"). Even prayer can be a form of delay and denial, as family members pray and hope the problem will go away without facing it squarely.

> Even whole churches can become codependent with a dependent family.

Shame and frustration are behind the cover-up. Unable to stop what is happening, family members accept the most bizarre behavior. Some children grow up thinking it's normal for dads to get drunk or to beat others or to have sex with their children.

Pastors and counselors will sometimes have to pry hard and long to get the true picture. Often this requires meeting with the whole family, particularly listening carefully to what the younger children say. One needs to proceed with caution, however, since prodding a child into telling the family secret may result in his being severely punished.

Understanding the nature of codependent systems, pastors, church leaders, and churches will need to give appropriate responses. Even whole churches can become codependent with a dependent family. Once we know about the family problem, we may do nothing about it, virtually joining the family in their denial and cover-up. In their efforts to help, people in the church may actually keep rescuing the family, protecting them and the troubled member from the consequences of the problem, enabling them to delay facing it.

> The good news for members of codependent family systems is that they can correct their family situation even though the problem person does not change.

Changing Oneself, Not Someone Else

The good news for members of codependent family systems is that they can correct their family situation even though the problem person does not change. This is done by breaking their enmeshment with that person and with one another. This disengagement doesn't necessarily mean that they throw out the person or move away themselves. It means that they will first stop trying to change the troubled person and work at changing themselves; second, they will cut the strong emotional tie that keeps their feelings tied to the problem person and his or her feelings; third, they will stop permitting the family and its members to revolve around the uncontrolled person; and fourth, they will break the family rules and begin to feel, to talk, and to trust. When this differentiation begins to take place they will feel like they have stepped out of a dark, musty, stale cave into the sunlight. Taking control of their own lives, they will rid themselves of the oppressive hopelessness that they have lived with. They will cease believing that happiness will only start for them "when Mom stops drinking" or when "dad stops calling me names."

INTERVENING IN CODEPENDENT, ADDICTIVE FAMILIES

Confrontation can be the most useful intervention technique in dealing with troubled family members. Most in need, of course, is the addicted person or the abuser. But sometimes the person who lives with an addict or abusive person needs to be challenged: "What are you doing to deal with your situation?" There are cases where we should confront a married couple or a whole family.

Church life offers many occasions for this to occur: within the context of one-to-one discipling programs, in small groups through sermons or informally, or during a breakfast or lunch meeting. More and more Christians are recognizing their accountability to one another and are building into the life of the congregation opportunities to lovingly point out one another's faults.

Churches should not only be alert to the needs of spouses of dysfunctional persons, but also to those of the children. Sunday school teachers, pastors, club leaders, or any in the church who are in touch with these children can help them greatly by talking to them about their family life. Often, we hesitate to do this because we think the child will be embarrassed. Instead, the child will most often be relieved that someone has brought up what he has been too ashamed to mention.

First, church leaders need to learn how to identify these children. Unlike what we might expect, they are not always troublemakers; instead, they are often compliant, quiet kids. Depression may cause them to be shy and withdrawn. Being absent or tardy a lot may indicate the disarray in their family life.

Once we broach the subject of their families, we can teach them how to differentiate themselves from the family problem and how to care for themselves instead of waiting for the family situation to change. We can teach them the process of disengagement just as we teach adults.

Troubled families may need assistance in getting an addicted family member into some sort of treatment program. The addicted person seldom responds to the ordinary pleading and threatening of other family members. Severe jolts like divorce, the loss of a job, or physical ailments can sometimes force an addict into recognizing that he or she has a problem.

A "planned intervention" can often push an addicted person into treatment. This is a carefully orchestrated, loving, but firm confrontation. A professional drug rehabilitation counselor prepares relatives, employers, and friends for a group meeting with the addicted person. After being hit with the facts, feelings, and stories about his or her problem, the addict is persuaded to immediately check into a treatment center.[4]

Cooperating with Treatment Centers

Many clergy and church laymen perform a great service to dysfunctional families by referring them to various treatment centers and then offering a support system during recovery. Rehabilitation treatment centers welcome the involvement of church leaders since most of these programs promote spiritual activity as part of recovery. By visiting a center or participating in one of their seminars, church leaders can easily learn how to become part of the recovery team. Parkside, a nationwide network of clinics, offers a course of study for church laymen that teaches them how to build connections between churches and treatment centers.

Providing Support Groups

A Baptist church board of deacons, after much heated discussion, voted to permit a local Alcoholics Anonymous group to meet in its facilities. Several months later they were surprised to find that four recovering alcoholics had received Christ and were attending their church on a regular basis. This had not happened because someone in the church had evangelized them, but simply because they were drawn to this church and its message because A.A. met there.

In another church in Nebraska, the board discussed whether or not they should permit a local A.A. group to meet in their church. During the discussion the board agreed that, although no one in their church of about 500 people needed such a group, as a service to the community they would offer a room to the support group. Later they were astonished to learn that six of those who attended the first meeting were from their church.

These two incidents are examples of what is occurring more frequently than ever: churches are playing an increased role in the rapidly growing support group movement. The Twelve Step program started by Bill Wilson more than fifty years ago is now a basis for all sorts of support groups: Addictions Anonymous (for drug addicts); Debtors Anonymous; Overeaters Anonymous; Workaholics Anonymous; and Shoplifters Anonymous are just a few examples. Churches merely offer these nationally based groups a place to meet. Though most have a spiritual basis, it is rather general: that is, they urge faith in a higher power, but allow each person to define for himself or herself what that means.

Schools and communities have also sponsored support groups for spouses and children of dysfunctional families: Alanon, for spouses of alcoholics; Alateen, for children of alcoholics from 11 to 18 years old; Children of Alcoholics, for young children; and ACOA, for adult children of alcoholic and other dysfunctional families.

> Churches are playing an increased role in the rapidly growing support group movement.

Many churches are getting caught up in the current "adult children movement" that is championing the personal recovery of adults who have come from dysfunctional families of origin. In order to have more Christian, biblical support, some churches have started their own support groups. There are national evangelical support group ministries, but many churches are forming their own groups, based on their own Christian convictions. The following is a list of current groups: Blended Families, Eating Disorders, Infertility, Multiple Sclerosis, Victims of Incest, Disabled People, Aids and HIV Victims, Men's Cancer, Children of Dependent Adults, Widows and Widowers, Chemical Dependency, Marriage Reconciliation, ACOA, Pre-Marriage, Victims of Breast

Cancer, Post-Marriage Support, Divorce Recovery, Codependency, Unemployed, Crisis Pregnancy, Single Parents, Parents of Teens, Abortion Recovery, and Financial Recovery.

Starting a biblically based support group is not complicated. Some organizations offer free literature that explains how.[5] Leaders can easily be found since in most churches there are already people who have attended community support groups and can be enlisted to lead a Christ-centered group.

COUNSELING MINISTRY

Providing counseling is not simple since it requires specialized expertise and vast amounts of time. Churches are responding to the demand in a number of ways.

Pastors as Counselors

That pastoral counseling is the most common approach is not surprising since research continues to show that a large percentage of people turn to the clergy for counseling.[6] Advanced training in counseling is not always required since pastoral counseling deals with spiritual matters that lie in the area of pastoral competency. But there are also physical, emotional, and mental dimensions about which the pastor may know little. Exactly which problems can be analyzed and treated spiritually and which need the insight of specialized psychologists and psychiatrists is a topic of hot debate in Christian circles. I offer the following generalization not to settle that debate, but to describe the situation.

First, pastors are being asked to deal with issues that often confound them. A Bible verse, spiritual insight, and prayer do not seem to be enough for so many of the problems presented to them; therefore, many pastors are reading and studying to prepare themselves to deal with these issues. Second, though many of them are gaining competency to deal with various issues and are being of tremendous help, their heavy schedules don't permit getting the expertise needed for dealing with all the issues they face, nor do they have the time to counsel people with these problems. Besides there being so many people with problems, many of the cases require months, even years, of treatment. Third, pastors are constantly referring people to clinics and counselors. Often, they can continue to see the referees on a limited basis, dealing with spiritual issues as a supplement to the professional counseling. Fourth, referral is not always possible because in some locations there are no specialists to refer to, and even when available, the

> Providing counseling is not simple since it requires specialized expertise and vast amounts of time. Churches are responding to the demand in a number of ways.

pastor can't always be sure the professionals will respect the spiritual life and values of the one referred. Often people do not have the money to pay for the professional care. The result is that pastors constantly face the solemn plea: "If you won't help me, no one will." When an overworked pastor refuses to continue counseling someone, that person often leaves the church. If the troubled person does stay, the pastor watches the situation (and often the whole family) deteriorate from week to week.

Because of this pressure, churches of all sizes that are actively trying to help people get good psychological care, use a number of approaches.

The Church Counseling Center

The least complicated but most expensive way is opening a counseling center at the church, staffed by a professional psychologist; however, few churches can afford it, even large ones. Counselors are soon swamped by too large a caseload and the church is back to where it was before. Churches can handle this by establishing a separate counseling center that uses the church facilities. It is under the church board, but has its own board and director as well. Fees can then be charged, resulting in several advantages. The caseload will be more manageable since the cost will keep away those whose problems are not serious or who are not serious about their problems. Persons with critical problems who are unable to pay, can still be provided for by charging them less. And with money being collected, new staff can be added as the ministry grows.

Collecting fees will also make it possible for a church to open a center without assuming responsibility for another staff salary. Christian counselors are sometimes willing to open a center in a church without a guaranteed full salary. They benefit from being provided with an office as well as obtaining a pool of clients within the congregation. Given some financial support to begin, a counselor can sometimes be fully supported by fees within six months.[7]

Problems are possible with this approach. Some church members object to paying fees. Hiring a counselor that agrees with the church doctrine and policies is sometimes difficult as is making sure he/she complies with it in practice. Disagreement over sensitive issues can create conflict between the church board and the center, and they may eventually drift apart.

Multiple Churches Center

When an individual church has trouble mustering the resources to start its own center, it can join other churches in doing so. In some cases, the churches join together to provide a salary and office. At times, the counselor can have an office in each church, arranging certain days of the week to be at each. At other times, the churches join together to pay the counselor until the collected fees reach the level of support. In either case, a separate organization with its own board is created since it would be awkward for a person to serve under two church boards.

Network Approach

A unique approach to church-related professional counseling is called: "The Network of Christian Counseling Centers, Inc."[8] It grew out of the Harold Wahking's successful experience as a counselor in a local church context. While working at a college counseling center, he began counseling referrals from local churches during the evening hours. Eventually, he quit his college-related job and became the Minister of Counseling for two churches.

Six months later he found himself with a full caseload, a waiting list, and another church that wanted counseling services. At this point, he found a partner and founded "The Network." It is not simply a community-based Christian counseling center to which churches can send their members. Rather, this organization helps churches get their own professional counseling program going by recruiting Christian counselors to recommend to churches. More than that, The Network supervises, trains, and supports those counselors. Churches that establish such a counseling ministry join the network and select someone to represent them on the network's board of directors.

Supplementing Counseling Fees

Churches located where there are reliable, nearby professional counselors are taking another approach toward relieving their pastors of the demand for counseling: they help people pay for treatment. In some cases, churches simply pay for the counseling, all or in part, from a special fund like a "Deacon's Fund." People who benefit are encouraged to contribute to the fund at a later time when they are able.

In some cases, groups of churches have created a fund that provides for those unable to pay for counseling. People are put in touch with the funds either by the pastor who suggests counseling, or the local counselors direct their clients to them. Sometimes the churches may, after creating the fund, establish links to Christian counselors who qualify to draw from them.

Lay Counseling

A promising new movement to provide therapeutic care is lay counseling. Of course, the concept is not new since nonprofessional people counsel one another all the time and always have. What is novel is that churches are training laypersons to do it and then pairing them up with those who need help. Not equipped to deal with all personal problems, these lay counselors are not a substitute for pastoral and professional counselors. They supplement the professional's work by handling easier cases and referring the more difficult ones to them.

Outside the church, the movement has been around for some time. In 1979 it was considered a revolution in the mental health field. For decades many in that community have complained that professionals, despite their increased numbers, cannot handle the demand for mental health treatment.[9] As a result, lay and peer counseling have spread to schools, colleges and universities, social agencies, businesses, and now also to churches.

In churches, three different models have emerged. In the "informal, organized model" people are given systematic training for counseling. They then counsel people in informal settings, not in a church office designated for it. The "formal, organized model," however, does have a local church counseling center that is staffed by these trained lay counselors (and perhaps by professionals as well). Counseling is done personally and by phone.

A third model is centered around the term "caring" rather than counseling and is being promoted by a national organization called "Stephen Ministries."[10] In this program people are trained for a lay caring ministry that involves helping people in various ways, including counseling. They particularly target people who are deeply hurting because of personal problems or life circumstances, such as the hospitalized, the bereaved, the elderly lonely or depressed, the terminally ill and their families, the home-bound or institutionalized, the disabled and their families, those in a job crisis, those experiencing a spiritual crisis, those dependent on alcohol or other drugs and their families, those separated or divorced, those experiencing an unplanned pregnancy, those affected by accidental or natural disaster, the imprisoned and their families, parents with children leaving home, those experiencing the birth/adoption of a child, single parents, those experiencing the stress of moving, etc. Stephen Ministries trains caregivers to support people in transitions and crises, which can easily lead to their counseling these people about the personal issues in their lives.

> Lay counselors are not a substitute for pastoral and professional counselors. They supplement the professional's work by handling easier cases and referring the more difficult ones to them.

Whatever the model, the key to a successful lay counseling program lies in the selection and training of the counselors.[11] Those selected for this role obviously need to be stable, mature Christians, though they need not always have been so. People who have been through some tough times and conquered personal problems themselves often have the ability to empathize with those in trouble. Above all, lay counselors, even before they are trained, should be above average in their interpersonal skills such as projecting acceptance, listening, and self-disclosing. They should have a strong interest in people, a fairly stable family life, rich life experience, and be dedicated to helping others. When selecting them, we might look for evidence of certain spiritual gifts: exhortation, wisdom, knowledge, mercy, and healing. And we should look out for those who have had previous counseling training in college, seminary or community groups.

The pastoral staff can do the training or they can enlist professional counselors to do so. Fifty hours of training seems to be the norm. The staff of

Stephen Ministries will actually train a church's lay carers through seminars they offer in different locations. Besides understanding the counseling process and then being trained in the skills involved, lay counselors learn about special problems, marital and family problems, and spiritual problems. They are also taught when they should refer their counselees to others.

Once taught, lay caregivers or counselors require ongoing supervision. An experienced counselor needs to meet with them as individuals or in a group from time to time to dialog with them about their ministry and their personal lives. A national survey showed that this interaction played a major role in increasing the competence of lay counselors.[12] Without it, they showed no improvement, suggesting a church should not have lay counselor training programs without considering whether or not they have the personnel to oversee and support them.

There are other issues to ponder, as well. Friends of the movement point out its hazards. Lay counselors can hurt counselees by giving simple, unrealistic advice or by manipulating or controlling them. They might violate confidentiality or get emotionally or sexually involved with a counselee. Counselors might be hurt as well, feel like failure, or get "burned out." The risks are intensified because some of them involve ethical and legal matters tied to counseling. In some states the title "counselor" should be used with caution because of licensing regulations. Churches may use titles such as "lay caregiver" or "lay helper" as substitutes.

Despite the risks, more and more churches—convinced that the greater peril lies in doing nothing at all—are initiating lay counseling programs. Many of them are seeing firsthand how Christians, trusting their Lord, can have a healing ministry to one another. Churches are increasingly looking like the therapeutic communities God meant them to be, which many claim is the heart of church revitalization. D. Elton Trueblood, longtime advocate of church renewal, has said as much. Of the Stephen Ministry, he predicted: "the church of the future will regard [it] as a turning point on the road to Christian renewal.[13]

SUGGESTED RESOURCES

Some support group organizations:

Al-Anon Family Group Headquarters
1372 Broadway • 7th Floor
New York, NY 10018
Phone: 800-245-4656

Overcomers Outreach
2290 W. Whittier Blvd., Suite D
LaHabra, CA 90631
Phone: 213-697-3994

Incest Survivors Anonymous
P.O. Box 5613
Long Beach, CA 90805-0613
Phone: 213-428-5599

National Association for Christian Recovery
P.O. Box 11095
Whittier, CA 90603

Resources for helpers of dysfunctional family members:

Friedman, Edwin H. *Generation to Generation*. New York: Guilford, 1985. • A profound, insightful discussion of family systems theory applied to the synagogue and church.

Gelles, Richard J., and Jane B. Lancaster. *Child Abuse and Neglect*. New York: Aldine de Gruyter, 1987. •Thorough and well done.

Heitritter, Lynne, and Jeanette Vought. *Helping Victims of Sexual Abuse: A Sensitive, Biblical Guide for Counselors, Victims and Families*. Minneapolis: Bethany House, 1989. •A thorough guide from an evangelical viewpoint, providing what one needs to counsel and support victims to recovery.

Leehan, James. *Pastoral Care for Survivors of Family Abuse*. Louisville: Westminster/John Knox, 1989. •Simply written guidelines for conducting a support group for the sexually abused.

Pellauer, Mary D.; Barbara Chester; and Jane Boyajian, eds. *Sexual Assault and Abuse: A Handbook for Clergy and Religious Professionals*. San Francisco: Harper & Row, 1987. •One of the first books to help clergy, containing much useful information.

Sell, Charles M. *Unfinished Business: Helping Adult Children Resolve their Past*. 1992. Video with discussion guide that can be used with study and support groups. Available from Trinity Evangelical Divinity School, 2065 Half Day Road, Deerfield, IL 60015. Call 708-317-8100.

Van Cleave, Stephen; Walter Byrd; and Kathy Revell. *Counseling for Substance Abuse and Addiction*. Waco, Tex.: Word Books, 1987. •Resource for Christian counselors that deals in depth with the nature of drug abuse.

Wilson, Sandra D. *Counseling Adult Children of Alcoholics*. Waco, Tex. Word Books, 1989. •Various issues that adult children face, examined from a Christian viewpoint.

Vande Kemp, Hendrika, ed. *Family Therapy: Christian Perspectives*. Grand Rapids: Baker, 1991. A treatment of major issues.

NOTES

1. Unpublished report by Don W. Hebbard, "Family Life Ministry" (Atlanta: North Atlanta Church of Christ, August 4, 1991).

2. "Guide to Stephen Series," Brochure of Stephen Ministries (St. Louis, 1993), back page.

3. Ibid.

4. This technique is dramatized in a free public service video, available from Blockbuster Video, entitled *How to Stop the One You Love From Drinking*. It is based on the book by the same name by Mary Ellen Pinkham (New York: G. P. Putnam, 1986).

5. See resources above for addresses and phone numbers.

6. Bill Hymna and Wayne E. Wylie, "Implications for Improved Pastoral Health Counseling," *Journal of Pastoral Care* 41 (1987): 162–68.

7. Harold Wahking, "A Church-Related Professional Counseling Service," *Journal of Psychology and Christianity* 3:3 (Fall 1984): 60.

8. Ibid.

9. George Albee, "Prevention—Here to Stay," *APA Monitor* 17 (January 1986): 17.

10. For information, write to Stephen Ministries, 8016 Dale, St. Louis MO 63117-1449 or call 314/645-5511.

11. For thorough, step-by-step instructions for starting a lay counseling ministry, see Siang-Yang Tan, *Lay Counseling: Equipping Christians for a Helping Ministry* (Grand Rapids: Zondervan, 1991).

12. M. O. Wiley, "Developmental Counseling Supervision: Person-Environment Congruency, Satisfaction and Learning," paper presented at the Annual Convention of the American Psychological Convention, August 1982, in Washington, D.C., cited in Tan, *Lay Counseling*, 136.

13. "Guide to Stephen Series," back page.

26 ◆

Developing Ministries to Singles and Families in Transition

Single adults often feel like misfits in the church. This is no doubt due to stereotypes they have inherited from the past. In the fifties, singles were talked about as being those who failed to marry. Marriage was normal; singleness was not. A study done in the early fifties concluded that only negative reasons kept singles from getting married. Those who did not marry had personal and social problems; they were hostile toward marriage or toward persons of the opposite sex, were homosexuals, or were in poor health or unattractive. Because of those and other reasons, it was assumed, they were passed over—unmarried because unselected. There was little suggestion in the study's findings that such persons might be making a positive decision not to marry, because it was assumed that any right-thinking person desires marriage.[1] Both married and single adults harbor hostile feelings because of these stereotypes. Married people get the impression singles are more anti-marriage than they are pro-single. And singles complain of being misunderstood and even maligned. They talk of being ignored and neglected, made to feel out of place. Like minority groups, they are treated like misfits in society and church.

This is in stark contrast to what is today's reality. More adults are single because of choice; singleness is "in." In fact, singles are not a minority group. Over half of all Americans are single, and not all of those are widowed, elderly people, or adults in their early twenties. One-third of all adults between the ages of twenty and fifty-five are single, and the majority of those are over thirty. Although most of those are single temporarily, planning to get married or remarried, the shocker is this: in 1982, one-third of the single men and one-fifth of the single women said they choose to be single because they like the lifestyle.[2]

> Single adults often feel like misfits in the church. This is no doubt due to stereotypes they have inherited from the past.

Since singles tend to cluster in large urban areas, many individuals and churches are not aware of the size of the problems or the potentials in the new wave of singleness. Within this wave are all sorts of singles. Few of them fit the typical picture of "swinger" or "loser." Sociologists classify singles into four types: the voluntary temporary single; the voluntary stable single; the involuntary temporary single; and the involuntary stable single.[3] The church can best minister to them by accepting and understanding them, incorporating them into the whole church family, as I have already mentioned. This is why even a small congregation without any specialized programs for singles can still make a major difference in their lives.

CHURCH MINISTRY TO SINGLES

Absorb Them Into the Church

First and foremost, the general rule of ministry to singles, whether this is a group of never-married or others, is this: Absorb them into the life of the church. The outcry of singles is that they are made to feel peculiar. A national questionnaire given to both married and single adults indicated that married people perceived that the number-one problem singles faced was sexual frustrations and expressions. However, the singles ranked sexual frustration fifth on their list. Their biggest frustration had to do with "being left out" or "not included in especially couples or family events."[4] Equality with other adults is what they most want. The church needs to affirm singles. In sermons, bulletins, and announcements the message needs to be: single adults are important in the family of God.

> Even a small congregation without any specialized programs for singles can still make a major difference in their lives. The general rule of ministry to singles is this: Absorb them into the life of the church.

Part of bestowing this sense of importance is done by opening up all parts of the church to them. J. Brittain Wood expressed the desire of singles well in the title of his excellent book on singles and the church: *Single Adults Want to Be the Church, Too*. Some of them feel that when the church establishes special "singles groups" it segregates the singles, suggesting they are not part of the mainstream of the church's life. Yet, singles want to belong to the church just as other members do, serving on committees and boards, involved in teaching and other ministries, and included in small groups and other church agencies.

Provide Family-Life Interaction

As stressed earlier in this book, when the church is like a family, singles can find the family that they need. They not only want involvement; they want close involvement. Singles, like other adults, will be untouched by a

> When the church is like a family, singles can find the family that they need. They not only want involvement; they want close involvement.

church that is highly institutional, where personal contacts are superficial and formalized. "Without access to intimate inclusion, the churches' response to the single who is lonely, disconnected, and unsure of his personal identity and worth is hypocritical," say two singles-ministry experts.[5] They urge the church to have more cross-generational activities and community forms of the church. They suggest that families invite singles into their homes to participate in non-single life experiences.

Provide Interaction in Homogeneous Groups

Those with long experience in ministry to singles maintain that along with involvement in church life in general, they also thrive within their own singles group. They need programs that focus on their special needs. The varieties of single adults and the differences in their ages will often require that the church have more than one singles group.

Perhaps one of the best ways to keep singles groups healthy and productive is to highlight the study of God's Word, directing them to a vital life in Christ. In addition to direct Bible study, seminars and classes can focus on their particular transitions and tasks.

Minister to the Different Types of Singles

The Never-Married

It's important to distinguish various types of singles among the never-married. First, there are those who fit the category, *creative singlehood*. This term is applied to those who carve out a special life for themselves as singles, either because they've just never married or because they never intend to.

Peter Stein discovered that these singles remained single because of negative attitudes toward marriage and positive attitudes toward the single life. Remaining single offers freedom, enjoyment, opportunities to meet people and develop friendships, economic independence, and personal development. Some, unfortunately, believe it also offers "more and better sexual experiences." No doubt, this attitude is more likely today because of the change in moral thinking. Both men and women in Stein's study mentioned that sexual availability of other persons was an important motivation for remaining single.[6]

But not all those who choose creative singlehood are sexually active. The powerful pull toward singlehood for many is embodied in the opportunity for personal growth, service, and fulfilling relationships with others. Usually these singles, if in church, tend to make a significant contribution. Many of them use the freedom from family ties to devote themselves to various Christian ministries.

A somewhat different group is the singles who are not married, but hope to be. These, too, are often heavily involved in church ministry, but if they haven't reconciled themselves to their unmarried state, they may struggle with dissatisfaction. We can speculate that they grew up planning to get married, with all the usual dreams of a wedding, home, and family. Somewhere along the way, hope was mingled with disappointment and anxiety. Some years after high school, perhaps, the first inklings of possible future singleness occurred. Each year that passes becomes a stepping stone toward what they suspect will happen. Probably, it is not the years but certain events—such as college graduation—that create milestones for them. *By the time I am through college, I will be engaged*, the person whispers to his optimistic self. With no marriage prospects at graduation, hope fades, but still remains. As the years pass, disappointment and depression sometimes set in. Confusion about the future is normal, especially for women. They question whether or not to settle down in a career and forget about marriage. "Should I go somewhere where the chances of finding a partner are greater or should I disregard that in making choices about what to do and where to live?" is a major question.

Yet the single life for such a person is not all dire and foreboding. Apparently many singles who at first want to marry decide, by a certain age, that they like being single better. Perhaps they go through a period of grief and struggle to come to that decision, perhaps not.

Above all, we should understand that singles are not so peculiar as certain myths suggest. They are not necessarily lonely, nor is their lifestyle particularly glamorous. Single men are not all irresponsible and not all single women want to get married.

> Singles' happiness is often determined by whether or not they have someone (a kindred spirit) with whom they can share their problems.

Young singles under age thirty-five do have some special concerns. First, they need to learn the skills of intimacy. Though singles in general have people to do things with, they don't always have meaningful, rewarding friendships. Their happiness is often determined by whether or not they have someone (a kindred spirit) with whom they can share their problems.[7]

For the younger ones, this lack of close friendships may be due to their immaturity in interpersonal relationships. Developmentalist Erik Erikson stresses the importance of intimacy in adult development. Learning to be intimate, in his scheme, is the major young adult (ages 18–39) task. Erikson maintains that young adults need to learn to be committed to close and lasting relationships and have the willingness to sacrifice and compromise as those relationships require.

Failure to learn the art of intimacy in young adulthood can be serious, for the only alternative to intimacy is isolation. Loneliness can be a tragic human condition. Erikson, along with other psychologists, claim that several psychological problems are related to isolation.

One of the major steps toward learning to be intimate is achieving a sense of identity. If a person feels reasonably sure about who he or she is, intimacy can then be possible. The relationships between identity and intimacy are most easily seen in the sexual realm. Intimacy means both giving and receiving. In order for a woman to give and receive sexually, she needs to have a certain confidence in her femininity. Sexual intercourse challenges personal identity. Honeymooning may be difficult for the person who is not sure who he is. In other words, the more secure the identity, the less there will be fear of failure and rejection in marital intimacy—and the greater comfort with intimacy.

Sexual identity is crucial not only for the married. Knowing and accepting one's sexual self is vital to success in all interpersonal relating. Young adults sometimes have trouble being close because they have rejected their own sexuality. That happens because they have not distinguished genital sexuality from affective sexuality. Genital sexuality, of course, refers to overt forms of sex behavior. Affective sexuality has to do with the physical aspects of compassion, warmth, and gentleness in any human contact. Touch does not have to be genital sexuality to be pleasurable and satisfying. A father may find pleasure in running his hand through his nine-year-old daughter's silky hair or friends may find pleasure in embracing one another at the sharing of good news.

For some young adults, sex is something to be controlled in order to build one's Christian character. We have found that many Christian young adults conceive of sex as only genital, and therefore fail to see the relevance of their sexuality. Counselor Clark Barshinger says that this leads them to attempt to deny a very significant part of their personality, causing "repression and an unhappy compartmentalization of oneself. The end product is seeing yourself as your own worst problem and a tendency to reject your very self as too sinful to be forgiven."[8] Barshinger urges churches to teach singles to accept their sexual feelings and fantasies so that they are released to engage in more open intimacy with others in nongenital ways. His conclusion expresses a powerful insight: "We have come to believe that it is our fear of our own sexuality that gives so much trouble in intimate relationships with others, regarding the question of purity. If the sexual part of me does not have to be rejected flatly, then I am free to meet you on a more mature, holistic basis."[9]

> Knowing and accepting one's sexual self is vital to success in all interpersonal relating.

Other aspects of establishing a personal identity include being more assured about one's values, abilities, and convictions. When these are more firmly in place, a person can be more free to be close to someone who is different from himself. Here is the difference between mature love and immature adolescent love: Youth's love is highly emotional and self-centered. Such love arises from three factors: (1) The loved object

> Divorced persons have different needs depending on what stage they are at in the process.

loves the youth ("Wow, this cheerleader really sees me as something special; I love her for that"). (2) The loved object satisfies the youth's need for prestige and status ("Think of how I look walking down the hallway with her"). (3) The loved object responds to some aspect of the youth's own idealized ego ("She really goes with my image of super-jock"). An adolescent athlete may feel threatened by having, say, a drama buff, as a close friend. The friend doesn't fit his image. However, after a young adult's identity is more secure, there will be no threat in having friends who are different. This is a major feature of mature intimacy: being able to be close to someone without demanding they be like you or that they enhance your image.

Other needs of the young single adult related to family life include sorting out dysfunctional family matters, understanding dating and the courtship process, learning about the nature of marriage, developing interpersonal relationship skills, and financial management. Many of these topics can be dealt with in a Sunday school class for college and career singles or in a special Sunday evening or week night singles meeting. Whenever the group is large enough, it is wise to form them into two groups by age: those under thirty and those above. Further age divisions can be made as the size of the groups grow.

The Divorced and Separated

More and more churches are forming groups for divorced singles. Most divorced people will be young adults, since most divorces occur prior to age thirty. Yet they will include adults of any age. It helps to see that divorced persons have different needs depending on what stage they are at in the process.

The first stage is the *distancing period*. These are people whose marital life is in such trouble that they are headed for a decision to separate or file for divorce. Regular marriage enrichment programs might reach these couples with help that will turn their situation around; however, most of them will require intervention in the form of counseling. Yet some churches are targeting special programs toward these people. When first conceived, Willow Creek "Rebuilders" was primarily a group for separated and divorced people. However, now they are finding that couples in trouble are coming to their sessions to try to find a way to deal with their problems. The leaders of "Rebuilders" are shuttling these people to special lectures and groups designed for couples in trouble. Even though a couple is separated, they are candidates for dealing with problems and reconciliation measures.

The *transition period* stage covers the time between filing for divorce and the eventual emotional detachment. Many of the people in the church programs like "Rebuilders" are at this stage, which lasts from the early weeks and months after the divorce to the first two years after the divorce.[10] In the early weeks, the formerly married are in desperate need of support. Their behavior may become irregular and troublesome. They may forget appointments, make purchases of things they don't need, etc. Loneliness is a major problem, as also are their emotions. They may be filled with anger and are in a mood to blame. If children are involved, they are usually greatly concerned about them.[11]

As time passes, other issues begin to emerge: concern for forgiveness and dealing with the anger and bitterness, handling the sense of failure, and overcoming the terrible feeling of shame. Reframing their personal identity is a crucial matter; they will have to think of themselves as single again. And of course there are all the practical problems of being single—handling finances, dealing with their sexuality, maintaining relationships with relatives. Divorced women report being overwhelmed by the quantity of tasks that face them. They say they do not have sufficient time or physical energy to deal with household maintenance, financial tasks, child care, and job and social demands.[12]

William H. Berman and Dennis C. Turk catalog the six major divorce stress areas as follows:

> *Former spouse contacts*: talking about money matters or about the children with them, visitation of children
> *Parent-child interactions*: talking with child about life, about the divorce, expression of feelings
> *Interpersonal relations*: making new friends, getting involved in social activities, having some degree of intimacy with others
> *Loneliness*: being depressed, being alone, feeling inadequate as a person
> *Practical problems*: cooking meals, keeping house, having enough time with the children
> *Financial Concerns*: having enough money, balancing the budget.[13]

Besides these are other issues to be faced. *Denial* is a major problem. Some refuse to believe the marriage has ended. Christian friends may sometimes nurture this denial by supporting the person's hope that reconciliation may be possible. Granted, we want to encourage reconciliation and hold out hope, but to urge others to hope after the situation is final only delays their recovery. When actual hope for reconciliation is gone, the divorced person needs to enter the grief process as soon as possible and put energy into going through its stages and facing the practical matters involved in recovery.

The next phase of divorce is *redirection*. Though divorce leaves its scars, the large number of divorced realize that they must move on. The restructuring of life for some includes dating and going through the courtship process, and it may eventuate in remarriage. Those who remain single or delay marriage set new goals for their lives. Some decide to start to school; others plan a new vocation. For many it is an opportune time for ministry to other single adults or to find a meaningful Christian service in other areas.

Many churches have special programs for those who have serious marital problems or are already separated or divorced. Among the names for these programs are "Rebuilders," "Fresh Start," and "Beginning Again." Their

> Single parent households can be wholesome; yet, at many points they are "at risk."

major goals are to provide acceptance and love to help heal their wounds and to help them through their difficult time of transition. Program objectives are: (1) To rebuild the marriage when possible; reconciliation, not breakup, being their first concern; (2) To establish life after a relationship ends. Through small group discussion or lectures in a large group, they deal with relevant topics to aid their recovery: the grief process, life restructuring, emotional issues, dynamics of single life, biblical and theological issues regarding divorce, etc.[14] Mixed with discussion of the topics is honest frank talk about their personal issues, creating a much needed support group for them.

Single Parents

Single parenthood may be the result of divorce, death, or unwed pregnancy. A single parent family can be an unhealthy place to be; however, this is not always true. A better perspective is one expressed by Shirley Hanson and Michael Sporakowski that single parent households can be wholesome; yet, at many points they are "at risk."[15]

A single parent's greatest stress may not be caused by parenting issues, but by how they got to be single parents. There are many types of single parents: divorced, separated, widowed, never-married, adoptive single parent, single parent without custody, and single parents with shared (joint) custody. The church's support for them tends to vary according to the type of situation. For example, attitudes toward a widowed single parent may be entirely different than those toward a never-married or divorced parent. Because there is more support from others, it is actually easier to face a single parent situation caused by a death, and a widowed parent doesn't have to deal with issues related to the ex-spouse.

The responsibilities of the single parent can be bewildering. A single parent must be disciplinarian, cook, teacher, nurse, handyman, maid, mediator, program director, counselor, nurturer, and pastor to his or her children.[16]

Single parents often participate in "divorce recovery" programs that help them deal with issues facing them, since the presence of children makes these issues even more difficult. There are economic matters, usually caused by decreased income. The source of their income may change to Aid for Families of Dependent Children, welfare, food stamps, or a second job. Changes may dominate their lives, including moving to another residence or community. In addition, they struggle with effective discipline, meaningful communication with their children, and other parenting matters. A speaker who has been a single parent may be the best one to instruct them.

> Blended families work out well when they are able to handle the unique challenges their situation creates.

The church can play a major part by providing child care to give them some relief from the constant demands of their children. Even a few hours of baby-sitting can give parent time off to go shopping alone or to relax. A church's weekday club program for their children can provide adult models as well as child care. A "buddy program" at the Chicago area Willow Creek Community Church also helps with opposite sex role-models for the kids. Those in the church's singles programs volunteer to spend time with a single parent's child periodically.[17]

Blended Families

When a single parent marries another single parent, the resulting blended family is not always a happy one. In the Wallerstein and Kelly study, five years after the divorce over one-half of the children did not regard their new family as an improvement over their predivorce family. Despite the failings of the predivorce family, those children would prefer to return to it.[18]

Yet many blended families work out well when they are able to handle the unique challenges their situation creates. The problems don't always revolve around having children from two different parents in the family, though these sibling situations can be difficult. A parent may have other children in the custody of an ex-spouse. He or she may be torn between the two sets of children, and visiting them involves interaction with the ex-spouse which sometimes creates tension in the new marriage.

Stepfathering is a difficult art to master. Apparently fathers who have not been given an opportunity to bond with their children constitute a risk group for abuse. Most men are not aware of the psychological and physical demands fathering can make on them when they enter a second marriage where children are already present.[19] Frustrated, they may direct their anger toward the stepkids.

CONCLUSION

Our society is not a hospitable place for all families. People in the various family forms mentioned in this chapter not only need practical help; they also need acceptance, understanding, and love. Richard Olson and Joe Leonard, who have specialized in working with such families, believe that congregations will creatively invent varieties of positive responses to changing families and their needs. "We are convinced," they assert, "that, both actually and potentially, the church is the best friend the family ever had!"[20]

SUGGESTED RESOURCES

Resources for church programming:

Convissor, Kate. *Young Widow: Learning to Live Again.* Grand Rapids: Zondervan, 1992. •A Christian perspective.

Fagerstrom, Douglas, ed. *Single Ministries Handbook.* Wheaton, Ill.: Victor Books, 1988. •Specific plans and programs for singles ministries of all kinds, including the divorced.

_____ . *Single Adult Ministry: The Next Step.* Wheaton, Ill.: Victor Books, 1993.•Issues and programs of singles ministry not dealt with in the 1988 book.

Olson, Richard P., and Joe H. Leonard, Jr. *Ministry With Families in Flux: The Church and Changing Patterns of Life.* Louisville: Westminster/John Knox, 1990. •Empathetic look at single-parent families, remarried couples, blended families, couples without children, and families with disabled members, with suggestions for how the church can help.

Books for singles and families in transition:

Bustanoby, Andre. *Single Parenting.* Grand Rapids: Zondervan, 1992. •Sympathetic and practical.

Conway, Jim, and Sally Conway. *When a Mate Wants Out.* Grand Rapids: Zondervan, 1992. •Guidelines, based on the experience of counselors, for those who want to save their marriage.

Cutler, William, and William Pearce. *Blended Families: Yours, Mine, Ours.* Littleton, Colo.: Serendipity House, 1990. •A short course that covers the bases.

Frydenger, Tom, and Adrienne Frydenger. *Resolving Conflict in the Blended Family.* Old Tappan, N.J.: Fleming H. Revell, 1991. •Highly recommended by those who have been helped by it.

Papernow, Patricia. *Bonds Without Blood: Stages of Development in Remarried Families.* New York: Gardner, 1987. •A thorough book on helping family members understand what blending is all about.

Reed, Bobbie. *Merging Families.* St. Louis: Concordia, 1992. •A brief paperback full of discernment.

Smoke, Jim. *Growing Through Divorce.* Irvine, Calif.: Harvest House, 1976. •One of the first books on the subject from an evangelical viewpoint and still making an impact.

NOTES

1. Manfred Kuhn, "How Mates Are Sorted," *Family, Marriage and Parenthood*, cited in Peter Stein, "Singlehood: An Alternative to Marriage," *Family Coordination* (October 1975): 492.

2. Jacqueline Simenauer and David Carrol, *Singles, the New Americans* (New York: Simon & Schuster, 1982), 322, 324.

3. P. J. Stein, "The Lifestyles and Life Changes of the Never-Married," *Marriage and Family Review* 1, no. 4 (1978): 3.

4. Carolyn Koons, "Today's Single Adult Phenomenon: The Realities and Myths," *Single Ministries Handbook*, ed. Douglas L. Fagerstrom (Wheaton, Ill.: Victor Books, 1988), 29.

5. Hendrika Van De Kepp and G. Peter Schreck, "The Churches Ministry to Singles: A Family Model," *Journal of Religion and Health* 20, no. 2 (Summer 1981): 152.

6. Stein, "Singlehood," 494.

7. Koons, "Today's Single Adult Phenomenon," 27.

8. Clark Eugene Barshinger, unpublished paper, "Living the Single Life: On Singleness, Intimacy and Maturity," 16.

9. Ibid.

10. William White, "Singles—The Formerly Married," *Single Ministries Handbook*, ed. Fagerstrom, 59.

11. Ibid.

12. E. M. Hetherington, R. M. Cox, and R. Cox, "Stress and Coping in Divorce: A Focus on Women," *Psychology and Women: In Transition*, ed. J. E. Gullahorn (New York: Wiley/Halsted Press, 1978), as cited by David F. Hultsch and Francine Hultsch, *Adult Development and Aging* (New York: McGraw-Hill, 1981), 273.

13. William H. Berman and Dennis C. Turk, "Adaptation to Divorce: Problems and Coping Strategies," *Journal of Marriage and Family* 43:1 (February 1981): 179–89.

14. For a more detailed list of topics, see Bob Burns, "Divorce Recovery," *Single Ministries Handbook*, Fagerstrom, 157–62.

15. Shirley M. H. Hanson and Michael J. Sporakowski, "Single Parent Families," *Family Relations* 35:1 (January 1986): 7, cited in Richard P. Olson and Joe H. Leonard, Jr., *Ministry with Families in Flux: The Church and Changing Patterns of Life* (Louisville: Westminster/John Knox, 1990), 48.

16. Jim Dycus and Barbara Dycus, "Single Parents," *Single Ministries Handbook*, Fagerstrom, 63.

17. For more specifics on programming for single parents, see Dycus and Dycus, "Single Parents," 61–64.

18. Judith S. Wallerstein and Joan Berlin Kelly, *Surviving the Breakup* (New York: Basic Books, 1980), 305–6.

19. Michael J. Garanzini, "Troubled Homes: Pastoral Responses to Violent and Abusive Families," *Pastoral Psychology* 36 (Summer, 1988): 4.

20. Olson and Leonard, *Ministry with Families in Flux*, 183.

◆ *Part Eight*

Administration of Family Ministry

Designing a Family-Life Conference

27

THE VALUE OF A FAMILY-LIFE CONFERENCE

Perhaps the greatest benefit of the conference approach is the broadest one. It raises the awareness level of the congregation. Devoting a weekend or a whole week to the subject of family signals that family life is important. The promotion beforehand, as well as the excitement during the conference, may produce in people a readiness to learn and change. They may be prodded to purchase and read books, discuss changes with other family members, try new approaches, seek counseling, and generally be more alert to the potential and problems of family life.

The conference is valuable, too, as a means of dispensing much information quickly. Not only can Christian teaching about marriage and family be communicated, but specialized instruction for members of all types of families can be offered. Besides dealing with marriage and family enrichment, workshops can handle topics related to blended families, single parents, alcoholic families, and the like.

It is not surprising that evangelism can be a major purpose of a conference on family life. So much of life's hurt happens in the family. This prompts many people to seek relief in a church meeting that promises to help them. Many persons find Christ in family-life seminars.

> Devoting a weekend or a whole week to the subject of family signals that family life is important.

Quidnessett Baptist Church in Rhode Island rented facilities outside the church for three evening lectures by the pastor on the topic of the home. Scores of outsiders were among the 400–550 people who were there each night when practical, biblical help on the family was shared along with the gospel message.

The emotional impact of a family-life conference is also worthwhile. Successful conferences are often measured by feeling-oriented statements: "Isn't the speaker wonderful?" "I was so inspired," or "Really terrific!"

Of course, this feeling orientation marked church conferences of the past. Whether the conferences were evangelistically oriented, Christian-education oriented, or missionary oriented, we often sought for purposes and plans to produce revival, inspiration, and dedication. The difference today lies in a careful explanation of what we mean by these terms. Contemporary conference planners speak more of feeling than of inspiration, by which they mean a change of perspective or values. And the exclusively speaker-oriented conference has given way to one that also includes various types of involvement. Experiencing is no longer equated with listening, even when people are listening to a proven powerful speaker.

The conference is valuable also as a medium for developing skills. Typical conferences usually include certain workshops in which people can get down to business in solving their problems or learning new techniques. This can be true of a family-life seminar, where individuals according to age groups or as whole families can be involved in practical, small-group-oriented sessions to equip them with new skills in family living.

Obviously, the skills to be mastered as well as the information and attitudes to be gained will depend on the specific purpose of a particular family-life conference.

The Conference Goals

Planners of family-life conferences are susceptible to formulating goals that are too broad and general. Broad goals may seem sensible, particularly when a church has never had such a conference. One speaker or more is summoned to the premises to paint in broad strokes the whole canvas called "The Christian Family," while the attendees look on admiringly and in awe.

It's hard to make a case against this tendency to drop the whole load. But as a starting principle for selecting a purpose, I would suggest choosing a purpose that is narrow in scope. By doing this, you will leave other family topics for future conferences, thus avoiding the continuous repetition of generalities. And in this way you can avoid causing believers to come to the conference and end up feeling bad about all areas of their family life because they were taught to do very little specifically. It would be better to select a goal related to communicating in the home, for example, rather than living in the home. By selecting the narrow topic, you can concentrate better on developing certain skills and on providing specific suggestions than you could if the subject were too broad. The effect on those attending may more likely be a sense of satisfaction in accomplishment and improvement than one of frustration and guilt.

> Choose a purpose that is narrow in scope. You can concentrate better on developing certain skills and on providing specific suggestions than you could if the subject were too broad.

Keeping all age groups in mind in conference goals is a good principle to follow. While the larger session may be given to broad topics, workshop sessions can be devoted to specific, age-related interests. Reference can be made to the list of objectives of family-life ministry given in chapter 7.

S. Autry Brown provides a list of possible goals that can stimulate conference planners. Among other goals, he includes these:

Retired adults. To help senior adults (1) face the problem of loneliness; (2) retain or develop a feeling of worth; (3) develop or maintain a sense of purpose in life; (4) face money problems peculiar to retirement; (5) handle physical problems and tasks; (6) face death with dignity.

Adults in their middle years. (1) To help prepare adults for "the empty nest," when children are gone; (2) to help parents effect healthy relationships with sons-in-law and daughters-in-law; (3) to help grandparents understand how to develop healthy relationships with their grandchildren; (4) to help adults keep their marriage exciting.

Parents with teenagers. To help parents of teenagers (1) keep the communication lines open; (2) accept their teenager's sexual maturity and to help their teenager in accepting his own sexuality; (3) understand the physiological changes and personality needs and characteristics of teenagers; (4) determine how much freedom a teenager should be given.

Parents of children in their preteen years. To help parents (1) develop healthy and consistent patterns of discipline; (2) develop skills in communicating with their children; (3) understand the developmental needs of children.

Young married adults. To help young adults (1) effect healthy communication patterns; (2) learn problem-solving techniques; (3) deal with problem areas in marriage. . . . (6) understand the physical and emotional needs of the family; (7) accept their roles in teaching religious and spiritual matters in the family.

Single adults who have been married. To help one-parent families (1) understand discipline problems peculiar to their situation; (2) work through grief caused by separation due to divorce or death; (3) resolve feelings of guilt, anger, and hostility; (4) effect satisfying social adjustment and recreational activities.

Single adults who are looking forward to marriage. To help single adults (1) recognize differences in expectations in marriage; (2) determine healthy bases for mate selection; (3) decide on the qualities they desire in a mate.

Teenagers. To help teenagers (1) understand and accept the physiological changes occurring in their bodies; (2) be aware of their feelings toward the opposite sex without having to explore them. . . . (4) communicate with their parents. . . . (7) develop proper attitudes toward love, sex, courtship, and marriage.

Children (Preteens). To help children (1) develop a respect for parental authority; (2) develop positive attitudes toward their parents; (3) develop healthy concepts regarding their bodies; (4) develop a sense of worth and of being loved; (5) feel that they are part of the family.[1]

This is not an exhaustive list of goals, but it suggests the potential practical purposes of a family-life conference for any member of the congregation.

Another guiding principle in planning the conference is that the purpose should arise out of the needs of the congregation. This is a sensible principle, but it is not easily achieved, especially in the area of family life where problems are not so apparent to outsiders. Also, family failure produces embarrassment and guilt, which cause people to be reluctant to admit deficiencies. Even the pastor and other church leaders are not fully aware of the areas in which certain families need help most.

> The purpose should arise out of the needs of the congregation. This is a sensible principle, but it is not easily achieved, especially in the area of family life.

Taking a survey is an appropriate way to begin planning a family-life conference. Questions need to be related and directed to each age group. Provide for ease of response by inserting blocks for checking on the questionnaires and by ensuring that questionnaires will remain anonymous. A respondent can be asked to give a value to his response by circling a number from one to six so that there can be a comparison of the degree of recognized need.

A planning committee can conduct individual interviews as another means of finding relevant goals. Or the committee can ask small groups or Sunday school classes to discuss conference subjects and then to submit reports.

Including representative people on the planning committee can provide further assurance that certain people or possible topics are not ignored in the conference goals. Two authors suggest this approach:

> Select one person who is newly married, one parent who has young children, another whose children are away from home (or who has never had children), someone past sixty, a couple of teenagers, two children under twelve, and a parent without a partner. Include persons from both sexes.[2]

However it is done, selecting needs that congregational members feel are most important may be the most crucial ingredient of a profitable conference.

Another principle in regard to selecting a purpose is this one: the purpose should determine the type and the program of the conference. Too often in church ministry we begin with a program, not a purpose. Our tendency is a photocopy approach: we copy successful programs or invite dynamic speakers in imitation of things others have done. Instead, we should begin with a carefully selected set of goals, then design a program to achieve those goals. Program format and speaker selections will more easily follow the determination of precise goals. Workshop leaders and platform speakers can be invited on the basis of their strengths in certain areas and not merely because of their general popularity.

The Conference Core

We can gather together under the term *core* a number of features of a family-life conference that are difficult to deal with separately because they are so interrelated. These elements, which grow out of the conference goals, are theme, program format, schedule, and methods. The conference planners usually need to have all of these things out on the table at the same time. An example will explain what I mean.

Suppose a family-life conference is planned for an evangelistic purpose—to present life in Jesus Christ as the basic answer to successful family living. This purpose should dominate all elements. First, the theme will of necessity be one that will attract non-Christians to meetings, yet it will accurately describe the contents of the meetings. Second, the program format will probably be speaker-oriented, with perhaps a more-or-less formal question-and-answer period following. Small-group participation will probably be too threatening for an evangelistic purpose. But small-group participation might be part of the format if such participation is in a nonformal, small-group interaction, with refreshments following the main meeting. This would give people a chance to meet first-time attendees, making personal contact that might become a bridge for sharing Christ eventually. Probably the meeting will include some special music and even testimonies as an added attraction to outsiders. And one can conceive of yet other elements in the format that would serve an evangelistic purpose.

Third, the schedule of the conference will be in keeping with the evangelistic motif. A rigorous schedule requiring a great deal of commitment will be rejected for one that majors on meetings that are convenient and brief. Fourth, the methods used will be aligned with the evangelistic purpose. The workshop approach might be used, with an expert and small-group discussion. But the biblically-oriented speaker or teacher in a large-group session might better serve the evangelistic purpose. Fifth, the purpose will determine the climate of the meetings. A cheerful, expectant climate may be most appropriate for an evangelistic purpose. This climate is built through the music, the personality of the speaker, the decoration of the facilities, etc.

The design of a family-life conference is the next matter to consider.

Determining the Theme

Even though the purpose of the conference may relate to many topics and a variety of persons, one major theme can hold the conference together and provide a basis for promoting it.

A theme can be chosen from an area of family life: the family's spiritual life, family roles, family use of leisure, family responsibilities, family problems and crises, or a Christian view of sex.

Or else the theme can be selected by considering the dynamics of family life. There are certain skills or attitudes involved in relating within a family that can provide the focus of the seminar: communicating love in a practical way, handling conflict, accepting, supporting, maturing together, studying and praying together, handling change, or dealing with crises and problems.

Selecting a theme in regard to the circumstances surrounding family life today can give the program a contemporary look and a relevant thrust. Some such themes are living with pressures of family life, handling cultural threats to marriage and family values, struggling with disintegrating factors in family life, understanding changing family patterns, identifying family roles in changing times, dealing with ethical issues related to marriage and family, and biblical teaching about the family in uncertain times.

> No single format is best for all churches and situations, but there are some practical guidelines to follow when planning the program.

Once a theme has been selected, it should be expressed in a relevant and brief way that can be used in advertisement. Expressing the theme in pragmatic and personal terms may be more effective than stating it in an academic fashion. "Facing Family Pressures," for example, is more effective than "The Family Under Pressure."

The theme can be the umbrella under which more specific topics fall. For example, if you are using the family pressure theme, you can schedule a workshop on family finances as well as one on sex relationships. Under this theme youth can be invited to participate in a workshop on selecting a mate, while the subject of facing health problems can be assigned to a senior citizens' session.

Designing the Program and the Schedule

No single format is best for all churches and situations, but there are some practical guidelines to follow when planning the program. First, it is wise to have a program that includes both large and small groups. Whether the large group assembly is for a speaker, a drama, a film, or a panel discussion, there are obvious advantages to having it. Visitors are more comfortable in an auditorium where they can remain anonymous if they like. Besides other benefits, the large session can generate enthusiasm and overcome some of the initial inertia that people bring along with them. The small group, however, provides its own distinctive. Elective workshops or seminars, each for a few people, permit interaction and the opportunity to ask relevant questions. Scheduling four or five workshops during the same period also make it more likely individual needs will be met.

Thus a Sunday morning conference schedule might look like this:

9:30–10:30: Worship service. Message: The Basis of Christian
    Family Life
10:45–12:00: Elective sessions for teens through adults:
    Developing the Family's Spiritual Life—"Homemade Piety"
    Handling Anger—"How to Have a Fair Fight"
    Building Family Oneness—"Falling Together Instead
      of Falling Apart"
    Expressing Feelings—"How to Avoid Emotional Divorce"
    Enjoying the Single Life—"The Unmatched Potential"

To make the conference as inclusive as possible try to offer subjects that deal with people of all ages and in all types of family situations. This can sometimes be done by making subjects broad. As an example, a session on handling anger could relate to teens as well as adults, singles as well as married people. Otherwise, subjects can be geared to special age groups. During the Sunday school hour, each class could deal with the same subject, perhaps "Communicating Feelings in Close Relationships."

Following this principle the schedule for a Friday-evening-through-Sunday-evening conference might look like this:

Friday: Covered dish supper for all.
    Speaker: "Developing Unity in Relationships"
    Intergenerational discussion groups follow the speaker.
Saturday evening:
Workshops:
    Preschool children: "Loving in the Family"
    Primary children: "Biblical Family Roles"
    Junior children: "Coping with Parent-Child Relationships"
    Junior high: "Teen Tensions at Home"
    Senior high: "Dating with a View to Marriage"
    College age: "The Good Ship Courtship"

The principle of including all may also be carried out by having an entire evening or morning relate to one particular group. In this case there is no expectation that everyone in the church attends every scheduled event. A men's Saturday breakfast could be held on the topic "Understanding My Wife." A luncheon for the wives on the same day could deal with "Understanding My Husband." Saturday evening could be called "Couples Night," during which time couples could hear a message and then be guided, as couples, through some exercise to evaluate their relationships.

Numerous churches are extending the family-life conference for a whole week, offering a chance to include everyone by addressing issues of many types of families and their struggles. The week includes all sorts of activities, such as family fun times and meetings for each age group. The following program is a good example of this trend. Such an extensive program could, of course, only be offered by a very large church. But even the creativity of leaders of small churches can be stimulated by a look at their broad and innovative programming.

FAMILY WEEK: Ward Presbyterian Church
TITLE: Home Improvement

Sunday

Morning Worship with message: "Foundational Matters: The Basics and Nature of the Family"

Evening Worship with message: "Harmonizing Clashing Coordinates: A Biblical View of Family Conflict"

Monday

HOME IMPROVEMENT WORKSHOPS:

"How to Create Memories with Your Children," Rolly and Sandy Richert, Youth for Christ

"How to Tell Your Kids Everything about Sex without Sweating It," Joanne Blake

"How to Have Successful Family Devotions," Rev. Brian Tweedie

"How to Find the Love of Your Life," Pamela Dodge

"How to 'Alcohol Proof' Your Children," Thomas Growth, Richard Deighton, Sis Wenger of Maplegrove Treatment Center

"How to Become a Bethany Foster Parent or Shepherding Home Participant," Cheryl Morian, Bethany Christian Services

"How to Home School Your Children," Gene and Robin Newman

"How to Live with Your Spouse after Retirement," Janice VandeBok, M.S.W.

"How to Welcome People into Your Home," Jack Skiver

"How to Leave Home for Good," Rev. David and Marsha Brown

"How to Build an Affair-Proof Marriage," Rev. Arthur Hunt

"How to Blend a Family," Doug and Jacques Bingham

"How to Save One Child at a Time," Diane Costlow, AAA Crisis Pregnancy Center

"How to Train Up a Child in the Way He Should Go," Dave Jones

Tuesday

On Tuesday, the church continued their regular programming, consisting of club programs for children and a special class for adults, "12-Steps to Practical Christian Growth."

Wednesday

On Wednesday, the church also continued their regular programming, in this case consisting of what they call Ward Presbyterian Wednesday School of Christian Education. Besides having programs for children and teenagers, they have adult electives. At the time of their family week, they were offering the following classes (Note that on an ongoing basis, the adult electives include family-life themes):

> **Family Dinner:** For one hour an evening meal is served to those who make reservations ahead of time.
>
> Continuing 16 week classes:
>
> "What to Do When Life Is Not All Song," study of 1 Peter
>
> "Life Care Ministries," a training program for lay caregivers
>
> "The 2:7 Series: A Discipleship Course," a program created by the Navigator organization
>
> 8 week classes:
>
> "The Discovery Series: A Survey of the Bible"
>
> "Effective Fathering"
>
> "Exploring Your Spiritual Gifts"
>
> "Christian Financial Concepts"
>
> "The Apostle Paul and His World"
>
> "Christians in the Age of AIDS"
>
> "Roots to Grow—Wings to Fly—Fundamentals of Christian Parenting"
>
> "Inquirers Class"

Friday

Family Week Showcase: This three-hour program included a session topic, "Helpful Help for Hurting Families/Relationships" by Dave Busby, followed by a musical concert by Kenny Marks. The showcase was designed to appeal to adults and teenagers.

Saturday

Stupendous Saturday: This was a fun carnival for families from 12 to 3:00 P.M. It consisted of games for all ages as well as refreshments.

Sunday

Morning Worship with message: "The Family Constellation," Ephesians 6:1–4

Evening Worship: Children's Musical Presentation and Slide Presentation of the activities of Family Week

Choosing Methods

A successful conference will also feature a variety of methods. Variety alone is not the measure of success, but variety is occasioned by a diversity of goals. Unfortunately, the majority of our evangelical family-life conferences have as their objective the dissemination of information; therefore, they are usually speaker-centered, large-group settings, where the educational method is limited to the lecture. Sometimes, though, a film or even a panel discussion is included.

Yet given the needs of contemporary families, a family-life conference should go beyond the mere transmission of knowledge. Methods that lead to evaluation, learning skills, and interaction on an emotional plane should be used. The planners should take into account, however, that any learning models that force family members to face each other in situations that demand open-

> A family-life conference should go beyond the mere transmission of knowledge and use methods that lead to evaluation, learning skills, and interaction on an emotional plane.

ness and honesty raise the threat level of a conference a hundred fold or more. We should use some methods with caution.

Methods can be categorized according to purpose. Methods used to communicate information include lectures, question-and-answer segments, panel discussions, films, dramas, symposiums, etc. Discussion, role playing, small-group working sessions, case studies, couple discussions, family-group discussions, and family-cluster discussions comprise the methods that are used to get people to talk about concepts. These methods are more threatening than lectures or films, but still are less threatening than the methods of the third dimension—personal evaluation and practice. They include evaluation questionnaires, expressing-feelings exercises, practicing-listening games, and other techniques suggested in the marriage encounter and parent-training chapters of this book.[3] The right atmosphere and advanced preparation are necessary for the successful use of these designs that cause people to face themselves and demand change. These educational strategies are of such value that effort should be made to include them in the conference. Some of the threat can be overcome by announcing before the conference that persons who attend the session will be asked to be involved in thinking through their own family life. Or an involvement exercise can be scheduled after a lecture session, with the understanding that only those who choose to participate in the exercise will do so.

Conference Administration

The administration of a family-life conference involves elements essential to any conference administration. One of the major matters to plan for is climate.

Establishing the Climate

The atmosphere of the conference is important to its success, especially in our emotionally sensitive era. But the climate is fostered by more than the musicians and speakers. The form of the promotion and the announcements about the conference determine the attitude that people have when they attend the first session. If the announcement is colorful, eye-catching, well-written, and couched in creative terminology, those who attend may have a light-hearted, expectant feeling. On the other hand, if the conference advertisement is forthright and serious, having little attractive embellishment, it will attract only those who sense a real need. Even the name you give to the conference will affect its climate. If you call it a workshop, people may come with a desire to participate, and this will result in making it easier to get them involved in discussion and creative activities.

The start of the conference also sets the climate. If there is a registration procedure, it should be handled efficiently and conveniently. Enthusiasm and momentum should characterize the first session. The purpose and nature of the conference itself determine the type of beginning session the planners use. If the intention is to get people involved in small-group activities, it may not be best to begin as if it were a Sunday morning worship service.

The physical environment is a climate factor, too. Banners and signs and special seating arrangements can generate a feeling of expectation. The places where individual meetings are held contribute to the success of the climate. A question-and-answer session might be hindered in a church sanctuary setting, where the people in the audience customarily do not speak. Small-group discussion is certainly less effective when people are sitting in pews than when they are sitting in a circle in chairs. The physical setting may also contribute to the forming of the attitude toward the subject. The climate produced by a church sanctuary is usually not conducive to a discussion of sex or conflict in marriage.

Providing "white space" for participants is important for the atmosphere. If the scheduling is too tight, there is little leisure for the participants to think over the subject matter they have learned and the exercises they have done. Even if the conference continues all day long, there are measures that can be taken to prevent overwhelming people with new information and ideas. Refreshment and discussion breaks can be inserted between major sessions. The methods used can vary to avoid monotony. Exercises and creative methods can follow lecture sessions. And concentrating on the same subject for a large block of time, approaching it from different angles and through various media, can avoid the pitfall of bombarding people with a wide range of unrelated concepts.

Securing Leadership

Obtaining mature and resourceful workshop leaders and speakers is obviously the most important factor in a productive conference. And yet it need not be the most difficult. Major platform speakers are available from seminaries, Bible schools, and other churches. Many pastors are now well-known for a family-life emphasis in their ministry. Workshop leaders can often be found in the local church congregation or the community: doctors, nurses, lawyers, social-service-agency personnel, guidance personnel from local schools, home economics and health teachers, college professors in psychology, child-development and family-life and educational personnel of preschool institutions, state family-life consultants and state age-group workers, institutional chaplains, professional family counselors, and educators.[4] Many of these are Christians who can share their Christian viewpoint along with the technical information from their fields. In fact, unless they have a biblical perspective, it would be unwise to utilize them since no subject is untouched by Christian principles.

> Obtaining mature and resourceful workshop leaders and speakers is the most important factor in a productive conference. Workshop leaders are often available within the local church congregation or within the community.

When workshops are designed to draw upon the resources of the participants or to interact with what a specialist has already presented, leaders can be enlisted from the congregation. The major requirements in this case are the ability and the training for guiding group activities and discussions.

Handling Finances

Costs for the conference can be met by taking offerings or by registration fees. A church will need good publicity and a very large constituency to draw from in order to finance the conference with such fees. Sometimes the costs can be handled by churches banding together to sponsor a conference with widely-known speakers. Though financially feasible, this method does reduce the amount of involvement the people can have during the speaker-dominated session, and fewer church members from individual churches will attend than would do so for their own local-church event. Usually a church will need to underwrite the conference expenses, preferably including them in the annual church budget.

Publicity

Publicity, too, is based on the purpose of the conference. An evangelistic thrust to members of the community will require an extensive promotional effort. Broad media coverage, including radio, television, newspapers, and paid advertisement, not only informs community constituents but also excites church members, who will be motivated to invite others. An attractive brochure and posters contribute to the conference whether the planners propose to reach outsiders or not. Announcements can be made in family-living classes at schools, at community agencies, and at service clubs. The quality of the brochure determines the attitude people will have toward the conference itself. An inexpensive, carelessly produced brochure may even give a negative image. All in-church promotion should portray the importance and the possibilities of such a conference. Public announcements, posters, mailings, and bulletin inserts should convey the importance of the conference by both message and appearance.

Evaluating the Conference

Since designing future conferences depends on careful assessment of a conference by those who attended it, evaluation is crucially important. Improvements in a specific conference need to be made on the basis of previous conferences. As in assessing needs prior to a conference, an evaluation after the conference may be taken in three ways. Committee members can meet to discuss how well goals were met. Or committee members can conduct brief personal interviews during the conference. The most thorough means is a written evaluation form. But if it is to be effective, this method needs to include certain features. The form should be distributed to a representative sample of the attendants. Not everyone who attends the conference needs to fill out a form if the committee is careful to get a select number of the attendants from each age group and from each type of person attending. Second, the form needs to provide printed answers for checking or circling. This takes extra time to prepare, but it standardizes the answers so that they can be easily counted. The results obtained from such a form can be easily tabulated and evaluated.

Third, an evaluation form needs to be reviewed wisely. Avoid taking the remarks of one outspoken individual as the sentiment of the whole group. Forms should be tabulated and compared to determine what the majority thinking or feeling was for any item. And finally, the evaluation should be as thorough as possible. Participants should be asked to review biblical conformity of content, practical usefulness of content, effectiveness of communication of speakers and leaders, effectiveness of discussion leaders, suitability and adequacy of methods, adequacy of facilities, effectiveness of scheduling, and relevance of subjects covered. Each of these areas can be covered by a list of questions calling for a *yes* or *no* response or by rating various aspects by encircling a number. Space can be made available for respondents to make suggestions for improving future conferences.

The accumulated impact of this information from the congregation, along with the committee's and church board's honest appraisal year by year, will probably—more than anything else—assure a productive family-life ministry through a local-church conference.

NOTES

1. *Church Family Life Conference Guidebook* (Nashville: Sunday School Board of the Southern Baptist Convention, 1973), 9–10.

2. T. Garvice and Dorothy Murphree, "Implementation Guide for Christian Home Week, May 7–14, 1972," *Church Administration* (April 1972): 25–28.

3. In his guidebook, Brown describes in detail a number of fine creative group activities (see *Church Family Life Conference Guidebook*).

4. Ibid., 16.

Steps to Family Ministry

The cartoon figure, a woman in a sloppy bathrobe, slumps in a comfortable chair, surrounded by piles of clutter. To her husband she confesses, "I didn't know where to start, so I didn't." The dilemma of this housewife is also that of the administrator, and it is nowhere more true than in the area of ministry to families. Facing so much to be taught, so many troubles to be dealt with, the frustrated church leader may turn away and do nothing. Yet there is so much to be done.

But what? Where do we start? The following chapter outlines a proven administrative process of six steps to planning and administering a family-life program.

STEP ONE: PUT SOMEONE IN CHARGE

Numerous larger churches are now creating special task forces to develop and oversee the church's ministry to families. Often, this group has board or committee status. In addition to this, many of these churches are hiring a specialist for this area of ministry. Smaller churches, of course, may not have the funds to hire a family-life pastor nor the personnel to appoint a special committee, but they can take another approach. They can assign the oversight of family ministry to an existing church board or committee. And they can appoint a lay person to supervise the family-life ministry. The point is this: many churches are convinced that the need for—as well as the breadth of—family ministry is so great that some person in the church must give special attention to it. The group is often dubbed "The Family Life Task Force," and the person, "The Director of Family Ministry."

The Family Life Task Force

Duties of Family Life Task Force

1. *Conducts special family life programs.* This group can be in charge of certain programs not relegated to others in the church such as conducting a family life week or planning marriage and family seminars. The group must be careful not to conduct too many programs itself and avoid getting bogged down in work that keeps them from broader duties.

> The need for—as well as the breadth of—family ministry is so great that some person in the church must give special attention to it.

2. *Formulates and articulates the church's philosophy of family ministry.* With this group lies the responsibility of grappling with the theological issues related to family ministry and articulating the principles that will govern it.

3. *Assesses the needs of the congregation and the community in regard to family life.* In a variety of ways, this group will get in touch with church and community people to find out what needs to be done for them.

4. *Formulates goals and objectives for family-life ministry.* This group must sort through the catalog of needs and determine the priorities for the church's undertaking, resulting in a list of short-range and long-range goals.

5. *Coordinates, stimulates, and promotes the church's family-related ministries.* It must be made clear to all church leaders that the Family Life Task Force is not the only church group that does family ministry. While, as we've seen, it may arrange for some special programs, its major function is to help all the institutions and groups of the church to be aware of how they can teach about family life and minister to families, just as, for example, the missionary committee stimulates all church groups to be "mission-minded" and isn't the only group doing missions. Urging all sectors of the church to be "family-minded," they will stimulate youth groups to involve parents and deal with family themes, the adult Sunday school to schedule family-related courses, etc. In addition, the task force is a coordinating body; they should be notified of all family-related activities of the church in order to regulate them so that there is no troublesome duplication or inappropriate action.

6. *Studies the social and political issues related to family and informs the membership about them.*

Constituency of the Family Life Task Force

Two crucial considerations should be applied to the selection of people for the task force. First, they should be representative of the families of the congregation. Since this group must be sensitive to all family-related needs, it is important—so far as it is possible—that people who represent those needs be present to speak about them: both men and women, single and married, young and old. It might be wise to have an adolescent member to speak for the youth of the church, a member of a blended family for such families, etc.

Second, members appointed to this group should have a burden and vision for family ministry and, if possible, some special gifts or expertise related to the area. A home economics teacher, for example, may bring all these things to the committee. Or a journalist might make it easy for the committee to keep abreast of social and political issues that affect the family.

It will be neither possible nor advisable to require that the committee membership represent all the church's groups and agencies. In most cases, having a member from each of these would create a committee far beyond the most effective number of six or seven. In addition, such representatives, who are already involved in a ministry, would be too busy to give the time necessary to the Family Life Task Force's duties. The task force requires that people who can do some in-depth study of family life look broadly at what is being done and contemplate and plan for the future. People already involved in week-to-week activities in some other church ministry will usually not have time for that kind of work.

The Family-Life Minister

"Dr. Sell, we need your help." The voice on the telephone was the chair of the Christian education committee of a sizable Presbyterian church. He was asking me to recommend a candidate for the position of family-life minister. "Our youth minister is resigning," he reported, "and we have decided not to hire another." The reason? "Youth programs are no longer as effective as they once were; either parents are not pressing their teens to be involved or else they take them away for weekends to their summer homes

> Churches are hiring family-life educators in place of youth- or Christian-education ministers.

or their boat on the lake." Their conclusion: "Unless we get parents involved in the spiritual training of their own children, it's just not going to be done." Their answer: "We want to hire a family-life director who can concentrate on building and strengthening Christian families."

This church is not the only one to come to this conclusion. Church leaders are constantly telling me that churches are hiring family-life educators in place of youth- or Christian-education ministers. And I keep hearing about youth leaders, who claim their attempts to foster faith and maturity in many teens are being thwarted by the negative influence of parents. Large numbers of them are changing from being youth directors to being family-life ministers. Or both youth leaders and Christian educators are adjusting their job descriptions to include more family ministry. Some seminaries have responded to this need, either creating specialized M.S. or M.Div. degrees in family ministry, or else including a sufficient number of family-related courses in their Christian-education degree programs.

The role of family-life director is so new that no standardized job description has emerged. The most obvious duty is that this person supervise the Family Life Task Force. As its chief administrative officer, the duties for this position would look like those of the task force.

At issue is how much personal and family counseling the director should do. Most churches place limits on this ministry, since the demand for counseling and the large amount of time it requires typically interferes with the family-life minister's work involvement in the educational and prevention programs, which are so crucial.

STEP TWO: DEVELOP A THEOLOGY AND PHILOSOPHY OF FAMILY MINISTRY

The next step in the administration of family-life ministry is the formation of the church's theology and philosophy of family life ministry. If the church has a Family Life Task Force, this will be its first task. Otherwise, this task falls to the church board or Christian-education committee or some other group. Parts 2 and 3 of this book could help facilitate this formulation. Several persons could read through the material and list questions to be decided. The following are just a few of them: What is family? What should be the relationship of church and family? What will be the church's policy toward divorce and divorced persons? What does it consider the major features of a functional family? What are the biblical roles of husband and wife?

Then there is the need to spell out exactly what the committee's philosophy of family ministry will be. This involves formulating the principles that will govern the church's programs in this area. Part 3 touches on these and includes questions such as: What role should therapy have in the church's ministry? What sorts of strategies shall we employ in training people for family life? What will be our role in developing singles programs? Will we stress the training of men for their roles as husbands and fathers? Do we agree with the church's sponsoring support groups? How will we relate to community family-life programs? Is it important that we provide a "family-like" group experience for people? Is intergenerational programming a priority?

STEP THREE: ASSESS NEEDS

The committee must uncover the most pressing family-related needs of the congregation and rank them according to importance. Otherwise, they will face two unwelcome and disturbing things. The first is frustration. Like the housewife facing scores of cluttered rooms, those attempting to do family ministry will be overwhelmed by the possible options. Knowing where to start is determined by discriminating between what could be done and what must be done. The second is irrelevancy, the committee's programs failing to address people's concerns. When committees guess at what people need or fail to take their needs into account, they typically end up creating programs that are familiar, easy, or what others are doing. They decide, for example, to conduct a parenting seminar because one of the members once participated in one or because someone knows a teacher who can lead one. Attendance is small and the seminar disappointing. A careful study of the church and community might have shown the task force that other needs were far more pressing.

Means of Assessing Needs

There are a number of ways to discover the needs of a congregation and a community. First, data can be gathered through questionnaires. In his book about the administration of family ministry, Royce Money includes a set of exhaustive surveys for this purpose.[1] Second, interviews could be conducted. Though not as easy to statistically

There are a number of ways to discover the needs of a congregation and a community.

tabulate, a great deal can be learned by formally talking to selected church and community people. The interviewer should prepare a list of questions that would be asked of every person in the say way. Besides learning a lot, the interviewers will be creating goodwill by signaling to people that they really care about them. Third, a group of people can be convened to discuss what they perceive to be the needs. If the church appoints a Family Life Task Force, the group will perform this task in its meetings. If there is no special group, one could be convened temporarily to compose a list. As with the case of the task force, this group should be made up of people who represent the various groups of the church to assure that the needs of some are not overlooked.

Items to Assess

All sorts of data can be sought to help assure the church's programs will be relevant and effective. Obviously, people could be given a list of programs and simply asked: "If our church conducted any of the following programs, which would you attend?" Valuable as a summary of the answers to this question might be, there is much more useful information to be discovered.

To portray both the kind of data to seek as well as the value of that data, a congregation assessment done in a large church in suburban Atlanta, Georgia, will be described below.[2] This survey utilized an adaptation of the questionnaire from Royce Money's book, *Ministering to Families*.[3] The survey form was completed by 729 adults, eighteen years and older during a Sunday morning worship assembly. It contained the following items:

Gender

Forty-five percent of the adults in the congregation are male; 55 percent are female. No surprise here since churches typically have more women than men. This information is especially helpful when combined with other data; for example, knowing how many of the women are single and whether there are a large number of older widows, etc.

Age

The congregation is rather young; 30 percent are in the 30–39 age bracket; a close second is the age group category 18–29. Adding the 40–49 group to these two groups, the percentage of adults under 50 years of age is 76 percent. Later, when the expressed needs of the congregation are discovered, it will be easy to see that they represent needs of younger adults of which this congregation is composed.

Educational Level

Not only is the church made up of well-educated people (86 percent of them have pursued education beyond high school), but the younger adults as a rule were more highly educated than the older ones. Combining this with what we know about adults of various educational levels, we can assume that the adults in this church will be more impacted by reading material and be more open to workshops and seminars than in churches with a great majority of adults who have not participated in higher education.

Occupational Association

Forty-one percent of the survey group are employed in professional and managerial occupations. Other findings related to occupation show that the adults in this congregation are heavily involved in work outside the home, a factor that will need to be taken into consideration when planning for family life. This was confirmed by the findings related to the following item.

Hours Worked Outside the Home

Almost half reported logging more than the typical forty-hour work week. Data showed that 73 percent of the adults were employed more than part-time, indicating that a great many of the women were employed full-time. In addition, 24 percent of all adults were working part-time. From this, the committee that did the study reported that they would need very creative programming to fit into the heavy work schedules, commuting time, and other features of the fast-paced suburban living of the members of their congregation.

Marital Status

Church programming would need to be directed toward married adults since 71 percent were in that category, though attention should be directed toward 18 percent who were never married. Only 3 percent were divorced and remarried, 5 percent divorced and not remarried.

Years Married

The surveyors were surprised to find that there was an even spread over three of the categories: newly married, middle married, and mature married couples. That programs would need to be geared to the recently married was evident from the fact that 25 percent of the married couples had been married for five years or less. Yet 22 percent of the couples had been married for over thirty years, which the researchers called "a remarkable milestone in marital history." This church may have a large pool of successfully married mature Christians from which lay counselors could be recruited. Also, it is evident that large numbers in this age group will be part of the "sandwich generation," with teenagers or young adults to deal with while at the same time being responsible for aging parents.

Church Attendance

The vast majority reported attending church more than two times per week, revealing the possibility that most would be available for some sort of family-life education.

Family Spiritual Time

When asked how often their family did anything at home of a spiritual nature, most (54 percent) replied that they did so once or twice a month or rarely, if ever. This was of grave concern to the committee, though this statistic is consistent with results from other studies. Most encouraging was the fact that 27 percent reported doing something spiritual more than once a week and 19 percent about once a week. However, the question was intended to be very general; it is possible that those who reported doing something spiritual on a regular basis may have been referring simply to saying grace at mealtimes. Nonetheless, the data may also show that a significant number of families are spiritually active in their homes, providing a pool of people who by example and in other ways can be encouraged to help others cultivate this area of family life. They may also be counted on to take the lead in spiritually-related activities in intergenerational events.

Presence of Extended Family

Behind this question about the location of extended family members was a desire to learn about two situations: the number of nuclear families isolated from kin, and the quantity of families that may have day-to-day issues related to extended family, such as adults relating to their parents or parents to their adult children. One fourth of those asked had no relatives living in the Atlanta area. Thirty-four percent had either parents or adult children nearby.

Top Areas of Training Needed by Families

Providing a list of forty-five items, the committee asked adults to report what areas of training they were most interested in. The top twelve on the list provided some useful data for program planning. They were:

Marriage Enrichment
Marriage Communication
Family Communication
Role of the Husband
Role of the Wife
Teaching Christian Values in the Home
Parenting Young Children
Marital Conflict Resolution
Leading Children to Christ
Marital Problem-Solving
Finances and Money Management
Family Worship

That people wanted help in their marriages was quite clear. Not only did the subject "Marriage Enrichment" rank first, getting 359 votes out of the 729 cast, but six marital themes appeared among the top ten, and marriage education was considered a priority by all age groups. Another helpful finding was that members of families of all types were asking the church to help them with spiritual matters. Many items checked clustered around putting faith and families together, such as "Teaching Christian Values," "Family Worship," "Leading Your Child to Christ," and "Ministering as a Family." It also discovered (as expected) that the younger adults wanted training for their role as parents.

Services Needed by Families

Along with the question about need for training, the committee asked: "For which of the following services do you, or does someone in your family, have a current need?" Out of the seventeen areas of needs listed, the three highest scorers were:

1. Daily quiet time (167 votes)
2. Marriage and family counseling (128 votes)
3. Personal counseling (106 votes)

The ones that followed these three were: relating to aging parents, single adult issues, premarital counseling, vocational guidance, baby-sitting, unemployment, and drug and alcohol abuse.

It was most striking that the adults asked for help in arranging for "Daily quiet time." Apparently, pressured and rushed by numerous activities, scores of stressed church members were unable to plan for spiritual reflection and oases of calm. The committee decided that helping with this problem would have to be their highest priority. Providing counseling, too, would be something they would have to give attention to.

Delivery Times

The committee wisely recognized that having an interest in or a need for training is not the only factor that determines whether people will participate in it. So they asked a number of questions that dealt with some of these matters. One was: "When would you like the church to deliver train-

> A church will not be able to meet all the needs, nor should it.

ing in family life?" They found the favorite time to be Sunday morning when they were already at church for worship. Next in line were Sunday and Wednesday nights, each receiving about the same amount of votes. Sunday afternoon received a fair amount of votes, but Saturdays were out for the majority of members, as were weekday evenings.

Delivery Methods

Since how training is done will affect who will participate in it, the committee asked what methods the church members preferred. Interest was highest in a class or series provided during the regular church services. Next came group meetings, followed by workshops and retreats.

Though I have described only a part of this church's survey, it is enough to show how getting a profile of the congregation or community is crucial to the next step: determining goals.

STEP FOUR: DETERMINE GOALS

There are a number of factors to consider when determining goals. The needs of the church and community, as we have seen, will be a major factor, but not the only one. A church will not be able to meet all the needs, nor should it. The philosophy of ministry will play a role in deciding which it will try to handle. Senior citizens in a community may need recreational programs, but a church may decide for reasons of its own that meeting social needs is not part of its mandate. Resources and personnel will also influence the choice of goals. A congregation may not have the money or building space to launch into a massive program for single parents even if the need is there. On the other hand, a church may decide to give priority to such a ministry, even though there are more pressing needs, because it just happens to have the space and required personnel. The gravity of the need will also be influential. The committee should ask questions like: "What will happen if we don't help in this area?" and "How high are the expectations of people that the church will do something?" All these considerations go into the mix when a committee prayerfully attempts to decide what should be done.

There are actually four different processes involved in goal-setting: (1) Developing a mission statement; (2) Listing overall purposes; (3) Choosing goals; (4) Determining objectives.

Developing a Mission Statement

A mission statement is a very broad statement of the focus of family ministry. It should be carefully written and only a few lines long. The mission statement of Trinity Baptist Church of Syracuse, New York, places a strong emphasis on helping families by the church itself being like a loving family:

> Our desire is to respond to the needs and interests of families within our community with the relevance of Christianity. We wish to foster an atmosphere that embraces the virtues of a loving family—acceptance, nurture, and forgiveness. In doing so, we will provide a place where singles, couples, parents, and children can enjoy a strong sense of belonging. Our task is to build Godly families through discipleship, that we might effectively bear the Gospel throughout every area of life and serve as beacons of light in a dark world. Trinity Baptist Church is committed to being "One Family Under God."[4]

Another mission statement, that of the Third Reformed Church of Kalamazoo, Michigan, centers around family development:

> The mission of the Marriage and Family Ministries of the Third Reformed Church is to glorify God by enabling families to experience the joy of living by His design and in His power.[5]

Formulating Purposes

The discussion necessary to conceive a mission statement will already have touched upon the purposes of family ministry. Now, they need to be enumerated in writing. Though more specific than the mission statement, they are still quite broad. A list for a family-ministry team may look something like this:

> That our church possess an atmosphere that is accepting, forgiving and supporting.
> That there be special education programs to train for family life.
> That families will be involved in spiritual activities in their homes.

That all organizations and activities of the church include the
   enrichment and participation of families.
That there be significant intergenerational contact within the
   congregation and meaningful opportunities for family members
   to interact with each other within the programs of the church.
That the congregation, where appropriate, and individual
   members act to preserve family values in the political and social
   structures of our community and nation.
That single people and members of families of various types will be
   included among those who are accepted and ministered to in
   our congregation.
That our church provide places where therapeutic ministry can
   take place.

Stated in another fashion are the goals of the Third Reformed
Church of Kalamazoo:

To EDUCATE persons about God's design for family life.
To EQUIP persons in essential family-living skills.
To INFORM families on issues and available resources.
To SUPPORT families who have special needs and concerns.
To REACH OUT in Christ's love to the community around us.
To INTERFACE with other churches and pro-family agencies.
To DEVELOP church policies on marriage and family issues.

Obviously, not all of the above stated purposes can be achieved
immediately, nor even attempted. With this list of what the committee hopes
to do, they are ready to decide what they will now plan to do; that is, they will
determine their operational goals.

Determining Goals

In this step, the term *goals* refers to the specific outcomes that the
committee would like to see achieved in the foreseeable future, both long and
short range.

Five years is considered a workable period of time for long-range
goals. The following are examples of what a group might decide to try to accomplish in the next five years:

That there be a significant awareness of the role of father and
   increased effectiveness of that role along the men of our
   church.
That people of our community will hear the Gospel message
   through appeal to their needs in the area of family life.

That the family members will have increased feeling of
belongingness to one another and intimacy through an
increase of intergenerational contact within the church body.

That more marriage partners will be aware of the importance of
their marriages and that they be equipped to develop their
relationships.

That single parents will be increasingly involved in our
congregation and be ministered to in appropriate ways.

That some parents in our community and congregation be more
effective in their roles.

That adults who have come from dysfunctional families will be
better able to deal with personal problems that may have
resulted from growing up in those homes.

That our congregation be better informed about political issues
related to family life.

A task force adopting the above long-range goals is now in a position to calculate what needs to be done in the next year toward reaching these goals, resulting in a list of short-range goals. This entails more than simply adopting one or two of the above goals. While it may choose to work especially hard on several of them, the committee also has to decide what needs to be done in the next year toward any of the above goals. For example, it may choose not to achieve a lot with fathers during the first year, but decide to learn about the needs of fathers during that year. Then they can determine what needs to be done the second year, etc.

Short-range goals may look something like this:

To learn about the needs and struggles of the fathers of our
community and church.

To involve singles in the programs of our church.

To attempt to reach some community people through family
ministry.

To decide whether or not to recommend the church establish a
counseling center.

To enrich some marriages in the church and community.

To inform the congregation about relevant political issues related
to the family.

Note that goals are what the committee attempts to accomplish. They have not stated how they are to be accomplished; that is what is included in objectives.

Stating Objectives

In managerial lingo, *objectives* are statements about what has to be done to reach the goals. For instance, something must be done to reach the goal of enriched marriages. The committee may decide on two objectives for the year: (1) To conduct a weekend marriage workshop; and (2) to provide several elective Sunday-school courses dealing with marital topics. Let's take one more goal to illustrate what I mean: Goal 6, which deals with informing the church about political issues. Objectives for this might be to (1) appoint a member of the committee to study family-related political issues; (2) publish quarterly a worship bulletin insert that describes several of these issues; (3) request that the adult-education committee consider including a course on political issues and the family in its elective course.

Since some objectives involve the creation of programs, our discussion of them has already taken us into the next step of the administrative process, the devising of programs. But programming is such a major part of administration, it is considered a separate step in the process.

STEP FIVE: DEVISE PROGRAMS

Here used in a very broad sense, the term *programs* refers to any sort of process or agency that the church employs to reach certain goals. The Family Life Task Force may prompt the church to start a father's group, a separate agency of the church to promote family ministry to men. As a process, a program may be as simple as enlisting shut-ins to pray for families of the church.

Since many programs have already been described, we will only offer here a few suggestions for selecting them. First and foremost, programs should be chosen to achieve goals. It's extremely important to know what is to be accomplished before deciding what to do. Instead, churches often use the Xerox approach, simply copy-

> Programs should be chosen to achieve goals. It's extremely important to know what is to be accomplished before deciding what to do.

ing what they have seen in other churches. If a group first resolves what it really wants to achieve, it will often find that it can design an easier or better way to do it than others have. Take, for example, the goal: "That the fathers of our church be more aware of their role and be more competent in it." After stating the goal, they should explore all the possible means of reaching it, before deciding on what program is best for them. Too often, a committee quickly decides an action—like sponsoring a Saturday seminar for fathers—before they talk specifically about what they want to do and creatively about how to do it.

What is best for their church will depend on their situation; that's the second guideline to follow in selecting programs. What works somewhere may not work in another situation. For example, according to what we learned from a survey of the North Atlanta Church of Christ, we would not expect a Saturday seminar for men to reach many of them. A third guideline is connected to resources: personnel, money, time, facilities, etc. The best way will at least have to be possible. Fourth, the committee should try to think broadly, considering all types of means of reaching its goals. Ordinary, obvious programs are too often relied upon: holding a seminar or offering an elective course, for example. Certainly these are normal, effective, educational strategies, but there are many others, as well. Consider, for example, the many self-study possibilities now available: books, cassettes, videos, home-study courses, and computer-related instruction. Circulating several dynamic videos among the church's fathers or promoting their viewing these in small groups might prove effective.

For emphasis, I want to repeat a principle stressed earlier about integrating programming with what already exists in the church. The committee should continually ask: "How can we reach this goal through what we are already doing?" A fine example of this is how Kalamazoo's Third Reformed Church injected family-life education into its Sunday school program, gearing relevant topics to various age groups:

> 6–8th grade: Sexuality, obedience to parents, peer pressure issues.
> 9–12th grade: Dating, career choice, knowing God's will.
> College and Career: Marriage choice and preparation, career
>   choice, knowing God's will, interpersonal communication.

They also planned occasional intergenerational groups during the Sunday-school hour and Sunday evening service. In addition, they created a new group of programs, listed here to show what can be done.

Family Enrichment

1. Dads Discipling Dads Program

> Yearly video conference
> 12-week one-to-one discipleship training
> Weekly encouragement/accountability group

2. Mother-to-Mother Program

> Monthly support/educational group
> A.M. group/P.M. group

Marriage Preparation

1. Loving for a Lifetime

> PREPARE Inventory administered to couples
> 12-week one-to-one discipleship training
> Reformed Engaged Encounter weekend

2. Preparing for Remarriage Seminar

> All-day Saturday seminar
> Examine all important issues of remarriage
> PREPARE-MC Inventory administered to couples

Marriage Enrichment

1. Marriage Builders Class

> Sunday school elective
> 4–6 week sessions on important issues in marriage
> Provides means for couples to explore issues, evaluate their
>   marriage, and set growth goals

2. Marriage Maintenance Seminar

> Friday night-Saturday day seminar
> Follow-up meetings in 3 months
> Pair couples who volunteer as accountability partners

3. Marriage Growth Group

> Monthly small group
> Goal is education-encouragement-accountability

In addition, they ambitiously made a list they called "Future Program Possibilities."

Future Program Possibilities

> Single Parent Fellowship
> National Family Week Celebration
> Family Camp Out

STEP SIX: EVALUATING

The final step in the administration process—evaluating—is one of the most strategic, yet is probably the most often skipped. After all, evaluation can be very painful. After investing prayer and energy in trying to accomplish something, it could be quite disappointing to look objectively at the results. It is easier just to hope our goals were achieved. Feedback is the chief basis for improvement, as every golfer knows. Change in a golf swing is made according to the measure of the last shot. And so it is with our church programs. Evaluation is essential to restyling our methods and programs and modifying our goals.

Evaluation can be carried out in a variety of ways. Checking attendance is one method since people vote with their feet. But when attendance is good, it doesn't necessarily mean that the goals of the program are being reached. People may enjoy or benefit from a program in ways that were not intended. A marriage seminar, for example, may be entertaining and interesting, but produce little change in the couples who attend.

To get feedback other than what attendance figures show, a questionnaire can be used. Be sure, however, that it asks the right questions. Avoid general questions, such as "What benefits did you derive from this seminar?" Be more specific: "Was there improvement in your family's communication since attending the seminar?" And ask for the kinds of data you can use in future planning. Ask, for example, what was beneficial: the lectures, the film, the discussion; the exercises you did as a couple, the handouts, etc.

> Evaluation can be very painful but it is essential to restyling our methods and programs and modifying our goals.

Interviews are an effective method of evaluating. Planned, systematic interviewing goes beyond listening to comments after an event. The process involves selecting representative individuals, making sure they include persons of various genders, age groups, marital status, etc., then asking each person the same questions so that answers can be easily compared. Sometimes interviewing can be accomplished easily immediately following a program by having committee members each talk to two or three different people. Or, even better, individuals can be phoned several weeks or months later in order to judge longer range effects of the program.

The simplest form of evaluating is done by the planning committee following the event. Setting aside an hour or so, they can compile lists of positive and negative observations and record these for use in later planning.

CONCLUSION

Described in writing, these six administrative processes may look cumbersome, more like obstacles to impede than steps to achieve. Yet they are designed to simplify—not complicate—ministry, and everyone goes through them countless times a day, even in ordinary, simple things of life, like going to work. We recognize a need (a distance to travel), formulate principles (means has to be fairly convenient, reliable, safe, and cheap), set a goal (want to get there on time), choose objectives and programs (commute by car with friends for six months), evaluate (check if program achieves goal and conforms to principles).

> **We are to plan each day with God's priorities in mind.**

Consciously following these steps helps us concentrate on doing what is most important and avoiding distractions that get us sidetracked. Otherwise, we look too much like the disorganized, diverted farmer who in the morning stepped out to feed the chickens. On the way he discovered a loose barn door hinge he had wanted to fix, so he went to the tool shed to get a screwdriver to tighten the screws. But getting there he realized he had left it on the tractor seat the day before when he was working on the tractor engine. Finding it there, he decided to start up the tractor to see if it was fixed, then drove it out of the barn. Outside he noticed a wagonload of hay he had not taken to the barn, so he got off the tractor and hitched up the wagon and drove toward the barn, but in the process noticed the broken window frame on the barn that needed fixing. En route to the tool shed to get a hammer, he remembered that he hadn't fed the chickens. To get the feed, he started toward the feed shed. Halfway there, he heard his wife call him for lunch.

An orderly management of life and ministry is suggested by the Psalmist's prayer: "Teach us to number our days aright" (Ps. 90:12). We are to plan each day with God's priorities in mind. Godly leaders govern their lives by these administrative steps. Jesus, during his three years of ministry, appeared to have a systematic plan toward selected goals. That the apostle Paul formulated objectives to guide his ministry is apparent from his statement that God is able to do "immeasurably more than all we ask or imagine" (Eph. 3:20). Though he expected God to do more, he did envision something and set out to accomplish it.

This book embodies a vision—for families and for ministering to them. Perhaps while reading it, you have formulated one of your own. To fulfill that vision you will have to overcome many obstacles and difficulties. In the final two pages I would like to alert you to some of the frustrations you will face.

SUGGESTED RESOURCES

Books on administration of family ministry are few. The following are brief treatments of the church's family ministry.

Garland, Diana, and Diane Pancoast. *The Church's Ministry With Families.* Waco, Tex.: Word Books, 1990.

Guernsey, Dennis. *A New Design for Family Ministry.* Elgin, Ill.: David C. Cook, 1982. •A very worthwhile look at the needs of families at various developmental stages.

Kehrwald, Leif. *Caring That Enables: A Manual for Developing Parish Family Ministry*. Mahwah, N.J.: Paulist Press, 1991.

Larson, Jim. *A Church Guide for Strengthening Families*. Minneapolis: Augsburg, 1984.

Money, Royce. *Ministering to Families: A Positive Plan of Action*. Abilene, Tex.: Abilene Christian University, 1987. •The most helpful book in this list for detailed administration.

NOTES

1. Royce Money, *Ministering to Families: A Positive Plan of Action* (Abilene, Tex.: Abilene Christian University Press, 1987).

2. "Status Report on the Family," unpublished report (Atlanta: North Atlanta Church of Christ), 1991.

3. Money, *Ministering to Families*, 183–90.

4. Contained in a letter to the author from pastor Samuel H. Schwenk, February 17, 1993.

5. Unpublished document of the Third Reformed Church, Kalamazoo, Michigan.

Conclusion

People already deeply involved in family ministry may enjoy a great measure of success, but not without some frustrations. Any Christian ministry, above all, calls for bold faith. God's purposes must be achieved by God's power. Without trust in him, we are likely to burn out, ravaged by feelings of defeat and disappointment that come to those who set out to help families. If you enter into family ministry, prepare yourself for some of these feelings:

Confusion. We will become confused simply because we are involved. Family problems are often puzzling, and family-life issues controversial. The only way to escape being perplexed by them is to avoid being involved with them. Often you will have to say to yourself, "It's okay to be confused. I have some answers; I will have to keep searching for others."

Disappointment. Almost every time I speak at a marriage seminar or family conference, I hear this lament from those who planned it: "There are so many people who should be here, but aren't." These leaders then describe some of these troubled family members, badly in need of help, who had promised to attend. It is discouraging to want to help people more than they appear to want to help themselves. Frustrated by this, we allow their pain to become ours and we become trapped by codependency. Helpers must continually fight any compulsion to "fix" people; always recognize that the responsibility to change lies with them and the power to change rests with God.

Anger. We will likely be upset in learning what is happening in some families. Abusive husbands or neglectful parents could make us angry. So we must be careful. Being indignant is okay—it motivates us to act. But we should not act in anger. "Anger," says the apostle James, "does not bring about the righteous life that God requires" (James 1:20). We may need to be tough at times, confronting those who are badly hurting their families. Yet, to be effective, confronting will have to be done patiently and lovingly.

Sense of futility. There are reasons why we will sometimes feel that ministry to families accomplishes little or nothing. For one thing, change sometimes is not apparent because it can come with agonizing slowness. Patterns of relating persist even when they are damaging; emotions linger even when they are painful. Results of our ministry may only become evident in the distant future. Knowing that change often takes time, we can hold out hope for troubled families when we are otherwise tempted to give up.

Another reason for feeling that our work is in vain is that we may not always be aware of its impact. Changes that take place in people and homes are often subtle, even though crucial. A father spends more time with a daughter; a wife's attitude toward sex gradually becomes more positive. Being private and very personal, these kinds of changes don't always show up on evaluation questionnaires. Family ministry is not sensational. In fact, there is nothing less dramatic than someone checking a book out of the church library: a parent on discipline, for example, or a husband on marriage. Yet the effect may be spectacular.

Overall, you may become frustrated by the size of the task. You may feel a bit dazed from reading all the suggestions in this book about what can be done. When I feel this way, I remember the words I heard in a speech given by the late Bob Pierce, the founder of World Vision, a Christian organization to aid nations in crisis: "Don't fail to do something because you can't do everything." Perhaps before you put down this book you might meditate on what that "something" might be. Ask yourself and God, "What can I do?" "Where can I start?"

You are probably doing something already and have learned that helping has its bright side. People do respond; the Holy Spirit does work. There are results and rewards: a family now praying together; a father no longer yelling at his children; a couple's marriage holding together because of a weekend seminar; a teenager gaining respect for her parents; people coming to Christ and to church, attracted by messages and programs that deal with their problems.

The impact will keep going and going, because what is done to influence today's families will help tomorrow's. Because strong families reproduce themselves, just as troubled families do, family ministry will affect generations yet to come. When tempted to quit, I paint a certain picture in my mind. It is of a child (usually a boy) who is living years after I have gone. He has warm, caring parents who listen to him, gently encouraging and guiding him. By word and example they teach him to love God and others while, by their deep love for him, they build in him a healthy respect for himself. This child is in a Christian family—in fact as well as in name. And I imagine him in that home because God used me one day to help his grandparents build a home. That thought keeps me going.

Scripture Index

Subject–Name Index

This index does not include the suggested resources listed at the end of chapters 16–28.

Enmeshment 141, 158, 311–13
Enrichment, marriage (226–54)
    and developing romance 235
    exercises for 243–50
    and finances 237–38
    goals for 242–43
    guidelines for 251–54
    and handling crises 238–39
    and marital sex 233–35
    methods for 243
    and planning 237
    topics for 226–33
    and spirituality 239–40
Erasmus 98
Erikson, Erik 325–26
Eros (sexual love) 110, 113
Eternity 73–74
Eternity Magazine 293
Evangelism 177, 199
Ezer (helper) 92

Fairchild, R. W. 62
Families, educational approaches toward
        dysfunctional (301–8)
    recovery of 306–8. *See also* Recovery
    teaching about impact of 302–3
    teaching about influence of 303–6. *See
        also* Codependency
Family
    aging 29–30
    anti-image of 40
    biblical form of 74
    blended 330–31
    camping 198–204
    and churches 13–21
    clusters 196–98
    community and 34, 36, 37
    companionship 37
    diverse 25–30
    dysfunctional 45–49, 138, 158, 177, 216,
        217. *See also* Families, educational
        approaches toward
    empowerment in 124–25
    extended 32, 33, 34, 78
    external duties of 91–100
    forces that shape 52–65
    ill-equipped 36
    importance and form of 71, 72–74
    instituted by God 77
    interactive 26
    intimacy 37–40
    instability 42–49
    isolated 33–37
    meaning of 157–58
    nuclear 32–40, 78–79, 80

Scripture that diminishes 71–72
    and search for norms 60–63;
    significance of 11–13
    social functions of 15
    structural-functional 26
    theology of 63–65
    in transition 146–47, 327–31
    traditional 37
    typical 26–27
Family Altar League of America 293
Family life
    task force 349–57
    minister 351
Family-like church
    benefits of 164–68
    biblical arguments for 162–64
    dysfunctional 161
    features of 159–60
    function of 160–61
    models of 160
Family ministry
    administering 335–65
    is biblical 18–19
    is discipling 17–18
    is evangelism 17
    is integration 62–63
    methodology of 137–42
    is moral 14–16
    neglect of 13–14
    persons emphasized in 143–47
    is prevention 19–21
    is spiritual 14–16
    subject matter of 129–35
    steps to
    and therapeutic strategies 140–42
Family Research Council 155
Family Resource Council 28
Finances 237–38
First Evangelical Free Church (Fullerton,
        Calif.) 177, 307
Focus on the Family 155
Forces
    economic 52, 54–56, 58, 154
    political 57–58; 152–54, 158
    social 52–60, 152–54
    technological 57
Francoeur, Robert 59, 60
Freud, Sigmund 209, 263
Friedman, Edwin 18

Gathering of Men 145
George, Carl 175–76
Ginott, Haim 259
Glasser, William 261–62, 263, 264, 265,
        266–67, 268, 270

marital 233–35
premarital 16, 43, 57, 154
Shakespeare, William 98
Sherrill, Lewis J. 291
Shorter, Edward 20, 34, 35, 37, 38
Simmons, Amos 45–46
Simmons, Brandon 46
Simmons, Dave 45–46, 144
Simon, Sidney 274
Singles, 27, 146, 149, 155
church ministry to 322–30
divorced and separated 327–29. *See also*
Parents, single
never-married 324–27
Sjogren, Enos 293, 294–95
Skinner, B. F. 264
Small groups. *See also* Growth group
as growth group 177–83
and primary relationships 175–77
and young people 183–84
Small, Dwight 83, 85, 87
Spitz, Rene 133
Sporakowski, Michael 329
Stein, Peter 324
Stephen Ministries 319, 320
Sterling, Alan 133
Stinnett, Nicholas 132, 140, 161
Strong, Augustus 266
Swain, Margaret 196-97, 198
Swindoll, Charles 177
Systematic Training for Effective Parenting
(STEP) 276, 277

Taylor-Johnson Temperament Analysis 222,
250
Theology, meaning of 65
Third Reformed Church (Kalamazoo,
Mich.) 358–59
Thomas, Chris 147
Timber-Lee (camp) 200
Training, skill: goals of 139–40
Trinity Baptist Church (Syracuse, N.Y.) 358
Trueblood, D. Elton 234, 320

Trueblood, Pauline 234
Turk, Dennis C. 328
Twelve Step programs 315

Udry, J. Richard 26
Unity, defined 104

Van Eck, Bea 244, 254
Van Eck, Bud 244, 254
Vander Haar, Del 250
Vander Haar, Trudy 195, 250
Venues for teaching skills 131–32, 142
von Rad, Gerhard 76

Wahking, Harold 318
Wallerstein, Judith 48
Ward Presbyterian Church (Livonia, Mich.)
342–44
Ward, Ted 21
Wenger, Walter 76
Werner, Hazen 42
Wesley, John 177
Wheat, Ed 220
Wheat, Gaye 220
Whitehead, Barbara 58
Whitfield, George 177–78
Wieman, Regina 53
Wilder-Padilla, S. 302
Willi, Jurg 35
Willow Creek Community Church (South
Barrington, Ill.) 174, 327, 330
Wilson, Bill 315
Wilson, Sandra 303
Winter, Gibson 227
Woititz, Janet 47
Women, working 27, 55–56, 58
Wood, J. Brittain 323
Wright, H. Norman 13, 220, 221, 236
Wynn, John 19

Yada (to know) 104
Yorburg, Betty 20, 33
Young Child Tax Credit 57, 153
Youth for Christ 144